ultimate DVD

ultimate DVD

The Essential Guide to Building Your DVD Collection

Peter M. Bracke

BERKLEY BOOKS, NEW YORK

B

A Berkley Book
Published by The Berkley Publishing Group
A division of Penguin Group (USA) Inc.
375 Hudson Street
New York, New York 10014

This book is an original publication of The Berkley Publishing Group.

Copyright © 2004 by Peter M. Bracke.
Cover design by Rita Frangie.
Cover photo by Tristan Pairot.
Text design by Tiffany Estreicher.

PRINTING HISTORY
Berkley trade paperback edition / August 2004

Library of Congress Cataloging-in-Publication Data

Bracke, Peter M.
    Ultimate DVD : the essential guide to building your DVD collection / by
Peter M. Bracke.
        p. cm.
    ISBN 0-425-19643-7
    1. Motion pictures—Evaluation—Catalogs. 2. DVD-Video discs—Catalogs.
I. Title: Ultimate digital video disc. II. Title.
PN1995.B69 2004
791.43'75—dc22   2003063740

PRINTED IN THE UNITED STATES OF AMERICA

10 9 8 7 6 5 4 3 2 1

Acknowledgments

When I first sat down to begin work on a book about DVD—just a little thing I thought a few people might get a kick out of—I wasn't quite prepared for the journey that was to come. Not that I thought it would be a snap, of course, but after four years of running the website I started in college, DVDFILE.com, I certainly felt I had a handle on what made a great DVD and what consumers wanted out of their purchases. Such are the best kind of happy accidents—ideas that start as larks and become passion projects, and then grant the greatest gift of all, long-running careers. But all the planning in the world still can't quite prepare you for the actual act of *doing* it. The road that followed was one filled with a great deal of pleasure and a little bit of pain—the joy of creation, an occasional tragedy, what seemed like a million typos and one heck of a lot of work.

Despite what the cover may say, no book is truly written by one person. It is a collaborative effort in the truest sense of the word, not only in getting the written word down on the page, but also in the entire conceptualization, development, production, editing, fact checking and proofing of the final product. And there is the emotional journey one goes through in attempting to create—out of thin air—an undertaking of this size. That is where the support of family, friends and loved ones is instrumental in the process. This may be just a little book about DVD, but it is also a testament to the time, effort and dedication of a great number of people who endeavored to produce something truly special, a reference work that would be meaningful, instructive and, hopefully, a lot of fun to read.

First and foremost I would like to thank Jeff Kurtti, who, during a casual lunch a couple of years ago, first expressed support and encouragement for my little idea to write a DVD book. He was also instrumental in introducing me to my agent, Garrett Hicks, who immediately saw the potential in the idea. In addition to his terrific feedback and guidance, Garrett also instilled in me the confidence that such a book had merit and could be enjoyed by a great many people. And he sure knew how to convince a lot of other people of its appeal as well. To both Jeff and Garrett, I am eternally grateful.

As I was putting the book together and formulating the basic content outline and what DVDs would make the cut, the public relations departments of all of the major studios and independents that are featured in this book were essential in getting me the information I needed as well as a generous supply of screeners. (Yeah! Free stuff!) In particular, I would like to thank Michael Felsher and Anchor Bay Entertainment, Roger Sauden and Buena Vista Home Entertainment, R. O'Donnell and The Criterion Collection, Josh Davison and Elite Entertainment, Kavita Smith and Columbia TriStar Home Entertainment, Missy Davy and DreamWorks Home Entertainment, Jennifer Sandler and New Line Home Entertainment, Martin Blythe and Paramount Home Entertainment, Ronnee Sass and Warner Home Video, and Kevin Tachman and Electric Artists/Universal Studios Home Video. This book would not have been possible without their support and cooperation.

As the book began to take shape, it became clear to me that the sheer volume of time, work, research and writing would be far too daunting of a task to take on all by myself. So it is with no small amount of applause that I have to thank my tireless research and writing assistants, Mark Keizer and Mike Restaino, for their incredible contributions to this book. Their input, ideas, effort, writing and feedback greatly shaped the final product, and what you now hold in your hands is as much a testament to their vision as it is to mine.

I would also like to thank the incredible array of filmmakers who generously gave of their time to talk with me for this book. The fact that so many proved to be fans of my work at DVDFILE.com, or simply took a chance on a pushy, unknown author and consented to an interview, makes my fledgling-writer heart glad. Sincerest thanks goes out to them, as well as to their helpful staff of agents, managers, publicists and assistants: Michael Bay, Laurent Bouzereau, John Carpenter, Bill Kinder, Jeff Kurtti, Charlie de Lauzirika, McG, Alan Parker, Michael Pellerin, Jeffrey Schwarz, Bryan Singer, John Singleton and John Waters.

As the book began to take shape and actual content started to flow out of my word processor, the fine folks at Penguin became my new extended family. I would like to thank my tireless editor and cheerleader, John Morgan, who put up with my endless goofy ideas, last-minute changes, neurotic panic attacks and the worst thing an editor wants to hear, "Just one more day. Really, just one more!" I'd also like to thank the highly talented and collaborative staff at Penguin, including the proofers, copy editors, artists and layout team who made my words look so good. And let me not to forget the unsung hero of the publishing business: the transcriptionist. I had a great team of three and must thank Camille Kaminski, Brian Lennox and Mike Restaino again for sifting through hours of my misguided ramblings and incoherent questions, often recorded in the worst conditions imaginable. They will forever remain underpaid.

Finally, I would be remiss not to thank all those in my life who offered their friendship, support, encouragement and love in frequent times of crisis. To my friends Michael Cidoni, Alex Garcia, David Hildebrand, Tyson FitzGerald, Mark Langlois, Aaron Reza, Ronit Mitchell and Scott Bullock, and Bret Wachter, I thank you for putting up with my frequent disappearances and days spent hiding out in my room, head hunched over a computer. I would also like to give special thanks to Daniel Farrands, who was a bedrock of support throughout the writing of this book. You helped me realize that it could be done, and without you, I would not have had the courage to follow my passion. And last but not least, very special thanks to my family, including my mother, Sharlene, my sisters and brother and many nieces and nephews, for never batting an eye at my strange predilections all throughout my life.

And last but certainly not least, thanks to you, the dear reader. If you've actually made it this far then you have made it all worthwhile. Now, stop reading the damn Acknowledgements section and go buy some DVDs. Enjoy!

Contents

Preface: A Five-Inch Digital Wonder 1
Introduction: Thinking Outside the Box 5

The 100 Ultimate DVDs

1. *20,000 Leagues Under the Sea* 21
2. *Abyss, The* 24
3. *Adventures of Indiana Jones, The* 27
4. *ALIEN Quadrilogy, The* 32

   ○ **Making *ALIENS* and Other Stories:**
   A Conversation with Charlie de Lauzirika 36

5. *All That Heaven Allows* 41
6. *Almost Famous: Untitled—The Bootleg Cut* 44
7. *Amadeus: The Director's Cut* 47
8. *American Beauty* 50
9. *American Graffiti* 54
10. *Back to the Future Trilogy* 57
11. *Black Narcissus* 60
12. *Blue Velvet* 62
13. *Bowling for Columbine* 65
14. *Boyz N the Hood* 70

    ○ **Higher Learning: A Conversation with John Singleton** 72

15. *Brazil* 76
16. *Bridge on the River Kwai, The* 79
17. *Butch Cassidy and the Sundance Kid* .82

18. *Carrie* 85

19. *Casablanca* 88

20. *Cast Away* 91

21. *Citizen Kane* 95

22. *Cleopatra* 98

23. *Close Encounters of the Third Kind* 101

O   Auto Focus: A Conversation with Laurent Bouzereau 105

24. *Dances with Wolves* 111

25. *Doctor Zhivago* 115

26. *Do the Right Thing* 118

27. *Dracula* 121

28. *E.T.—The Extra-Terrestrial* 124

29. *Exorcist, The (25th Anniversary Edition)* 128

30. *Fantasia Anthology, The* 132

O   The Pixels of Pixar: A Conversation with Bill Kinder 136

31. *Fatal Attraction* 141

32. *Fight Club* 144

33. *Forrest Gump* 148

34. *French Connection, The* 151

35. *Gladiator* 154

36. *Godfather Collection, The* 157

37. *Goldfinger* 161

38. *Gold Rush, The* 164

39. *Halloween (25th Anniversary Edition)* 167

O   Prince of Darkness: A Conversation with John Carpenter 171

40. *Hard Day's Night, A* 175

41. *Harry Potter and the Sorcerer's Stone* 178

42. *It's a Wonderful Life* 182

43. *JAWS* 184

44. *Jurassic Park* 188

45. *Lawrence of Arabia* 192

46. *Lord of the Rings, The: The Fellowship of the Ring*
    (Extended Edition) 195

O **To Middle-Earth and Back: A Conversation with
Jeff Kurtti and Michael Pellerin** 199

47. *Mack, The* 204
48. *Magnolia* 208
49. *M*A*S*H* 211
50. *Matrix, The* 214
51. *Memento* 218
52. *Metropolis* (Restored Authorized Edition) 221
53. *Mildred Pierce* 224
54. *Monty Python and the Holy Grail* 226

O **It's the Film That Counts: A Conversation with Alan Parker** 230

55. *Moulin Rouge!* 235
56. *National Lampoon's Animal House* 238
57. *Night of the Living Dead* (Millennium Edition) 241
58. *Once Upon a Time in the West* 245
59. *One Flew Over the Cuckoo's Nest* 249
60. *Peeping Tom* 252
61. *Pink Flamingos/Female Trouble* 255

O **Shock Value: A Conversation with John Waters** 258

62. *Pirates of the Caribbean: The Curse of the Black Pearl* 263
63. *Platoon* 267
64. *Princess Bride, The* 270
65. *Producers, The* 273
66. *Psycho* 276
67. *Pulp Fiction* 279
68. *Rebecca* 283
69. *Red Shoes, The* 286
70. *Right Stuff, The* 289
71. *Rocky* 292

O **Automat for the People: A Conversation with Jeffrey Schwarz** ..296

72. *Rocky Horror Picture Show, The* 301
73. *Royal Tenenbaums, The* 305
74. *Saturday Night Fever* 308

75. *Scarface* 312

76. *Singin' in the Rain* 315

77. *Sixth Sense, The* 318

78. *Snow White and the Seven Dwarfs* 321

79. *Sound of Music, The* 325

80. *Star Trek II: The Wrath of Khan* (The Director's Edition) 328

81. *Star Wars Episode II: Attack of the Clones* 332

   O Full Throttle: A Conversation with McG 336

82. *Straw Dogs* 340

83. *Stunt Man, The* 343

84. *Sunset Boulevard* 347

85. *Superman: The Movie* 350

86. *Taxi Driver* 354

87. *Terminator, The* 357

88. *Thing, The* 360

89. *Third Man, The* 363

   O Kinetic Energy: A Conversation with Michael Bay 367

90. *This Is Spinal Tap* 370

91. *Toy Story: The Ultimate Toy Box* 374

92. *Traffic* 377

93. *Treasure of the Sierra Madre, The* 380

94. *TRON* 383

95. *Usual Suspects, The* 387

   O X Marks the Spot: A Conversation with Bryan Singer 390

96. *Valley Girl* 395

97. *Vertigo* 398

98. *West Side Story* 401

99. *Willy Wonka and the Chocolate Factory* 404

100. *Wizard of Oz, The* 407

   Appendix A: The Shape of Things—
   What Is an Aspect Ratio? 411

   Appendix B: Glossary of Terms 423

A Five-Inch Digital Wonder

March 25, 1997. Small black boxes began to appear in seven test cities across America. These little devices could play shiny, five-inch digital discs that looked a lot like CDs, but they played movies instead. It was an inauspicious debut: the industry snickered, the press yawned, and almost all of the studios balked. And then it happened. Little ripples, at first on the Internet, then trickling into the mainstream, began to crest into waves. A shift of seismic proportions was about to occur. The digital age in home entertainment was finally here . . .

DVD has quickly become the most successful new product in the history of the consumer electronics industry. It's sleek. It's sexy. It's convenient and affordable. So collectable it is addictive. It's your VCR on steroids, humming with the kind of power thought impossible just a few short years ago. It finally brings the home theater experience within reach of the average consumer. And it has completely redefined the way we watch, listen to and interact with movies.

It was not always this way. The act of going to the movies has, throughout most of its history as a commercial medium, been a linear, "watch once," entirely of-the-moment experience. The early nickelodeons at the turn of the nineteenth century were the original cinematic dime-store theaters, unspooling short little mini-dramas all shot with one camera and with no edits. Then, rapidly, a series of advancements gave way to the birth of the classical Hollywood narrative: editing, sound, color, special effects and large-screen exhibition. The lavish movie emporiums of the 1940s would become a monument to this brief golden era, when audience attendance was at its highest. But the monopoly Hollywood held over American tastes and trends was soon toppled by the advent of television. The decline was as swift as the gimmicks were desperate: 3-D, Odorama, drive-ins, sometimes-outlandish wide-format and multichannel surround sound "inventions"—all of which were designed to lure audiences away from the boob tube and back into the theaters. The counterattack didn't work. By the late 1960s, movie attendance was at its lowest in history. Even the loosening of censorship regulations and the creation of the Motion Picture Association of America (MPAA) did little to reclaim Hollywood's dominance over popular tastes and trends. And through it all the industry's modus operandi had always been the same: to entice ticket buyers to share in a communal experience, one that was elusive and intangible, and could not be captured, taken home, rewound and watched over and over.

Enter the video cassette recorder. In the early 1970s the VCR, and to a lesser extent, cable television, shattered the old paradigm. Movies were suddenly beamed, "live" and uncut, into homes across the country. Consumers could snap up and rent magnetic tapes that offered an unheard-of level of control. While the technology was antiquated and the quality negligible, it was an event that sent shock waves throughout the industry. As with the introduction of the television, industry pundits predicted utter collapse and the major studios panicked. Lawsuits were filed and court battles waged, but when the dust settled, a whole new industry was born.

It all coalesced in the 1980s, the age when video fully penetrated our shared cultural consciousness. America embraced anything remotely futuristic: video games, MTV and the personal computer taught a new generation that life could be disseminated as a series of bits and bytes. Kids could now be found at home in front of their VCRs and Ataris instead of at the local soda shop. The boob tube became the hearth of the modern American family, and driving it was the corner mom-and-pop video store, which had become as ubiquitous as the gas station. Movie fans could stop by their local Kmart and pick up the latest Hollywood megahit for less than it cost to buy a movie ticket, some popcorn and a Coke. No longer did fans have to wait for years until their favorite film popped up on cable or network TV, often poorly edited and constantly interrupted by commercials. And Hollywood wasted no time in exploiting America's newfound love for the videotape. Theatrical-to-video "release windows" became so short that home video replaced the second-run theater and the drive-in as the primary afterlife for the theatrical motion picture. By 1986, video revenue topped theatrical ticket sales and generated billions in profits. Americans still loved watching movies. But now they loved watching them at home even more.

For the film buff and collector, prerecorded home video formats have been nothing short of a miracle. What once seemed impossible—owning an incredible library of your favorite movies—is now within easy reach. And DVD has taken it to the next level. A level of quality unimaginable just a few short years ago is now at the fingertips of the average consumer. DVD player prices have fallen below the magical $100 mark, and DVD movies are routinely sold for budget prices at every major retailer across the country. A DVD collection is not just a high-class status symbol or a luxury item for the wealthy. It is now a part of the cultural lexicon and a new form of communal interaction. Friends brag to other friends about the DVDs they just bought. Families gather around the DVD player on Saturday nights, sharing laughter, excitement and tears. Potential mates size each other up as they walk in the door with a backward glance at the A/V cabinet. A person's DVD collection reveals as much about their personality as the clothes they wear, the car they drive and the food they eat.

That is why *Ultimate DVD* exists. It is designed to be the ultimate starter guide to building your DVD collection. It is written by someone who loves movies, loves technology and loves the format—not a day has gone by in the past six years when I haven't thought about DVD at least once. Many will undoubtedly take issue with the one hundred selections included herein; rest assured that none has been chosen with a cavalier attitude, because the excitement in building your own DVD collection is that it is entirely of *your* choosing—you just may need a little help sorting through all of the endless marketing hype and hard-sell tactics. Every single one of the one hundred DVDs here has been selected for three very simple reasons: because it is a film of lasting importance, is representative of the best the format has to offer, and delivers tremendous insight into the art and craft of filmmaking. The irony of DVD is that you don't even have to love the movie (or even like it) to become completely immersed in its DVD. The format has redefined how we experience the motion picture—the movie truly is only the beginning.

This book offers a little bit of everything. An introduction to the DVD format's capabilities and interactive features. The ABCs of some of the more complex and intimidating aspects of the technology. Intimate conversations with some of today's top filmmakers and DVD producers. And one hundred terrific titles to begin building your very own DVD library. Now is truly a most exciting time to be a movie fan and a movie collector. So don't be intimidated. All you need is the power that comes with knowledge, the knowledge to make the most informed choices possible. And choice is what DVD is all about.

So step into a whole new world and a whole new way of looking at movies. DVD is truly a phenomenon. It has revolutionized an industry, allowed filmmakers to more fully realize their visions than ever before, and even inspired many to pursue their own dreams of a career in the industry. It has certainly changed my life, and I think it will change yours, too. Or, at the very least, provide you with years of fun, excitement and entertainment. What could be cooler than that?

Thinking Outside the Box

WHAT IS DVD?

DVD, or Digital Video Disc, is the next generation in optical disc storage technology. It is the ultimate convergence medium, designed to supplant videotape, laserdisc, the CD-ROM disc, the video-game cartridge, and the audiocassette. It is a dynamic portal to the Internet, connecting our computers and our content to the World Wide Web. It is video and audio quality of the highest degree, allowing us to bring professional-caliber excellence into our homes at affordable prices. It is a versatile, flexible storage medium that encompasses movies, music, computer data, the written word and still images. It is a revolution in how we experience, collect, appreciate and understand the creative arts. Regardless of where you live, work, and play, DVD will impact your life. It *is* the future, available today.

If you are reading this book, it may be because you have been attracted to the idea of buying your first DVD player, want to upgrade to a better system, or just want to get more out of the equipment you already own. It is easy to step into your local electronics store and be intimidated by racks of hi-tech-looking black boxes covered in lights and buttons and accessed by extravagant remote controls. Or to sit down with your DVD player's manual, bewildered by all the options and choices at your fingertips. And even after you have become an expert on how to hook up, use and enjoy your new player (or your computer's DVD-ROM drive), a trip to the local video store can still be a frightening experience. Tens of thousands of movies, music titles, TV shows, special interest programming and computer applications are now available on DVD, all for the taking. The choices seem endless and exhausting.

That is where this chapter comes in. It is broken down into eight easy-to-digest subsections, telling you everything you need to start building your own DVD collection and getting the best out of your home theater. It has been written with a minimum of techno-babble, and all of the big words are *italicized*—if any of them are confusing, refer to the Glossary in Appendix B for more help. So, are you ready? Let's go!

1. Do I Need to Know What DVD Means?

Not really. In the early days of the DVD format's development, its makers, the *DVD Forum*, coined it "digital video disc." Soon, manufacturers and studios hoping to promote the interactive capabilities of the format attempted to change it to the more all-encompassing "digital versatile disc," although the name never stuck. (Both are now used interchangeably.) But just as we all know how to use our VCRs and CDs regardless of what the letters stand for, you, too, can get the full benefits of DVD irrespective of acronym.

2. How Does DVD Work?

DVD is like a CD, only better. It looks the same, measuring five inches across and less than a centimeter thick. But a DVD can deliver more than music. It can hold video, audio, computer data, words, pictures—just about anything that can be dreamed up and prerecorded, DVD can store. And unlike a CD, DVD was designed to supplant yesterday's antiquated, *analog*-based technologies, including the videotape and the laserdisc, and to greatly improve on the limited storage capabilities of CD-based computer storage formats, including CD-ROM and its recordable and rewritable offshoots, such as CD-RW and CD-RAM.

DVD is *digital*. It works its magic with two little but very powerful tools at its disposal: ones and zeros, or *digital data*. Analog technology is very different. In the real world, our senses are constantly stimulated by information overload—sound waves bouncing across walls, light rays emanating from movie screens, vibrations from your neighbor's boom box shaking the floor. Analog recording technology works by making small changes in a physical media, such as the grooves on a vinyl record album, magnetic particles on a cassette or silver halide crystals on film, all susceptible to degradation, decay, damage and interference. Digital information is instead simply a picture—a snapshot (or a *sample,* the process called *sampling*) of an analog value that is then translated into a numerical equivalent, a set series of ones and zeros.

What this means is that digital information does not suffer from most of the drawbacks of analog. It can be transferred, processed and copied over and over again with no loss in quality. Digital data will still, eventually, have to be converted to analog before it hits your eyes and ears—the sound will still have to come out of a speaker, the picture still has to form an image on a television set. But the big advantage of digital technology, and DVD, is that it is so durable. All those snapshots, those millions of ones and zeros, regardless of how many times you cut and paste them, transmit them or burn them onto a DVD, will still be the same snapshots for you to use, reuse and enjoy.

3. How Does DVD Fit So Much Stuff on a Little Five-Inch Disc?
DVD's biggest trick is not that it uses digital technology to store video and audio—CDs and CD-ROMs have been doing it for years. It is the miracle of *compression* that allows a DVD to store so much data in such a little space. All those ones and zeros, if they were to be encoded on a single disc in uncompressed form, would never fit—the disk would be able to hold about five minutes of video and maybe two hours of audio. Compression looks for *redundancy,* areas of a single picture that are the same. Say a movie has a shot of a clear blue sky, made up of one thousand blue dots. Each dot, or *pixel,* in its uncompressed form would require a numerical value to be repeated one thousand times, even if it is the same value. But DVD allows for a

shortcut: instead of encoding the numerical values of all those blue dots, one value can be encoded to represent all one thousand of them. Voilà! A lot of information in a much smaller space. And DVD is smart enough that it can look for redundancies over time. Say that blue sky lasts for ten minutes. Even more information could be compressed, all with no perceptible loss in quality. And it works just as well for audio, too, or computer data. Anything that can be encoded as digital information.

The compression scheme DVD uses is called *MPEG-2* named after the Motion Picture Engineering Group. It is the next generation above MPEG-1, which CD-ROM technology is based on. Even better, DVD is a *variable bit rate* technology, meaning the rate at which it compresses is imminently malleable; a DVD content provider (the folks, like the studios and computer software companies, that make DVDs) can exert total control over how much material to squeeze onto a single disc, or, depending on the material, multiple discs. It can all get a bit complicated, but all you need to know is that it works. And works brilliantly.

4. What Kinds of DVDs Are There?

Like CD technology, the DVD format was conceived with more than just one application in mind. So just as CD begat multiple formats, such as CD-ROM and various CD-R and recording formats, so, too, has DVD.

Will a single DVD player or DVD drive play all of these formats? Not exactly. Compatibility issues, especially among rival DVD recordable formats, remains the thorn in DVD's side. All DVD-Video players (still the dominant and biggest-selling type of DVD playback device) will, of course, play DVD-Video discs, and 99.9 percent will also play all of your old CDs. A growing majority of commercial DVD-Video playback devices also support DVD-Audio and even MP3 playback. And currently, DVD set-top players and drives that can both write to and play back DVD-R and DVD-RW formats are the fastest growing sector of the DVD world, as compatibility issues continue to be worked out and prices fall to affordable levels.

The following is a rundown of all the major DVD formats. Before deciding on any purchase, it is best to check with the manufacturer to make sure exactly which formats the player or drive will support.

1. DVD-Video: The standard for delivering MPEG-based video and audio. Designed to provide constant access to time-based content. Can support multiple audio formats, including Dolby Digital and DTS. The dominant DVD format for delivering movies, music video and television-based material.

2. DVD-Audio: An audio-only standard for high-quality storage and reproduction, including uncompressed material. Can support multiple proprietary audio formats and has limited DVD-Video capabilities, including the ability to present stills and subtitle information.

3. DVD-ROM: Stands for Read-Only Memory. Can hold any type of digital data, including computer applications, but cannot be recorded on.

4. DVD-RAM: Stands for Random Access Memory. A version of DVD-ROM that can be erased, recorded and rerecorded on more than once.

5. DVD-R: A variation of DVD-ROM that allows for data to be recorded on a disc only once. Similar to CD-R.

6. DVD-RW: A rewritable version of DVD-R.

7. DVD+RW: An erasable and rewritable format, based on existing CD+RW technology and created for computer-based applications. Is not supported by the DVD Forum and is no longer in wide use.

5. What Is a DVD "Layer"?

As phenomenal a storage medium as DVD is, even its space is finite. To stretch the capacity of the format even further, the developers of DVD planned ahead to ensure it would be a multilayer format. The physical DVD disc is comprised of two plastic *substrates,* coated with a polymer resin (an icky, gooey substance) and bonded together. Each substrate can be made of up to two layers.

Thus, four permutations are possible, each given their own disc code by the DVD Forum:

1. DVD-5: Single-sided, single-layer

2. DVD-9: Single-sided, dual-layer

3. DVD-14: Double-sided, one dual-layer and the other single-layer

4. DVD-18: Double-sided, both dual-layer

All DVD players and drives bearing the DVD logo must be able to play all four disc types. On average, a single layer of a DVD-Video disc can hold about two-and-a-half hours of high-quality video and audio. A dual-layer DVD-Video disc can hold a little over four hours of high-quality video and audio (this reduction is due to the second layer boasting a smaller surface area). All DVD players and drives automatically refocus the laser from one layer to the other during playback. Note that this layer change can be seamless; however, access times vary by player so you might experience a short still frame or hiccup during the switch. No DVD player or drive currently on the market is able to access all four layers of a DVD disc without requiring the user to manually flip the disc over. Sorry, couch potatoes.

6. What Can DVD Do?

Everything! That five-inch little digital wonder that you hold in your hand combines the best of CD technology with a host of new innovations—multiple audio track and subtitle capabilities, enhanced playback modes, multiple angles, variable aspect ratios and more.

It is up to the content provider to actually include any and all special features and material on a disc. Just because the DVD format is capable of presenting a movie in a "director's cut" or from multiple angles does not necessarily mean that such content will be on the disc. Check the back packaging and all promotional materials carefully for what special features, if any, are included on a disc.

The following is a rundown of the DVD-Video format's most exciting special features and capabilities:

○ Direct Access: Similar to tracks on a CD, chapter stops can be encoded on any DVD program, allowing instant access to specific portions of a disc. (Movies are usually indexed by scenes, music programming by song.) Direct access also encompasses all supplementary content, including featurettes, documentaries, trailers and music videos, or any other video- or audio-based material encoded on a disc.

○ Menu-Based Navigation: This is the heart of a DVD. Video and audio setup options, supplemental content and other access controls can be arranged on a disc through a hierarchical navigation system, comprised of a series of still and/or animated screens. Such navigation allows for an unprecedented level of interactivity and user control.

○ Variable Aspect Ratio Support: This is one of DVD's most powerful capabilities; video material can be presented in multiple *aspect ratios* (or screen shapes), including that of a film's original theatrical presentation, either via letterboxing or anamorphic encoding. (See Appendix A)

○ Multiple Audio Tracks: Up to eight separate audio tracks can be encoded and stored on a DVD disc. Common applications include presenting alternate language dubs, proprietary audio formats (such as Dolby Digital and DTS), filmmaker's commentary, karaoke versions, and isolated score and effects tracks.

○ Subtitles/Captions: A DVD can store up to thirty-two subtitle text "streams" or tracks, which can play simultaneously with the video and audio. Words, text, simple graphics and overlays can be placed anywhere on the screen and in up to eight colors. Common uses include language subtitles, trivia, song lyrics, menu overlays and navigational graphics, icons and cursors.

○ Enhanced Playback: Also called "multistory seamless playback." Up to eight separate video streams can be encoded on a disc. "Seamless branching" allows for additional material to be accessed with no interruption in playback, such as an alternate "director's cut" or a re-rated version of a film. "Extended branching" will interrupt playback of the main program to access a separate program, and then return to the same location where the branch began (such as activating the remote control when prompted to watch a supplementary featurette, then returning to the same point in the movie).

○ Multi-Angle: Similar to enhanced playback, this is used for on-the-fly access to alternate video and audio material. The user can "toggle" through up to eight alternate video and/or audio tracks via the remote control or the DVD player's on-screen controls. Common applications include alternate angles, takes or camera setups. Access times will vary based on the playback device.

○ Still Playback: DVD allows for direct access and manual control of individual still frames. Users can stop, still-step, navigate and perform other basic controls.

○ Interactive Games: DVD's powerful interactive capabilities and limited random-access memory can allow for user-controlled, real-time activities, usually game-based features. Popular applications include simple trivia challenges (that can branch off to video or audio segments depending on the answer chosen), basic video game–like programs with simple graphics and cursors, and memory-based quizzes and children's games.

○ ROM/PC Enhanced Interactivity: This is one of the most powerful capabilities of the DVD format. Proprietary software can be encoded on a disc that allows for Internet connectivity and material stored in other locations (such as a website or web server) to be unlocked. Common applications include access to exclusive content, live web events (including chats and alternate audio and text commentaries) synced with real-time DVD playback, voice-controlled menu navigation, screenplay viewers with direct scene access, and advanced software applications including editing studios and interactive games.

7. Why Are There Different Aspect Ratios and Sound Formats?

One of the most exciting and powerful capabilities of DVD is variable aspect ratio selection and the ability to access different sound formats at the touch of a button. The topics of aspect ratio, widescreen and letterboxing are comprehensively discussed in Appendix A, so please refer to that section for more information. But what about all those cool-sounding, whiz-bang surround-sound formats advertised on the back of DVD boxes and at electronics stores? What are Dolby Digital and DTS? And PCM?

Dolby Digital and DTS (Digital Theater Systems) are both proprietary standards that deliver multichannel audio in the home and theatrical environments. Both use MPEG-2 to squeeze all of that information into a small little space; however, DTS utilizes higher bit rates and less compression, which has led many to proclaim it superior to Dolby Digital. Others, however, either don't hear an appreciable difference, or any at all. And DTS tracks, due to their higher bit rate, eat up more space, leaving far less room for all of those great supplemental features DVD fans love so much.

In the early development stages of DVD, there was much debate over which sound format—Dolby Digital or DTS (or neither)—would be chosen as the de facto standard. Dolby Digital won. Any DVD-Video disc bearing the label *must* carry at least one Dolby Digital soundtrack in order to maintain compatibility across all equipment and software. (That way, when you pop a disc in, at least you'll hear *something*.) But DTS wasn't going to go away without a fight. DTS proponents waged their own successful battle to be included as an optional sound format in the DVD spec. Today, DTS has carved out an appreciable niche as an alternative to Dolby Digital. While the contentious debate over which is better can't be decided here, note that as DTS is optional, the vast majority of titles released in North

America do not contain DTS soundtracks. However, if you are a DTS proponent, or just curious, you can still readily enjoy a DTS soundtrack as long as you have the appropriate equipment: a DVD player that can decode or pass along the DTS bit stream (commonplace today even among low-end players), a DTS decoder somewhere in your system (either inside the DVD player itself or in your audio/video [A/V] receiver) and enough speakers to handle all of those channels of sound.

So how do you actually start enjoying surround sound at home? You'll need a decoder (either Dolby Digital or DTS, preferably both) somewhere in your system. (Many DVD players come with them built in and even the cheapest A/V receivers will support at least Dolby Digital; or you can invest in a stand-alone outboard decoder instead.) You will also need A/V cables and wire to hook it all up (consult your instruction manuals) and six speakers: three in the front (left, right and center), two in the back (left and right) and a subwoofer (which only delivers low-bass frequencies). These six channels of audio information make up what is called a 5.1 soundtrack—which replicates a theaterlike sonic experience in your home with one full-frequency channel of audio for each speaker (left, right, center, and two rear left and right channels) and the low-bass subwoofer (the ".1" in "5.1"). Note that you can get by without buying all of this at once. The DVD-Video specification requires all players and drives to "downconvert" a Dolby Digital multichannel soundtrack. That means regardless of how many speakers you have—even just that one in your lowly black-and-white television— your player will take all of that sound and crush it all down into just the right number of channels to match your setup. (And remember, like all those great interactive features described above, it is up to the content provider to include a full multichannel soundtrack on a DVD. Just because Dolby Digital *can* deliver up to 5.1 channels of high-quality audio doesn't mean it *will*. Many DVD soundtracks, especially of older material produced before the advent of surround sound, will be presented in Dolby Pro-Logic, two-channel stereo or even mono.)

Things got a little trickier with the recent introduction of the

Dolby Digital Surround EX and DTS ES 6.1 formats. The concept is an exciting one. A Dolby Digital EX track matrixes in, or embeds, frequencies into the two surround channels that, when extracted, create a third rear channel that delivers a more enveloping, near 360-degree experience. To enjoy this, you will need to upgrade your A/V receiver to one that supports EX (or buy an outboard EX decoder) as well as purchase an extra back center speaker. DTS ES goes one better by offering two flavors: the matrixed option just described, or a fully *discrete* (full bandwidth) extra surround channel encoded as part of the bit stream. However, unlike an EX or matrixed ES soundtrack, a discrete DTS ES 6.1 mix is not backward compatible. (Matrixed tracks can still be played on existing 5.1 equipment; the matrixed surround information is simply distributed to the existing two rear speakers.)

Finally, what about PCM? Many music fans decried the lack of any support for a completely uncompressed sound carrier on DVD, which they said would seriously limit the format's ability to accurately play back high-quality audio, primarily music. So they, too, fought a battle and won. PCM stands for pulse code modulation and is just a fancy way of saying that any DVD-Video disc can store (and any DVD-Video device can play back) up to two channels of completely uncompressed audio. Everybody's happy.

8. What Is Region Coding?

In order to control the geographic distribution of their products on DVD, the motion picture studios teamed up with (some would say strong-armed) the DVD Forum to implement *region coding*. All DVD-Video players and DVD-Video discs are flagged with a single-digit region code (0 to 8), a number that designates what area of the world a disc *should* be played in. Attempting to play a disc with a different region code than that of the playback device will result in an error or no playback at all. The average consumer in North America, however, should not be too concerned with region coding. The continent by far gets the vast majority of new Hollywood releases first; only great enthusiasts of foreign films or of material that does not benefit from wide distribution in the United States (such as overseas television and special interest programming) may want to consider investing in a region-free player.

Region coding was established to prevent mass import/export of DVD titles into areas where, in many cases, they had not yet been released or would break previous licensing and distribution agreements. The matter can get even more serious in many parts of the world, including significant territories in Europe: objectionable subject matter, such as pornography (or even mainstream movies rated "R" in the United States), is routinely banned, its use, purchase, importation or exportation often punishable by law with hefty fees or even imprisonment. While region coding remains one of the most controversial topics in DVD, one should think carefully before attempting to "break" any region code barriers. (Note: Although region code "hacks" routinely appear on the Internet, modifying your DVD player or drive instantly voids the warranty and is not recommended.)

The following is a list of the nine region codes as established by the DVD Forum and the major studios:

○ Region 1: North America (including the United States, Canada, Bermuda, Puerto Rico, and the Virgin Islands and surrounding areas)

○ Region 2: Japan and Europe, and also including South Africa, Turkey and the Middle East (Iran and Egypt)

○ Region 3: Southeast Asia (including Hong Kong, Indonesia, Macau and South Korea)

○ Region 4: Australia, New Zealand, and Central and South America

○ Region 5: Northwest Asia and North Africa (including Russia and all its former territories)

○ Region 6: China

○ Region 7: Unassigned

○ Region 8: Special venues, primarily airlines

○ Region 0: Any disc or playback device marked "Region 0" is simply not flagged; such a disc can be played in any device throughout the world.

the 100 ultimate DVDs

20,000 Leagues Under the Sea

DISTRIBUTOR: Buena Vista Home Entertainment
DVD RELEASE: May 2003
THEATRICAL RELEASE: December 1954
RUNNING TIME: 127 Minutes
MPAA RATING: G

*2*0,000 Leagues Under the Sea was a milestone for The Walt Disney Studios. Its first attempt at a full-length, live-action theatrical feature, the blockbuster success of this 1954 adaptation of the Jules Verne classic allowed the studio to expand its empire beyond the bounds of animation and proved that classic literature could be successfully adapted into a mainstream entertainment without diluting any of its intelligence, thematic relevance and excitement. 20,000 Leagues Under the Sea also earned its place as a pioneering achievement in motion picture craftsmanship, remaining a majestic and unforgettable combination of mechanical, optical and practical effects wizardry.

> "A prisoner has a right to escape, hasn't he? And a guest don't need to. So I guess that makes us a little bit of both?"

Yet what continues to earn 20,000 Leagues Under the Sea its status as a genuine classic is its single-minded devotion to inspiring awe and wonder. Disney's choice of Verne's timeless tale would prove to be a prescient one and in perfect alignment with what is still Disney's overriding sensibility: to disguise a sometimes thinly veiled spiritual parable as commercial entertainment. Like Verne's novel, Eric Felton's tight script treats the undersea milieu as more than just a new location in which to stage action sequences. It is almost as if we are visiting another planet, the film's series of breathtaking, balletic montages of undersea life an evocative allegory for man's own continuing need to explore, discover and—rare for a Disney feature, the implications grow darker—plunder and destroy.

It is inevitable that for today's audience, the visual thrills of

20,000 Leagues Under the Sea will seem antiquated. But much of the fun comes from the incredible passion the cast and filmmakers invest in the material. James Mason's anarchist spin on Captain Nemo is a devilish delight and anchors the picture. In self-imposed exile aboard his submerged ship *Nautilus,* he is truly inspired in his use of stiff formality and polite manners to mask a growing madness—his glee is also ours as he relishes in the tormenting of his captors, and his back-and-forth banter with a mangy Kirk Douglas is priceless. Director Richard Fleischer (*Fantastic Voyage, Tora! Tora! Tora!*) also smartly plays up the performances while not belaboring the action sequences, mixing in elements of espionage, sci-fi, suspense and sly comedy ("It seems you can't do anything on this boat without getting wet," quips a dry Peter Lorre). Less successful is the film's stodgy narration and the occasional misguided foray into light musical comedy. But with a mix of great source material, terrific performances and sharp direction, *20,000 Leagues Under the Sea* transcends its age and remains truly wondrous.

The Goodies Years in the making, the supplements Disney has produced for this two-disc special edition of *20,000 Leagues Under the Sea* are simply marvelous, and this remains one of the most underrated and overlooked DVD releases of all time.

"The Making of *20,000 Leagues Under the Sea*" is an amazingly thorough, incredibly comprehensive eighty-seven-minute look at what was originally a huge risk for the Walt Disney Studios. The movie's sheer size and scope exceeded even Disney's biggest animated features, and the task that faced the production was daunting. Contributing new interviews are director Fleischer, who is still sharp and humorous, along with the always-dignified Douglas, effects pioneer Bob Broughton, Roy Disney and other key collaborators. Further paying tribute to the film's pioneering effects are a series of featurettes that are a must-see for anyone even remotely interested in the craft and history of motion picture special effects. These are a virtual treasure trove of never-before-seen, on-set material, the majority shot on 16mm and restored to such a superb condition as to rival the quality of the main feature. Among the newly-recovered gems? The infamous "Sunset Squid Sequence," reassembled from production footage and complete with excerpts from Paul Smith's rousing score, as well as a striking, previously lost animated sequence by Disney artist Joshua Meador meant to precede the squid battle. And as conceived by Harper Goff, the *Nautilus* itself remains one of the most brilliantly realized miniatures in movie history. "Touring the *Nautilus*," an elaborate computer generated recreation of the film's famous vessel reconstituted from more production footage, shows us why it is a benchmark in the history of fantasy and science-fiction filmmaking.

Supporting the video-based material is a new screen-specific audio commentary by director Fleischer and author Rudy Behlmer that is wholly comprehensive. Behlmer provides the historical context, Fleischer the nuts and bolts of what would become a highly complex and arduous shoot. A gallery of storyboards offers a glimpse at the construction of key scenes; animatics reveal more of the standout special effects; copious amounts of publicity and promotional materials flesh out the extensive still galleries; hundreds of pages of rare production documents and script excerpts have been newly unearthed; and a clutch of trailers and rare lost "trims" are simply an embarrassment of riches.

The Presentation Just as fabulous as the extras is the first-class restoration. Presented in the film's original expansive 2.55:1 theatrical aspect ratio, the sweeping, panoramic vistas of *20,000 Leagues Under the Sea* are tailor-made for the DVD format. The film's special effects have inevitably dated: the many composited matte shots suffer from obvious grain and reduced detail, and the inserted stock footage can often be painfully obvious. Otherwise, this is a luxurious transfer minted from a clean, sharp and detailed print, with strong, solid colors and a lush, three-dimensional appearance. The wonders of the deep have rarely looked so good.

The remixed Dolby Digital 5.1 surround track is not quite as successful as the transfer but it is still a laudable effort. At last removed are much of the defects that marred previous video incarnations, including dialogue hiss, noise and dropouts. Paul Smith's lush score now flows as smoothly as a fine vintage wine, and the inventive sound design is given new life and presence. However, the mix is not incredibly enveloping with little in the way of surround presence, but it is otherwise quite effective.

Additional Recommendations In 2001, Disney launched its "Vault Disney" series, a collection of the studio's most beloved live-action classics, each of which has received the deluxe two-disc treatment. Standouts include the *Escape from Witch Mountain* series, *The Apple Dumpling Gang, The Love Bug, Old Yeller, Pollyanna* and the perennial favorite, *The Parent Trap*. While the studio has subsequently dropped the moniker, the results speak for themselves: all are fabulous special editions every Disney fan should check out.

The Abyss

DISTRIBUTOR: Fox Home Entertainment
DVD RELEASE: March 21, 2000
THEATRICAL RELEASE: August 1989/August 1993
RUNNING TIME: 146 and 171 minutes
MPAA RATING: PG-13

A rare misfire for James Cameron, the auteur behind *The Terminator, True Lies* and *Titanic, The Abyss* landed with a thud. For a filmmaker often compared to Steven Spielberg, it should have been his *Close Encounters of the Third Kind,* a sweeping, exciting, romantic, awe-inspiring adventure. But something happened on the way to dry dock: when Cameron's would-be epic finally surfaced in August 1989, critics responded with indifference and audiences were apathetic. The 141-minute theatrical cut, shorn of nearly 30 minutes of material, was only a work in progress—key subplots were left on the cutting room floor, entire effects sequences abandoned and most of the

> "When you're hanging on by your fingernails, you can't go waving your arms around."
>
> —Virgil "Bud" Brigman

hoped-for Spielberg-like wonder all but absent. *The Abyss* was lost at sea.

Three years later, still seething from his first box office failure, Cameron convinced Twentieth Century Fox to invest even more millions to restore his lost vision. Excised footage was restored, key special effects sequences completed and a theatrical rerelease, complete with a new marketing campaign, gave his tarnished masterpiece a shot at redemption. The result was *The Abyss Special Edition*. And it was a film reborn.

Critical consensus has often branded Cameron a calculated control freak long on craft but short on emotion. But *The Abyss Special Edition* goes a long way toward silencing the skeptics. Cameron has always been ambitious, and with *The Abyss* he attempted to tell not just one but three interlocking stories: a tale of our first contact with an underwater alien species, an intimate, poignant drama of a lost love at last rekindled, and a suspenseful story of a world high above on the brink of apocalyptic catastrophe. These seemingly disparate threads simply did not come together in the theatrical cut. The exposition was clunky, the pacing disjointed and even the strong cast, led by Ed Harris and Mary Elizabeth Mastrantonio as the sparring lovers, were undermined by the severe cuts. It is hard not to blame Cameron for the initial failure of *The Abyss,* but here is a genuine rarity, a film that was granted a second chance and deserved it.

The Abyss is truly a film that has been rescued by home video. And the *Special Edition* makes a strong case for supporting the revisionist filmmaker. The *Special Edition* is no mere vanity project, or just another excuse to spruce up an inferior film with needless new effects. *The Abyss* at last sings, soars and sweeps us off our feet with its grand love story, epic scope and breathless action sequences. *The Abyss Special Edition* is a lost treasure at last recovered.

The Goodies As conceptualized by Cameron's longtime DVD producer Van Ling, this two-disc set is vast in scope and almost fanatical in its devotion to detail. The disc's elaborate, highly creative menus let you know right away that you are in for something special—they come with their own on-screen instruction manual that runs several pages. But *The Abyss Special Edition* packs more than just gimmicks. At the heart of this set is the landmark sixty-minute documentary, "Under Pressure: Making the Abyss," which has been widely hailed as one of the best of its kind ever produced. Filmmaker Ed Marsh was granted unprecedented access to the production and has crafted a documentary as emotional, exciting, dramatic and suspenseful as the film itself. Cameron called *The Abyss* "the toughest shoot in movie history," and the auteur's legendary ego only added fuel to the fireworks. Scenes unfold like Murphy's Law. Hampered by production delays and budget overruns, the shoot extends from weeks to months. A waterlogged cast and crew reach the breaking point—Harris nearly dies during the filming of a crucial underwater scene, while Mastrantonio explodes in a fit of rage and stomps off the set. Cameron's perfectionism and the film's then-pioneering computer-generated effects cause endless delays, resulting in missed release dates and millions of dollars in lost box office. The intensity of "Under Pressure" is sometimes so raw it is almost unbearable. But it is a testament to Marsh—and Cameron, for having the guts to reveal all—that "Making the Abyss" has now become required viewing for anyone even remotely interested in the hard realities of filmmaking.

If "Under Pressure" were the only extra on this set, it alone still would be worth the price of admission. But the amount of additional material amassed is staggering. Ready for exploration is "Mission Components," which takes us on a complete tour of *The Abyss*'s many creatures, locations and vehicles. Additional "Vidmatics" reveal the secrets behind the film's pioneering effects work, including the landmark all-computer-generated-imagery creation, the "Pseudopod." Massive still galleries include a variety of storyboards, conceptual art, publicity photographs and advertising materials that encompass the film's entire gestation from page to screen. You can also track the development of the screenplay with excerpts and full drafts, as well as discover a variety of hidden easter eggs scattered throughout the menus. And an excellent twelve-page color booklet notes all of the differences between the theatrical and Special Edition cuts of the film.

The Presentation Fox Home Entertainment and THX came under considerable fire from DVD enthusiasts with *The Abyss,* as they chose to present the film in its original 2.35:1 theatrical aspect ratio but without anamorphic encoding. Despite this disappointment, it is still a strong presentation with much to recommend it: rich, deep blacks, excellent contrast and vibrant colors awash in bold blues and greens. Some noticeable digital processing has been applied in an attempt to increase apparent sharpness, which does distract—it is certain that an anamorphic transfer would have improved the level of apparent detail and clarity, especially in the murky underwater sequences. Less questionable is the very dynamic Dolby Digital 5.1 soundtrack, which is highlighted by aggressive surround activity and thunderous low bass. Atmosphere is integral to the effectiveness of a film like *The Abyss,* and this soundtrack delivers a highly enveloping and engaging experience.

Additional Versions Fox Home Entertainment has released three versions of *The Abyss* on DVD: this two-disc *Collector's Edition,* as well as separate single-disc widescreen and pan-and-scan versions, both of which simply drop the second disc of supplementary material. Despite the higher list price, the two-disc set is by far the superior choice.

The Adventures of Indiana Jones

DISTRIBUTOR: Paramount Home Entertainment
DVD RELEASE: October 21, 2003
THEATRICAL RELEASE: 1981/1984/1989
RUNNING TIME: 359 Minutes
MPAA RATING: PG and PG-13

It was the sand castle that changed the world. Two old friends, both world-renowned, fabulously successful filmmakers, were on holiday on a beach in Hawaii and decided to make a bet. They would build a sand castle and, if it was still standing by the time the tide came in, then their latest epic—the tale of a rogue archeologist with a hankering for lost religious artifacts—would be a hit. If it wasn't, well . . .

The filmmakers were, of course, Steven Spielberg and George Lucas. And the epic was *Raiders of the Lost Ark*. "The next morning," said Lucas, smiling, "not only was the castle still there, but it was there when the tide came back in the next afternoon."

A throwback to the Saturday afternoon serials and B-movie cliffhangers that so inspired the pair as children, Indiana Jones (named after Lucas's malamute dog) gave audiences the perfect hero to usher in the Reagan-era 1980s. Indy was a rogue, a chauvinist and not without moral ambiguity—he had no qualms about ducking a swordfight with a single, well-placed bullet—but idealistic enough to plunder for passion, not profit. And Harrison Ford brought to Indy the scruffy good looks of a 1930s serial star and the rakish, smug charm he perfected as Han Solo in *Star Wars*. Moviegoers around the world ate it up, and a new icon was born.

The first in the trilogy, *Raiders of the Lost Ark* shined up the pulpy conventions of old-school serials with wit, aplomb and nonstop derring-do. The glee in watching Lucas and Spielberg's nostalgic pastiche today is to marvel at the state-of-the-art, pre-computer-generated-imagery effects. Indy outruns boulders. Indy drags himself beneath speeding trucks. Indy beats up big bald guys and blows up airplanes. All done live and without a digital net.

Raiders also gives us the best of the Indy girls. Cut from the same cloth as the best old-school Hollywood heroines, Karen Allen's spunky, tough-talkin' and beer-slingin' Marion Ravenwood generates real sparks with Ford and helps balance out the inherent misogyny of the Indy character—she is the only one of his leading ladies who could duke it out with him, quip for quip. If the film's bland Nazis and forgettable Belloq (Paul Freeman) don't quite rank as the most memorable of movie villains, well, no matter. Spielberg and Lucas's obvious love for sheer pop-culture whiz-bang and nonstop action make *Raiders of the Lost Ark* one of the best films of its kind ever made.

By 1984, anticipation was at its highest for another go-round. But Spielberg and Lucas gave new meaning to the term "box office gross" with *Indiana Jones and the Temple of Doom*. After a bravura, Bubsy Berkeley–inspired opening number, the left turn into the dark, doomy and intense dungeons of *Doom* left many audiences and critics shell-shocked. Watch as a heart gets ripped out of a body, laugh as victims are dropped into flaming pits of lava or feast on a dessert of chilled monkey brains. But such outlandish, EC Comics–inspired touches now seem comparatively tame and the breathlessly extended climax—never has a film piled cliffhanger on top of cliffhanger so extensively—is still a total rush. We don't go on roller coasters for depth, just for fun, which, despite its showiness, *Temple of Doom* delivers in spades.

Stung by the criticisms leveled at *Temple of Doom,* Spielberg and Lucas recoiled with 1989's *Indiana Jones and the Last Crusade*. Returning to the style and tone of *Raiders, Last Crusade* couldn't hope to recapture the freshness and inventiveness of the original, and even lifted the former's entire structure and restaged key sequences. Only the inspired casting of Sean Connery as Indy's father—a sly acknowledgment of the debt the trilogy owed to James Bond—raises *Last Crusade* above the level of merely serviceable sequel. Connery's vocal sparring with Ford is inspired, witty and poignant; the scene where they realize they have each shared the bed of the same woman is a classic. And Spielberg's staging of the action is, as always, breathless and thrilling. *Last Crusade* may be the weakest of the Indy movies, but it still proves to be a fitting capper to one of the most well-conceived trilogies of all time. And with Spielberg and Lucas continuing to threaten an *Indiana Jones 4,* it is more than enough.

The Goodies The Indiana Jones films have become such an iconic part of cinema history that even the most mundane details of their making have become priceless artifacts amongst fans. Lucasfilm originally produced a television special on the production of each film at the time of their original theatrical releases, but material since has been scarce. So anticipation for a DVD release of the Indy trilogy grew to a fever pitch until, after a six-year wait, Lucasfilm and Paramount Home Entertainment finally released *The Adventures of Indiana Jones* on DVD in October 2003. This four-disc box set features remastered versions of each film plus a bonus disc containing exclusive new documentaries and featurettes.

Over the course of nearly a year, the Lucasfilm vaults were raided by longtime Spielberg documentarian Laurent Bouzereau and his team, an expedition that uncovered hundreds of hours of rare and never-before-seen behind-the-scenes footage, publicity interviews and screen tests. The heart of the fourth disc is the 126-minute "Indiana Jones: Making the Trilogy" documentary. Bouzereau and Lucasfilm have gone beyond the usual talking-heads interviews to create a mosaic that makes the most of these unearthed treasures. Over and over and over, the documentary treats viewers to a fascinating story or specific production detail from a cast or crew member, only to then cut to actual footage of the incident—a genuine rarity on a DVD for a film produced over two decades ago. The doc is also evenhanded, giving each film equal weight and nicely balancing all aspects of the production, from personal stories to on-set tomfoolery to the nuts-and-bolts logistical challenges.

Four additional featurettes, each running about 12 minutes, further examine the films' stunts, special effects, sound and score. What the filmmakers were able to accomplish, especially on *Raiders,* with its incomprehensibly low $20 million budget, set the standard by which all future blockbusters would be judged. John Williams's score has also become an undisputed classic, and he is seen here in candid moments, both during the composition process and later scoring sessions. And some of the flights of fancy leave one questioning the mental health of the average stuntman—with no digital magic at their disposal, what these brave (or foolish) men and women achieved simply astounds.

Theatrical trailers are also included for all three films, plus teasers for *Raiders* and *Last Crusade*. (The only disappointment is the lack of any deleted scenes or a still gallery.) The included six-page color booklet is also far too slim for an otherwise expansive box set.

The Presentation Working under the auspices of THX and Lowry Digital Imaging, Lucasfilm and Paramount have outdone themselves with *The Adventures of Indiana Jones*. Each film has undergone a painstaking frame-by-frame restoration. The removal of a few hundred thousand specks of dirt, a "serious scratch" that marred a good portion of *Raiders,* and some digital tweaking—many of the films' intrusive mattes lines are gone, as is the famous "snake reflection" seen in the "Pit of the Souls" sequence in *Raiders*—required hundreds of hours of meticulous effort. The results are exemplary. The level of detail and sense of depth will be a revelation for those who grew up with the trilogy on television. Fans could spend virtually hours going through each film, discovering fine details previously imperceptible. Colors have also been restored to their former luster, from the glorious amber fleshtones of *Raiders* to the vivid reds and oranges of *Temple of Doom* and the lush greens and deep blue skies of *Last Crusade*. And Paramount and Lucasfilm have wisely given each film its own disc, with no intrusive extras to steal precious data space. The result is smooth, sharp and artifact-free transfers.

The remixed Dolby Digital 5.1 soundtracks are equally impressive. Both *Raiders* and *Temple of Doom* were produced with mono surrounds; *Last Crusade* is the only truly discrete mix in the bunch. All three have been greatly expanded with more lush, robust frequency response and more consistently active surrounds. The action scenes now rumble with deep low bass. And none of the original soundtracks—including *Raiders*'s, which won an Oscar—have been altered with newly recorded or processed sound effects. *The Adventures of Indiana Jones* is the Holy Grail for Indy fans.

The ALIEN Quadrilogy

DISTRIBUTOR: Fox Home Entertainment

DVD RELEASE: December 4, 2003

THEATRICAL RELEASE: May 1979–October 2003

RUNNING TIME: 502 Minutes

MPAA RATING: R

A*LIEN*'s most iconographic scene is also one of the most glee-fully perverse and just plain disgusting in all of cinematic history. The crew of the Nostromo, after having just discovered a seemingly benign alien species, is on its way back to Earth. But one of their crew is playing host to a biomechanical terror like nothing they could have imagined. When the little bugger finally makes its entrance, it is a moment so shocking, so visceral, so horrific, that audiences were left literally gasping for breath. Few who saw it back in 1979 can re-member the next few minutes of the movie, so unnerving was its impact. *ALIEN* did more than just what every great horror movie should—actually horrify us—it also spawned a "quadrilogy," one still unparalleled in the annals of the genre.

> "You've been in my life so long, I can't remember anything else."
>
> —Ripley, to the Alien

With the cold and austere aesthetics of the original, Ridley Scott crafted an art film out of borrowed parts, a heavy metal *Ten Little Indians* dripping with gore and ooze. Critics were mixed or down-right cool, calling the movie too derivative, too bloody, too manip-ulative. But soothed by the more benevolent visions of Stanley Kubrick's *2001*, George Lucas's *Star Wars* and Steven Spielberg's *Close Encounters,* audiences turned out in droves. *ALIEN* would define 1980s xenophobia. A parable for AIDS? A warning about the dangers of military totalitarianism? Or, in an idea explored even further in its first sequel, 1986's *ALIENS,* a new Vietnam waged in space against an enemy we could defeat? While Ronald Reagan was getting ready to launch his Star Wars program into orbit and

Rambo was preaching a renewed jingoism, Ripley (Sigourney Weaver, in the role of her career) and her motley crew were battling an enemy from both far, far away and deep within. With acid for blood and rows of sharp metallic teeth, the alien of *ALIEN* again gave paranoia a good name.

James Cameron built solidly upon the mythology created by Scott, then turned it inside out. A balls-to-the-wall action film, 1986's *ALIENS* brought back Ripley, gave her plenty of ammunition and let the best bitch win. It was the rare sequel that not only didn't suck, but is also widely considered to be even better than the original. But Cameron, as highly technical a filmmaker as he is, has always been intent on mixing hardware with heart, and so gave Ripley more than just better ammunition and bigger aliens to fight: she became the most beloved and influential female action hero in the history of science fiction. The reward? Weaver brought home an Oscar nomination for her efforts, the film made millions, and at last we got a happy ending. Or so we thought.

ALIEN³ released in 1992, couldn't help but suffer by comparison following the one-two punch of Scott and Cameron; music video whiz kid David Fincher turned out a dark, meandering film ripe with religious allegory but short on the action and the terror that made its predecessors so memorable. *ALIEN³* was certainly a film of its time, and nihilistic and ballsy enough to attempt the impossible: end the most famous sci-fi horror trilogy on a downbeat note and "kill off" the franchise. Audiences and critics balked—many admired it, few embraced it. *ALIEN³* landed with a thud.

An attempt to rinse the bad taste from the mouth left by Fincher's much-maligned box office bust, 1997's *ALIEN Resurrection* was an emotional cul-de-sac of a movie. French auteur Jean Jeunet, filtering his pre-*Amélie* sensibilities through a big-budget, American action spectacle, and the always-game Weaver couldn't save a convoluted script and warmed-over special effects. And Winona Ryder, woefully miscast as a mangy crew member, top lined a supporting cast not nearly as memorable as those in the earlier installments. And *Resurrection*'s capper, clearly designed to leave the door open for yet another sequel, felt contrived and manipulative.

The Goodies *The ALIEN Quadrilogy* must set some kind of record: forty-five hours of supplemental material! A case of more is more, or overkill? Yes and no. Because, yes, the extras are so massive that they do require the kind of time commitment usually reserved for a marathon viewing session of *War and Peace*, and it is also an effort to fully adjust to the languid pacing—the twelve hours of documentaries take their time and not a minute is rushed. But no, beacause despite the sheer volume of material, nothing feels gratuitous or extraneous. *The ALIEN Quadrilogy* is the equivalent to a book on DVD: sprawling, expansive and impossible to digest in one sitting. Which is a good thing.

Each *ALIEN* opus is presented in its original theatrical version and an expanded cut, although arguably only *ALIENS* and *ALIEN³* benefit from the added footage. Cameron trimmed a considerable subplot for the theatrical cut of *ALIENS,* one that greatly fleshed out the relationship between Ripley and Newt. The 156-minute expanded cut reinstates this key plot detail and heightens the emotional impact considerably. Fincher's film was a disaster, compromised by ugly, contentious battles with the studio. But, surprisingly, despite the opportunity offered here to revisit his most maligned film, Fincher passed—the 125-minute expanded version presented here (30 minutes longer than the theatrical version) is a prerelease edit completed without the director's involvement. Regardless, it gives tremendous insight into Fincher's original intentions and what might have been. Each film also includes optional "Special Edition Markers" denoting the newly inserted footage.

The twelve hours of new documentary material created exclusively for the *Quadrilogy* are staggering. Each film receives its own three-hour documentary. Scott's longtime DVD producer Charlie de Lauzirika has created an epic—his passion and commitment is evident in every frame. The sheer number of participants, including Scott, Cameron, and Weaver and most of the key cast and technical crew members, is thrilling. (Only Fincher is sorely missed.) Each documentary is extensive and focused, a unique story well told. And the additional cast and crew commentaries, one for each film, astoundingly are not redundant of the documentaries. Each group track includes interview excerpts and screen-specific material, expertly integrated with not a second of dead space. Each is also accessible and informative enough that it is hard to resist them even after immersing yourself in the documentaries.

Extensive still galleries for each film—easily over one thousand images strong—break down in minute detail all facets of the productions, from H. R. Giger's groundbreaking creature designs and the special effects to amusing vanity photo shoots. There is also a collection of additional deleted scenes and, on a bonus *ninth* disc(!), more theatrical trailers, a sixty-minute abbreviated version of the *ALIEN* documentary, and even more Electronic Press Kit promotional materials. *The ALIEN Quadrilogy* is a landmark and, hands down, delivers the most bang for your buck of just about any DVD set in history.

The Presentation The quality of the supplementary material is matched by all four of these stupendous, THX-certified anamorphic transfers. The integration of the expanded footage is seamless, and each film is a study in different styles and textures. Restored and reconstructed for its twenty-fifth anniversary theatrical rerelease, *ALIEN* is revelatory: Scott's clinical surfaces and ominous, vast landscapes are incredibly three-dimensional and infused with color. *ALIENS,* shot on high-contrast film stocks, has long been plagued by excessive grain and abrasive contrast on video, but here it is smooth, clean and filmlike. Both *ALIEN³* and *ALIEN Resurrection* are the most recent and polished, but they, too, benefit greatly from stronger colors, heightened detail and prints that are as clean as a whistle. A stunning collection.

Each film has also been remixed and remastered in Dolby Digital 5.1, and *ALIEN* and *ALIEN Resurrection* also include DTS options. Scott's esoteric leanings on *ALIEN* are most intriguing: previous video versions suffered from muffled dialogue and a harsh, abrasive sound, which here has been greatly minimized or completely eliminated. Minute, subtle sonic details and ominous effects now emanate from the surrounds for an eerie, effective experience. *ALIENS* features heavy, rumbling low bass if more sporadic directional effects

MAKING *ALIENS* AND OTHER STORIES: A CONVERSATION WITH CHARLIE DE LAUZIRIKA

Charlie de Lauzirika has quickly established himself as one of the top documentarians in the business. He first came to prominence for his continuing collaboration with filmmaker Ridley Scott, crafting all of his landmark special editions—*Gladiator, Thelma & Louise, Black Hawk Down* and the nine-disc *ALIEN Quadrilogy* among them—before branching out with some of the most progressive and pioneering releases yet seen on the format, from the Five-Star Collection of *Speed* to James Bond and *Die Another Day*. This USC graduate is also an accomplished filmmaker in his own right, having written numerous screenplays and directed commercials and music videos.

You first came to prominence as "the Ridley Scott guy." Do you think that affiliation hurt, hindered or had no effect on your career?
It definitely helped. Without a doubt. He basically handed me the keys to the car and let me take it for a drive. It's a responsibility I take seriously and I take his opinions very seriously about the discs I've worked on. I have Ridley to thank for getting me started. Certainly those first couple of years, he was the only person in my court who was helping me get things done. Fortunately, after a few discs it got easier!

How involved is Ridley Scott in the conception process, and is he typical of most of the filmmakers you have worked with?
I think I mostly have free rein. Because if it exists, I'll try to put it on the disc. Occasionally, there will be a little more discussion about it—like on *Matchstick Men*, Ridley and I talked about it way early on, before shooting and pre-production, how to document the film in a way he [had] never done before on any of his films. We had an all-access pass, basically. That's the most he's ever been involved, and he was very involved with the editing of the documentary—pointing out things he liked or disliked or that he wanted to change.

But usually with a filmmaker, you try to find one who supports you and what you are trying to accomplish, but isn't micromanaging, either. Hopefully they trust you. Only on occasion, when I come across material that might be sensitive or something they wouldn't want to show, I run it by them and make a case for why it should or shouldn't get on there. But generally, for me it's a no-brainer. You just try to find the best material you can and load the disc up with it.

Your work on *The ALIEN Quadrilogy* was certainly amazing. Did you have any apprehensions about taking on a project so massive?

Yes, and not just because of the scope of it. But because those are four very different movies with very different expectations. When I look at something that big, I try to bring uniformity to it so it makes sense. Here you have four films that really don't make sense together. They are very unique pieces of work.

On the *Quadrilogy*, there is so much information you almost have to allow for multiple entry points and various navigational options. How did you approach that?

I actually didn't plan on the documentaries to be over three hours long—they just turned out that way! I like to watch a documentary from beginning to end. I don't like this Screen Actors Guild–mandated, thirty-minute rule. That's the main reason for the "Play All" option. It is a necessity for legal, but with *ALIEN,* because it was so epic in scope, I wanted to break that up with different phases of production, which I don't normally do.

That's the only difference this time. For me, designing the disc and doing the flow-charts—that's the most fun. That's when it's easy. It's like when you're writing a script for a movie—you're not really spending money or anything. It's just you. It is so much fun.

For the *Quadrilogy,* you were able to assemble an amazing roster of talent. Do you think you would have been able to pull that off three or four years ago?

Talent is hipper to DVD, and that's both good and bad. They take DVD seriously now. They actually return your calls and show up for interviews and commentaries. (laughs) But by the same token, they want more control over it, and there have been reports that people want money.

Have you found that, in general, talent are more willing to talk about something they did a long time ago as opposed to something new and potentially more sensitive?

Time heals most wounds. In terms of *ALIEN*, I think we got some much more interesting stories about the conflict and the tension between various parties. That's fascinating. It wasn't all a big picnic. It was tough. There were a lot of conflicting emotions. I do think that as time goes on, people feel a little freer to talk about it.

Do you think there is a natural and perfectly understandable resistance to getting the real "nitty gritty," so to speak, on behalf of the filmmakers, or the talent, or the studio?

It depends on the filmmaker. They can go a long way in getting you that access and getting that onto the disc. It's tough but not impossible. It depends on the politics involved—what actually happened and if any feelings were hurt. If it was a great project and there were no problems, that's the honest making of the movie. It's not as interesting as seeing dirt like in *Hearts of Darkness*, [a legendary documentary detailing the ardu-

ous production of Francis Ford Coppola's *Apocalypse Now*] but it's possible.

Do you think that what you were able to accomplish on the *ALIEN* set is indicative of the general direction that the format is going in, in terms of more is more?

Some studios do want to load on as much as they can because they love all those bullet points on the back. Other studios actually are pulling back from that and want quality over quantity, believe it or not. And that's interesting.

I like to find a balance. I want a lot of good stuff. I want to give people as much as they want or expect out of a special edition disc as long as it's good. For that one fan out there who gives a damn about *Legally Blonde 2*, they want to know everything about it. The people who don't care about it won't buy it anyway.

Did you consciously think while putting together the *ALIEN* set that perhaps a line could be crossed into overkill? It is certainly something that cannot really be watched and absorbed in one or even a few sittings.

Is there ever too big of a library? When you go, you want a selection. You don't have to read every book, but it is nice to know that it is all there.

I don't think there's such a thing as too much, but there's something to be said for digital gluttony. Viewers are trying to force-feed themselves with all this stuff—slow down! Take your time and enjoy the experience. If you're one of those people who pick up *The Lord of the Rings* and power through it in one day, you might get burnt out, but if you know it's there on the shelf, and you say, "Oh, I want to learn about miniatures today," then there it is.

Free of budget or time constraints, what do you think are the basic components that make up a great DVD?

In general terms, a really good documentary is at the heart of it all, but it depends on the title. What are the quirks of that particular movie? Maybe a particular deleted scene has to go on there or lost footage or an artifact of the film that everyone's been dying to see. You have to find that. That is what helps flesh out the rest of the experience.

There are a lot of DVDs that have been called "a film school in a box," and that is a phrase I don't care for much, because I don't think it is any particular movie's responsibility to teach you how to make movies. It's the disc's responsibility to tell you how *this* particular movie was made.

What do you think is the future of DVD?

I don't think people are tired of it yet. My concern is that DVD is going to get dumbed-down to the point where it's not going to be interesting to anybody. There was one home video executive who said that DVD might go back to the VHS/LaserDisc paradigm, because you'll have the kind of snotty, expensive Criterion edition, and then you'll have the vanilla Wal-Mart version for five bucks, and that's what keeps the industry going.

I don't think enough is being done to educate consumers. Not just about widescreen, but in terms of a more sophisticated home theater experience. It is just product that they're spitting out. I wish there was a little more thought and a little slower pace so people could put more thought into it. Movies themselves are being cranked out these days just to make that opening weekend and then they disappear. I wish everything would just calm down a little bit and that people would be more thoughtful. I don't mean that in terms of DVD producers, because most DVD producers want to do the best job they can, but they're being cut off at the knees by marketing.

Perhaps we've all gotten a bit spoiled by sets like *The ALIEN Quadrilogy*?
Everyone has been spoiled by DVD. Consumers have been spoiled, producers have been spoiled, but in different ways. It would be nice if things got more thoughtful in the process. ○

---

but excellent reproduction of James Horner's kinetic score. *ALIEN³* is the only of the four to suffer from damaged original elements; some portions are so poor that optional subtitles appear onscreen in place of dialogue that is too muffled to discern. Otherwise, both *ALIEN³* and *Resurrection* feature highly inventive sound design and, in their best sequences, create a completely convincing 360-degree soundfield. They are scorchers.

Additional Versions *The ALIEN Quadrilogy* is the second trip to DVD for the *ALIEN* saga. Fox Home Entertainment's initial release in 1999 was called *The ALIEN Legacy* and featured the theatrical cuts of all four films except *ALIENS,* which was presented in its expanded 156-minute form only. The set also contained a solo audio commentary by Scott on *ALIEN,* and a bonus fifth disc with an original, 60-minute documentary. *The ALIEN Legacy* has since been discontinued and is no longer in print. Each film in *The ALIEN Quadrilogy* is also available separately as a two-disc set; the ninth disc is available only in the *Quadrilogy* box set.

All That Heaven Allows

DISTRIBUTOR: The Criterion Collection
DVD RELEASE: September 12, 2001
THEATRICAL RELEASE: January 1956
RUNNING TIME: 89 Minutes
MPAA RATING: Not Rated

German émigré Douglas Sirk was the Rodney Dangerfield of 1950s cinema. He received no respect: not from the critics, not from the intelligentsia—who would rarely, if ever, lower themselves to see any of his bourgeois potboilers—nor from his peers, as few would publicly applaud a skilled and brilliant European. And Sirk was working in a disreputable genre. Under contract during the waning heyday of the studio system, he would be routinely tossed the typical women's weepies relegated to B-filler, yet transformed them into slick, flamboyant, populist melodramas. Sirk raised the lives, loves and repressed passions of the lowly to the level of the operatic. But

"I don't apologize for wanting you."

—Howard Hoffer

it would only be in the intervening decades, as a new generation of movie brats rediscovered his work at revival houses and on television and video, that Sirk would reemerge as the finest dramatist of his era. The reappraisal may have been too late, but it wasn't too little.

Sirk first hit his stride with 1954's *The Magnificent Obsession,* a box office hit, and followed it up with a series of pictures that refined his unique skills as a social observer and ideological maverick: *Written on the Wind* (1955), *A Time to Love and a Time to Die* (1958) and *Imitation of Life* (1959). But 1956's *All That Heaven Allows* is his most archetypal. Jane Wyman (recently divorced from Ronald Reagan) stars as Cary Scott, a middle-class widow enjoying a life in the fictional anytown of Stoningham, New York. She lives a "perfect" existence: well-off, encased by a close circle of socialites and a regular at dinner parties and the local country club. Then she meets Ron Kirby (Rock Hudson), fifteen years her junior, the handsome young man who tends to her garden. Their attraction is instant and mutual; she is as elegant and refined as he is rugged and clear in purpose (his bible, Thoreau's *Walden,* never leaves his side). But society has other ideas. In melodrama, fate always has the upper hand.

What separates *All That Heaven Allows* from typical '50s pulp is not only Sirk's style, which is formidable, but also his ability to facilitate multiple points of entry and modes of interpretation. Sirk was a true subversive, and *All That Heaven Allows* is representative of his best work—it can be taken as high drama, camp, satire or thriller. The plot is highly formulaic, with all of the standard obstacles: Cary's eager suitor Harvey (Conrad Nagel), for whom she feels no passion; the gossipy Mona Nash (Jacqueline de Wit), who will set the wheels of tragedy in motion; and the disapproving glances of the stifled, desperate townspeople. But Sirk excels by reaching for deeper meaning while still delivering on the required conventions of the genre.

With Sirk, style is not merely substance. His eye for composition, pacing and structure is arguably as great as that of the masters, and he layers symbolism on top of theme in a manner that remains influential. His surfaces are just slick and artificial enough to remind us that his world is slightly surreal, and then he betrays it with an underlying critical eye and satirist's wit. Subtle and delicate, arch and heavy-handed, such seemingly contradictory impulses are, in Sirk's hands, oddly complementary, which remains key to his appeal and importance. He was a true artist and one of the first American auteurs, not just pushing the envelope of what the modern drama was capable of, but ripping it wide open.

The Goodies In the included illustrated essay, the great Rainer Werner Fassbinder sums up what may be the reason Sirk continues to prove so influential: "Only in Sirk's movies do you see women think instead of react." Interspersed with an extensive still gallery of rare production and publicity photos and ad materials, Fassbinder is joined by a legion of top directors, who all make a strong case for why Sirk was a criminally underrated genius far ahead of his time. Joining Fassbinder in their praise are, among others, Quentin Tarantino and Laura Mulvey.

But the star extra is the nearly sixty-minute "Behind the Mirror: The Life of Douglas Sirk," which may strike some as too slim, especially as it does not focus specifically on *All That Heaven Allows*. But this series of interview excerpts from 1979 were among the last to be recorded with the late auteur and are invaluable in assessing his place and importance in the modern pantheon of great filmmakers. Almost shocking is his admission that he didn't really much care for melodrama, just another example of how the limitations of the genre prevented many from seeing the full facets of his talent and the intricacies of the stories he chose to tell.

The Presentation Is *All That Heaven Allows* just another example of Sirk dressing up a mediocre romance novel with splashy Technicolor? Whatever the case, as presented here in 1.78:1 anamorphic widescreen, it looks gorgeous. Appearing more painted-on than filmed, the colors are first-rate and incredibly vivid and stable. Blacks are deep and the contrast uniformly excellent. While the source material can suffer from some minor age-related defects, it excels given the film's vintage and detail is often three-dimensional. The film's original mono soundtrack is preserved here; it does not distract from the material but is otherwise undistinguished.

Additional Recommendations For more classic Sirk, see Criterion's *Written on the Wind,* also wonderfully restored in fabulous Technicolor, as well as *Imitation of Life* and Todd Hayne's critically acclaimed Sirk homage, *Far From Heaven,* starring an Oscar-nominated Julianne Moore. The latter pair are both available from Universal Studios Home Video.

Almost Famous: Untitled—The Bootleg Cut

DISTRIBUTOR: DreamWorks Home Entertainment

DVD RELEASE: December 4, 2001

THEATRICAL RELEASE: September 2000

RUNNING TIME: 162 Minutes

MPAA RATING: R

Filmmakers have been trying to channel the untamed spirit of rock 'n' roll onto celluloid for decades, with largely dismal results. So leave it to Cameron Crowe, one-time rock critic and the pied piper of post–Baby Boomer generation angst—he penned *Fast Times at Ridgemont High* and directed *Say Anything*—to at last get it right.

Almost Famous—and even better, its expanded 162-minute version, *Untitled*—is a quasi-autobiographical, swaggering and just plain rowdy love letter to rock 'n' roll. It is also Crowe's richest, most fully realized work. Yet, despite critical raves, it was a commercial bust upon first release, its intricacies lost on those who pegged it as just another plotless, meandering slice of nostalgia. At least Academy members threw Crowe a bone: he picked up the Oscar for Best Original Screenplay. But it did little to spark further profits. *Almost Famous* was still the Almost Hit.

At first, Crowe's unique brand of cinematic storytelling seems like nothing more than simplistic, manipulative button-pushing, but that is only because his subtlety and lackadaisical nonchalance hides a deeper meaning. Take what will be our first introduction to the world of backstage rock 'n' roll. Our protagonist, the young Crowe stand-in William (Patrick Fugit) is trying to sneak into the inner circle of the Black Sabbath tour machine. In a bravura and amazingly compact five-minute sequence, Crowe adroitly weaves story, character, theme and milieu in a way that recalls the best work of Crowe's idol, Billy Wilder. William's sexual liberation, growing frustration and ultimate triumph of self-confidence is played out like its own minimovie (or rock video),

> "Rock stars have kidnapped my son!"
>
> —Elaine Miller

all smothered in the cotton-candy levity of *Apartment*-era Wilder. *Untitled* is filled with scenes like this, each a small treasure.

There are those who argue that the rhetoric in *Almost Famous* is overly naïve and not biting enough (there are no drugs in these backstage arenas, and the sexual debauchery is kept largely offscreen), but let them eat Crowe. He is far too ambitious a filmmaker to reduce *Untitled* to the level of a tabloid expose of boring rock excess. He's distilling the very essence of rock 'n' roll, then reformulating it into a nostalgic, slice-of-life entertainment for the masses. And the DVD format was tailor-made for experiments like *Untitled*—box office failures now given a new life and a new avenue in which to find an audience. The reward? A great film that reveals more with every viewing. Don't be scared off by its pretentious title, for *The Bootleg Cut* is apt; *Untitled* is nothing more than an old, worn-out vinyl LP. Let it sit on your shelf for a while and gather some dust, and then whenever you get hungry for a little hip, shake and swagger, pull it back down, fire up the air guitar and let 'er rip.

The Goodies Cameron Crowe has long been a huge proponent of DVD, and *Untitled* may be his best yet. *The Bootleg Cut* successfully reproduces the look and feel of a real collector's item on DVD, which is no easy feat in today's era of cookie-cutter studio product. Crowe is certainly a great fan of the communal audio commentary, which here is even more poignant and personal. Joining in is his mother, Alice, and their banter is by turns hilarious and touching. Even more unusual, representatives from Vinyl Films (Crowe's production company) and DreamWorks chime in with insight on the challenges of getting such an outrageously personal and ultimately uncommercial project to the big screen. What a great track—there certainly are few out there like it.

Adding a bit of strangeness to the whole affair is a variety of seemingly arbitrary and unrelated vignettes. Crowe hides audio introductions all over the place on this two-disc set, weaving in everything from a short interview with rock legend Lester Bang to a demo version of Nancy Wilson's "Love Comes and Goes"—set to a montage of behind-the-scenes footage—and short "B-Sides," all DV material shot by Crowe and his team, which run the gamut from auditions and rehearsals to other production shenanigans and outtakes. Additional extras include even more deleted scenes and a fifteen-minute performance by Stillwater (the film's fictional answer to Led Zeppelin) that is cleverly edited as if it were a real-life concert. Just another inspired touch in a special edition full of them.

Crowe is not without a sense of humor when it comes to DVD, and *The Bootleg Cut* at last includes the holy grail of *Untitled* outtakes, the infamous "Stairway to Heaven" scene—a pivotal, seven-plus–minute sequence built around the Led Zepplin masterwork as heard in its entirety. If this had actually made its way into the film, it would have probably earned *Almost Famous* that elusive Oscar nod for Best Picture. But Zeppelin is loath to grant clearance rights to their crowning achievement, so Crowe had to leave the scene on the cutting room floor. So how does he get around it here? I won't spoil the joke, but it is one of the cleverer and slyly comic uses of the DVD format's "interactive" capabilities ever attempted. It is, like *The Bootleg Cut* itself, the ultimate in lo-fi meets hi-fi.

Rounding out this smart collection is another rarity on DVD, a wealth of text-based biographical and historical information. Interested in Cameron Crowe the "rock writer"? Survey his Top Albums of 1973 and seven selected articles from his Rolling Stone days, plus extensive production notes and filmographies. And no "bootleg" DVD would be complete without an easter egg—here a lovely, aborted scene with Kate Hudson and a mysterious girl named "Leslie." It has to be seen to be believed. Still want more? Also slipped in the package is a six-song Stillwater CD. Rock on.

The Presentation *Untitled* features nearly forty minutes of additional footage excised from the original theatrical cut of *Almost Famous,* and it has been reintegrated here seamlessly. (The original 127-minute release version is also included on the second disc in this set.) Presented in a lush, 1.85:1 anamorphic widescreen transfer, *The Bootleg Cut* is awash in nostalgia. It looks and feels like a memory, enticing us with its supple amber hues, rich detail and near three-dimensional concert sequences. This is likely the most pristine, impeccable example of a "director's cut" you are likely to see on DVD.

Alas, *Almost Famous: Untitled—The Bootleg Cut* is not perfect. The theatrical cut is blessed with both DTS and Dolby Digital 5.1 surround tracks, yet the DTS option has been dropped from *Untitled*. The Dolby mix is certainly kick-ass—the concert sequences here are as dynamic as any you are likely to hear—but *Almost Famous* ultimately becomes the preferred sonic experience. The DTS track is a bit more boisterous, roomy and aggressive. Unfortunately *Untitled* is so much more complete of an experience that it is hard to watch the theatrical cut again, which makes the lack of a DTS track a surprising omission. Otherwise, *The Bootleg Cut* is as close to DVD perfection as you are likely to get.

Additional Versions DreamWorks Home Entertainment first released *Almost Famous* on DVD in March 2001. It contained the theatrical cut of the film, a short featurette and a Stillwater music video (none of these extras appear on *Untitled*). The two-disc *Bootleg Cut* followed by the end of the year. Both remain in print.

Amadeus: The Director's Cut

DISTRIBUTOR: Warner Home Video
DVD RELEASE: September 14, 2002
THEATRICAL RELEASE: April 2002
RUNNING TIME: 180 Minutes
MPAA RATING: R

Milos Forman's *Amadeus* is more than just another Hollywood biopic, however brash and brilliant it may be. It is indeed a dissection of the life and times of Wolfgang Amadeus Mozart. It is also an astonishingly intimate character study. And a historical saga of exceptional proportions. But what elevates *Amadeus* to the status of a true classic—and here it is even more amazing in its restored 180-minute *Director's Cut*—is that it is a biting, satiric parable on the very act of creation itself. *Amadeus* lays bare the most painful truth every artist must eventually accept: that genius trumps craftsmanship every time.

When Salieri (F. Murray Abraham, who won an Oscar for his performance) begins the film

> "Forgive me, Majesty. I am a vulgar man! But I assure you, my music is not."
>
> —Wolfgang Amadeus Mozart

with his haunting confession to his priest, we realize this isn't going to be a pretty story. Salieri works like a dog day in and day out, perfecting his ultimately mediocre operas. Mozart, meanwhile, gets drunk, beds as many loose women as he possibly can, then wakes up in the middle of the night and spends five minutes writing the greatest piece of music the world has ever heard. Such is life, and no, it is not fair. But you can't blame Mozart. Salieri, however, can. And to what ends he will go to avenge such a cosmic injustice forms the dark heart of *Amadeus*.

Winner of eight Academy Awards including Best Picture and Best Director, *Amadeus* was originally released theatrically in 1984 with a runtime of 160 minutes. When it was announced that Forman would be revisiting the film in *The Director's Cut,* with an additional 20 minutes of material reinstated, eyebrows were raised. Why try to improve upon a film already considered a classic? Yet Forman did it. *The Director's Cut* allows us to better appreciate some of the finest performances of the past couple of decades. Unlike Abraham's universally praised portrayal of Salieri, Tom Hulce's Mozart was lambasted by some for being too juvenile and bawdy, but here his garish grandstanding is better tempered by scenes revealing his latent fear, insecurity and self-loathing. And young Elizabeth Berridge, virtually cut out of the theatrical release as Mozart's long-suffering wife, is a revelation. *Amadeus: The Director's Cut* is just as much of a testament to its cast as to Forman.

Yet whether or not it is viewed in its expanded form, *Amadeus* remains one of the most mean-spirited and uncompromising films to ever hit mainstream Hollywood. All the more shocking is that the evil in the hearts of its characters is not transformed into the monstrous or blunted by farce—no easy laughs or horror-movie clichés are offered to shield us from the consequences. *Amadeus* is a film with bite and flavor and made with undeniable passion, an unforgettable story of lives graced by the beauty of music but ultimately hollow and fueled by spite and malice. The questions Forman dares to ask continue to resonate.

The Goodies Pioneer Entertainment released *Amadeus* on laserdisc in the mid-1990s, and it was a box set so lavish that it quickly became a benchmark for the format. In preparing the DVD release of *The Director's Cut,* Warner Home Video has not produced much in the way of new material; the majority of the extras here have been pulled from the Pioneer set, albeit in slightly altered form.

The audio commentary is a scorcher. Forman and screenwriter Peter Shaffer, who adapted his own stage play, are edited together from two separate commentaries (Forman's is culled from the laserdisc). Despite the lapse of time and no specific mention being made of *The Director's Cut,* it is a very strong track. Rarely do we get such insight on the development of a screenplay: Shaffer is intelligent and articulate about the challenges involved in such an undertaking, while Forman makes no bones about what was often an arduous and emotionally demanding shoot. A first-class commentary.

On the set's second disc, we get a comprehensive sixty-minute documentary "The Making of Amadeus," which has also been repackaged from the laserdisc. It is a near-perfect companion piece to the commentary and remarkably free of any redundancy. Insightful cast and crew interviews flesh out the human drama, from casting to production to the eventual Oscar windfall. Although the remaining extras are slim—the obligatory theatrical trailer, an awards listing and pithy filmographies—and any sort of still gallery is completely absent, the combined might of the commentary and the documentary more than redress any imbalance.

The Presentation *Amadeus* is a beautiful and haunting film, impeccably photographed and a triumph of costume design and art direction. But it also poses a considerable challenge for the DVD format. Although newly remastered, this 1.85:1 anamorphic widescreen transfer is an often soft, even fuzzy-looking presentation. It is the colors that impress the most: they are rich, vibrant, clean and glorious. Shot primarily with natural light, the majority of the film suffers from a lack of true detail, and scenes bathed in shadows—of which there are many—lack the sharpness of the best modern-day transfers. There is even some intrusive edginess throughout. Yet this doesn't ruin the party: *Amadeus: The Director's Cut* retains a classic look, a bit dated but appropriately timeless.

    Amadeus certainly lives and dies by the strength of its score, and *The Director's Cut* has been appropriately remixed in Dolby Digital 5.1 surround. It is generally superb. The classical compositions are given a renewed sense of breadth and depth, with a consistent surround presence and heftier low end. A minor complaint: dialogue and some of the brash, brassier instruments still sound too harsh and cramped. Otherwise, *Amadeus: The Director's Cut* would do Mozart proud.

Additional Versions Warner Home Video originally released *Amadeus* on DVD in 1998. It contained the theatrical release version but was hampered by a poor transfer and no supplementary material. It has since been discontinued.

American Beauty

DISTRIBUTOR: DreamWorks Home Entertainment
DVD RELEASE: October 29, 2000
THEATRICAL RELEASE: October 1999
RUNNING TIME: 115 Minutes
MPAA RATING: R

American Beauty is a primal-scream movie, bursting with rage, pain and unfulfilled desire. That it was made at all is some sort of minor miracle: Hollywood does not usually honor those who try to bite the hand that feeds them. But *Beauty* pulled off the impossible. It convinced the very culture it mocked to proclaim it a masterpiece. It is a movie that defies easy classification. Is it a comedy? A horror movie? A thriller? It certainly isn't a mystery. We know our protagonist, Lester Burnham, will be dead in less than a year's time. It is one of the many vicious conceits of *American Beauty* that he will be both our narrator and our surrogate. He tells us what we already know the minute we first meet him, because we already recognize it in ourselves. He is lost, alone, unloved by his family and unnecessary at work. We are forced to stare deep within the abyss of his and our shared spiritual emptiness . . . and laugh.

American Beauty challenges us to "look closer." It could only have been written by an artist fed up with a culture that revels in the banal, the mediocre and the shallow. After years toiling in the trenches of Hollywood, screenwriter Alan (*Six Feet Under*) Ball put poison pen to paper and discovered manifest destiny in the mundane. His is an audacious, even arrogant, polemic. Somehow, in *Beauty,* Ball is able to convince us that our lives are ultimately meaningless, but that if we only embrace our insignificance we will achieve transcendence. And that we should be grateful to him for such precious illumination. It is easy to balk at such a stern lecture, but before we can get too angry, Ball delivers on his audacious promise: he tells us where we are going before we get there. And he's right.

> **"Welcome to America's Weirdest Home Videos."**
> —Ricky Fitts

"There's a secret life behind things." Even a plastic bag floating in the wind. *American Beauty* is a rare breed, a commercial pop masterstroke that does more than just straddle the line between art and commerce; it completely bridges the gap between the two. That it walked off with eight Academy Awards may be the ultimate joke. There is likely some sort of great irony in the fact that both Ball and director Sam Mendes, a theater veteran, were first-timers. And that Mendes, a Brit, made one of the best American movies of the past couple of decades. Even more absurd? *American Beauty* was shepherded by DreamWorks and Steven Spielberg, a filmmaker not known for his dark visions of middle-class suburbia. But somehow, it all makes some sort of bizarre sense. *American Beauty* is an unclassifiable, fiercely independent, utterly dazzling original. An instant classic.

The Goodies Hot on the heels of its eight Academy Awards wins, DreamWorks Home Entertainment unleashed the *American Beauty Awards Edition*. Although the extras are comparatively slim for a film of such stature, the lack of lengthy bullet points on the back of the box is indeed deceptive. Once again, you have to look closer. It is the quality, not the quantity, that impresses.

There is nothing particularly wrong with the twenty-four-minute featurette "Look Closer . . ." other than that it is utterly formulaic. Kevin Spacey and Annette Benning landed the roles of their careers with *Beauty,* and the film also introduced a trio of rising young stars in Thora Birch, Mena Suvari and Wes Bentley. But this electronic press kit does not do them justice, nor Mendes and Ball, nor certainly the late cinematographer Conrad Hall, who capped a glorious career with his amazing work on *Beauty*. Made up of the usual quick-cut, on-set interviews and behind-the-scenes clips that barely scratch the surface, "Look Closer . . ." makes the same fatal assumption most press kits of its type routinely do: that you haven't already seen the movie you just bought.

Rescuing the Awards Edition are the remaining two extras, which more than make up for the lackluster featurette. The screen-specific audio commentary with Mendes and Ball (also both Oscar winners for Best Director and Best Original Screenplay, respectively) is notable for its lack of ego. Recorded after the Academy windfall, both remain wry, humble and articulate, if forgivably fawning over their cast. The conversational tone covers the entire arc of the production—casting, rehearsals, working with the sometimes fiery Hall, a rejiggered ending and a mentor (Spielberg) with an unusual amount of faith in his first-time charges. But even better than the commentary is a truly one-of-a-kind feature: Mendes and Hall provide a full-length "Storyboard Presentation" which, at first, doesn't instill much confidence. Just another bland and perfunctory still gallery? Hardly. The pair completely breaks down the film, scene by scene, shot by shot, and it is like eavesdropping on an intimate conversation with the masters. This kind of depth and detail simply is inconceivable on any other video format and raises the Awards Edition to the level of the truly indispensable.

The film's theatrical trailer and a nice liner essay by Mendes round out the set.

The Presentation Conrad Hall does not waste a single shot. Evocative and haunting and awash in bold, thematic uses of color, every last inch of the frame is utilized, each shot suitable for framing. Presented here in 2.35:1 anamorphic widescreen, this is a rich, highly detailed and very filmlike transfer. It can also be moody—film grain is sometimes apparent and some scenes have a dark cast. But colors retain a vibrant purity and no distracting edge enhancement or other digital processing has been applied. A fitting monument to one of history's finest cinematographers.

DreamWorks has also included both Dolby Digital and DTS 5.1 options, with the DTS a better realization of *American Beauty*'s intricate, often deceptively simple sound design. Nothing here dazzles or distracts us with sonic bombast. Thomas Newman's minor-key, minimalistic score sneaks up on you, blending seamlessly with the sparse effects and low-key dialogue. And the increased resolution of the DTS format provides the more enveloping experience, with the rear channels more full-bodied and alive and dialogue crisper and more natural. This quintessential dramatic soundtrack proves you don't need explosions to engage the senses.

Alternate Versions DreamWorks Home Entertainment has also released a 4:3 full-screen version of *American Beauty,* which includes the same extras and sound formats.

American Graffiti

DISTRIBUTOR: Universal Studios Home Video

DVD RELEASE: September 30, 1998

THEATRICAL RELEASE: August 1973

RUNNING TIME: 112 Minutes

MPAA RATING: PG

There is something intoxicating about the warm glow of nostalgia. It is able to convince us that even the most mundane moments of our lives are somehow integral to the fabric of the universe. We are endlessly fascinated by our own quintessential rite of passage into adulthood—whether to go off to college, off to war, off to Europe, or off to get married. And as a culture we love to revel in the shallow, too. We worship hot rods—meaningless symbols of out-of-control masculinity—and preferably ones that drive really fast and look really cool. George Lucas seemed to understand all of this when he made what remains his best film, *American Graffiti*.

Lucas's tale of a group of 1960s high school seniors, cruising the ship on the edge of their last night of innocence, remains the preeminent example of the underdog movie, the one no one wanted but that became a blockbuster. Only producer Francis Ford Coppola believed in its potential:

> "You can't stay seventeen forever!"
>
> —Steve Bolander

Universal Studios, so sure they had a bomb on its hands, dropped it into theaters with a thud. But *American Graffiti* proved so popular it inspired its own subgenre, the Plotless Examination of Bored Youth. Indeed, nothing much of great importance seems to happen. Teens cruise the strip and cruise one another. They swap stories at the hop, play pranks and whisper secret crushes. They talk of big dreams and ideals and the future. There are some vague threads of a story. Curt Henderson (Richard Dreyfuss) frets about going off to college. Childhood sweethearts Steve Bolander (Ron "Ronny" Howard) and Laurie Henderson (Cindy Williams) break up, make up, and break up again. Terry "The Toad" Fields (Charles Martin Smith) attempts his first big score with Debbie Dunham (Candy Clark). And perpetual senior John Milner (Paul Le Mat), stuck with pint-sized cargo Carol (MacKenzie Philips), confronts his long-standing rivalry with Bob Falfa (Harrison Ford) in the big drag-race finale. Poignancy is only achieved with the end title cards as we find out the fate of each: innocence must always be lost.

Before he turned to the geeky sci-fi of *Star Wars* and its even more mechanical sequels, Lucas seemed to be one of the American cinema's last great hopes. In this galaxy far, far away, he was a humanist filmmaker, telling real stories about real people. His restraint and passion are evident in every shot of *American Graffiti*. Its brilliance is in its simplicity. Acted in a largely improvisational manner and captured with a natural authenticity by the sharp cinematography of Haskel Wexler, it transcends its meager narrative by refusing to let us off the hook. We all must eventually confront our own destiny. "It doesn't make sense to leave home to look for home. To give up a life to find a new life. To say good-bye to friends you love just to find new friends." *American Graffiti* achieves relevancy because it understands that however much we might want to hold on to the past, we have no choice but to embrace our destiny. Such is the allure of nostalgia.

The Goodies American Graffiti does not seem to have much going for it as a DVD. There is only one major extra, the seventy-eight-minute documentary "The Making of American Graffiti." But sometimes a great documentary is enough.

"The Making of American Graffiti" is like a Hollywood High who's-who yearbook—it is even divided into its own little chapters ("Genesis," "Casting," "Production Stories," "Final Words"). Frequent Lucas documentarian Laurent Bouzereau has enticed everyone to return: Coppola, Dreyfuss, Howard, Williams, Ford, Smith, Le Mat, Clark, Kathleen Quinlan, Suzanne Somers, editor Walter Murch, casting director Fred Roos, screenwriters William Huyck and Gloria Katz, and more. While faces like Dreyfuss, Ford and Howard remain familiar, the shock at seeing others is disorienting, an often uncomfortable reminder of our own mortality and the ever-flickering passage of time. (Even more jaw-dropping: The vintage screen tests that feel like artifacts of a lost era.) Without even trying, "The Making of American Graffiti" reinforces the very themes of the movie it documents. Fueled by the power of nostalgia, even the simplest of on-set stories ooze with poignancy. "I wanted to chronicle the end of an era, how things change, of life passages," Lucas says. And that is what we get here, a true mosaic of ambition, youthful enthusiasm and just a little bit of blind luck. An essential document of a seminal American masterpiece.

The Presentation With its naturalistic, neodocumentary style, *American Graffiti* does not have the sharp, glossy veneer of more modern, big-budget fare. Lucas wanted his film to "look like a jukebox," shot largely in real locations and with little in the way of controlled lighting. So those new to *Graffiti* may find this THX-certified, 2.35:1 anamorphic widescreen a bit lacking. But given the film's intended style—and certainly compared to the horribly cropped, incredibly murky transfers that routinely show up on broadcast television—it is a revelation. Blacks are rock solid, colors deep and rich and, despite frequent grain due to the use of high-contrast film stocks, the source material is near pristine. Just perfect.

American Graffiti also remains a landmark because of its soundtrack. It pioneered the "song score" and gave Hollywood a whole new way to market its movies. Packed wall-to-wall with classic 1950s pop tunes, the film is devoid of any original score or even incidental cues. Thus this DVD's Dolby 2.0 surround track is more than adequate. Rear presence is just about nil, as the limited fidelity of the vintage songs requires a more traditional stereo mix. Dialogue is of primary importance and it remains firmly rooted in the center channel, always clear, distinct and audible. But it all only adds to the charm. *American Graffiti* remains gloriously lo-fi. As it should.

Back to the Future Trilogy

DISTRIBUTOR: Universal Studios Home Video

DVD RELEASE: December 17, 2002

THEATRICAL RELEASE: May 1985/November 1989/May 1990

RUNNING TIME: 342 Minutes

MPAA RATING: PG

If television's *Family Ties* turned Michael J. Fox into a star, *Back to the Future* shot him into the stratosphere. Robert Zemeckis's zippy tale of DeLorean-fueled time travel was the perfect match of actor, director and material. In an era when going to movies meant splitting up the family at the local gigaplex, *Back to the Future* brought them back together. Fox played a pint-sized conservative that freaked out his ex-hippie parents on *Ties,* Zemeckis was a pop-culture brat who grew up on TV, the Beatles and matinee serials, and Ronald Reagan had just been inaugurated in his second term as president. *Back to the Future* did more than just bridge the generation gap, it welded it shut.

With its Spielberg-sanctioned sentimentality and post–*Star Wars* love of hokey B-movie conventions, *Back to the Future* is the blockbuster that proves, without a doubt, that the 1980s was the decade of cozy nostalgia. If Indiana Jones was a bit of a bad boy, Fox's Marty is the kind of guy you could bring home to Mom. Watch as Marty plays out a host of vaguely Freudian complications as he hitches up his not-so-hip-to-be-square parents—despite Mom's amorous advances toward *him*—and introduces 1950s teens to rock 'n' roll. And watch how Zemeckis gets to have it both ways. Played to stammering perfection by Fox, Marty teaches the teens that maybe being like their parents isn't such a bad thing after all—and reassures the boomers that their kids are going to grow up just fine after all. . . to be just like them.

> "Wait a minute, Doc, are you trying to tell me that my mother has got the hots for me?"
>
> —Marty McFly

But Zemeckis and Spielberg couldn't leave well enough alone, and four years later *Back to the Future* became a trilogy. *Part II* was—

and still is—one of the loopiest follow-ups of all time. Gone was the more-or-less linear narrative of the original as Zemeckis went post-modern. Audacious if calculated, a jagged series of set pieces bounced across three time zones as the movie simultaneously pandered to and skewered Reagan-era greed. The return of almost all the familiar old faces did little to warm up the ice-cold irony, and most audiences and critics left the theater scratching their heads. And that "To Be Continued . . ." cliffhanger ending sure didn't help, either.

Slowing things down after the genre-bending antics of *Part II*, Zemeckis returned to the safe and familiar with *Part III*, setting Marty and Doc Brown down in the Old West. More a remake of the first film than a fresh climax, the folding-back-on-top-of-themselves gags were still charming, but even a sweet romance for Doc and more nifty effects weren't enough to satisfy audiences after six hours of build-up: *Part III* grossed the least of the bunch. *Back to the Future* as a trilogy may have suffered from the law of diminishing returns, but it deserves a reevaluation. Here is the rare popcorn trilogy that improves with age—intelligent, ambitious and thoroughly entertaining.

The Goodies When a studio releases a movie trilogy on DVD as a single, you-gotta-buy-'em-all box set, it usually means studio marketeers are trying to unload a bunch of crummy sequels at one way-too-high price. But here is one that actually makes sense—the sequels add new layers of complexity to the first, and improve on their own with every viewing.

Longtime Spielberg documentarian Laurent Bouzereau is again at the helm of this three-disc set, but Zemeckis makes him shake up the formula. Along with co-scenarist Bob Gale, Zemeckis, a one-time Spielberg prodigy, hosted a Q&A at his alma mater University of Southern California that is reedited here into three separate audio commentaries, one for each flick. (The sequels get the short shrift, however, with only partial tracks that simply cut out midway.) The lively format adds an element of spontaneity missing from most other commentaries, forcing Zemeckis and Gale to openly discuss many of the rumors that have long dogged the trilogy. And the frequent charges of narrative inconsistencies leveled at the filmmakers often prove hilarious. Also supplying a more traditional, nuts-and-bolts, screen-specific audio commentary for each installment is Gale again, along with coproducer Neil Canton. But wait, there's more! Three "Did You Know That?" subtitle fact tracks fill in additional trivia, cast and crew tidbits, and useless pop-culture throwaways. Talk about information overload.

Zemeckis, Gale and Fox contribute new interviews in three "Making the Trilogy" segments on each film, and Fox further discusses life with Marty in his own solo interview. Additional vignettes cover the effects, stunts and gadgets with a variety of archival, before-and-after, and test footage. The 1990 *Behind the Back to the Future Trilogy* TV special (hosted by Kirk Cameron!) lends the appropriate retro feel, while an extensive selection of deleted scenes, stills, music videos and trailers round out the package for completists. The only glaring omission? Eric Stoltz, originally cast as Marty, shot a few key scenes before being unceremoniously replaced by Fox. Long the Holy Grail among *Back to the Future* fans, the footage is sadly not included. Lost in a time loop somewhere?

The Presentation Each *Future* flick gets the remastered 1.8:1 anamorphic widescreen treatment, and if ever the phrase "so good, it is too good" proved true, it is here. One of the ironies of the DVD format is that its clarity renders the effects of the pre-CGI era painfully fake. But despite many an obvious matte painting, composite outline and rotoscoped-in animation, each flick looks bright and poppy, especially the candy-colored second installment and the warm western motif of the trilogy's capper. Equally impressive are the Dolby Digital and DTS 5.1 remixes. Heightened surrounds and an overall expanded sonic palette give the trilogy a new lease on life; dig the surprisingly punchy LFE and some clever uses of the rear channels. Pretty nifty.

Black Narcissus

DISTRIBUTOR: The Criterion Collection

DVD RELEASE: January 30, 2001

THEATRICAL RELEASE: December 1947

RUNNING TIME: 100 Minutes

MPAA RATING: Not Rated

Emeric Pressburger and Michael Powell's *Black Narcissus* may be as timely and relevant today as it was in 1947. It has often been dismissed as a "women's prison picture," but it is far more than that. The story—lust and unrequited physical longings at play between nuns and mountain men in a remote Himalayan convent—may sound exploitative, sensational or merely trite. But *Black Narcissus* insists that its viewers look beneath its dazzling surface at the passions and desires that will play themselves out with tragic consequences. It endures because it asks a fundamental question that continues to plague the secular world: what happens when our desires interfere with our devotion?

Based on the novel by Rumer Godden (who reportedly disliked the adaptation), *Black Narcissus* does not pull any punches despite having to, at times, tiptoe around censorship restrictions of the time. It is truly a film that deepens upon repeated viewings. The sensual aspects are never played for titillation or easy moralizing. Godden's novel was a potent allegory, but Pressburger and Powell's staging is so adroit and inventive that they are able to transform the book's episodic structure into a more coherent and rewarding whole. And their often startling use of symbolism—visual, aural, thematic—rivals anything by Luis Bunuel. Pressburger and Powell may have simplified some of Godden's characters and situations, which likely contributed to his disappointment, but they have stripped away none of his story's power and meaning.

> **SISTER CLODAGH:** "Well, I don't really know what to do."
>
> **MR. DEAN:** "What would Christ have done?"

Black Narcissus is also one of those great movies you show to your friends to try to trick them. Full of lush, exotic locations, grand exteriors and scrumptious detail, it hides an amazing secret: it was shot entirely in a studio. Certainly, any self-respecting cineaste will be able to identity most of the film's backdrops as matte paintings and other visual trickery at play. But fifty years after the fact, Jack Cardiff's mesmerizing color photography remains as smooth, seamless and spectacular as ever. Every frame of *Black Narcissus* is a work of art.

The Goodies Michael Powell's and Martin Scorsese's screen-specific audio commentary here is essential. It is a track that film lovers will want listen to at least twice, if only to study the work of the three grand masters, Powell, Pressburger and Cardiff. *Black Narcissus* is one of Scorsese's all-time favorites and his passion comes through with great impact, as this is a filmmaker who has obviously studied every frame. But truly poignant is Powell, who speaks eloquently of his late partner and also in great detail about the intricacies of staging a production that seemed so simple on the surface but was vastly complex behind the camera.

Cardiff also gets his full due in a lovely thirty-minute documentary. "Painting with Light," produced specifically for this DVD, is a fitting tribute to one of history's greatest cinematographers, whose symphonic visual style continues to influence and inspire. Touching on his early days, his landmark work on *Black Narcissus* and his further collaboration with Powell and Pressburger, it is a comprehensive mix of interviews, archival footage and stills.

Other extras include a strong collection of production stills and a sharp liner essay by critic Dave Kehr.

The Presentation *Black Narcissus* is a beautiful film and, despite some minor print flaws, looks beautiful here. It is the incredibly vibrant and bold colors that linger the most in memory; they are strongly rendered with the stability and sharpness that only the DVD format can deliver. The favorite of purists, Criterion's approach has always been to respect the filmmaker's original intentions, which usually means not upgrading or remixing monophonic soundtracks. Such is the case here—the elements are slightly cleaned up but still noticeably dated. Dialogue can sound distorted, and audible hiss is frequent. But the quality of the transfer is near-definitive and makes *Black Narcissus* an essential DVD.

Blue Velvet

DISTRIBUTOR: MGM Home Entertainment
DVD RELEASE: June 18, 2002
THEATRICAL RELEASE: September 1986
RUNNING TIME: 121 Minutes
MPAA RATING: R

The movie that introduced an unsuspecting public to the S&M bedroom antics of Middle America, David Lynch's delightfully twisted *Blue Velvet* is still one of the most influential and important American movies ever made. And one of the most polarizing, a love-it-or-hate-it proposition that still has the power to provoke, disturb and disgust. If you're not absolutely hooked by Lynch's thoroughly unique vision within the first three minutes, you might as well hit Eject because it is not going to get any easier.

Not convinced that a single film could be so simultaneously loved and hated? *Premiere* magazine's 1990 International Critics' Poll named *Blue Velvet* the best film of the 1980s by a landslide. Yet Roger Ebert *still* gripes about the movie being one of the fifty worst pieces of trash he's ever seen. In a breathless series of op-ed pieces, feminist scholars either berated or praised Isabella Rossellini's fierce, naked portrayal of Dorothy Vallens—surely one of the most vulnerable performances ever seen on screen—as a misogynistic caricature or a bold reinvention of the classic (and outdated) noir femme fatale. And the film's lack of box office and

SANDY WILLIAMS: "I can't figure out if you're a detective or a pervert."

JEFFREY BEAUMONT: "Well, that's for me to know and you to find out."

scattershot award recognition only underscored its duality and cemented its notoriety. It was an instant cult classic despite poor grosses. The Academy would honor Lynch with a nomination for Best Director, even while many of its members publicly campaigned against giving it a Best Picture nod. It is precisely this dichotomy that has kept *Blue Velvet* alive and fertile as the ultimate cineaste think piece.

What continues to provoke about *Blue Velvet* is that Lynch did more than just stretch the limits of what was permissible on-screen in a mainstream, R-rated studio picture. Like other similar lightning rods for controversy—David Cronenberg's *Crash,* Adrian Lyne's remake of *Lolita*—Lynch's sex games were branded cold and impersonal, ugly illustrations of a filmmaker interested not in healthy, sensual (consensual?) adult sex but in how sex could be used to brutalize, humiliate and coerce. That some were turned on by the now-infamous "interaction" between Rossellini and Dennis Hopper—*Blue Velvet* resuscitated his career—only further enraged detractors. In an excruciatingly long, dimly lit wonderland of scary shadows and even scarier sexual indulgences, Lynch transforms the erotic into the uneasy and dangerous. Terrifying, exhilarating, campy. This wasn't sex. This was a war zone.

That *Blue Velvet* continues to reek of unease is what continues to intrigue. Few, if any, mainstream motion pictures have dared to skirt the territory Lynch gleefully reveled in. So why even have *Blue Velvet* on your shelf? You'll have to see it for yourself. Movies don't come any more daring or provocative than this, and just the fact that Lynch was able to play such a wild card at all remains cause for celebration. The ultimate coffeetable DVD.

The Goodies Produced by Jeffrey Schwarz and Automat Pictures, "Mysteries of Love" is a benchmark documentary. It starts off a little slow—typical of full-length documentaries ("Mysteries" nearly exceeds ninety minutes) the luxury of the run time allows participants to linger on subjects a bit too long. But once the humdrum introductions are out of the way, "Mysteries" pulls back the curtain for a revealing look at a production shrouded in secrecy. While Lynch is rumored to be defiantly against "special features," and here declined a new interview, he did approve the use of extensive archival footage as well as never-before-seen material and stills. And no key scene is left untouched—who can forget the infamous seduction scene with Rossellini spreading her legs, which we learn here was done sans underwear, much to the shock of the seasoned Hopper. In addition to Rossellini and Hopper, also contributing new interviews are Kyle MacLachlan, Laura Dern, Dean Stockwell, composer Angelo Badalamenti and more.

The original cut of *Blue Velvet* Lynch delivered to Dino De Laurentis reportedly ran four hours. While none of this footage, still much buzzed about among Lynch-ians, has been restored, an amusingly titled "Are You a Pervert?" montage has been assembled that hints at what the "lost cut" may have contained. It is hardly definitive, with most of the legendary trims only represented with still photographs, if they're represented at all. One can accept Lynch's claims that the scenes have long since been destroyed—"Why keep them around?" he has always reasoned—but it only makes being a pervert that much more frustrating.

Highly entertaining is an excerpt from the "Siskel & Ebert" show, with Roger Ebert's virulently negative response to the film and a near rave from Gene Siskel. It runs only ninety seconds, but is a hilarious must-see for Lynch cultists. Other extras include the film's theatrical trailer, TV spots and some cute if repetitive easter eggs.

The Presentation *Blue Velvet* may be a difficult film for some to watch, but as a purely visceral experience it is an unequivocal masterpiece. Fredrick Elmes's influential photography is sometimes soft and blurry by design, but his evocative uses of color, especially deep reds and midnight blues, come through with great clarity. And Lynch has always been a master of using symbolism and expansive widescreen compositions to reveal the subtleties of story and character hidden by his obtuse dialogue. Here, at last, *Blue Velvet* has been restored to its proper 2.35:1 theatrical framing and will prove to be a genuine thrill for those who have experienced the film only on badly cropped VHS copies and cable airings.

More controversial is the new Dolby Digital 5.1 surround remix. Supervised by Lynch himself, it cannot be accused of discrediting Alan Splet's highly inventive sound design. However, comparisons with the also included Dolby 2.0 surround track reveal few differences. Only a handful of effects sound truly discrete, and the lack of powerful surrounds will likely disappoint those hoping for more. But if this is the way Lynch wants us to hear his film, it is, after all, his universe.

Additional Versions MGM Home Entertainment originally released *Blue Velvet* in a movie-only, budget-priced edition one year prior to the special edition. Both remain in print.

Additional Recommendations Sadly, much of Lynch's filmography remains unavailable on DVD, including two of his most incendiary works, *Wild at Heart* and *Lost Highway,* which as of this writing are mired in licensing quagmires. Those that are in print include some of his most influential—*Mulholland Drive, The Straight Story, The Elephant Man* and *Eraserhead*—although all but the latter are, at Lynch's request, devoid of extras. *Twin Peaks* fans can enjoy the cult series' entire first season (sans pilot) and a special edition of the poorly received theatrical prequel *Fire Walk with Me*.

Bowling for Columbine
DISTRIBUTOR: MGM Home Entertainment
DVD RELEASE: November 2002
THEATRICAL RELEASE: August 19, 2003
RUNNING TIME: 125 Minutes
MPAA RATING: R

Although it's tragic that a film like *Bowling for Columbine* needed to be made, it's a good thing Michael Moore is around to make it. Moore, in his liberal uniform of T-shirt and baseball cap, has crafted a blistering, hilarious, rambling essay on America's preoccupation with guns, focusing partly on the media's desire to scare citizens into believing a crazed African American killer is perched on every doorstep, ready to kill.

Moore's jumping-off point is the 1999 Columbine High School massacre, in which twelve children and one teacher were murdered by gun-wielding students Eric Harris and Dylan Klebold (there is even eerie surveillance footage of the killers as they stalked the school's cafeteria). Moore approaches the problem with satirical knives sharpened, rejecting the Conservative axis of evil: music, TV and movies. Moore even discusses the issue with shock rocker Marilyn Manson, which leads to one of the most honest exchanges in the film:

JAMES NICHOLS: "When a government turns tyrannical, it is your duty to overthrow it."

MICHAEL MOORE: "Why not use Gandhi's way? He didn't have any guns, and he beat the British Empire."

JAMES NICHOLS: "I'm not familiar with that."

> MOORE: "If you were to talk directly to the kids at Columbine . . . what would you say to them if they were here?"
> MANSON: "I wouldn't say a single word to them. I'd listen to what they have to say. That's what no one did."

Taking a broader look at gun violence in America, Moore asserts that Canada has equal access to guns, yet gun-related deaths there are drastically lower. To help explain this, he strikes at the media, specifically the television show *Cops,* with its culture of fear, and local news, with its philosophy of "if it bleeds, it leads." After a live report on the death of six-year-old Kayla Rolland, shot by a fellow first-grader, the reporter wonders aloud if he needs more hairspray. This has always been one of Moore's most effective weapons: letting the subjects hang themselves.

As watchable, entertaining and thought provoking as he is, Moore does not always play fair with the audience, a fault that goes beyond a liberal documentarian making a liberal-minded documentary. Given that he holds the camera as well as the keys to the editing bay, no subject is safe from agenda-serving manipulation. The mother of Kayla Rolland's killer worked at a restaurant owned by Dick Clark. When Moore ambushes Clark regarding the restaurant's use of welfare-related tax breaks, there is nothing Clark can say to satisfy someone with so strong an agenda. In fact, his silence better serves Moore's dramatic purpose: he looks as if he's hiding something. Maybe he is. But maybe he just chooses not to be bullied into a debate while about to make a speedy exit in a van. Picking on a celebrity target like Dick Clark is easier than asking why the shooter's uncle had a gun lying around the house for a six-year-old to find.

But Moore overcomes any criticism with his humorous approach and Everyman appearance. His films are as far from *The Sorrow and the Pity* as one can imagine. He is brilliant at layering his humanist approach with clever angles. Toward the end of the film, Moore escorts two survivors of the Columbine massacre to Kmart, where bullets are available for seventeen cents apiece. Both boys still have bullets lodged in their bodies (one is between the boy's aorta and spine) and Moore goes to Kmart hoping to get them a refund on the bullets. Surprisingly, a day later, Kmart announces they will stop selling bullets in all of their stores.

Moore is not subtle, but he knows subtlety won't play to a mainstream American audience. It's this provocateur's spirit that makes him an important and necessary filmmaker in a confused and difficult time. The success of *Bowling for Columbine,* which won the 2002 Academy Award for Best Documentary, lies in the message and the messenger.

The Goodies Moore's opinions as populist mouthpiece cannot be confined to one disc, so MGM Home Entertainment gives us a second one full of entertaining extras that cover a wide range of thematic ground. *Bowling for Columbine* is also one of the few documentaries to receive any sort of special edition treatment, which in itself makes it noteworthy.

Most unusual is the audio commentary by the various receptionists, interns and production assistants who worked on the film. While it may read funny on the back of the packaging, it is likely not for everybody, and many will complain that little information is actually insightful or interesting. And it is a little disappointing that Moore chose not to record his own commentary track, where he could have directly addressed some of the criticisms made against the movie and his filmmaking techniques. This track certainly won't help him win points with his detractors, but it rates as the only weak spot on an otherwise fine set. Interns, however, should love it.

The second disc contains the rest of the supplements and, true to Moore's nature, he starts with the most controversial subject. Sitting on a picnic bench, somewhere in Michigan, Moore justifies his Oscar acceptance speech, where he told the Kodak Theater crowd, "We live in a time when we have a man sending us to war for fictitious reasons. We are against this war, Mr. Bush. Shame on you." Moore was roundly reviled for using the Academy Awards as his platform, and on the *Bowling for Columbine* DVD he claims, "It not only was something I said, it was something I had to say." Moore's performance here is reasoned, sincere and, most impressively, completed in one, fifteen-and-a-half-minute take.

Ever the traveling activist, Moore spoke at the University of Denver on February 26, 2003, and twenty-five minutes of his standard rhetoric is presented in "Return to Denver/Littleton—6 Months After the Release of *Bowling for Columbine*." The very next day, February 27, Moore gave an interview to Joe Lockhart, former press secretary for Bill Clinton. The DVD presents twenty-one minutes of excerpts from that appearance. The best of the interview-related extras is Moore's appearance on *The Charlie Rose Show*." Rose is not willing to let Moore proselytize, which leads to a spirited discussion. The last TV excerpt includes footage from Moore's unjustly ignored and occasionally hilarious show, *TV Nation*. The segment from which the footage was lifted is presented here in its entirety. It concerns a research lab that tested chemicals on humans without notifying them of possible side effects. The piece is not one of the show's best, although it does include a visit from the always-entertaining Crackers: The Corporate Crimefighting Chicken.

There is also a rather intriguing and predictably controversial DVD-ROM supplement called the "Teacher's Guide," which provides educators with *Bowling for Columbine*–related topics to discuss with their students. There is much thought-provoking subject matter for young adults, although Moore's detractors will find firepower here for their attempts to prove that he is ultimately trying to indoctrinate, not educate, students with his political philosophy.

Rounding out the more notable extras are a Marilyn Manson music video, a photo gallery and sixteen minutes of Moore cavorting around various film festivals.

The Presentation Like many documentaries, *Bowling for Columbine* contains video from multiple sources, some new, some archival. This 1.85:1 anamorphic widescreen transfer looks terrific considering the material, although it cannot quite overcome the limitations of the source material. There is no problem with the picture that cannot be traced back to production and the quality of the vintage footage. Grain is an issue in some scenes, otherwise blacks are rock solid and colors are a tad mute, but Moore is operating in some pretty drab locales. Detail and sharpness are quite good and the print is generally free of dirt and admirably free of edge enhancements. Barring the unlikely event that Moore starts shooting documentaries in 35mm, the medium won't get much better than this transfer.

MGM can be thanked for providing viewers with a Dolby Digital 5.1 mix; however, with the exception of a few scenes, this still sounds like a documentary. The soundscape is limited with very frugal use of the surrounds. And even when the opportunity arises for an improved presentation, as in the songs and the cartoons, they don't sound as full as they should. But most important, dialogue sounds as good as the source audio, which most of the time is very clear.

Boyz N the Hood

DISTRIBUTOR: Columbia TriStar Home Entertainment

DVD RELEASE: September 3, 2003

THEATRICAL RELEASE: July 1991

RUNNING TIME: 120 Minutes

MPAA RATING: R

It has always been incumbent upon the motion picture art form to take us someplace we've never been, to tell us something we didn't know. But American white, middle-class audiences have long preferred to learn of contemporary social injustice from foreign films, of the marginalized and the downtrodden in places safely removed from the superficial splendor of life in the First World. Films like Lee Tamahori's *Once Were Warriors* or Phillip Noyce's *Rabbitproof Fence* have broken out of the foreign film ghetto, but even their success has been treated like a backhanded compliment. We all share a collective cry for those poor, poor people so very far away, and then run home to the warm, womblike comfort of *Friends*.

In 1991, one American film dared to break through and depict a ghetto in our own backyard. *Boyz N the Hood* forced us to acknowledge a war-ravaged part of the world that most white, middle-class Americans, to paraphrase Doughboy (Ice Cube), didn't know, didn't show or didn't care about. *Boyz N the Hood* is about kids with guns. It's about mothers mourning their sons. It's about 34.61 square miles of urban battlefield that could no longer be ignored. It's about South Central Los Angeles.

> "Either they don't know, don't show, or don't care about what's going on in the 'hood."
>
> —Doughboy

America, and the Academy, had to pay attention. The script, by first-timer John Singleton, was too good. The performances were too real. The story was too heartbreaking. *Boyz N the Hood* played it smart. It didn't bash. It didn't blame others. Characters dug their own graves, or earned their own redemption. It wasn't a policy statement. It was an artistic statement. Oscar gave Singleton a nod for Best Director, the youngest person ever to be awarded such recognition. The film exploded at the box office and created the most important minority movement in cinema since the days of blaxploitation, the "urban drama." B*oyz N the Hood* was one of the most important films of the 1990s, and its repercussions are still being felt throughout the industry.

Most commercial movies ask us to look back in time to learn a lesson and take our medicine. *Boyz N the Hood* asked us to look across the street. It didn't shove our face in its story, nor did it back away from its implications. At the beginning of the film, words on the screen inform us "1 out of 21 Black American males will be murdered in their lifetime." Maybe the eye-opening power of films like *Boyz N the Hood* can reduce that number to 1 in 20. Or 1 in 19. It's not much. But it's a start.

The Goodies This two-disc special edition begins with John Singleton, who provides a conversational and interesting audio commentary, open and honest about how his script paralleled his own life experience. Singleton's mother shipped him off to live with his father, who once shot at a burglar, both of which events made it into the film. The commentary is also by turns amusing, an example of how odd a world Hollywood can be. Singleton recounts meeting Laurence Fishburne on the set of the CBS television series *Pee-Wee's Playhouse,* where Fishburne was a performer and Singleton was a production assistant. To think . . . Pee-Wee paved the way for Ice Cube.

The second disc contains the rest of the supplements, including the forty-three-minute documentary "Friendly Fire: The Making of an Urban Legend." It takes the viewer from Singleton's original script, through his attempt to get it made during his stint at the University of Southern California to a difficult and dangerous low-budget shoot. Producer Steve Nicolaides recounts having to pay gang protection money to insure the safety of the crew and that Singleton warned him he'd probably be the only white person on the production. Admirably, the documentary doesn't ignore the gang violence that erupted in some theaters. Singleton tells of seeing a Crip walk into a theater he knew to be populated with Bloods. The young di-

HIGHER LEARNING: A CONVERSATION WITH JOHN SINGLETON

At the tender age of twenty-four, John Singleton became the youngest nominee in history to score a Best Director nomination for *Boyz N the Hood*. A diverse, challenging and highly acclaimed body of work followed, from the more personal, highly charged dramas *Poetic Justice* and *Higher Learning* to his hit remake of the 1970s blaxploitation classic *Shaft* and the $125 million–grossing *2 Fast 2 Furious*. He remains one of the most original and diverse voices working in cinema today.

What was it like to attend the Oscars at twenty-five?

It was cool. In retrospect, I'm happy that I didn't win because if I had won off this first movie, it probably would have meant the end of my career—too much too soon. It's phenomenal that after all these years, this film still has so much power to it.

Do you feel like the "Godfather of the Urban Movie," given the rash of imitators that followed in the wake of *Boyz N the Hood*?

They made too many of them afterward. All these other movies were influenced by the success of this movie. No matter how much they try to deny it, those films are a response to this picture.

MTV has certainly come to embrace hip-hop and rap in a way it didn't at the time *Boyz N the Hood* was made. And it has, conversely, spawned a whole new generation of filmmakers who grew up on fast-cut MTV imagery and videos . . .

I think so. We have the MTV generation, where everything is quick, quick cuts, and then you have great filmmakers like M. Night Shyamalan, who creates his own time frame upon which a movie can flow that is slow and laborious, but it's captivating. The fact that he's taking time is a revolutionary step.

There's nothing wrong with narrative film. I don't think it's changed very much. Most of the guys who are making all these rapid-cut films are not really saying much and nobody's really listening to the work they're doing, because it's not coming from anyplace. There's a difference between what David Fincher did with *ALIEN³* and what David

Fincher did with *Se7en*. *Se7en* is a classic. I can watch that movie every night of the week.

Looking at your films, many of your characters share a similar trait: they're trapped in a place or a situation and then they try to break out of it. Is that a theme you've consciously explored?

No. I just think every film I've done is a personal reflection on myself. In film school, the teachers would say that you can't hide who you are as a person because from watching your films, any person will know who you are.

Back when you were trying to get *Boyz N the Hood* made, you were still finishing up your degree at USC and the opposition was certainly fierce. Did you ever think back then that you would make it this far?

Yes, of course. I knew I was going to have a career as a filmmaker. I wasn't just going to make one movie and be like, "I made my movie," and go back. I wanted a career. I saw *Star Wars* when I was nine and that was what made me want to make movies.

Were there any filmmakers who you were particularly inspired by?

Steven Spielberg, George Lucas—the big movies of the '80s. And then when I was in high school, I started exploring other filmmakers like Woody Allen and Martin Scorsese and Francis Coppola. That's what made me want to make films. These movies really had serious subject matter to them.

Martin Scorsese recently said that the industry is at a point where you need to make one movie to have the hit, and then you can make another for yourself. In the past few years, you have balanced the bigger budgeted movies like *Shaft* and *2 Fast 2* Furious with smaller films like *Baby Boy*. Do you find yourself emulating what Scorsese was talking about?

I want to do films that are huge Hollywood pictures and I want to do films that are smaller Hollywood pictures that are more personal. All those films—no matter the size of the picture, I put a lot of personal energy into it and they're still aspects of me.

As a filmmaker, why is it so attractive to do DVD commentaries and featurettes and things like that?

It's because it makes everything interesting. People watching the films want to learn more about the background of making a film. When I'm watching these movies, I want to learn more about the stories behind them. I was watching the making of *Casablanca* the other night, and I have seen the movie so many times, I sometimes don't look at the movie—I look at the documentary on the making of the movie and I go from there.

I looked at the documentary on the making of *Sunset Boulevard*. It is phenomenal. They are what filmmaking is all about. Films take on a life of their own after you see them. What I really appreciate about *Boyz N the Hood* is that it has a life. It continues to have a life. It continues to evolve and affect people.

What is your approach toward the growing trend of director's cuts, deleted scenes and alternate endings on DVDs?
I don't do any alternate editing of my movies because I'm like, "This is what the movie needs to be. And the final edit is what it is." When I'm making a movie, I'm making a movie. I'm not even thinking about the DVD yet, unless we're making a gag reel or

something. The gag reel for *2 Fast 2 Furious* is hilarious. All the funny stuff between Paul Walker and Tyrese, and those guys goofing off—it's crazy.

So you'd never go back and do a new cut or add CGI to any of your movies?
No!

In terms of digital filmmaking, have you ever wanted to shoot anything on DV and give that a try?
Nah. It's still video. It doesn't have the flaws that film has. It's too perfect. It's a problem. We shot stuff on videotape when we were there, but I'd much rather shoot something on film. I'd rather shoot something on Super-8. To smell the film, to cut the film—that's great.

Do you ever worry that DVD will take too much from filmmaking, that it will siphon away some of the magic?
No, because the magic of filmmaking is to get a whole group of people together in a theater and having a collective experience to a movie and reacting emotionally to what's happening on screen. That can never be taken away.

rector immediately left the theater and saw cop cars drive up as he drove away.

Two deleted scenes are included, each an extended dialogue exchange, that better flesh out a couple of characters. There are also two music videos, "Growin' Up in the Hood" by Compton's Most Wanted and "Just Ask Me To" by Tevin Campbell, that predate MTV's eventual embrace of hip-hop and movie tie-ins. No less than eight theatrical trailers complete the set.

The Presentation Columbia TriStar Home Entertainment presents *Boyz N the Hood* in its original aspect ratio of 1.85:1. While this anamorphic widescreen transfer is good, it can't overcome the limitations of the film's budget. Overall, the picture is grainy and flat. There is the occasional spot of dirt on the print, which should have been cleaned up. Light edge enhancements are a problem, but colors are quite accurate and detail surprisingly good. Columbia should have dropped the full-screen transfer also crammed on the disc; it is unnecessary and its omission would have left more room for a better transfer.

The audio is also representative of the source material. There is no 5.1 track, but the Dolby Digital 2.0 surround mix provided is quite acceptable. However, when you consider the thumping rap music, the helicopters flying and the bullets blazing, a 5.1 would have proven a truly enveloping experience. There is some nice imaging to be discerned, mostly general neighborhood noise and some helicopter and bullet sounds. Dialogue is very understandable, but lacking power. Bass action is good, but considering how heavily rap music relies on bass, it should have been really kickin'. Although one wonders what might have been, the track does justice to the film's tough, gritty nature.

Brazil

DISTRIBUTOR: The Criterion Collection
DVD RELEASE: July 13, 1999
THEATRICAL RELEASE: December 1985
RUNNING TIME: 142 Minutes
MPAA RATING: R

Terry Gilliam's *Brazil*—a film unceremoniously butchered by its studio and dumped into the marketplace, only to rise, phoenix-like, from the ashes to emerge as one of the biggest cult movies of all time—remains as prescient, exuberant and dazzlingly original as it did nearly twenty years ago. Gilliam created a one-of-a-kind futuristic fantasy, a world so unlike any other that it ranks as one of cinema's greatest genre achievements. Love it or hate it—and many do hate it—you cannot say that you have ever seen anything else like it.

Gilliam's tale of bureaucrat Sam Lowry (Jonathan Pryce), who, in trying to correct an administrative error, finds himself labeled an enemy of the state, is similar to George Orwell's *1984* and Aldous Huxley's *Brave New World,* as well as a number of other literary works that dramatize the

> **"Mistakes? We don't make mistakes."**
>
> **—Archibald "Harry" Tuttle**

plight of modern man in a futuristic dystopia. Yet Gilliam infuses his vision with a rock 'n' roll sensibility, tossing out only a little dry exposition and refusing to explain just how and why his future works the way it does. But it is this opaqueness that allows Gilliam to paint in broad, allegorical strokes and playfully riff on the oddities of his alien locale. Gilliam and Tom Stoppard's screenplay is certainly dramatically sound, but its open-endedness is what liberates *Brazil* from being just another sci-fi totalitarian nightmare.

Some blamed Gilliam's *Monty Python* past for what they saw as his masturbatory impulses toward juvenile comedy, but it only proved him an expert at making a decisive and biting social statement under the guise of a slapstick satire. *Brazil* remains so jolting because it balances extremes so adroitly—cheerful and fatalistic, depressing and hilarious, heavy on the symbolism yet light on overt meaning, all at the same time.

With both *Brazil* and his *12 Monkeys,* another instant cult classic, to his credit, Gilliam has proven himself one of the most underrated futurists around. And one misunderstood by the Hollywood machine. *Brazil* was severely truncated from its intended 142-minute form for its original American theatrical release; the European cut was less damaging if still incomplete. But on DVD, at last, Gilliam's original vision has been restored. You won't find a more oddly frightening, utterly entertaining, impeccably realized universe on film than the one depicted in *Brazil*.

The Goodies With this landmark three-disc box set of *Brazil,* Criterion has set a new standard in the quality and depth of supplemental material. Never before has form, function and format come together in such a thoroughly satisfying way. Gilliam contributes a screen-specific audio commentary for the fully unexpurgated 142-minute cut of the film on disc one. It is a marvelous commentary. Gilliam is smart and cheeky, and discusses all of the major facets of the production, from the film's autobiographical elements to the complex visuals, the labyrinthine studio machinations that resulted in the disastrous American cut and the film's eventual impact on his career. It is one of the best commentaries ever recorded.

The second disc houses two documentaries. "What is *Brazil*?" runs thirty minutes and was created at the time of the film's original production. It is amusing to see how the studio attempted to sell such a complex and ultimately uncommercial movie. Absolutely essential viewing is the now-infamous "The Battle of *Brazil*," a fifty-six-minute epic that rips wide open the true story of Universal's butchering of *Brazil* and Gilliam's ultimate vendetta against the conglomerate. As a documentary it is a bit talky, and the studio execs were not particularly helpful in providing the required archival documents and materials needed to truly burn themselves at the stake. But this tumultuous, highly charged documentary is so full of jaw-dropping stories and unbelievable treachery that it remains one of the most searing assassinations of Hollywood stupidity ever produced. Also included on disc two is the "Production Notebook," a vast collection of storyboards, deleted scenes, drafts of Gilliam and Stoppard's script, special effects footage and more.

Despite such heavy subject matter, *Brazil* the DVD is not without its sense of humor. Disc three contains the ninety-minute television version of the film, dubbed the "Love Conquers All" cut. It is unwatchable, so why include such a travesty? *Brazil* scholar David Morgan recorded a new commentary that, while rather academic, is also sadly hilarious, as Morgan explains with a very dry wit what changes were required and why. It completes the last piece of the *Brazil* puzzle and remains a searing indictment of a Hollywood that seems impossibly stupid.

The Presentation While director approved, sadly *Brazil* was produced in the early days of the DVD format and boasts a 1.85:1 widescreen transfer that is not anamorphically enhanced. It is still a very fine transfer, struck from a clean print with strong colors and a surprising amount of detail. However, some compression artifacts are apparent, another indication of how far the DVD format would come in just a few short years. Hopefully, Criterion will rerelease *Brazil* with a definitive restoration.

In keeping with its corporate philosophy only to present films the way they were originally intended, Criterion also has not remixed the film's original Dolby 2.0 surround track in 5.1. Still, it sounds fine, with a fairly involving presence, but one can only hope that, like a restored transfer, someday fans will see a fully remixed 5.1 soundtrack.

Additional Versions Universal Studios Home Video initially released *Brazil* on DVD in the slightly longer "European Cut." It then licensed the title to Criterion for this three-disc box set. Universal's original, movie-only DVD remains in print.

Additional Recommendations Gilliam fans can have a field day with many of the director's best works having received extensive DVD special editions. Criterion has released two-disc sets of *Time Bandits* and *Fear & Loathing in Las Vegas,* while Universal made amends for *Brazil* with an excellent special edition of the director's Oscar-nominated *12 Monkeys.* Only the excellent laserdisc box set of *The Fisher King* has not been retooled for DVD.

The Bridge on the River Kwai

DISTRIBUTOR: Columbia TriStar Home Entertainment

DVD RELEASE: November 21, 2000

THEATRICAL RELEASE: December 1957

RUNNING TIME: 162 Minutes

MPAA RATING: PG

The Bridge on the River Kwai is about a different kind of war: it's about a war of wills. What is most wounded is pride. What is most at stake is honor.

Its two combatants are British Colonel Nicholson (Oscar winner Alec Guinness) and Japanese Colonel Saito (Sessue Hayakawa). They are armed not with guns, but with their egos and a cultural and military code that stresses dedication to the point of intractable stubbornness. Nicholson is the leader of a defeated British battalion taken to a Japanese POW camp, run by commanding officer Saito, who instructs his new captives that they will begin building a bridge across the Kwai River, helping

SAITO: "Do you know what will happen to me if the bridge is not built on time? . . . I'll have to kill myself. What would you do if you were me?"

COLONEL NICHOLSON: "I suppose if I were you, I'd have to kill myself . . ."

complete a railroad meant to ferry Japanese troops and supplies from Bangkok to Rangoon.

Nicholson challenges Saito by invoking the Geneva Convention; Saito responds by grabbing Nicholson's copy of the Convention guidelines, slapping him across the face with it and placing him in "the Oven," a torturously small metal shack that sits in the broiling sun. It's the first salvo in a fascinating cultural showdown. The ever-so British Nicholson is willing to die for his wartime principles; Saito is unwilling to back down, lest he lose face. And while Nicholson sits in "the Oven," the film's other story line takes shape as Shears, the camp's American POW (William Holden), miraculously escapes and finds his way to a local village. This story strand was not in Pierre Bouelle's (*Planet of the Apes*) original novel, and while it's not as interesting as the Nicholson/Saito showdown, it opens up the film by taking it out of the camp and is integral to how the plot ultimately plays out.

In one of the best scenes in the movie, Saito brings the emaciated and trembling Nicholson to his quarters. Internally, Saito begins to question the ability of the Japanese lieutenant assigned to the bridge, as well as the possibility that the British could do a better job. Saito capitulates, releasing all British officers, who are no longer required to perform manual labor. As the POWs cheer Nicholson's victory, Saito sits in his quarters and weeps, his honor wounded. But Nicholson, whose men still must complete the bridge, decides to use the expertise of his officers to build the best bridge possible. To some, it's tantamount to collaborating with the enemy. For Nicholson, a twenty-eight-year veteran of the service, it is to be his legacy. However, at British headquarters, Shears has been given new orders: return to the camp and destroy the bridge. It will be this showdown that brings the film to its stunning conclusion, one of the greatest climaxes in motion picture history.

The Bridge on the River Kwai, released in 1957, is considered director David Lean's transition from more intimate films (like *Great Expectations* and *Summertime*) to the full-blown Technicolor wonders of his later career (his next film would be *Lawrence of Arabia*). And while the movie, which won seven Oscars, has an epic scale featuring World War II as a backdrop, the film's primary relationship is quite intimate. Nicholson and Saito thrust and parry using the swords of their respective military and social cultures. Their intractable nature and egomaniacal attachment to conformity and honor make them two of the cinema's most fascinating foes. And, in the whole of this unforgettable war movie, neither of them fires a gun.

The Goodies Columbia has provided an outstanding set of supplements, all of which are contained on a second disc. The premiere extra is a fifty-three-minute exploration of the film's difficult birth, "The Making of *The Bridge on the River Kwai*," directed by noted DVD documentarian Laurent Bouzereau. It dissects the adaptation of Boulle's novel, its use of blacklisted screenwriters Michael Wilson and Carl Foreman, and the studio's insistence on creating a role for an American star. Shooting was arduous, as logistics and weather created problems on location in Ceylon, an island at the southern tip of India. Although the film's major participants are now dead, the documentary includes interviews with surviving crew members as well as vintage stills and archival footage.

Also included are two very enjoyable, very vintage featurettes. "Rise and Fall of a Jungle Giant" is a six-minute black-and-white piece chronicling the building of the bridge (at the time the largest structure ever built for a motion picture) and its subsequent destruction. Loads of great archival footage is included. The other vintage supplement is a sixteen-minute University of Southern California production on film appreciation. Introduced by William Holden, the short uses *Bridge on the River Kwai* to teach basic lessons in filmmaking.

The other notable extras are another eight-minute "appreciation" of the movie by filmmaker John Milius, a photo gallery set to Malcolm Arnold's score and the film's theatrical trailer. And be sure to read the reprint of the original *Bridge on the River Kwai* souvenir book, produced in 1957, which is a fascinating artifact of old Hollywood.

The Presentation Columbia has done a masterful job restoring *Bridge on the River Kwai* in this often beautiful 2.55:1 anamorphic widescreen transfer. However, be warned: the opening credit sequence has a fair amount of scratches and dirt. Once you get past that, it's a wonderful picture that honors the film's vast CinemaScope panoramas. Colors are reproduced beautifully, retaining a good amount of vibrancy considering the age of the film. Detail, contrast and shadow delineation are fantastic. The picture itself, especially the big, outdoor vistas, is bright and eye-popping. Fans will be elated.

Audio is available in Dolby Digital 5.1 and 2.0 surround. The effort to upgrade the film's soundtrack to a truly discrete mix has paid off: *Kwai* sounds great and, more importantly, not artificial. The rears are effective in conveying ambient jungle noise while the front speakers handle the rest with finesse. Dialogue is very clean, although Sessue Hayakawa's heavily accented English is occasionally shrill. Much better is Malcolm Arnold's Oscar-winning score, which is reproduced with great energy and, as an added bonus, is also available isolated on a separate track.

Alternate Versions Columbia TriStar Home Entertainment has also released *The Bridge on the River Kwai* in a single-disc edition that drops the second disc of extras. Both remain in print; the two-disc special edition is well worth the extra investment.

Butch Cassidy and the Sundance Kid

DISTRIBUTOR: Fox Home Entertainment
DVD RELEASE: May 16, 2000
THEATRICAL RELEASE: September 1969
RUNNING TIME: 129 Minutes
MPAA RATING: PG

B*utch Cassidy and the Sundance Kid* is reality inflated into legend. And in the hands of director George Roy Hill (*The Sting*), events become exploits. Exploits become Hollywood cinema. And Hollywood cinema becomes . . . reality.

The Wild West has churned out its fair share of oversized characters memorialized in film and folklore: Wyatt Earp (who survived well into the twentieth century) and Jesse James (who did not) are arguably the most enduring. But Hollywood has always told such stories primarily in standard, dramatic fashion (with the exception of 1959's *Alias Jesse James,* in which insurance salesman Bob Hope is mistaken for James). But the story of Butch and Sundance, two of the most famous outlaws who ever lived, is here reimagined in a revisionist fashion. And better for it, because of the lighthearted way in which its story was told made it one of the biggest hits of the 1960s, and it has since achieved the status of beloved classic.

There is no doubt that Butch Cassidy and the Sundance Kid really lived, but there's also no doubt they didn't live *quite* the way they were portrayed in this 1969 Best Picture Oscar nominee. ("Not that it matters, but most of it is true!" read the tagline.) For starters, they didn't have William Goldman writing their dialogue. And although Goldman, in his indispensable Hollywood book *Adventures in the Screen Trade,* famously criticizes his script by claiming, "The entire enterprise suffers from a case of the cutes," the fact is "the cutes" are what keep the film fresh and enjoyable thirty-five years after its release. Audiences didn't clamor for tickets to see Paul Newman and Robert Redford in a depressing, true-to-life tale of crime, punishment and capture. They paid to see two larger-than-life stars saddle up, shoot guns, get the girl and ride off into the sunset.

> "He'll feel a lot better after he's robbed a couple of banks."
>
> —Butch Cassidy, on the Sundance Kid

Butch Cassidy and the Sundance Kid is a seemingly contradictory pastiche, a sun-drenched, nostalgic biopic of notorious bandits who meet a violent end, a sort of sepia-toned *Bonnie & Clyde.* It is about the end of an era, a fictional one, maybe, but one no less important than the real thing. It is an idealized vision of what we imagined, in our shared cultural dreams, that the warm and cozy Old West should have been like. The film isn't funny, per se, or campy; it is merely larger than life. It is unabashed, unapologetic entertainment. And the kind of Hollywood reality we love to believe in.

The Goodies While a Robert Redford and Paul Newman audio commentary will always be a dream, Fox Home Entertainment has ponied up a fine array of extras that pays fawning tribute to these two stars, the legends that they played and the film that glorifies them.

The audio commentary by director George Roy Hill, lyricist Hal David, associate producer Robert Crawford and cinematographer Conrad Hall is a dry and pieced-together affair, but there are still plenty of juicy nuggets to be mined from it. Lengthy gaps of silence drag the pace, and some of the more famous passages come and go with no comments at all. Yet there is still something compelling about what is said, a team of misty-eyed filmmakers recalling perhaps their most successful and beloved achievement. Despite the poor editing job, this commentary is cozy nostalgia.

But the real home-run supplement is the forty-two-minute documentary "The Making of *Butch Cassidy and the Sundance Kid*." It is a video diary before there were video diaries, compromised completely of on-location production footage and vintage photos, with voice-over primarily by director Hill. He is blunt and honest in a way that no director could ever be today, freely admitting what scenes he didn't like and what actors he thought were miscast. This 1968 documentary ends with Hill saying, "If audiences don't dig it, I think I'll go out of my fucking mind." He need not have worried.

In 1994, a twenty-fifth anniversary laserdisc was released including interviews with all the principals, and they're all here. Newman, Redford, Katherine Ross, William Goldman and Burt Bacharach contribute recollections of varying degrees of interest, with Newman classy, Bacharach jovial, Goldman stuffy, Redford reserved and Ross effervescent as always. Rounding out this set are a collection of vintage production memos and three theatrical trailers.

The Presentation Sometimes the DVD for a thirty-five-year-old film will looks better than does the DVD for a brand-new film. That's the case here, as Fox really hit it out of the park. The film is presented in its original aspect ratio of 2.35:1 and the sprawling western vistas captured by Hall have never looked better. The film begins with a sequence in sepia, which looks suitably worn. However, it's not until the film literally fades to color that the beauty of the transfer takes hold. The exterior browns and greens are warm, very filmlike and fully saturated, although purposely a little dusty. The skies are not only as blue as can be, but they're also without dirt or specks. Overall detail is terrific in the close-ups, good in the long shots. Interior night scenes falter at times, with some grain, average shadow detail and occasional muddy blacks. Still, it is a gorgeous transfer.

The quality of the audio is no match for the impressive video, but it's still quite acceptable. Sound is mono, which means if you can understand the dialogue, that's all that matters. And here, the dialogue is clear and distinct. There is some tearing when characters scream, and whispering characters may prompt a volume adjustment. But for a mono presentation, it does the job very well.

Carrie

DISTRIBUTOR: MGM Home Entertainment
DVD RELEASE: August 28, 2001
THEATRICAL RELEASE: September 1976
RUNNING TIME: 98 Minutes
MPAA RATING: R

Carrie is the ultimate fantasy-revenge flick, a grand guignol tale of teenage angst and fury so single-minded it instantly earned its place as a horror landmark. Audiences and critics expecting just another shoddily constructed, no-budget exploitation cheapie were literally shocked out of their seats: produced independently for less than $500,000, it boasted no major stars and was based on a novel written by a then little-known horror novelist named Stephen King. Its director, Brian De Palma, had previously helmed a few critical favorites but audiences had paid little attention, and the studio, United Artists, had so little faith in the picture it was

> "I should have given you to God the day you were born!"
>
> —Margaret White

backed by virtually no advertising campaign. But hell hath no fury like a telekinetic teenage girl scorned.

Over twenty-five years later, *Carrie* is a virtuoso horror epic, an example of how style, wit, intelligence and craft can elevate even the most potentially exploitative B-movie material to the level of art. King's first novel had a hook as simple as it was undeniably primal—our glee in watching a tortured innocent at last exact her revenge upon the status quo. It was also infused with the elements of King's best work: a vaguely supernatural story staged in a mundane, believable milieu, tapping into our everyday fear of shame, alienation, abandonment and untimely death. And although De Palma's dizzying cinematic bravura is sometimes excessive, it elevates *Carrie* to the rarified plateau of a King adaptation that actually improves upon the original. De Palma pulls out every trick in the book in crafting the film's many now-famous set pieces. Highly complex, minutes-long sequences are staged in one shot. Clever uses of deep focus and extreme foreground and background disorient our sense of perspective. Slow and fast motion keep the pace from lagging. Inventive split screen (especially in the climatic prom massacre) facilitates a rarity in a mainstream genre picture—multiple entry points for audience identification. It is an ingenious trick, allowing us to both empathize with and be terrified by Carrie's horrific revenge. Showy, yes, but the perfect marriage of theme and technique, style and substance—it deepens the film to the level of genuine Greek tragedy.

De Palma's subsequent career has been dogged by comparisons to Alfred Hitchcock, and he has even been accused of ripping off his own style in his later thrillers. In *Carrie* he freely lifts from the master but does so with such incredible finesse that he is able to distill his influences and King's sensibilities into a single, unified whole. He may resort to the occasional cheap shot—the film's highly influential shocker ending is a stunner if a narrative dead-end—but when it works, it works beautifully. *Carrie* is one of the most seminal horror films ever made.

The Goodies Thankfully eschewing the usual gimmicks that clutter up even the best DVDs, frequent De Palma documentarian Laurent Bouzereau has wisely chosen to focus on *Carrie*'s most impressive qualities, its direction and amazing cast, by way of two terrific forty-five-minute documentaries.

"Visualizing Carrie" is the more straightforward of the two, exploring De Palma's baroque techniques and the conceptualization, production and editing of several key sequences. Despite his reputation as a master of suspense, De Palma is never egotistical, even humble about what he perceives may have been an overabundance of style and an eagerness to break barriers instead of serve the story. Most revelatory is unearthed footage of the much-rumored flashback scene, deleted from the final cut, showing Carrie as a young girl. Despite the slim raw material available, Bouzereau successfully recreates much of the sequence by deftly intercutting interviews with De Palma and production designer Jack Fisk, plus storyboard and screenplay excerpts and stills. It is a very strong examination of how important craftsmanship is to creating an effective horror film.

It is a testament to the durability of *Carrie* that so many have returned to revisit the film that launched their careers. Sissy Spacek, as Carrie, delivers a wrenching and emotional performance that won her an Oscar nomination; Piper Laurie also earned a nod for her inspired turn as Carrie's fanatical mother (her over-the-top interpretations of loopy dialogue are still hysterical and have turned her into a true cult icon). Also a part of the impressive ensemble: John Travolta, Amy Irving, William Katt, Betty Buckley, PJ Soles and Nancy Allen (who would also go on to marry De Palma). "Acting Carrie" features all save for Travolta. Interesting tidbits? De Palma shared casting sessions for Carrie with George Lucas, who was also casting a low budget little sci-fi film called *Star Wars*. Carrie Fisher as Carrie? Amy Irving as Princess Leia? William Katt as Luke Skywalker? The twenty-odd years since *Carrie*'s release lend a sense of poignancy and perspective so sadly lacking in most DVD retrospectives.

Adding a bit of whimsy is the slim ten-minute "Carrie The Musical." (Yes, they actually turned Carrie into a big-budget stage show, complete with lasers, explosions and musical numbers such as "Rothouse Whiskey.") But notable by his absence is Stephen King, an unfortunate omission Bouzereau attempts to make up for with a short text summary, "Stephen King and the Evolution of Carrie." It is this disc's only weak link and not particularly satisfying. Additional extras include a still gallery montage that runs six minutes, plus an eight-page color booklet of facts and trivia.

The Presentation Awash in bold, rich colors and backed by a baroque score by frequent De Palma collaborator Pino Donnagio, *Carrie* has been remastered in 1.85:1 anamorphic widescreen and remixed in Dolby Digital 5.1. The soundtrack is very strong and a clear improvement over all previous, generally atrocious video releases. Gone is all the distorted dialogue and muffled effects—surround use can be frighteningly effective, with the classic, climatic prom sequence a real shocker. Unfortunately, the transfer is a little less impressive if still visceral enough to scare. The source print is scratchy and dated and leaves the film with a flat appearance, but the quality of the color reproduction compensates, especially the vivid, bloody reds. *Carrie* looks just good enough to take to the prom.

Additional Recommendations De Palma's string of thrillers in the 1970s and the early 1980's helped define the era. The best of the lot are 1973's *Sisters* with Margot Kidder, the wonderfully lurid *Dressed to Kill,* and his *Vertigo* homage/pastiche/rip-off *Obsession*. Sadly, perhaps the director's best film, 1981's *Blow Out,* also starring Travolta and Allen, has been released solely as a movie-only edition.

Casablanca

DISTRIBUTOR: Warner Home Video
DVD RELEASE: August 5, 2003
THEATRICAL RELEASE: November 1942
RUNNING TIME: 102 Minutes
MPAA RATING: PG

Casablanca is more than a classic. It is an institution. It contains so many famous lines, characters and scenes even those who have never seen it feel like they have because of osmosis; it is *that* ingrained in our shared cinematic consciousness.

The iconic moments from Michael Curtiz's 1942 masterwork are what cineastes remember most—"We'll always have Paris," "Here's looking at you, kid"—but what continues to startle, sixty years on, is

> "Of all the gin joints in all the towns in all the world, she walks into mine."
>
> —Rick Blaine

just how well constructed and imminently watchable it is. Yes, the famous parts are justifiably classic examples of writing, direction, performance and editing, but check out all that lies between the film's obvious masterstrokes: Curtiz's subtle use of camera movement, the expressive melancholia of Max Steiner's musical score, Claude Rains's shady but lovable turn as Bergman's would-be suitor—these may not be the moments that continue to get spoofed on retrospective TV specials and American Express commercials, but they do confirm that it is impossible to imagine ever getting tired of watching *Casablanca*.

Ingrid Bergman and Humphrey Bogart deserve a lot of credit for the success of the film, for it is their indelible chemistry that continues to send hearts soaring six decades on. Never has emotional pathos and closely guarded, barely contained physical longing been so eloquently apparent. And when they have to say good-bye to each other at the end of the flick? There is not a dry eye in the house.

But *Casablanca* is also more than a movie; it is also a place, and a state of mind. Its misty, darkly lit streets and haunted piano bars remain figments of our lost dreams and future hopes. Bogart and Bergman have, despite changing tastes, fads and fashions, remained our romantic ideal, the perfect pair of lovers who must, as fate decrees, part for now but perhaps not forever. It is one of those moments when all of the planets aligned perfectly, to capture the pure essence of human fragility, love and longing in a single, iconic moment. It may be a predictable choice for the best film of all time, but *Casablanca* is really that good, that important and that seminal.

The Goodies To honor the sixtieth anniversary of *Casablanca*, Warner Home Video has produced an excellent two-disc set that is a shining example of how to craft a special edition for a film when, sadly, most of the participants have long since departed. After a predictably sappy introduction by Lauren Bacall, most of the rest of the supplements are exemplary. Two separate audio commentary tracks, the first by famous critic Roger Ebert, the second by historian Rudy Behlmer, excel by virtue of the passion and knowledge of both participants. Behlmer's may be the more engaging discussion, as his ability to dissect even the smallest details is almost awe-inspiring—it is hard to imagine someone who had no connection with the production of a film knowing so much about it. Ebert, as always, is animated about a film he is passionate about and offers a more all-encompassing perspective on the film's impact and influence.

The set's second disc contains the majority of the video-based supplements, including two excellent documentaries. "Bacall on Bogart" is an extensive ninety-minute discussion with the legendary actress, who reminisces on Bogie and how he made his trek from lowly Broadway character actor to Hollywood legend. "A Tribute to Casablanca" is a nice thirty-minute television special originally produced for Turner Classic Movies that examines in brisk if comprehensive fashion the film's legacy, and features a wealth of lovely recollections from various historians and collaborators. A third featurette, "The Children Remember," is unfortunately too saccharine. The two leads' offspring Stephen Bogart and Pia Lindstrom (Ingrid Bergman's daughter) talk about what the film meant to them growing up and how it has affected their lives since. Unfortunately, insight into the real lives of Bogart and Bergman is painfully slight.

A variety of unique extras round out the set: two deleted scenes and a montage of outtakes (both without sound); an audio-only Screen Guild Theatre Radio Show version of the film in which Bogart, Bergman and Paul Henreid reprise their roles; eight more audio-only "Scoring Stage Sessions," an absolutely surreal eighteen-minute condensation of a Warner Brothers made-for-television update of Casablanca set in the Cold War, entitled "Who Holds Tomorrow"; an extensive "Production Research" gallery containing memos, still photos and publicity materials; eighteen minutes of Casablanca-inspired Looney Tunes shorts; "A Great Cast is Worth Repeating" series of text pages that chronicles the many collaborations of the film's key players and original theatrical and re-release trailers.

The Presentation *Casablanca* looks extraordinary. Faithfully preserved in the correct 1.37:1 theatrical aspect ratio, this painstaking restoration is a marvel. Arthur Edesons highly influential black-and-white photography has at last been restored to its original brilliance—the clarity of the print and the level of detail are awe-inspiring. Perfectionists may find the occasional print anomaly and some dirt and grain if they choose to nitpick, but this is a truly gorgeous restoration.

Warner has also stuck with the film's original mono soundtrack, and no digitally processed stereo or surround remixes are offered. Nevertheless, such simplicity suits *Casablanca* perfectly. The elements have been appropriately cleaned up, and the all-important dialogue is at last free of the excessive distortion and weak frequency response that has so often marred television broadcasts and previous video releases. *Casablanca* looks and sounds wonderful.

Additional Versions Three previous editions of *Casablanca* have been released on DVD. All were largely inferior movie-only releases, and none featured the newly remastered transfer and soundtrack of the Sixtieth Anniversary Edition. All of the previous editions remain out of print.

Cast Away

DISTRIBUTOR: Fox Home Entertainment
DVD RELEASE: June 12, 2001
THEATRICAL RELEASE: December 2000
RUNNING TIME: 143 Minutes
MPAA RATING: PG-13

Isolation may be the most unlikely of subjects to power a mainstream Hollywood blockbuster. Who wants to watch a man alone and lost on a desert island for two-and-a-half hours? Yet Robert Zemeckis's *Cast Away* is a movie that is at its most compelling when it accepts this challenge and runs with it. For most of its 143-minute run time (nearly 100 minutes of which occur virtually without dialogue), *Cast Away* is quiet, meditative and almost abstract but always absolutely riveting. It is a film that understands how time, and our perception of it, informs every single choice we make.

Cast Away is a movie of contrasts—between civilization and isolation, sound and silence, modern technology and antiquated technique. After a spectacular plane crash sequence that ranks as one of scariest and most visceral in screen history, we share in the isolation of Chuck Noland (Tom Hanks) for the entirety of the film's lengthy second act. Hanks and Zemeckis take a huge risk, confident that they can hold our attention. This second act is split into two halves, shot nearly a year apart; Hanks underwent a rigorous physical routine to gain and then lose the necessary pounds to make Noland's transformation believable. Hanks earned his Oscar nomination, matching Zemeckis's passion for exploring not just the physical but emotional, intellectual and spiritual consequences of alienation. It is hard to recall a performance as transformative.

> "This package saved my life. Thank you."
> —Chuck Noland

Much was made in the press of *Cast Away*'s pioneering use of CGI effects to convince us that, yes, Tom Hanks really is stranded on that island, thousands of miles from civilization. Yet the film moves us not because of its razzle-dazzle but because Zemeckis is so meticulous in melding visual trickery and story that the effect is transparent. We are never overwhelmed; we simply don't realize how much of the film exists nowhere but inside the computer. If the film's third act is not as riveting—as the trailers had no shame in spoiling for us, Noland eventually returns home to reconcile with his lost love (Helen Hunt)—the climactic shift does not violate any of the themes Zemeckis set up in the first act, but in fact deepens the film's ultimate impact and meaning. With *Cast Away,* as in *Forrest Gump,* Zemeckis continues to prove himself as one of the rare mainstream Hollywood filmmakers who uses technology to enhance his stories. He is the most decent of filmmakers, Hanks the most decent of actors, and *Cast Away* the most decent of movies—a drama made for and about adults, one with something to say and that, upon repeated viewings, gives more and more.

The Goodies *Cast Away* is an example of a DVD that doesn't reinvent the medium, but the story it has to tell—of a production so unique and inventive that it is a story all its own—makes up for any lack of freshness. Spanning two discs, the supplemental features are straightforward and presented in a classy, unobtrusive manner. The screen-specific audio commentary is an edited collection of interviews with the technical team, director of photography Don Burgess and, from a Q&A discussion at his alma mater, the University of Southern California, director Zemeckis. It is largely focused on the considerable technical hurdles the production faced in shooting a film that was in some ways two movies in one. Hanks was required to pack on the pounds; then the production shut down and restarted months later as the newly svelte star returned to close the island; bound passages of the film. Shooting on location has always proved to be one of the greatest challenges in filmmaking; finding a suitable location and then augmenting it with modern CGI effects gives the making of *Cast Away* a unique spin and makes for a compelling commentary.

These aspects of the production are explored in even further detail in a series of video-based featurettes and vignettes. The twenty-four-minute "HBO First Look Special" is the weakest but transcends the ordinary due to extensive on-set footage, some of it from the tough location shoot. Better are more specific, shorter featurettes: "S.T.O.P.: Surviving as a Castaway," also twenty-four minutes, explores the physical and emotional struggles Hanks faced in playing an island survivor; the fourteen-minute "The Island" reminds us why filmmaking is not nearly as glamorous as it sounds; and the amusing "Wilson: The Life and Death of a Hollywood Extra" exposes the real story behind Hanks's on-screen inanimate costar, who may be the most emotive volleyball ever seen. A series of short "Special Effects Vignettes" reveal the considerable effort that went into camouflaging the fact that there exist no locations in the world today completely untouched by civilization (or at least none that are amenable to a film production). While these before-and-after breakdowns of *Cast Away*'s extensive use of models, blue screen, rear-projection and compositing are nothing new on a DVD, they are more impressive than usual because they aim not to create the fantastical or other-worldly but to completely fool us with the photorealistic.

Additional extras include a twenty-four-minute interview excerpt with Hanks from *The Charlie Rose Show,* a series of video and still galleries chronicling most of the production, additional conceptual and storyboard artwork, and various trailers and TV spots.

The Presentation *Cast Away* remains one of the best-looking and best-sounding DVDs ever released and is considered by many to be one of the top demo discs of all time. The THX-certified, 1.85:1 anamorphic widescreen transfer is astounding in its depth, clarity and sense of detail. Director of photography Burgess's effective use of natural light—especially in the nighttime sequences—requires ab-solute perfection, as even slight errors in color timing, contrast and brightness can destroy the intended effect. Short of high definition, it is hard to imagine an image as three-dimensional and lifelike. And *Cast Away* sounds just as terrific as it looks. Featuring both Dolby Digital EX and DTS ES soundtracks, the DVD presents a film whose power comes from subtlety, not bombast. The complex sound design is seductive—the middle third of the film is awash in atmosphere, subtle ambience and intricate aural texture. (The single lapping of a wave upon the shore is enough to elicit chills.) *Cast Away* is a reference-quality presentation.

Additional Versions Fox Home Entertainment has released *Cast Away* in three DVD editions: the widescreen two-disc set covered here, as well as single-disc widescreen and full-screen versions that drop the second disc of supplemental material. It is a shame that the packaging on all three makes little note of any differences; pay close attention to the back labeling, as it is about the only indication of which version you are buying. Go with the two-disc set—it is worth the investment.

Citizen Kane

DISTRIBUTOR: Warner Home Video

DVD RELEASE: September 25, 2001

THEATRICAL RELEASE: December 1941

RUNNING TIME: 119 Minutes

MPAA RATING: PG

Citizen Kane needs no introduction. Having been torn apart and put back to together again for over fifty years, it is hard to imagine any film class that does not include *Kane* on its syllabus, yet its reputation has almost ruined it for the uninitiated. You *have* to like it or else risk the scorn and hu-

> **"I think it would be fun to run a newspaper."**
>
> —Charles Foster Kane

miliation of every film critic in the world. But what is so often forgotten about Orson Welles's unrivaled landmark is just how much fun it is to watch, to savor, to revel in. This is not just a homework assignment: it is great, grand, glorious entertainment.

Armed with the most lucrative motion-picture contract in history, Welles in 1941 wrote, directed and starred in his definitive masterpiece—all at the tender age of twenty-four. It would be not only a staggering achievement of youthful chutzpah, but also a technical benchmark that invented its own cinematic language. Working with his director of photography Gregg Toland, Welles pioneered a host of new techniques—photographic, editorial, narrative. In a single bound, this boy wonder and *enfant terrible* leaped so many technical hurdles that *Kane* is the most oft-quoted and ripped-off film in history.

Loosely based on the life of publishing tycoon William Randolph Hearst (not loosely enough, it seemed, to appease Hearst's lawyers, who promptly waged legal war on Welles and RKO Pictures), the story of *Kane* echoes not only Hearst's life but also Welles's. Kane, Hearst and Welles were each child prodigies who lacked a loving home and quickly rose among the ranks of the privileged to amass their own empires. And each one ultimately lived out his final days as a fallen idol, exiled to his own Xanadu, unlucky in love and a prisoner of his own legacy. The film's mosaic of differing perspectives mirrors the disparate opinions of Welles, an eventual pariah of an industry that blacklisted him as difficult, uncommercial and tyrannical. In *Kane,* film and filmmaker became one.

The film's classic, haunting final image, "Rosebud," is both ironic and tragic and rightfully the most famous parting shot in all of cinema. *Citizen Kane* is more than a work of art. It's a monument to lost genius, faded glamour and promises unfulfilled.

The Goodies Much of the material on this wonderful, two-disc Sixtieth Anniversary Edition of *Citizen Kane* will likely already be familiar to Welles's vast legion of admirers. But Warner Home Video has produced a number of exclusive new supplements that complement what is one of the greatest documentaries ever produced about a motion picture.

To pay tribute to Welles's ultimate achievement, esteemed critic Roger Ebert and Oscar-winning filmmaker Peter Bogdanovich each contribute a new screen-specific audio commentary. Bogdanovich, who worked with Welles and acted as his personal confidant, has spoken on numerous occasions about his relationship with the idiosyncratic auteur but reveals much here that is revelatory. It is an often poignant, even sad commentary, with the highly articulate Bogdanovich open and honest about the albatross *Kane* eventually became for Welles. Ebert delves more into the technical and the preeminent place *Kane* holds in film theory and history. Combined, they form an essential four-hour aural history of a cinematic landmark.

Disc two is reserved entirely for "The Battle over Citizen Kane." It is an amazing documentary and required viewing for every film lover. This 113-minute special, originally produced for The Turner Network, chronicles the legendary campaign Hearst launched to try to destroy the film . . . and Welles. *Citizen Kane,* like many films that went on to become classics, was not unanimously heralded as a masterpiece upon first release—it was a box office bust and failed to garner a single Academy Award despite six nominations. But it attracted enough attention to incense Hearst, who subsequently wielded his immense wealth, power and influence to bury the film under an avalanche of acrimonious lawsuits and, allegedly, yellow journalism. This incendiary story is told adroitly via newsreel and rare archival footage and interviews of surprising candor. "The Battle over Citizen Kane" masterfully recounts a story that is as fascinating as the film itself.

Additional materials include theatrical trailers, extensive production notes, two archival newsreels, a gallery of storyboards and a fascinating collection of over one hundred rare stills: publicity and production photos, alternate ad campaigns, memorabilia, studio "call sheets" and never-before-seen letters from Welles.

The Presentation The story of *Citizen Kane*'s difficult road to the screen is one fraught with ego, vanity and retribution. Jack Warner, then head of Warner Brothers, was reportedly so incensed by Welles and *Kane* that he had the film's original negative destroyed. The real story remains clouded by history and rumors of dubious veracity, but *Kane*'s negative remains lost. However, just in time for this landmark's sixtieth anniversary, Warner's restoration team located a new print of the film, one far better than any found before. The result is magnificent. Newly restored with the help of the latest in digital technology, this DVD is a revelation.

Kane has been seen throughout the years in a variety of rereleases and restorations, and none can compare to the experience of this DVD. It's that good. Today's digital technology has cleaned up the print to virtual perfection—gone are any traces of blemishes, dropouts, nicks or other anomalies. Blacks are pitch perfect, the film now detailed and rich where before it was flat and lacking in sharpness. At times the sense of three-dimensionality is jaw-dropping— Toland's gorgeous black-and-white photography remains an unparalleled achievement. This may be the best restoration ever seen on a DVD.

In a decision to maintain the integrity of Welles's original vision as well as appease the purists, Warner decided to forgo creating a new 5.1 remix for *Citizen Kane*. Included is the film's original mono soundtrack. But it is clean as a whistle, with an expansive sonic palette that is generally clear, full-bodied and free from any major aural defects.

Cleopatra

DISTRIBUTOR: Fox Home Entertainment
DVD RELEASE: October 21, 2003
THEATRICAL RELEASE: 1963
RUNNING TIME: 248 Minutes
MPAA RATING: G

Behold "Cleopatra's Procession," the centerpiece of a film often called the biggest flop in Hollywood history. Still one of the most impressive sequences ever captured on celluloid, watch as Elizabeth Taylor sits atop a thirty-foot statue, wheeled in front of tens of thousands of extras. But they are not screaming "Cleopatra!" They are screaming "Liz!" It is the epitome of Hollywood excess: we don't sit in awe of what is happening on the screen, we recoil, slack-jawed, at what it all must have cost. Such excess is an example of Hollywood's worst if most enduring tendency—a never-ending zeal to not just sell us style as substance, but style as better than substance.

> "Queens, queens. Strip them naked as any other woman, they are no longer queens."
>
> —Marc Antony

Like stopping to gawk when you drive by an accident, it is hard to look away from the screen despite *Cleopatra*'s interminable 248-minute run time. Pompous, bloated, largely unnecessary and often little more than a vanity vehicle for stars Taylor and Richard Burton, none of this detracts from the fact that *Cleopatra* is immensely entertaining. Here is a film that offers far more than the usual guilty pleasures of the camp classic—the bad dialogue, ridiculously gargantuan sets, bombastic action scenes and pompous sense of self-importance. It is pure narcissism itself burned onto celluloid. It isn't just the way the camera worships Taylor—never has a major Hollywood movie lavished so many fawning, unnecessary close-ups on its star—but the movie itself seems to think it exists to do the audience a favor. It is as if both the filmmakers and Twentieth Century Fox—which greenlit this catastrophe to rescue itself from a disastrous real estate venture—thought if they created enough lavish sets, dragged out the run time to four hours and exploited the tabloid controversy swirling around the unmarried Taylor and Burton, they didn't need to make a good movie.

Cleopatra is not without its genuine pleasures. It is so big, so extravagant, so over-the-top ("The motion picture the world has been waiting for!" the tagline screamed) that it is hard not to be impressed by the sheer spectacle of it all. And with decades of even worse would-be epics taking away some of the sting, *Cleopatra*'s staggering desperation to dazzle now seems quaint and charming. Even the film's reputation as the biggest money loser in Hollywood history is not entirely accurate; it actually made a fair amount, grossing $112 million back in 1963, a considerable sum when tickets cost about three bucks. Too bad it just cost so damn much. *Cleopatra* is one of the great cautionary tales, a reminder that in Hollywood, more is indeed less.

The Goodies The success of the DVD format has created something of a strange phenomenon. With mainstream consumers now so hungry for behind-the-scenes material and distributors realizing that even the most marginal of films can sell in considerable amounts if they come packed with supplemental features, we are now seeing the worst movies in history getting the kind of extravagant treatment previously lavished only on the true classics. Eyebrows are raised when a movie like *Cleopatra* gets a mammoth three-disc set like this, but sometimes even the worst movies can make for the most fascinating—and juicy—DVDs.

The ninety-minute documentary "*Cleopatra*: The Film That Changed Hollywood" is by turns hilarious, heartbreaking and infuriating. *Cleopatra* certainly did change Hollywood—it proved that there is no such thing as a guaranteed blockbuster, and that while millions starve all around the world, Tinseltown doesn't bat an eyelash at spending millions on catering alone. But we get to have the last laugh, as everything that could possibly go wrong with a motion picture did on *Cleopatra*—it was the cinematic equivalent of Murphy's Law. And what makes "The Film That Changed Hollywood" even more relevant today is that the industry hasn't learned much in the intervening four decades. It is a town still obsessed with the sure thing, that so worships stars more concerned with perks and pampering than performance that it will concede to their every whim, no matter how outlandish. That Fox, a studio then undergoing enormous financial woes, would hang its entire future on a single motion picture may not be all that surprising; but what is surprising is that that no one—not during the film's disastrous pre-production schedule, not during a six-month shoot that makes James Cameron's now infamous *Titanic* production look like a pleasure cruise, not as relentless casting changes made the film the laughingstock of the industry—ever thought to just pull the plug. "The Film That Changed Hollywood" is compulsively watchable: sardonic, impeccably researched and dripping with new interviews, rare outtakes, screen tests, premiere footage and extensive stills. And with so many DVD documentaries these days being more PR events than true making-ofs, there is a certain glee in watching so many major Hollywood players actually telling the truth. Most telling are shots of this would-be epic's gargantuan sets, many of which went unused as the production suffered setback after setback, being toppled, smashed to the ground and, ultimately, turned into firewood. What a fitting epitaph.

Also included is an audio commentary with Chris and Tom Mankewicz, sons of director Joseph Mankewicz, and actor Martin Landau and studio publicist Jack Brodsky. After the documentary, it feels like overkill: the real importance of *Cleopatra* as a historical document is in the big picture, not the small details. And given the snooze-inducing 248-minute run time, the commentary is best left for masochists and Taylor completists only. Far more amusing is the fawning 1963 featurette "The Fourth Star of Cleopatra," which in hindsight plays as ridiculous. Rounding out this three-disc set is footage of the film's New York and Hollywood premieres, and a still gallery that serves as a fitting tribute to the film's costumes, sets and production design. They are the one element of *Cleopatra* that has re-mained unfairly overshadowed by the film's ill repute.

The Presentation One of the few genuine pleasures of *Cleopatra* is its sheer visual majesty. Fox Home Entertainment, under the aus-pices of THX, has bestowed *Cleopatra* with a restoration befitting a queen. This 2.35:1 anamorphic widescreen transfer—to watch this movie panned and scanned seems beside the point—certainly re-stores it to its once-former glory. The source material has been nicely cleaned up, with colors now lush and vivid and the sense of detail palpable (if only better to enjoy Taylor's endless costume changes). A nice Dolby Digital 5.1 remix can't compensate for the dated ele-ments of the soundtrack, but the surround channels are aggressive enough to at least give some sense of envelopment and atmosphere. Some may argue that such a fine effort is more than *Cleopatra* de-serves, but here is a film better remembered as a technical exercise than as a successful narrative. It certainly is a film that will never be duplicated. Or so we can hope.

Close Encounters of the Third Kind

DISTRIBUTOR: Columbia TriStar Home Entertainment
DVD RELEASE: May 29, 2000
THEATRICAL RELEASE: December 1977
RUNNING TIME: 137 Minutes
MPAA RATING: PG

For U.S. cinema, 1977 was the year of science fiction, when a genre long since relegated to C-grade schlock at last reclaimed the box office. It was bookended by two blockbusters: George Lucas's *Star Wars* and Steven Spielberg's *Close Encounters of the Third Kind*. Lucas's nostalgic space opera became, arguably, the most important and influential cinematic phenomenon of the twentieth century. And it left Spielberg's more benevolent tale of our first contact with ex-traterrestrials as the also-ran. While still a huge hit—and considered by many to be the superior film—only the passing of twenty-five years has been able to redress the balance. While Lucas's original trilogy has suffered a reevaluation due to its poorly received prequels, *Close Encounters* has enjoyed a new position of preeminence as a genuine epic as influential, awe-inspiring and revolutionary a film as *Metropolis, 2001: A Space Odyssey* and *Blade Runner*.

Spielberg's masterpiece flew in the face of all that audiences expected out of their mainstream science fiction. It married a Disney-like sense of enchantment and idealism with a metaphysical exploration of faith and religion. It was the first new-age movie, reimagining spiritual transcendence as extraterrestrial contact. Blue-collar suburbanite Roy Neary (Richard Dreyfuss) became another in a long line of Spielberg protagonists, an ordinary man trapped in extraordinary circumstances. Like many classic religious figures, he becomes a pariah and an outcast, alienated from his family, friends and coworkers, finding redemption only after connecting with fellow "disciples," all of whom share a common vision and spiritual quest. Pauline Kael wrote of the film, "This isn't nuts-and-bolts, *Popular Mechanics* science fiction, it is beatific technology—machines from outer space deified." When the film climaxes at Devil's Tower as first contact is made, Neary sacrifices his life and his earthly responsibilities—man, husband, father—to ascend to a new level of consciousness. This unconventional ending has, over the years, caused much consternation, most of all from Spielberg himself, who has since reevaluated *Close Encounters*'s place in his body of work. "It is the film that dates me the most." But even Spielberg's own ambivalence does little to diminish *Close Encounters*'s status as one of the most intelligent, ornate and visionary science fiction epics ever made.

LACOMBE: "You felt compelled to be here? What did you expect to find?"

ROY: "An answer."

Close Encounters of the Third Kind opened on December 17, 1977, with a run time of 135 minutes and was an immediate sensation. But Spielberg remained dissatisfied with the final product; an accelerated post-production schedule, enforced by the studio to capitalize on the lucrative holiday box office season, led him to dub the theatrical cut a "work in progress." In 1980, Columbia granted Spielberg the then unheard-of opportunity to revisit his epic and craft the Special Edition, which he shortened to 132 minutes. He removed entire scenes, trimmed and reshaped others, and completed several "dream shots," at a cost of over a $1 million. But there was a concession: Columbia forced Spielberg to shoot an extended finale taking us inside the mothership, a sequence that, while expertly executed, did not advance the narrative and that the director publicly decried for nearly two decades. The Special Edition, like the original theatrical cut, eventually proved to be another rough cut. Finally, in 1997, for the film's twentieth anniversary rerelease, Spielberg returned to his masterpiece yet again to create what he called his definitive director's cut. Scenes were again added and reshaped and the extraneous "inside the mothership" climax finally excised. The book on *Close Encounters* at last seemed to be closed.

The Goodies Although originally produced in 1997 to celebrate the film's twentieth anniversary, the ninty-seven-minute documentary "The Making of *Close Encounters*" was not released on DVD until 2001. That the material was not really conceived with the format's interactive capabilities in mind is readily apparent: the menus and arrangement of the supplements is entirely linear, and there is no option to watch the various cuts of the film via seamless branching (only the Spielberg-approved 137-minute cut is offered, with eleven deleted scenes—including the much-maligned "in the mothership" finale—presented separately). Additional materials are also slim two theatrical trailers, brief filmographies and the original 1977 featurette, which runs a scant five minutes.

But the sheer size and ambition of the documentary makes up for the static presentation. With a narrative arc missing from today's fast-cut, vignette-based DVDs, "The Making of *Close Encounters*" evokes a style of storytelling common to laserdisc. The documentary may sometimes feel stiff and stodgy, but it is an evocative snapshot of a culture undergoing a massive paradigm shift, one that was developing a new conception of extraterrestrial intelligence, moving away from organized religion and hovering on the brink of a techno-logical revolution.

It is these three fascinating threads that form the core of "The Making of *Close Encounters*." Spielberg is eloquent about how risky his labor of love really was. He was not yet Hollywood's golden boy, the director of such future blockbusters as *Raiders of the Lost Ark, Jurassic Park* and *E.T.,* and *Close Encounters* would prove to be his most personal work up until *Schindler's List*. His faith in the project would border on near-obsession and aptly parallel the quest of his protagonist; recollections of the cast and crew, including Dreyfuss, Melinda Dillon, Teri Garr and director of photography Vilmos Zsig-mond, poignantly reflect their director's often fragile state of mind and describe a set where emotions ran high.

Just as arduous was the extended shooting schedule, made no easier by the film's pioneering effects, all done before the advent of CGI. The brilliance of the visual trickery of *Close Encounters* is that it suggests more than it shows. While in Bombay prepping the film's complex India sequence, Spielberg observed a vast power station that astonished the young director, with tens of thousands of high-wattage lightbulbs arranged across a giant steel mesh struc-ture. This image inspired the design of his film's extraterrestrials and their mind-bending "mothership." Working with *2001: A Space Odyssey*'s Douglas Trumball, Spielberg created in *Close Encoun-ters* a landmark of innovation but also the first of a dying breed—doomed by the emergence of computer-generated imagery effects twenty years later. "The pure art of misleading the eye, of control-ling where the viewer looks and gets to see," Spielberg lamented, "those days are gone." "The Making of *Close Encounters*" is a fit-ting tribute to an age of awe and wonder the cinema screen will never see again.

The Presentation *Close Encounters of the Third Kind* has never been very well represented on home video, until now. Zgismond's Oscar-nominated photography—so delicate and subtle—was virtually de-stroyed by the low resolution of the analog VHS and laserdisc formats and hacked to bits by pan-and-scan television broadcasts.

AUTO FOCUS: A CONVERSATION WITH LAURENT BOUZEREAU

Over the past decade, Laurent Bouzereau has emerged as one of the most acclaimed and recognizable names in DVD. His style—reverential, graceful and steeped in the classical tradition—has earned him enduring collaborations with many of world's most renowned filmmakers, including Steven Spielberg, George Lucas, Peter Bogdonavich, Brian de Palma and the estate of the late Alfred Hitchcock. In addition to having produced over seventy-five DVD titles, he is also the author of eight books, including *The De Palma Cut, The Cutting Room Floor, Ultraviolent Movies, The Alfred Hitchcock Quote Book* and *Star Wars: The Annotated Screenplays*.

Your name has become one of the first to be recognized by the DVD-buying public. And rare for this industry, you have been able to sustain a long-lasting relationship with specific filmmakers, like Steven Spielberg. Have you ever analyzed why this has happened and what it is about your style that seems to be so attractive to these filmmakers?

I kind of got hooked up with Steven by chance when Amblin and Universal were looking for someone to work on the laserdisc for *1941*. They heard of me through Criterion, where I had done a couple of laserdiscs, and my name came up as somebody who hopefully did good work and who was passionate about Steven's work, and particularly *1941*.

It happened organically that way in that I have been there ever since. I understand the way Steven works. I understand the kind of relationships he has with his colleagues, so I know what he expects from a documentary. And I know his cinema so well that when he watches [the documentary], it's like he's looking at some choices he would have made. And I have done so many that it's kind of easy to just keep on doing it!

However, I think in this business I do not take anything for granted. I never expect to be on the next film. I always ask. And you never know—I might not be on the next one for whatever reason. I have seen it happen with filmmakers. You cannot assume anything. I go one film at a time with them. That helps me be humble and respectful and always give 500 percent. And I do not want to get too comfortable.

Your work is commonly regarded as the most well researched in the business. What are the basic steps you take when starting a project?

I really embrace the film. I watch it and I write up a continuity in the order of the scenes, and then for each scene. With *Indiana Jones*, for instance, [there's] the opening sequence and you have the sound, you have the music, you have the special effects, you have stuff that was shot on location, stuff that was shot in the studio, you have some stunts. I do that with every single movie I work on, and that helps me right off the bat to sort of make a list of interviews or more research that I need to do beyond what I have.

You also have exhibited an amazing talent in terms of your interviews, not only in who you are able to attract but the depth and honesty of their recollections. How would you describe your technique?

It all comes from the film itself. Unless you understand the film really, really well, you're not able to ask good questions. And the way my questions are structured, they also follow the story of the film so that it is easy for the actors who, for example, are sometimes the hardest interviews because they're not really necessarily involved with any aspects of preproduction or the history of the film. You really have to create an environment for them that is going to be easy for them to remember and relive that moment. So you tell them the story of the movie. It sounds a little too literal, but that's the way you walk them through it.

Many pronounced the longform documentary dead with the arrival of DVD. Yet you've been able to successfully marry your style with the technology in unique ways. For example, your pacing and ability to "break up" your work in fresh ways has proven to be highly influential.

I am really cool with splitting things up when you do a documentary, into featurettes where you can either play them all or play them separately. The intention of my work is always to have people watch the movie, watch the documentary and then go back and watch the movie—that back and forth as opposed to digesting it all in one sitting and then never looking at it again. It also forces me to be a little more structured and a little more cognizant of the audience. "Let's make this a full thought about acting in *Scarface*. Let's make this a full thought about special effects in *Indiana Jones*." Whereas if they were part of a big documentary, you would touch upon it in a more overall view as opposed to a detailed view.

That aspect of things I do like. Even though it was a transition for me going from really long form—when you think about *JAWS*, that's two-and-a-half hours worth of stuff. Having to split that up was a bit of a decision creatively for me, but I like it better. In working with my editors, I can see they like it better also.

Some fans continue to demand more interactivity, such as commentaries and branching vignettes. How do you cope with all these varying opinions and still stay true to your own spirit? When I get feedback from the press or people who watch my work, I really feel sometimes that I get a little pissed about certain comments. They are judging the stuff based on technology. "Oh,

you can do commentaries? So let's do a commentary." You can't do that. You have to consult people creatively. If they want to do it, they do it. If they do not want to do it, they do not do it. Just because the technology is there doesn't mean it has to be done.

I feel they want everything and the kitchen sink, and it's like this geeky thing of having everything. But part of what we do is having respect for the mystery and being very structured in what you decide to talk about and have a through-line as opposed to anything goes.

Perhaps there is a correlation between your continued success with filmmakers like Steven Spielberg and Brian de Palma and your respect for this mystery? I do not know if there is a correlation there, because I certainly asked them to do them on people's requests. We've had discussions about it. I, for one, do not push for that. I am glad these filmmakers want to work with me. [Roman] Polanski is another one I have started to work with, and we are doing several projects. And, like Spielberg, he doesn't want to do commentaries. And I am so glad.

However, having said that, after I did some—with Peter Bogdanovich, especially—I really enjoyed it because he was a film critic prior to being a filmmaker, so I think he could interview himself without a problem. So with him, it is a slightly different approach.

Do you have a preference for working on a new film, which might be easier to assemble talent and footage for, as opposed to a catalog title with more of a history but less material at hand?

It's two different approaches and they both have their pluses and minuses. When you work on a current movie, you can only blame yourself if you do not have enough material at the end of it because you had the opportunity to get everything on the set and talk to everyone. That makes it really exciting for me, because in the case of working for someone like Steven Spielberg or M. Night Shyamalan or anything I do with Kathleen Kennedy and Frank Marshall, I start setting up my ideas for the DVD from day one.

That's really exciting because you really get to do that stuff, and so quickly now that it's a real luxury to be on set. However, I think that in terms of interviews, I do not think you get the historical perspective that you get on a library title years later. Frankly, they're in the middle of making a movie, and for filmmakers to analyze what they're doing at that moment, it's hard to get that perspective. The movie's not out yet, it's not complete, they're still working on it.

The problem with a library title, on the other hand, is that some of the people are gone. Like on *JAWS*—Robert Shaw is not around anymore, Verna Fields, the editor, is not around anymore, and it's hard to find archival images. It still wasn't much of a problem, but I had to clean up the negatives of the pictures because at the time, they didn't want to show the shark, so most of [the source materials] them had been killed, basically. Finding B-roll is very challenging, and if you go even further and work on titles like Hitchcock's—I am about to tackle other titles of his, where absolutely nobody is around—it is very challenging because you want to be definitive and you want to be faithful to the stories.

So it is a challenge in both cases, but makes for two different experiences, and I love the fact that I am able to bounce back and forth on both. I think I'd get a bit frustrated if I was just doing old movies and I think I'd be a bit frustrated if I was just doing current movies.

How involved are filmmakers, such as Spielberg, during your post-production process?

To me, I am just a messenger to these directors, so their input is essential. Because I know them personally and because I have discussed things with them as I go, hopefully there has never been a case of delivering something that was not living up to the original discussions and expectations that we had. I have been very lucky in that I have been able to match our initial goals, saying, "This is who we are going to interview and these are the featurettes we are going to do and this is how the documentary is going to be." All the people I am involved with have been really very involved with the development and the result. It is amazing to get feedback—even if it is a change—from someone like Steven Spielberg or Brian de Palma. I will take that any day. And I welcome that. They know their movies. They know better than anybody else.

How much of an impact have legal restrictions had on your work?

I have a dialogue with them right away. I ask them what the rules are because each studio is very different and I have never had a problem—and I am knocking on wood as I am saying this—but I have very, very specific dialogue with them when I get on board. Like in the case of *Indiana Jones,* I had meetings with them before I even starting interviewing people and I told them exactly what I was going to use. I told them exactly what I intended to do. They asked me questions—"Are you going to showcase other movies? Are you going to use songs? Are you going to use other scores?"—so I pretty much know what to stay away from to make my life easier. I am not going to suddenly have a Madonna song to a montage because I know we are going to run into clearance issues.

Given that some of the titles you have worked on have proved controversial, how do you handle interview material that may not be entirely laudatory or is even mean-spirited?

I am very careful. I do not want to sound like I censor things in the work I do, but I am not going to have somebody on screen say, "So-and-so is an asshole." It's just a question of . . . what are you trying to accomplish? I am not doing sensational documentary filmmaking. I have no interest in that. Not to say that doesn't have any value but that's not me. I am interested in film history and creating an inspiration for people. When you have that kind of ethic and respect for the work, I have never been in a situation where I was going to use something that was offensive or that would hurt somebody's feelings or destroy somebody's career. That doesn't even compute because I would not even go there.

With DVD now mainstream and more and more pressure being put on filmmakers and the film's themselves to justify elaborate DVDs, where do you think the future for the format is headed?

I think it is going in the right direction. It is the movie that lives as opposed to a fan-driven type of thing. Let's make sure that what is on the DVD is an inspiration for people and is definitive as far as its director is concerned and that it makes people want to watch the movie again. That is the function of DVD, to have this constant thirst for information about this film and wanting to watch it again. It's an exciting time, and at the same time it is a little frightening because there is so much happening with the technology . . . all those possibilities. But let's not lose sight of the movie itself, of the work of art, because that is where it really lies. That is where the answer is. It is in the movie. ○

This THX-certified, 2.35:1 anamorphic widescreen transfer is as close to the theatrical experience as one can get outside of the cinema. Zsigmond's intelligent use of light, depth and texture no longer looks like colored mush; here fine detail is at last discernible, colors richer, and blacks rock solid. Much of the dirt and excessive grain that marred previous transfers have been greatly reduced or eliminated entirely. Also stunning are the included Dolby Digital and DTS 5.1 surround tracks. *Close Encounters* delivers some of the most incredible low bass ever heard in a motion picture; the extended frequency response of both tracks, especially the DTS, creates a knockout experience. You just may think a UFO is landing in your living room.

Dances with Wolves

DISTRIBUTOR: MGM Home Entertainment
DVD RELEASE: May 20, 2003
THEATRICAL RELEASE: 1990
RUNNING TIME: 236 Minutes
MPAA RATING: R

To quote another Academy Award–winning, world-famous film-maker, there once was a time when Kevin Costner could have proclaimed, "I'm the King of the World!" That was in 1992, when Costner was at the end of a ten-year odyssey: *Dances with Wolves,* his labor of love few thought would ever get made, had just finished a six-month theatrical run that grossed over $250 million worldwide. It won six Academy Awards, including Best Director and Best Picture, and defied the naysayers who, throughout its troubled production, dubbed it "Kevin's Gate." It was the Hollywood dream movie: a deeply felt, highly personal film that defied the odds and clicked with critics and audiences alike. Costner was the new king of Hollywood. Too bad it is a town that loves to dethrone its royalty.

The subsequent decade was not an easy one for Costner. A string of disappointments and charges of rampant egoism tarnished his image and turned the actor-producer-director into box office poison, which makes it easy to forget what a stunning epic *Dances with Wolves* really is. Based on the novel by Michael Blake, it reinvigorated a genre long thought dead by inverting all of its most cherished conventions. Confederate solider John Dunbar (Costner), fearing the destruction of the union, embarks on the classic heroic quest. Wanting to "see the frontier before it is gone," he will eventually befriend a tribe of Sioux Native Americans, an action that is treasonous and forces Dunbar to make a choice between his conscience and his country. Dunbar eventually becomes a member of the tribe and fights to save them from extermination. *Dances with Wolves,* by all reasonable estimates, should have been another offensive, stereotypical Hollywood polemic about the destruction of the wild frontier. That Americans flocked in droves to see a film about a white man who sides with Native Americans to protect the onslaught of westernization remains nothing short of amazing,

> "The strangeness of this life cannot be measured: in trying to produce my own death, I was elevated to the status of a living hero."
>
> —John Dunbar

but Costner did not pander to western sensibilities of backhanded justice. Instead, he painted the most realistic portrait ever seen on screen of Native American culture. While still a white man's view, *Dances with Wolves* is subtle and delicate: the attention to detail, the respect for custom and (in what was considered a move of commercial suicide) the decision to let the Sioux speak in their own native tongue elevate the film far above the typical revisionist history lesson. It is an adventure both highly intimate yet grandly archetypical.

Politics aside, *Dances with Wolves* remains a blistering and passionate western, one filled with gorgeous panoramic vistas, high adventure and romantic longing. Many of its most grandiose sequences have become classics: the "Buffalo Stampede" is both a thunderous action sequence and a triumph of low-budget filmmaking. That Costner was able to craft such a complex, sprawling epic on less money than most big-budget, brain-dead Hollywood action spectaculars eat up at lunch is a testament to the power of the independent spirit. And that the film proved to be such a success only reaffirms one's faith in the intelligence of the movie-going public.

Too bad, then, that Costner's subsequent vilification in the press may continue to tarnish the reputation of *Dances with Wolves*. For it is more than just a great western. And more than just a heavy-handed purging of a society's collective guilt over its treatment of a native culture. It is the ultimate heroic story of the power of humanity to overcome difference, violence and intolerance. And one of the most important American movies of the 1990s.

The Goodies Originally produced by the now-defunct Orion Pictures, *Dances with Wolves* jumped like a hot potato from distributor to distributor before MGM picked up the rights in the late 1990s. Long one of the studio's most highly requested titles, MGM at last issued *Dances with Wolves* on DVD in this expanded special edition, which integrates over forty minutes of material excised from the theatrical release, with a total run time of 236 minutes.

Given the movie's six Academy Award wins, many questioned Costner's decision to make such significant additions to a film that needed no improvement. Costner addresses these charges in a written introduction in this set's included eight-page collectible booklet, refraining from calling the expanded version a true "director's cut." It is neither better nor worse than the original theatrical version, rather just an alternate look at a film that has quickly become a modern classic. The extensive array of additions range from minor dialogue and scene extensions to entirely new sequences, all reassembled on film and fully scored and completed.

This two-disc set spreads the expanded 236-minute cut across one DVD-18; a second disc contains the supplementary material. Costner and producer Jim Wilson contribute a new screen-specific audio commentary that runs the entire length of the picture, as do director of photography Dean Semler and editor Neil Travis on a second track. These rank as two of the finest commentaries around. Even those who are not fans of Costner will find his candor and humility refreshing; *Dances with Wolves* is proof that the low-budget, personal project can still be made in Hollywood and fulfill the expectations of even the most optimistic makers. Wilson, Semler and Travis give full due to the film's entire cast and crew but rise above the typical schmooze-fest to offer a powerful primer on how arduous and unglamorous low-budget filmmaking can be. And Semler and Travis serve as an important reminder of what is required to tell a story efficiently and without pretense. These commentaries are, ultimately, as much a testament to independent film as *Dances with Wolves*.

The eighty-two-minute documentary "The Creation of an Epic— A Retrospective" puts a face to the many names paid tribute to in the commentaries. Documentarian J.M. Kenny has crafted an appropriately reverential, loving tribute that weaves many disparate threads and themes into a cohesive whole. The making of *Dances with Wolves* meant many things to many people—it was a personal labor of love for Costner, a daring and bold inversion of classic western clichés for Blake, a monument to a culture destroyed by imperialism for Native Americans, and a tale of an often arduous production for its cast and crew. Each of these facets is explored with considerable depth, a deftly assembled combination of new retrospective interviews, never-before-seen production footage (much of it from Costner's personal collection) and still material. However, "The Creation of an Epic" suffers from a growing tendency of the major studios to chop up what should be full-length documentaries into more digestible bits. Sometimes the approach can work, but here it is intrusive, requiring far too much button pushing that can only be alleviated thanks to the "Play All" option. But Kenny's passion and restraint mirrors that of Costner's, and comes through in every shot.

More extras include a ten-minute photo montage offering a fairly comprehensive overview of the film's production in chronological order, an ad materials gallery that is a bit slim, various theatrical trailers and TV spots, and a music video that is essentially a still montage set to the film's score.

The Presentation Winner of the 1992 Academy Award for Best Cinematography, Semler's evocative photography is lushly reproduced here. The film's expansive 2.35:1 widescreen compositions are awash in rich, vibrant oranges, browns and splashes of blue and red—never has the American flag looked so striking. *Dances with Wolves* is imbued with a golden sense of nostalgia tailor-made for DVD. The sense of depth is almost three-dimensional, and the integration of the additional footage is seamless: never do any of the changes and additions reveal themselves, which carries over to the soundtrack. The biggest beneficiary of the new Dolby Digital 5.1 remix here is John Barry's evocative score, which is nicely spread out across the entire soundfield. The film's thunderous action scenes, especially the classic buffalo stampede, are rendered with great force and clarity. The increased heft of the .1 LFE channel delivers a highly engaging experience, and surround use is consistent and creative. The only disappointment? No DTS option, which would have enhanced the film's effectiveness even more. Otherwise, it is hard to imagine *Dances with Wolves* looking or sounding better.

Additional Versions Before MGM acquired the Orion library, Image Entertainment licensed the rights to release *Dances with Wolves* on DVD. Image issued two versions of the film's 180-minute theatrical cut: a single-disc Dolby Digital version and a two-disc set with a full bit rate DTS track. Both are now out of print. As of this writing, MGM has not yet released or announced a DVD reissue of the theatrical cut.

Doctor Zhivago

DISTRIBUTOR: Warner Home Video
DVD RELEASE: November 6, 2001
THEATRICAL RELEASE: December 1965
RUNNING TIME: 200 Minutes
MPAA RATING: PG

Leave it to David Lean to make the grandest, most expansive Cinema-Scope epic out of the simplest, most threadbare story he could find: *Doctor Zhivago* is a three-and-a-half hour motion picture about two people who just want to get it on.

Such a statement is not meant to demean the importance of the vast historical backdrop *Doctor Zhivago* is set against, nor the rich metropolitan Russian culture the film so evocatively depicts. But the greatest compliment one can offer *Doctor Zhivago* is that in spite of, or perhaps because of, its pretense and desire to elevate the mundane to the level of epic, it is sometimes easy to forget—and forgive—that at its core it is a tale of illicit passion and sexual

> "There are two kinds of women, and you, as we well know, are not the first kind. You, my dear, are a slut."
>
> —Victor Komarovsky

indulgence, played out against a backdrop of political intrigue that really has nothing much to do with anything else.

Aiding the effectiveness of *Doctor Zhivago* significantly—aside from Lean's usual grand imagery—is that it is hard to imagine any couple on this planet as physically appealing as Omar Sharif and Julie Christie. The camera worships her—check out the way Lean finds any excuse he possibly can to highlight her mesmerizing blue eyes. But the film is more than just gorgeous wallpaper: Christie and Sharif generate true chemistry and their most passionate scenes are highly erotic. Scoff at all the melodramatic contrivances that bring them together ("He's *married*!"), but who cares when a film burns off this much heat? This isn't Rock Hudson and Doris Day wooing each other in *Pillow Talk*. It isn't even Jimmy Stewart and Donna Reed getting all witty about wanting to get married and be "together" in *It's a Wonderful Life*. The reason *Doctor Zhivago* achieved the level of timeless romance is that it revolves around two people who are so hungry for each other that they simply cannot contain it no matter the consequences.

And the end. Dear God, the end. It is patently ridiculous, and even Lean's greatest admirers shot daggers at the director for such a manipulative and cheesy conclusion. I would wager that those new to *Doctor Zhivago* will absolutely *scream* with shock and sadness at what happens to Sharif. It is over-the-top and shamelessly melodramatic. But *Doctor Zhivago* is a movie made for people who like to read poetry to their lovers in bed, who can't resist cuddling together on a cold winter morning and who get teary-eyed while watching the snow fall. *Doctor Zhivago* is the ultimate mushy movie romance, so epic and grandiose that the only possible course of action after watching it with someone you love is to get a little mushy yourself. And make no apologies.

The Goodies *Doctor Zhivago* has received the deluxe two-disc treatment courtesy of Warner Home Video. It is a Valentine's Day card to the film, to Lean and to its two beautiful leads.

After a pleasing introduction by Sharif, we can sit down for a screen-specific audio commentary with the actor and Lean's last wife, Sandra. Rod Steiger also pops up to interject a few comments on this commentary track, and if, at over three hours, it is a sometimes a tough slog, the trio is so game to hold our interest it is a compulsive listen. Steiger's cranky comments are the most fun—he seems to be channeling his most over-the-top performances—and nicely balance out the far more polite and earnest Sharif and Lean. The auteur's widow is predictably loving and warm, and possesses a fine memory for recalling specific details of the lengthy shoot, and Sharif is also full of insight. There is also a welcome addition in a second track containing Maurice Jarre's beautiful score isolated in Dolby Digital 5.1 sound, which means fans no longer have to spend extra money on the film's soundtrack CD.

On disc two, we have "*Doctor Zhivago*: The Making of a Russian Epic," an impressive sixty-minute documentary narrated by Sharif. The scope is grand and a wealth of excellent new interview footage is intercut adroitly with some brief if tantalizing on-set footage and a wealth of stills. The lack of Christie's involvement is an admitted disappointment, but more than making up for her absence is an impressive roster of other collaborators, including Geraldine Chaplin, screenwriter Robert Bolt and, again, Lean and Steiger.

Rounding out the edition are eleven vintage featurettes. Such time capsules are, as always, a mixed bag and often more intriguing as proof of how far the art of movie documentary–making has come. But the footage of Lean is a priceless find for fans, especially given his usual press-shyness. The remaining extras include a theatrical trailer, an awards list, and far too brief cast and crew filmographies.

The Presentation Even if it had lacked any extras at all this DVD release of *Doctor Zhivago* would be a classic just by virtue of its stunningly remastered 2.35:1 anamorphic widescreen transfer. Colors are lush and vivid and leap off the screen; the amount of detail in the image is extraordinary. Blacks are rock solid and the sheer clarity of the print just about flawless. Lovers will undoubtedly burst into tears after watching this one.

The Dolby Digital 5.1 remix is a bit less impressive than the transfer but still sounds quite good. The film's old monaural soundtrack has been nicely opened up—surrounds are a bit subdued but the overall sound field is more full and expansive. There are a few noticeable and quite effective discrete effects apparent, and Jarre's lush and evocative score is at last done justice. Separation is exploited nicely, and the film's monaural dialogue and effects are nicely spread across the front channels.

Additional Versions *Doctor Zhivago* is also available in a limited collector's edition set that includes the same two-disc set, plus a collectible Senitype and its corresponding 35mm film frame, six limited edition photo stills, eight lobby card prints and an original theatrical poster (27 by 40 inches).

Do the Right Thing

DISTRIBUTOR: The Criterion Collection
DVD RELEASE: February 20, 2001
THEATRICAL RELEASE: June 1989
RUNNING TIME: 120 Minutes
MPAA RATING: R

Spike Lee's *Do the Right Thing* is a film that dares to ask a question with its title, not make a declarative statement. When the movie's main character, a lazy but generally well-meaning pizza delivery man named Mookie (Lee), picks up a garbage can and throws it through the window of Sal's Famous Pizzeria, it is one of the most galvanizing moments in recent cinema history. Whether moviegoers viewed Mookie's actions as misplaced anger or as a justifiable response to the death of one of the main characters depended upon who was watching the film. African Americans had a different reaction than did white Americans. Korean Americans had a different reaction than did Latinos. But one thing is certain: everyone had a reaction.

The center of the film's universe is Sal's, for twenty-five years the pizzeria of choice on Stuyvesant Avenue in Brooklyn. Owner Sal (a riveting Danny Aiello in an Oscar-nominated performance) is proud of his restaurant and has little problem with the mainly African

American clientele. Sal's sons are the racially tolerant Vito (Richard Edson) and the blatantly racist Pino (John Turturro), who longs to leave the neighborhood to the "animals" who live there. The teachings of Martin Luther King Jr. and Malcolm X figure prominently in the lives of the African American residents. *Do the Right Thing* chronicles one sweltering hot day in this neighborhood, and as it progresses, Lee masterfully builds tension. And when that tension is inevitably released, the viewer scrambles to process an opinion. But Lee doesn't make it easy: although every character is given sympathy and motivation, blame is evenly distributed, black and white. And admirably, Lee does not provide any answers, nor is it fair to expect him to. He is there only to pose the question.

The Bed-Stuy depicted here seems hyperreal: talented cinematographer Ernest Dickerson paints with the red-hot colors of a boiling summer day. Characters have odd nicknames like Da Mayor (Ossie Davis), the old drunk who patrols the neighborhood, and Mother Sister (Ruby Dee), the object of his affection. Samuel Jackson plays Mister Señor Love Daddy, a radio DJ who provides running commentary from behind the safety of his glass booth. Of the local residents, Buggin' Out (Giancarlo Esposito) is most clearly the bomb looking for a ground zero. And he finds it when demanding that Sal adorn his pizzeria walls with pictures of famous African Americans, instead of the Italian Americans whom Sal admires. Buggin' Out's major ally is Radio Raheem (Bill Nunn), who carries an enormous boom box and wears matching brass knuckles that spell out "Love" and "Hate." At times, Lee will stop the action as characters face the camera and purge their feelings (one arresting montage sees each character spewing a litany of racial epithets).

> "Hey Sal, how come you ain't got no brothers up on the wall?"
>
> —Buggin' Out

Lee has always been an aggressively provocative filmmaker, but in *Do the Right Thing* he creates the perfect racial petri dish and still one of the most searing and incendiary portrait of intolerance and its consequences ever seen on the screen. It is clearly one of the great films of the modern era, a devastating social and political powder keg that, unfortunately, will never stop being relevant. No matter how many viewers experience *Do the Right Thing,* no two people will see the same movie.

The Goodies The Criterion Collection has once again lived up its reputation as the premiere producer of DVD product with an outstanding array of supplements on this expansive two-disc set.

First is a low-key but informative audio commentary from Lee, director of photography Ernest Dickerson, production designer Wynn Thomas and actor Joie Lee. Dickerson and Thomas speak on a more technical level, whereas Lee tackles some of the film's thornier moral questions. He pulls no punches, so even his most fervent detractors should listen to this commentary with open ears and open minds.

Lee is admittedly notorious for documenting his productions on video. And here it pays off with "The Making of *Do the Right Thing,*" a wonderful sixty-minute behind-the-scenes trip from pre-production to teardown of the major sets. Directed by St. Clair Bourne, the documentary includes interviews with local Bed-Stuy residents (some of whom complain about the inconvenience of filming in their neighborhood) as well as copious amounts of production footage. "Behind the Scenes" contains amazing video footage shot during preproduction and production. Most notable is the footage of the read-through, which offers a remarkable view of the actors as they begin to discover and inhabit their characters. Another worthwhile addition is the press conference held after the film's premiere at the 1989 Cannes Film Festival. See a bunch of French journalists trying to and understand a quintessentially American film.

Odds and ends include Public Enemy's "Fight The Power" music video, an interview with editor Barry Brown, storyboards for the riot sequence and the film's theatrical trailer.

The Presentation Dickerson painted Lee's sweltering portrait in vibrant swatches of brown and red, a stylistic conceit requiring a top-notch transfer or else all would have turned to mush and murk. And Criterion has delivered with a stunning effort, presented here in 1.85:1 anamorphic widescreen. The digital transfer was created on a high-definition Spirit Datacine from the 35mm intermediate positive. Colors are blazing but never oversaturated or smeared, and flesh tones are accurate right down to the sweaty brows and three-day stubble. Blacks are deep, and shadow detail and contrast excellent. The only criticisms worthy of mention are the transfer's occasional soft look and some very minor print flaws. Otherwise, this outstanding film has received an outstanding transfer.

Audio is available in Dolby Digital 2.0 surround and, very rare for a theatrical feature, uncompressed PCM stereo. Both tracks sound excellent, but the PCM effort gets the nod for its ability to better reproduce the finer audio details. In both mixes, the left and right speakers are sprinkled with ambient street noise and there are plenty of directional effects involving dialogue. Said dialogue is always easy to understand, and generally there are no pops, hisses or other audio anomalies. The pizzeria riot is the most complicated audio sequence and both mixes handle it very well, although the PCM is able to present more aural flavors. And the low end really kicks in whenever the film's anthem, Public Enemy's "Fight the Power," plays on Radio Raheem's boom box.

Additional Recommendations Spike Lee has been very well represented on DVD. Some of his best include *Malcolm X,* which, while lacking in extras, remains his most epic achievement. Other notable releases include *Clockers, Mo' Better Blues,* his Academy Award-nominated documentary *4 Little Girls,* and the underrated *25th Hour.*

Dracula

DISTRIBUTOR: Universal Studios Home Video
DVD RELEASE: December 21, 1999
THEATRICAL RELEASE: February 1931
RUNNING TIME: 75 and 104 Minutes
MPAA RATING: Not Rated

There is something about Count Dracula, isolated in his ominous, empty castle, that cuts a figure both strangely tragic and deliciously ghoulish. He is a little bit silly, cloaked in his black cape, long spidery fingernails and pale white skin, but is a character and a mythology that has survived the decades, regardless of shifting tastes, trends and societal mores. Dracula is the godfather of the horror movie, the grand ghoul of the cinema. And that you must respect.

Given the elasticity of Bram Stoker's original tale, it is probably unwise to suggest a definitive retelling. Many cite F. W. Murnau's seminal *Nosferatu* (1921), with its surreal, expressionistic dutch angles and a chilling performance by Max Shrenk as the titular bloodsucker, although as many modern viewers are likely

> **"There are far worse things awaiting man than death."**
>
> —Count Dracula

to favor more recent interpretations, such as Francis Ford Coppola's ornate, stately *Bram Stoker's Dracula* (1993), which boldly explored the story's sexual undercurrent. Stoker's dark, mysterious, sexy creation was primal and basic enough to tap into something truly universal and scary, which has since allowed filmmakers a wide latitude in updating its lore and legend for modern audiences. That poor Drac eventually succumbed to parody (*Abbott and Costello Meet Dracula*? *Vampira*? *Blacula*?!) does not signal the character's deterioration so much as it reminds us that he has fully crossed over into legend. Regardless of how many spoofs, satires or parodies attempt to dethrone him, his appeal remains neverending. He will always come back stronger, smarter . . . and scarier.

There are two real stars in Tod Browning's 1931 version of *Dracula*, Bela Lugosi and cinematographer Karl Freund. Lugosi, he of the permanently arched eyebrow—and as cheesy as anything at your local haunted house—may be a period creation, but awash in Freund's gloomy, gothic interiors, he still radiates a primitive, deeply disconcerting sense of menace and evil. Audiences in 1931 screamed, fainted and ran for the exits at the sight of him. Today, Lugosi and *Dracula*'s very quaintness is campy and cornball, but with just enough creepiness that, well, you will not want to watch it with the lights off.

The Goodies What a frightfully wonderful special edition this is! In 1999, Universal Studios Home Video launched its *Classic Monsters Collection,* a growing series of the best and most terrifying horror films in its vast library. The first eight included such all-time greats as *Frankenstein, The Wolfman, The Mummy* and, of course, *Dracula.* These are eight of the reasons why DVD was invented.

At the heart of this special edition is David J. Skal, film historian and "monster" expert. Highly animated and with an infectious energy, he contributes a new screen-specific audio commentary that is the best of the Classic Monsters Collection. His appreciation for the material and vast knowledge of the subject is rather amazing. He dissects not just Browning's adaptation but the Stoker novel, the various stage-bound productions, and Drac's continued impact and influence on the genre film. As fascinating are Skal's comparisons of the original script and the final film, as well as the 1931 Spanish version, filmed concurrently on the Universal lot, complete with the same sets and costumes, and directed by George Melford. (This 104-minute Spanish version is also included on this set in its entirety.)

Skal returns for more with the excellent documentary "The Road to *Dracula,*" which should, once and for all, silence those who believe that you cannot create a great documentary for a film almost as old as Dracula himself. Skal has enticed an amazing array of filmmakers and historians to contribute new interviews, including John Balderston (son of Lugosi), producer Dwight D. Frye, filmmaker and horror icon Clive Barker, makeup guru Rick Baker, actress Lupita Tovar Kohner and many more. Here Skal sticks close to the subject at hand, the making of Browning's *Dracula* and its amazing legacy, and also touches upon the "lost" film *Dracula's Death,* a must for horror fans and vampire addicts.

A sharp still montage includes rare promotional and production photos and poster concepts, and remaining extras include extensive production notes, filmographies and *Dracula*'s vintage theatrical trailer.

The Presentation Even Dracula isn't immune to the ravages of time, but the print for the 1931 version is in solid shape, with considerable grain and a lack of detail, but nothing inconsistent with a film of the period. Freund's black-and-white photography still sparkles in many scenes, with only some pronounced fading lessening depth and some patchy bouts of dirt and scratches to take us out of the narrative.

The film's mono source elements have been cleaned up but still sound dated. There is constant hiss, if reduced, and the score is abrasive. However, Philip Glass and the Kronos Quartet have recorded a new Dolby 2.0 surround soundtrack especially for the 1931 American version. Oddly, while it is technically far superior to the original mono, it is so good it can be distracting: we are too aware of the disparity between such a modern soundtrack and a well-worn classic. As a surrealist piece, however, it works very well played at a high volume—*Dracula* was never been so slick and, well, kinda trippy.

The included Spanish version looks a bit worse for wear, in both video and audio quality, but also excels for a film of its vintage.

Additional Recommendations Universal has released two separate Classic Monsters collections, the first an eight-disc set with such landmarks as *Dracula, Frankenstein, The Invisible Man* and *Creature from the Black Lagoon*; the second another eight discs of double features largely comprised of sequels: *Dracula's Daughter/Son of Dracula, Son of Frankenstein/Ghost of Frankenstein* and *The Mummy's Hand/The Mummy's Tomb*. All titles in the collections are also available separately.

E.T.—The Extra-Terrestrial
DISTRIBUTOR: Universal Studios Home Entertainment
DVD RELEASE: October 22, 2002
THEATRICAL RELEASE: June 1982/March 2002
RUNNING TIME: 115 and 122 Minutes
MPAA RATING: PG

If you have never seen *E.T.—The Extra-Terrestrial,* then in a way you are very lucky, because you can still experience it for the first time. Steven Spielberg's enchanting masterpiece is pure childlike wonder itself, that rare blockbuster to capture the hearts of both critics and audiences alike and become a worldwide phenomenon. It is a film that changed lives, left millions weeping in the aisles and, like *Star Wars,* created its own merchandising empire. But it is the film's heartfelt message and simple goodwill that has caused it to endure. *E.T.* is the reason they invented movies in the first place.

While Spielberg's love of old-fashioned sentimentality and unabashed romanticism has suffered a reevaluation in our current age of postmodern irony, his vision for *E.T.* is a far darker and more complex one than has been acknowledged. Aided by Melissa Matheson's pitch-perfect script (for which she would take home an Oscar), Spielberg delivered a movie personal and intimate yet universal in its appeal. The sense of wonderment in the film comes from the small details—every scene is a masterpiece of lighting, composition, editing, sound and performance. And Spielberg's natural rapaport with child actors has never paid so many dividends. *We* believe in E.T. because *they* believe in him. As constructed by makeup legend Carlo Rambaldi, the squishy, bug-eyed, clumsy E.T. is a creature obvious in his artifice but still a marvel, not merely of technology but of that intangible quality called *magic*. We can almost see the seams but it hardly matters. It is impossible not to love E.T.

Given the film's extraordinary success, it's unfortunate that Spielberg himself eventually fell prey to today's mad, mad rush to repackage every acknowledged

> **"I've been wishing for this since I was ten years old."**
>
> —Keys

classic with newfangled CGI effects and needless additional scenes. *E.T.* returned to theaters in March 2002 in the heavily marketed and reedited 20th Anniversary Edition, but audiences proved far more resistant to his charms twenty years later. The rerelease proved to be one of the rare financial disappointments in Spielberg's long line of guaranteed blockbusters, which in hindsight is no surprise—with *E.T.,* it was never about the effects, only the magic. Twenty years later, he can still take us for a ride across the moon. And make our hearts soar.

The Goodies Universal Studios Home Video has released *E.T.—The Extra-Terrestrial* in no less than three editions: widescreen and full-frame two-disc sets with identical supplements, plus an even more extensive four-disc, limited edition box set. Amid much controversy, the original, untouched 1982 theatrical version of the film was at first only to be included in the expensive four-disc set; but at the last minute Spielberg wisely relented and now all versions contain both the original and rerelease cuts. The original is still the more satisfying experience. The added effects of the anniversary edition distract, and the two additional scenes—including a cutesy throwaway with Elliott introducing an all-CGI E.T. to the joys of water—add little to the narrative. *E.T.* was just perfect the first time around . . . Why change it?

In bringing *E.T.* to DVD, Spielberg has once again chosen to work with his longtime producer Laurent Bouzereau. It is a perfect fit. As always, Bouzereau is inclined to be reverential, but does it with such class and style that this is yet another impeccably constructed lineup of documentaries. Both the two-disc and three-disc editions feature the seventeen-minute "The 2002 World Premiere" and eighteen-minute "The Reunion" codas. The three-disc set goes three better with the exclusive fifty-seven-minute "The Evolution and Creation of *E.T.*" (pared down to a twenty-eight-minute "The Making of *E.T.*" digest version on the two-disc editions) the ten-minute "The Music of *E.T.*," focusing on Williams's essential contributions and the surprisingly candid and introspective "*E.T.*: A Look Back," essentially a thirty-eight-minute interview with Spielberg.

Just a few of these features on their own would make for an impressive package; combined, they form one very cohesive, comprehensive retrospective. While there are plenty of other making-ofs with more technical razzle-dazzle, Bouzereau's strength as a documentarian has always been his insistence on focusing on the personal. Filled with surprisingly intimate and honest recollections, the documentary goes beyond the backstage goofs and gaffs; Bouzereau is able to pull out the deepest of emotions from his subjects. The three-disc set is an especially effective evocation of the overall experience of making a movie; the nuts and bolts are there, from conception, casting and creating *E.T.* to its eventual blockbuster release and the 2002 retooling, but more importantly, so is the heart.

The Presentation Listening to the complaints of historical revisionism from purists, Spielberg wisely does not give short shrift to the original theatrical version of *E.T.* in terms of presentation. The transfer of the original on all three releases is generally preferable to the CGI-enhanced reissue. Both have seen their original masters cleaned up and smoothed out; but the original cut appears less processed and more filmlike, retaining a moodiness that the new version sacrifices for hi-tech gloss. *E.T.* has never looked better—colors are bold, and the level of detail is impressive for a film so dark. At last, Allen Daviau's impeccable, award-winning cinematography can be appreciated in all its glory.

Alas, the audio options on the various editions are downright confusing: the two-and three-disc sets (the latter also featuring a bonus soundtrack CD of Williams's Oscar-winning score) feature differing audio configurations. The 2002 cut included on all the versions features excellent Dolby Digital and DTS 5.1 surround remixes, plus the highly touted "live score" recorded at the film's 2002 World Premiere at the Shrine Auditorium. Conducted by Williams himself, it's a unique way to experience the film and surprisingly effective on the home screen. However, for some inexplicable reason, on the three-disc set only, Universal decided to forgo a DTS track on the 1982 cut in favor of French and Spanish Dolby 5.1 options even though a DTS track *is* included on the two-disc editions! It's too bad that true collectors—the prime market for the box set—have to go without the DTS. Nonetheless, despite its high list price, the three-disc set is a must for fans of this extraordinary motion picture.

The Exorcist (25th Anniversary Edition)

DISTRIBUTOR: Warner Home Video

DVD RELEASE: December 1998/December 2001

THEATRICAL RELEASE: December 1973

RUNNING TIME: 121 and 132 Minutes

MPAA RATING: R

One of the most disturbing, visceral and just plain nauseating horror films ever unleashed upon the movie-going public, *The Exorcist* revolutionized the genre, a tale of demonic possession and green pea soup that so shocked audiences around the world even atheists called it the work of the devil. Based on the best-selling novel by William Peter Blatty, *The Exorcist* was the kind of cultural lightning rod that Hollywood dreams about. It was so controversial in its day that even the Vatican was forced to answer public outcry and condemn it, and all the fuss shot ticket sales through the roof: while the film intelligentsia dismissed it as lowbrow entertainment, all the critical brickbat did little to soil the film's enduring reputation, and audiences ate it up. Even today, thirty years later, *The Exorcist* is widely considered the scariest movie of all time.

> "What a lovely day for an exorcism."
>
> —The demon Pazuzu, through Regan McNeil

Much of the credit for the film's effectiveness goes to director William Friedkin, whose beginnings in documentary filmmaking gave *The Exorcist* its palpable sense of reality. Fresh off of his Oscar triumph with *The French Connection* (1971) winning Best Picture and Best Director, Friedkin wisely downplayed the more episodic structure of Blatty's novel—which many critics carped was nothing more than trite, exploitative hokum—dropping many of its extraneous subplots and melodramatic "happy" ending. Freidkin's legendary, irascible off-set behavior (which included firing off a loaded gun between takes to scare the actors) may have bordered on the tyrannical, but he was able to manipulate audiences into buying what is essentially a wafer-thin tale of lapsed Catholicism. The film's detractors—and there were many—vilified Friedkin and Blatty for pummeling audiences into submission with its bevy of stomach-churning illusions of demonic possession. Yet *The Exorcist* remains so terrifying precisely because it is more than just an effects freak show. It did what all great horror movies must do: ground a super-natural, rather ludicrous story in such a genuine and believable real-ity that we forget it is absolutely ridiculous.

But the story of *The Exorcist* would not end with its blockbuster release (the film remained Warner's biggest moneymaker until *Batman* in 1989). For nearly twenty-five years Blatty publicly expressed his displeasure with the completed film, complaining that Friedkin's minimalist approach stripped his story of its essential spiritual un-derpinnings. After haranguing Friedkin in interview after interview, in the fall of 2000 Blatty finally got his wish: Warner spent a reported $2 million to restore the film and reinstate over ten minutes of footage Friedkin had previously excised. Premiering in September 2000—to the tune of over $100 million in worldwide box office—*The Exorcist* was back in *The Version You've Never Seen*. But bigger does not always mean better.

Fan sentiment was divisive regarding the changes, with the ma-jority favoring the original theatrical cut, an opinion this author shares. Some of the reinstated material does flesh out what was ar-guably too oblique in Friedkin's cut; unfortunately, also gone is most of the subtlety and eerie ambiguity that was key to the film's im-mense impact. Worst of all is Blatty's preferred happy ending, which feels tacked on and is fairly ridiculous given all that has gone before. (Friedkin, for his part, claimed the new version was not a "director's cut" but a mere concession to please his old friend Blatty, although he was only too happy to help repromote the release during an ex-tensive publicity tour.) Audiences turned out in droves, and the infa-mous, long-thought-lost "Spider Walk Sequence" left many a packed theater cheering. Yet such trumped up scares only emphasize the ul-timate flaw with *The Version You've Never Seen*: by making overt the underlying themes that the original cut let audiences discover for themselves, it dilutes the spiritual resonance Blatty tried so desper-ately hard to achieve.

The Goodies *The Exorcist* is a film that, like the devil himself, will never die . . . or at least will keep getting resurrected on DVD release after DVD release. Warner Home Video originally issued the film as a bare-bones DVD edition in March 1997. This lackluster presentation (now discontinued) was thankfully replaced by the much-anticipated 25th Anniversary Edition in December 1998. This excellent double-sided set remains the version to buy.

The wealth of supplements are a devilish delight. Two audio commentaries by Friedkin and Blatty are highly informative, especially because of the ever-chatty director. Following a post-1970s career slump, Friedkin came to regard *The Exorcist* as his "one true classic," and he is as blunt as always on the film's legendary shoot that stretched over six months. While Blatty's displeasure with Friedkin's cut of the film is evident, his recollections on the development of the story are fascinating, making both tracks a must-listen. Hollywood grudge matches have rarely been this much fun.

Flip the disc over and it's an embarrassment of riches. Considered by some to be the best making-of documentary ever produced about horror film, the seventy-five-minute "The Fear of God: The Making of *The Exorcist*" reunites all the main cast and crew, including Friedkin, Blatty, stars Ellen Burstyn, Linda Blair, Max Von Sydow and Jason Miller, and most of the crew. Just as fascinating as the phenomenal reaction to the film is Friedkin's legendary perfectionism. Who else would slap a Jesuit priest across the face to get the reaction he wanted? Friedkin's approach was more akin to waging a war than making a movie—both Burstyn and Blair ended up with back injuries, while the score that original composer Lalo Schifrin submitted so incensed the young Friedkin that he called it a "piece of shit" and promptly threw it out of a third-floor window. And most notorious was the "Exorcist curse," long rumored to have resulted in mysterious accidents and three fatalities. Fact, fiction or pure nonsense? When it is this delicious, who cares?

Additional extras include numerous deleted scenes (including many of the sequences that were reinstated in *The Version You've Never Seen*), an often contentious back-and-forth interview with Friedkin and Blatty, and extensive amounts of promotional materials including publicity and promotional stills, conceptual art, and a series of hysterical vintage trailers and TV spots.

The Presentation The 25th Anniversary Edition sports a sharp new anamorphic widescreen transfer and a highly effective Dolby Digital 5.1 remix. For years, this horror classic has suffered from rather poor full-frame transfers and scratchy, badly aged source elements. This somewhat grainy, neodocumentary appearance is retained, but Owen Roizman's criminally underrated cinematography is at last given its proper due. His subtle use of shading and color is preserved, as evocative dark reds, purples and greens are now visible and the sense of detail is a vast improvement over all previous video incarnations. Highly effective (and scary, too) is the remixed soundtrack, which spreads the guttural, extremely disturbing vocal effects across the entire 360-degree soundfield and still delivers chills. Don't watch this one alone.

Additional Versions and Recommendations Warner Home Video has also released *The Version You've Never Seen* on DVD in a shockingly poor pseudo-special edition. While the transfer and Dolby Digital EX soundtrack are slightly improved, the lack of extras is a major disappointment. The disc has become legendary for containing one of the worst audio commentaries ever recorded, with Friedkin virtually reciting the film verbatim, scene by scene. *Exorcist* masochists can also check out the ludicrous sequel *Exorcist II: The Heretic* and the Blatty-directed *Exorcist III*, both available from Warner in nice-looking if supplement-starved budget releases.

The Fantasia Anthology

DISTRIBUTOR: Buena Vista Home Entertainment

DVD RELEASE: November 14, 2000

THEATRICAL RELEASES: November 1940/January 2000

RUNNING TIME: 219 Minutes

MPAA RATING: G

In 1940, Walt Disney realized a one-of-a-kind fusion of animation, music and theatrical presentation. It was called *Fantasia*. It would be the mogul's most unusual, risky and personal film. The concept was challenging—a lyrical, dialogue-free combination of drawn image and classical music, as conducted and arranged by the famous Leopold Stokowski, that would be positioned as not merely a movie, but an event. Opening exclusively in only a dozen specially equipped theaters and presented in the first stereophonic exhibition format (which the Disney team dubbed "Fanta-Sound"), *Fantasia* generated enormous expense—and swift reaction. Critics were confused, audiences indifferent. In what would become the only major defeat in a career full of triumphs, Walt's grand experiment failed. *Fantasia* was a bust.

> "The stimulus for any individual to listen to music, fully engaged, with their imagination working, is really what this is all about."
>
> —Conductor James Levine, 1999

Despite all its daring and sophistication, *Fantasia* remained unappreciated in Walt's lifetime. Unlike many of the Disney Studio's full-length animated features, subsequent theatrical rereleases for the movie were sparse. Because of *Fantasia*'s epic length—125 minutes—and lack of dialogue, it appealed little to television networks, and only a small cult kept the film's memory alive. Yet *Fantasia* continues to be widely cited as a seminal influence on artists working in disciplines as far-ranging and disparate as computer-based animation, world music and Broadway musicals, and a new generation of Disney artists applaud it as their major inspiration for pursuing a career in animation. And the film's most well-known image—Mickey Mouse, adorned as a sorcerer's apprentice, wand high in the air—has become an icon synonymous with the Disney brand throughout the world.

In 1940, Walt originally intended for *Fantasia* to be a traveling roadshow; sequences could be retired and replaced and the film rereleased for new generations. But box office failure caused Walt to abandon his vision. Then, decades later, came the home video revolution. How ironic that what would resurrect *Fantasia* would be videotape, the very medium once thought to be the death knell for the animated motion picture. *Fantasia* was released for the first time on VHS in the mid-1980s, and it astonished everyone, most of all Disney itself, by selling a staggering 20 million units. This success, timed with the reemergence of Disney as a box office powerhouse, not only inspired Roy Disney, Walt's nephew, to pay homage to his uncle's most overlooked accomplishment but also cement his own legacy as rightful heir to the kingdom.

A decade in the making, *Fantasia 2000* hit IMAX screens in early 2000. Reviving only the famed "Sorcerer's Apprentice" sequence from the original, the film's remaining seven segments are all dissimilar in tone and style but connected by a shared theme of hope and renewal. Some of the sequences, such as the majestic "Pines of Rome," with its balletic flying whales, and the closing, eco-friendly "Firebird Suite," perfectly capture the surreal beauty of the original. Others, such as the slighter "Pomp and Circumstance," a comedy starring Donald Duck in an adventure set aboard Noah's Ark, and the jazzy "Rhapsody in Blue," are a bit spotty. Only "Allego" falls flat, altering the ending of the classic Hans Christian Andersen story of a steadfast tin soldier out to win the affections of a beautiful ballerina, but still not doing enough to create a truly worthy retelling. Yet if *Fantasia 2000* failed to fully recapture the ingenuity and majesty of the original, it was still successful enough, both as an artistic complement to the original and a box office success in its own right, that a return engagement—if not quite the traveling revue originally envisioned by Walt—seems an inevitable proposition. And a most promising one.

The Goodies Before DVD became a lucrative revenue stream for the studios, DVD producers were allowed greater freedom to experiment as the stakes were not high, yet the format was successful enough that the majors could invest considerable resources into producing extensive supplemental content. *The Fantasia Anthology* was born out of this era, one that many DVD enthusiasts have already begun to proclaim the format's "golden age." The production team of Jeff Kurtti and Michael Pellerin, key players behind the majority of Disney's finest laserdisc releases, may have created their definitive masterpiece with *The Fantasia Anthology,* as this three-disc set is as inventive, comprehensive and impeccably constructed as any ever produced.

From the minute you pop the disc in your player, it is readily apparent why this set is a cut above: the menus, design and elegant presentation are extremely classy and, well, just look really, *really* expensive. Hosted by Roy Disney, this collection offers documentaries, featurettes, archival footage, stills and interactive vignettes dripping with passion. Each film receives its own disc with enough extras to serve as a special edition in its own right, while the third compliments them both by further exploring the individual suites that make up the anthology.

Two fifty-minute documentaries, "The Making of *Fantasia*" and "The Making of *Fantasia 2000,*" offer a comprehensive overview of the entire saga. Friends, family and collaborators talk poignantly of what would become the biggest disappointment in Walt's career, while Roy is eloquent and candid about the highly personal investment he made in at last reviving his uncle's original vision. Generations of Disney animators and collaborators, as well as some of the biggest names in the field, including Pixar's John Lasseter, set out to prove that *Fantasia* is no mere footnote—it has earned its place in the pantheon of the all-time greatest animated films, up there with classic Disney films like *Snow White, Sleeping Beauty* and *Cinderella*. And no less than four audio commentaries—two for each film, each hosted by Roy Disney and featuring a cacophony of segment directors and producers, plus historian John Canemaker, conductor James Levine and restoration expert Steve MacQueen—reveal far more than anyone could ever possibly want to know about the *Fantasia* legacy. Amazingly, there is little redundancy with the documentaries, resulting in nearly ten hours of essential viewing.

The additional supplemental material spread across the three discs is an embarrassment of riches. Each sequence of both films is analyzed, torn apart and then put back together again via an extensive collection of story reels, character designs, storyboard-to-film comparisons, effects breakdowns and a wealth of never-before seen material, including abandoned concepts, development notes and an orchestral demonstration from *Fantasia 2000*.

But perhaps most exciting for *Fantasia* completists is "The *Fantasia* That Never Was," a lost ark of abandoned sequences that have finally been reconstructed, including the legendary "Clair de Lune," which has also been rescored. An assortment of theatrical trailers and TV spots and a sharp full-color booklet round out a terrific box set.

The Presentation Undergoing a meticulous, frame-by-frame restoration, *Fantasia* remains a vibrant, vital and virtuoso experience of animation and music. The attention to craft and detail is what continues to impress. Presented in its original 1.37:1 full-screen dimensions, the source materials look about as good as one could hope; some grain and slightly desaturated colors still mar the original *Fantasia,* but the sense of depth, texture and detail sparkles. Inevitably, *Fantasia 2000* looks superior to its predecessor and is one of the most glorious transfers ever of an animated film. Colors are so rich, pure and vibrant they threaten to stain the television screen. The sense of depth is three-dimensional and the immaculate print simply dazzles. And unlike the original, *Fantasia 2000* was composed for 1.85:1 and is presented here in anamorphic widescreen, which further improves the level of clarity and detail.

But Walt's most unsung moment sings as well as soars. Each film has been newly remixed in Dolby Digital and DTS 5.1 surround, and they are stunning. The sequel again trumps the original in sheer sonic power and presence. But *Fantasia* impresses with just how good it sounds for a film that is over sixty years old. Surround use is surprisingly alive and electric, with noticeable discrete effects and the

THE PIXELS OF PIXAR: A CONVERSATION WITH BILL KINDER

A graduate of Brown University, Bill Kinder studied film, sound and photography at Rhode Island School of Design before joining the birthplace of electronic cinema, Francis Ford Coppola's American Zoetrope. There he oversaw post-production of a diverse slate of feature films, including *Jack*, *Mi Familia* and *Theremin: An Electronic Odyssey*, and innovated Coppola's electronic storyboard department. Kinder joined Pixar in 1998, where he oversaw production for such megahits as *A Bug's Life*, *Toy Story 2* and *Finding Nemo*, and all of their highly acclaimed special edition DVDs. Kinder is also an accomplished filmmaker, having directed an Emmy-nominated documentary and produced numerous television news shows and specials.

Pixar's rise has almost been on an equal curve with the explosion of DVD. How has your approach to the format changed over the years?
Back when *A Bug's Life* first came out, DVD was really a novelty. I think the assumption at that point was that it was just going to be like a stepson to laserdisc, which had gone as far as it was going to go. And then DVD came along . . . and no one at that point knew it would take off and become the huge consumer format that it is.

But I think everyone at Pixar had always been huge laserdisc fans and appreciated the extras— the look at the filmmaking process, the behind-the-scenes stuff, the interactive features and, of course, the quality. [Now] we are starting at the beginning, making sure we squirrel away bits and pieces of stuff that will contribute to the making-of as we go. And we can always review what we've got and if it helps to tell the story of the way the thing got made, or if it's of entertaining value and it measures up to the film, we can include it.

What are the initial steps you take when deciding on the direction the DVD will take?
We start with the film. You really can't have a great DVD without a great film—DVD is really an extension of that. With *Finding Nemo*, we started by talking to the direc-

tor, Andrew Stanton, asking, "What is it about the movie? What should we pay attention to? What would you like to see?" And I remember, for instance, in that first discussion, him saying that he really wanted to convey the sense of majesty of the ocean. And he goes on in rapture about this environment that he's been immersed in, literally and figuratively for years, and you get inspired: "How is that going to transcribe to the DVD medium?"

It sounds like a very immersive approach and one indicative of the way DVD is headed. Kids today almost demand that the DVD return them to the world that they loved in the movie.

That is how we came up with the idea of the menus. On *Nemo*, you have the same kind of ocean environments—modeled and lit and rendered by the same brilliant people who worked on the film. We just took it a step further and said, "What if we could allow viewers to turn the text off the menus, so you could just make these living environments fill up their rooms? And finish it off with enveloping 5.1 sound?" It really just takes its lead from the director's vision of the film.

One of the prime challenges a Pixar release has to face is that it must appeal to a very broad range of consumer—both children and adults.

I have kids and I talk to parents all the time, and they really enjoy taking their kids to a Pixar film. I know of a lot of films that parents dread having to take their kids to, or they do it as a naptime for themselves. But teens and parents and nonparent adults—every kind of demographic likes to go see a Pixar film because it works on so many different levels. There is something for everybody. That is a philosophy, that is a real approach. It is not easy, but it is exactly what we try to do on the DVDs as well—offer something for everybody.

For example, again the way we address that on *Nemo*, disc one is largely organized around the kinds of things that film lovers would want. The director's commentary may not ever be something a six-year-old wants to sit through, but that's okay. I don't think that excludes kids, but it's probably not for the four- or five-year-olds. Disc two has the material that appeals to families and kids. I don't think it excludes adults, either. I've seen adults playing the "Fish Charades" game and having a great time! Hopefully it just cuts across. But it is definitely a challenge we face.

One of the most comforting aspects of a Pixar release is that you know if you pick one up, it is going to be stuffed to the gills and not feel like just a prelude to another, better release. Is that an intentional part of the Pixar philosophy?

I never want to say never, but we certainly don't have plans like that. It builds on all the experience we've had since *A Bug's Life*. But we're not "double-dipping" people. Sometimes studios plan to do multiple-stage releases. It holds you back from buying it: "Well, I'll just wait for the super-special edition."

It's the same editing decision-making you go through when you're making a film. It may mean some great bits get left out but the overall result is better for it. If something doesn't make it on there, it's not good enough. Just do it right the first time.

How important is the ROM- and PC-enhanced side of the equation for Pixar? Is that something you would like to explore further in the future?

We talk about it and it is interesting. Quite honestly, what I've seen is mostly stuff that you can do with a browser, so at that point I would rather just know the URL and go there myself. And having to have the DVD in my player in order to get there seems extraneous. They are not really related. I have heard descriptions of things that could be much more interactive and updated and I think that is interesting, but we just decided not to spend a lot of time developing something like that right now.

The other thing that sometimes cuts out opportunities on the ROM side is that I think it should be platform agnostic. If it requires you to have a certain type of computer, again, there has to be something there for everybody. And if it requires XYZ and XYZ is something I don't have, it doesn't matter to me and all of a sudden, it is a strike against the consumer.

Pixar made DVD history with *A Bug's Life*, which was the first digital-to-digital video transfer, directly from the source files, of a major theatrical motion picture. What are some of the benefits, and challenges, of creating a pure digital presentation?

It's funny—when things get virtual,

when it's not a physical medium that you're moving around with your hands, when it's something you handle over a network, it is easy to lose sight of what is going on.

Film work is done at a resolution and a color space that is particular to that medium. And there is also digital cinema. It is very similar to the process that we undertake when transferring to a standard-definition video master. But digital cinema requires us to take the frames that were originally at film resolution and put them in the correct resolution, and then do color correction *for* that particular medium. You're in a different color space and you're looking at a different medium. Even if you have a video projector and are looking at reflected light, you're still on a completely different brightness scale, and gamma, and all these other considerations. We have an in-house color correction system that our director of photography sits down at and manipulates while looking at the actual output that he or she is aiming for. (It has to be) corrected in real time. That is probably the biggest single effort we undertake.

Pixar has also broken barriers by presenting most of your titles in two aspect ratios—both the original theatrical composition and a recomposed version in 4:3 full screen.

That is standard routine for us now. The 1.33:1 aspect ratio is entirely reframed with a 1.33:1 camera. It's recomposing characters, plus in most cases it heightens the frame and exposes more of the background. It is not inexpensive, and it takes far more work.

Does Pixar feel that the original theatrical aspect ratio is preferable and the recomposed version is just a concession for the marketplace, one that often dislikes or has not been educated on just why those "black bars" are there?

I think it's debatable. If you took a poll at Pixar, most people would say the former, that the movie was made for widescreen, but I know there are people here who would say that market realities aside, there are technical realities: Most people are going to see this thing on a 4:3 monitor and accepting that as fact, you have to say, "What is the best presentation those people can have? Is it to cut off a bunch of their monitor, or should we give them more picture because we can?"

There are definitely people who think that it is more than just pandering to the lowest common denominator. Stanley Kubrick released his films in full frame and he's no dummy. There are reasonable cases on both sides. And when you have multiple tastes to address like that, why not address all of them?

So we just take that tack: here it is both ways. Some people are rabidly, passionately anti–full frame, and that's okay. They don't have to watch it. But for people who say, "What are those black bars, honey? I don't get it." Then they get the full frame. You serve both extremes.

Is that frustrating that you have to give up such a huge amount of disc space to another version of the film, which could be used for more extras, a DTS soundtrack or the like?
Yes, true. Although I've heard some people say, "Hey, I got two copies of the movie instead of one!"

Looking at a DVD like the ultimate toy box, it is hard to imagine what else you could include on there. Do you think DVD has hit the saturation point?
It sure seems like the bar keeps being raised. When I first saw my parents get a DVD player it seemed like we hit the tipping point. The stuff is here to stay. Honestly, if you got a stripped-down DVD with no extras on it, I can't imagine that you wouldn't be disappointed. That's what people expect now.

What do you think the appeal of DVD is?
DVD is a great film history tool, even if the movie isn't so great. It is a dream to get this stuff preserved and distributed in a mass way, even if it's not a mass product. There are labels out there now doing work on such ephemeral films. There is weird random stuff that you wouldn't be able to see otherwise. But that is what this medium allows you to do. It is a film student's dream. ○

---

classic Stokowski arrangements given a new lease on life. Watching and listening to *Fantasia* here is like watching and listening to it for the first time.

Additional Versions Buena Vista Home Entertainment also released *Fantasia* and *Fantasia 2000* as single-disc versions concurrent with

The Fantasia Anthology box set; each remains on the market and includes the same extras as their respective discs in the set, sans the third disc of additional supplements.

Fatal Attraction

DISTRIBUTOR: Paramount Home Entertainment
DVD RELEASE: April 16, 2002
THEATRICAL RELEASE: September 1987
RUNNING TIME: 119 Minutes
MPAA RATING: R

atal Attraction is the ultimate high-gloss slasher flick. It did for infidelity what *JAWS* did for sharks, *Psycho* did for taking a shower and *The Exorcist* did for green pea soup. The plot is pure Hollywood high concept—a story that can hook you in one sentence. Upper middle-class schlep (Michael Douglas) has the perfect wife (Anne Archer), cheats on her anyway in a moment of unbridled passion (oops!), then pays the price when psycho-from-hell (Glenn Close) exacts her revenge, all leading to the grand guignol climax, complete with the-killer-isn't-really-dead-and-must-come-back-for-one-last-scare ending. Yes, it is shameless, manipulative, cheap, lurid and trashy. But oh, how we love our stories about men who can't help but put their hand in the cookie jar . . .

Everything about *Fatal Attraction,* on the surface, is a class act. Douglas, Archer and especially Close are terrific—Close virtually defined the modern nonmonstrous psycho—and Adrian (*9½ Weeks, Indecent Proposal*) Lyne's direction is incredibly stylish. The first two acts of the script by James Dearden and Nicholas Meyer are so tightly wound, they give new meaning to the phrase *nail-biter*; this movie is so compulsively watchable that we are completely absorbed in its world and characters. But test audiences were cool on the original climax (included on the DVD as an alternate ending), where Close offs herself, implicating Douglas for the crime. They wanted to see Close killed *violently,* and to relish every second of her demise. Hell hath no fury like a test audience scorned.

Fatal Attraction was controversial at the time, but it remains relevant today because the fuss wasn't just about how scary it was (boiled bunnies!), the buttons it pushed (erotic infidelity!) or its questionable morality (cheating is wrong, but it is not your fault if you do it with a psycho!). Why it still matters is because it is the preeminent example of a film created by the test-screening

> "Well, what am I supposed to do? You won't answer my calls, you change your number. I mean, I'm not gonna be ignored, Dan!"
>
> —Alex Forrest

process, where a movie is shown, the audience polled and changes made to ensure maximum box office. The production of *Fatal Attraction* mercilessly stalked the line between art and commerce, and the movie's success paved the way for a sea change in how Hollywood engineered its movies. It wanted it both ways and got it—to be an intelligent, perceptive thriller but also deliver the audience the cheap thrills and stock clichés to satisfy their bloodlust. Freddy and Jason are nowhere to be found in *Fatal Attraction,* but they should have received an Oscar for their unaccredited contributions.

Most feminists hated *Fatal Attraction,* but its impeccable direction, design and cast make it impossible to dismiss as a mere fad movie or the product of excessive hype. We wouldn't still be talking about *Fatal Attraction* if it were *merely* a great thriller. It perfectly exploits two of our most basic fears—abandonment and loss of family—and expertly frames them in a story of infidelity and betrayal. That it comes under the guise of a glossy slasher flick exemplifies Hollywood at its lurid, exploitative best. And its ultimate epitaph? "Hopefully people will realize," producer Sherry Lansing quips in the supplements, "that when you sleep with somebody, at least you owe them a phone call afterwards."

The Goodies To celebrate the film's fifteenth anniversary, Paramount Home Entertainment produced a glossy special edition as desperate to justify the movie's place as a true cinema classic as it is a blatant admission of the film's shameless commercialism. Rarely has a filmmaking team been as honest as they are here, admitting with no hesitation that they openly pandered to the lowest common denominator in the name of box office success.

Director Adrian Lyne contributes a new screen-specific audio commentary, and he is as passionate about the material as he is articulate about his choices, both stylistically and thematically. But Lyne solo is not nearly as fascinating as the amusingly titled "Forever Fatal: Remembering *Fatal Attraction*." This twenty-nine-minute featurette is just like the movie—classy and seductive, even while it shamelessly tries to manipulate you into siding with its ideology and ignoring most of its moral complexities. Never has the test-screening process so affected the outcome of a film. "What happened is that nobody could anticipate the anger that the audience had for the character Glenn Close played," says Douglas, without irony. "You knew the audience wanted some revenge!" And the filmmakers were more than happy to give it to them. Watching these fresh interviews with all the principals—Douglas, Close, Archer, Lyne and producers Lansing and Stanley Jaffe—it is easy to believe them when they claim they had no idea the maelstrom their movie would ignite. Only Close, who fought "for weeks" against the rejiggered ending, stands the high ground, and the simmering animosities are still palpable. Anyone curious as to the thought processes that go behind making a movie by committee must watch "Forever Fatal."

Four more featurettes are included: "Social Attraction," a ten-minute examination of the film's impact with insights from various cultural historians and clinical psychologists, often hilarious; "Visual Attraction," a look at the film's style and a bit long at nineteen minutes; and two vignettes that cannot be missed—a rough assemblage of rehearsal footage between Douglas and Close (she's a stunner) and the infamous alternate ending, which is indeed a downer if more emotionally satisfying than the over-the-top climax that so thrilled moviegoers. Also a treat? An audio recording Lyne made in a packed theater of terrified patrons screaming along to the new bloodthirsty finale. Scary!

The Presentation *Fatal Attraction* was one of the most stylish thrillers of the 1980s, but has been given only a good, not great, remaster here. The source material is not pristine, and suffers from a slightly dated look. Colors are nicely reproduced but the picture can look a bit soft; daylight scenes tend to look the best with more appreciable detail. Otherwise, the transfer has a pleasing sense of depth and is still attractive. Much better is the film's moody and highly effective soundtrack, remixed here in Dolby Digital 51. surround. Maurice Jarre's underrated score expertly combines sound effects with very subtle motifs and cues, which are so well integrated it's impossible to tell where one ends and another begins. Enveloping and engaging, this soundtrack is a standout that, like Close's character, will not be ignored.

Additional Recommendations Fatal Attraction spawned a slew of "victim from hell" copycat thrillers that all had the same plot. A recently scorned, borderline psychotic returns for revenge against his or her unwitting instigator. While none approached their progenitor's box office, the short-lived trend did produce a few guilty pleasures, all available on DVD (though most sans extras, as if they deserved any): *Single White Female* (roommate from hell), *The Hand That Rocks the Cradle* (nanny from hell), *Unlawful Entry* (cop from hell), *Pacific Heights* (tenant from hell) and perhaps the most gleefully ridiculous of the lot, *The Temp* (self-explanatory).

Fight Club

DISTRIBUTOR: Fox Home Entertainment
DVD RELEASE: June 6, 2000
THEATRICAL RELEASE: October 1999
RUNNING TIME: 139 Minutes
MPAA RATING: R

It's hard to feel sorry for Tyler Durden, but he feels sorry for you. In today's Starbucks Nation, where we are what we drive and adult men flip through the pages of a Pottery Barn catalogue the way they used to flip through *Playboy,* Tyler champions a reclaiming of men's place as feral, sinewy, hunter/gatherers whose ultimate expression of maleness is to give into evolutionary desire and beat the crap out of other men. In David Fincher's provocative *Fight Club,* Tyler uses his sledgehammer approach to bitch-slap a generation of guys too eager to be defined by pop culture. "We've all been raised on television to believe that one day we'd all be millionaires and movie gods and rock stars," Tyler opines. "But we won't." That Tyler is portrayed by millionaire movie god Brad Pitt is ironic, inevitable and just one sharp example of how the film constantly folds in on itself.

Edward Norton is the narrator, another nameless victim of the consumer wars. Suffering from insomnia, he finds emotional release in attending support groups for diseases he doesn't have. There he meets Marla (Helena Bonham Carter), another "faker" who enjoys support group meetings for their voyeuristic value. Then, on what he describes as the worst day of his life, he meets soap salesman Tyler Durden (Brad Pitt), who convinces him to shed the shackles of his consumer coil and return to the safe havens of the primordial male, where men express their desires in underground fight clubs. But Tyler is not content to preside over bare-knuckled pummeling contests and soon begins to envision a cultural apocalypse and resetting of our consumer compass.

> **"The things you own end up owning you."**
>
> —**Tyler Durden**

In an era when studios are loath to make a film that incorporates more than one original concept (especially if you can save another one for the sequel), it's admirable that screenwriter Jim Uhls and Chuck Palahniuk, author of the original book, refused to limit their ambitions. The first half of *Fight Club* promises a stinging polemic aimed squarely at the feet of the institutions that bankrolled it: that every commercial pitch is a hard droplet of rain, falling until we're so buried by commercialism and the lifestyle it expects us to live that we're forced to learn to breathe underwater. We then expect the second half to deliver the expected payoff—Norton and Pitt unleashing anarchy and staging a revolution, taking down this monument to mass commercialism that has destroyed the spiritual center of our lives in a maelstrom of audience-pleasing fire and brimstone. But what is so exciting and subversive about *Fight Club* is that Uhls,

Palahniuk and Fincher are too smart for that; they deliver a sucker punch by challenging what previously seemed to be their point—that revenge, destruction and vigilantism are the only sane and just responses to totalitarianism. *Fight Club* is in fact a deeply moral film whose use of graphic violence is justified by its necessity to the film's themes. Those who dismissed Fincher's style as a masturbatory exercise in high-tech showboating—that instead of supporting and enhancing the story, his visual exegesis instead *became* the story—missed the point. Just as a Vietnam epic needs a body count to make its point that war is hell, *Fight Club* needs its bone-on-concrete esthetic to make its final point, that while destroying society in order to save it is a romantic notion, it's simply wrong. Much of what *Fight Club* has to say has been said before. But never like this. And it won't stop until you sit there and take it like a man.

The Goodies The irony of using fancy cardboard packaging and almost two dozen supplements to sell the DVD for a film about anti-consumerism is lost on no one. The release of *Fight Club* was also an important moment in DVD history; it was one of the first two-disc special editions produced for the format and is considered by many to be a benchmark as yet unsurpassed.

The supplements are spread across two discs, with the "only" extras on the first one being four audio commentaries. Sometimes an embarrassment of riches is just embarrassing, but each of these commentaries is actually worth listening to. One from Fincher, another from Palahniuk and Uhls, the next with director of photography Jeff Cronenweth and the design team, and the final one the best of the bunch, a fun and informative track with Fincher, Pitt and Norton. It is incredibly lively, wry and sarcastic; Helena Bonham Carter also appears on this last track, but her separately recorded comments are edited in and stick out a bit too much.

The second disc contains the rest of the supplements, the majority video-based. Practically everything there is to know about *Fight Club* can be found here. The extras are split into five sections: "Crew," "Work," "Missing," "Advertising" and "Art." It is now obvious why many feel *Fight Club* set such a standard: the "Crew," "Advertising" and "Art" sections are comprehensive in a manner all but required on today's biggest releases, but it was done here first. "Work" and "Missing" are the most interesting. The former further breaks down into "Production" (six featurettes), "Visual Effects" (nine featurettes) and "On Location" (a single five-minute vignette), which combined cover all aspects of the film's creation in a fast-paced, slick style that again has proved to be an enormous influence on DVD today. "Missing" contains seven deleted or alternate scenes, some of them almost identical to the final cut with interesting tonal changes the only difference, and which offer an important insight into Fincher's directorial style and approach.

The Presentation With *Fight Club,* Fox Home Entertainment has produced one of the most impressive transfers ever created for home theater. The film's wide 2.40:1 aspect ratio contains an abundance of dark, shadowy scenes that were a challenge to reproduce without excessive grain and pixelization. Thankfully, the blacks are absolutely fantastic, and even more impressive is how they don't impinge upon color reproduction; shadow detail is wonderful. No matter how dark the scene, colors come through with full saturation and no chroma noise or bleeding. Print flaws are almost nonexistent and detail is very impressive. Those with the appropriate gear may want to turn down the lights to get the full effect of this reference quality, THX-certified transfer.

And while you're turning down the lights, you may want to crank up the volume, because *Fight Club* includes a very impressive Dolby Digital Surround EX mix. The soundscape is a heady, highly creative stew of dialogue, music and effects and each is rendered extremely well. Dialogue is clean, easy to understand and occasionally comes through the side speakers, a nice change from most DVDs, which direct every spoken word dead center. The electronic score by The Dust Brothers utilizes the full spectrum and it sounds incredibly pure and clean. Bass is especially floor-rattling, and surround use is employed to great effect. A highly aggressive and engaging soundtrack that every home theater should experience at least once.

Forrest Gump

DISTRIBUTOR: Paramount Home Entertainment

DVD RELEASE: August 28, 2001

THEATRICAL RELEASE: July 1994

RUNNING TIME: 141 Minutes

MPAA RATING: PG-13

Just as Forrest Gump, the slow-witted native of Greenbow, Alabama, can't live without his beloved Jenny, *Forrest Gump,* the Oscar-winning Best Picture of 1994, can't live without Tom Hanks. In a pitch-perfect performance free of irony, guile or canned sentiment, Hanks, who also won an Oscar, provides an emotional center to a movie that would otherwise be a simplistic sociopolitical travelogue through time. And while the film itself is thematically ambiguous, sometimes frustratingly so (it seems to want to say more but can't clearly articulate what), there is so much quality filmmaking on display that *Forrest Gump* remains a unique movie about one of the cinema's most interesting characters.

From the 1950s to the 1980s, Gump lives through and participates in the shedding of America's innocence. As a child, he teaches Elvis Presley to swivel his hips when he dances. As a college student, he witnesses Governor George Wallace try to block African Americans from entering the University of Alabama. As a Vietnam vet, he calls the front desk when he sees burglars breaking into a room at the Watergate Hotel. And through it all, he remains full of optimism despite the war, racism and political strife raging around him. He is everything we want to be: honest, unwaveringly loyal, a global man/child whose desire and resilience overcome his immaturity.

Forrest's strongest attachment is to his childhood sweetheart and the character most his opposite, Jenny (Robin Wright Penn). It is she who gives him his best advice: "If you're ever in trouble, don't try to be brave, just run away." And it is Jenny, the political activist and drug addict, who sticks

> "I'm not a smart man. But I know what love is."
>
> —Forrest Gump

with guys who slap her around. But Forrest, in his childlike longing to be good and do good, sees the best in everyone. And when their destinies finally merge, we hope the resulting child (Haley Joel Osment) combines the best of the both of them.

Upon its release, the film garnered much attention for its use of computer-generated effects. CGI scenes of Forrest interacting with Presidents Kennedy, Johnson and Nixon are exemplary moments, and were a better choice than casting actors in those roles. But Robert Zemeckis, who won a Best Director Oscar for the film, wows the viewer with visual trickery and still has plenty left in his creative tank to engage our emotions. Granted, the audience-pleasing sentiments ladled out in Eric Roth's script (adapting the Winston Groom novel) are hardly subtle. But for Zemeckis, *Forrest Gump* was the culmination of a creative process that began with 1988's *Who Framed Roger Rabbit?* That film also combined brilliant special effects with a story and style that would have thrived even if the film had used a stuffed bunny to play Roger Rabbit. In *Forrest Gump,* the effects are special. But so is everything surrounding them.

And that's all I have to say about that.

The Goodies One of the last studios to fully embrace the DVD format, Paramount Home Entertainment made Forrest Gump its first comprehensive DVD release, with two discs to prove it.

Disc one contains two audio commentaries. The first is by Zemeckis, producer Steve Starkey and production designer Rick Carter. Zemeckis's comments were lifted from a Q&A session and edited onto the track with Starkey and Carter. It has become a common choice for Zemeckis, and sometimes it works (as on *Back to the Future*), but here it would have worked better had he actually been watching the movie. Otherwise, there is no lack of insight, even if Starkey and especially Carter can get a bit overly technical, which is only exacerbated by the film's long run time. The second commentary by producer Wendy Finerman takes a different angle, eschewing technical details for a more thorough look at the book's journey to the big screen. It is a very strong track, although the gaps of silence become epic in length.

The remainder of the extras are on the second disc and are split into four sections. "Through the Eyes of Forrest Gump" is a standard-issue, thirty-minute documentary, originally seen both on television and the old Gump laserdisc. It is mostly clips and sound bites, but luckily the additional five featurettes here take up the slack. The more in-depth vignettes focus on the film's production design, sound design, visual effects and makeup, and benefit from strong editing and an abundance of behind-the-scenes and raw effects footage. Screen tests of Robin Wright Penn and Haley Joel Osment are the most interesting. There are also two trailers and a throwaway photo gallery.

The Presentation Paramount's 2.35:1 widescreen edition is excellent, the best *Forrest Gump* has ever looked on home video. Colors run the gamut, from the green jungles of Vietnam to the blue skies of Forrest's cross-country run—all are crisp and vibrant and smooth. However, as Gump makes his way across history, the film purposely varies in color and brightness and, in the cases where Gump is reinserted into newsreel and archival footage, it looks intentionally grainy and degraded. Still, the transfer is very sharp and detailed (the nighttime exteriors in Vietnam are particularly impressive), with only some edge enhancement evident on occasion.

As hardworking as Mr. Gump is the new Dolby Digital 5.1 remix, which veers between the appropriate sonic maelstrom (mainly in Vietnam, where explosions rip through all available speakers and the low-end rumbles nicely) and subtlety during the dramatic moments. Alan Silvestri's amazing score is evocative and beautifully rendered, and dialogue, so important to *Gump,* is generally clear and distinct, although spoken lines can struggle against louder ambient sounds. Overall surround use is less than ideal but better that than a showy mix that would cheapen the material.

The French Connection

DISTRIBUTOR: Fox Home Entertainment
DVD RELEASE: September 25, 2001
THEATRICAL RELEASE: October 1971
RUNNING TIME: 104 Minutes
MPAA RATING: R

The French Connection is all nervous lines and blurry edges. Dialogue comes in whispered clumps and heavy strokes of street slang. Its pulsing energy seems haphazard, and sometimes is. But it has an underlying structure and form that keep it from getting too messy. In most films, the viewer is aware that performers and crew members are pulling the strings, manipulating fiction to imply reality. The story of a film is the story of the making of the film. *The French Connection,* which paved a pothole-filled road for the urban ugliness of *Mean Streets* (1973), *Death Wish* (1974) and *Taxi Driver* (1976), breaks down that wall. It just *is*. Today, shaky cameras chronicling the exploits of racist cops are a cliché. In 1971, mainstream American audiences had never seen anything like it.

In the film, a fictionalized take on a true story, New York City cops "Popeye" Doyle (Gene Hackman) and "Cloudy" Russo (Roy Scheider) discover that 120 pounds of heroin have entered New York in the rocker panels of a Lincoln Continental, which had been shipped in from France. Capturing the mastermind behind the shipment and the men behind its local distribution lead to what was then the largest narcotics bust in American history.

> "I'm gonna bust your ass for those three bags. Then I'm gonna nail you for picking your feet in Poughkeepsie."
>
> —"Popeye" Doyle, arresting a suspect

Director William Friedkin began his film career doing documentaries, most notably the 1962 film festival favorite *The People vs. Paul Crump*. He was the perfect choice for *The French Connection*. He kept the camera low most of the time, better to give a street-level feel to such streetwise characters. He would occasionally rehearse the cast and the camera crew separately and have the camera follow the action as if covering a news story. The locations were New York City's garbage-strewn, crime-encrusted corners that tourists and film crews never journeyed to. The famous chase scene, as Doyle's car races to catch an elevated train rolling through Brooklyn, is a masterwork of guerilla filmmaking and editing prowess and puts the computer-enhanced car chases of modern films to shame.

Ultimately, what ties the film together is Hackman. In an Oscar-winning performance, he positions Popeye as an angry and single-minded cop whose racism seems a natural reaction to life as a New York City detective. As a character, Popeye is not particularly likable, yet we envy his bravado, his commitment and his acumen. Hackman receives terrific backup from Scheider, who earned an Oscar nomination, and from Fernando Rey, a Spaniard cast to play a Frenchman. Friedkin's vision is supported by Don Ellis's jazzy, experimental score, Jerry Greenberg's Oscar-winning editing and Owen Roizman's urgent, handheld cinematography. *The French Connection* was nominated for eight Academy Awards. It won five, including Best Picture, beating out *Fiddler on the Roof, A Clockwork Orange* and *The Last Picture Show*.

The Goodies Lots of DVDs claim to be special editions, which can mean nothing more than the inclusion of a couple of trailers and a flaccid electronic press kit. Even two-disc sets can seem painfully undernourished. But Fox Home Video's Five-Star Collection of *The French Connection* is the real thing.

There are two audio commentaries, one by director Friedkin, and the other with actors Hackman and Scheider. Friedkin's effort is quite illuminating, as he is conversational, articulate and always riveting. Hackman and Scheider's comments are not scene specific, despite the claim on the DVD packaging. Pieced together from an interview, their comments run back to back and are about twenty-five minutes each. So just have the remote handy, as it is a great coup to listen in on these premiere actors.

"Poughkeepsie Shuffle" is a comprehensive fifty-minute documentary produced by the BBC that begins by telling the story of Eddie Egan and Sonny Grosso, the New York City detectives who broke the French Connection case. Host Mark Kermode takes us to some of the actual film locations and manages to round up many of the major players, except for Egan, who died of cancer in 1995. Admirably, "Poughkeepsie Shuffle" doesn't hide from the controversy, delving into, among other things, Hackman's reticence at delivering Popeye's racist dialogue.

"Making the Connection: The Untold Stories" runs fifty-four minutes and originally aired on the Fox Movie Channel. While it smacks of vertical integration, "Making the Connection" is actually pretty terrific, highly detailed and guaranteed to surprise even the most hard-core fan. Vintage photos and footage of Egan, interviewed on a local talk show, mix with some surprising facts, including how Egan was friends with gossip columnist Walter Winchell, who'd get Egan's busts in the newspaper, inflating his legend.

There are also seven deleted scenes, which can be played individually, all in a row or as part of a separate supplement that comes with lucid, insightful introductions by Friedkin. Rounding out the set are trailers for the film and its 1975 sequel, and a still gallery broken up into "Behind the Scenes," "Unit Photography" and "Poster" sections, totaling about fifty images in all.

The Presentation Flaws become virtues in Fox's stellar anamorphic widescreen transfer of *The French Connection*. Much of the film exhibits fair amounts of grain, but it's inherent in the source material and essential to the look of the film. Never has grit looked so great. Shadow detail, which was wanting in 1971, is no better now, but its absence adds to the ambience. While the picture was never intended to be slick and pristine, the transfer thankfully lacks any obvious errors or defects—there is no edginess to the image, compression artifacts or major dirt and debris. Things get murkier with the audio. Dialogue levels can waver at times, with whispering characters hard to hear and lines that were dubbed in later easy to spot. Still, this Dolby 5.1 remix comes to life during the famous chase scene and for the occasional explosions and gunshots. While hardly a revelation, this soundtrack is appropriate and true to the source material.

Additional Recommendations Friedkin has enjoyed a wildly varied career, veering from such blockbusters as *The Exorcist* and *The French Connection* to the lows of *The Guardian* and the widely disparaged *Jade* (both available on DVD with commentary by Friedkin). Also available in special editions are the director's hit military drama *Rules of Engagement* and, in what many consider an unofficial follow-up to *The French Connection,* the 1980s cult favorite *To Live and Die in L.A.* Sadly, two of the director's most underrated thrillers have gotten the short shrift: *Sorcerer,* which has been released sans extras, and *Cruising,* which has yet to be released at all.

Gladiator

DISTRIBUTOR: DreamWorks Home Entertainment
DVD RELEASE: November 21, 2000
THEATRICAL RELEASE: May 2000
RUNNING TIME: 155 Minutes
MPAA RATING: R

Gladiator makes you want to dress up in a skirt and chain mail, arm yourself with a long sword and indulge in some heavy-duty primal scream therapy. It is the kind of epic tale Hollywood isn't supposed to make anymore, a *movie*-movie about grand themes (honor, loyalty, revenge, destiny) played out across vast vistas, all old-school melodrama blown up to epic-sized proportions and dressed up in state-of-the-art spectacle. *Gladiator* doesn't just ask the same question as one of its most memorable lines, "Are you not entertained?!" It makes sure that anyone foolish enough to answer in the negative is drawn, quartered and fed to the lions.

In the role that made him a star (and earned him an Oscar), Russell Crowe is Maximus, a decorated military commander and the son Emperor Marcus Aurelius (Richard Harris) never had. After leading his troops to a bloody victory "for the dream of Rome," Maximus returns a hero, only to be double-crossed by the sniveling Commodus (Joaquin Phoenix, also an Oscar nominee). Maximus's wife and child are executed, and the hero exiled to the gladiator pits. But revenge is a dish best served cold and, in the hands of director/visual stylist Ridley Scott, a delicious excuse to stage some of the most visceral, relentless and just plain noisy battle scenes ever seen on screen.

Gladiator is big, bloody, bone-crunching fun. Crowe commands every second he is on the screen and proves himself to be a star of the first magnitude. *Gladiator* also served as the vehicle for the long-awaited return

> "I don't pretend to be a man of the people. But I do try to be a man for the people."
>
> —Gracchus

of Scott, a true filmmaker in the tradition of the *gesamkuntswerk*—those who create a total work of art. After a string of disappointments (*1942: Conquest of Paradise, White Squall, G.I. Jane*), in *Gladiator* he at last found the perfect material to match his bravura visual style. And *Gladiator* is a milestone for the state of the art in computer-generated special effects. CGI settings had already become de rigueur by the time of the movie's production, but *Gladiator* was the first to successfully integrate the fake within a historical milieu, turning artifice into high art. So convincing was the illusion that when star Oliver Reed died late into filming, no one batted an eyelash—they simply digitally lifted his face from one shot and stuck it over another. Are you not entertained?

Yet despite a nearly $200 million domestic box office haul and twelve Oscar nominations (with four wins, including Best Picture), *Gladiator* was not universally well received. Many critics carped that its pumped-up action, bombastic soundtrack and Scott's typically impeccable visuals simply glossed over a standard-issue revenge tale. But *Gladiator* is the rightful heir of old Hollywood—should a film be penalized for its own virtues? Who cares when you can't catch your breath for a second—and there are 93,339 of them in the film—to even ask such a question?

The Goodies *Gladiator* was one of the first of the DVD blockbusters. A two-disc behemoth, it set a record as the first to ship a million copies and was, at the time, called the greatest DVD ever made. Today, it still holds up smashingly well.

Before he suffered an Academy snub for Best Director (and a worldwide audience of three billion watched him pout), Scott recorded this grump-free, screen-specific audio commentary. He is his famously low-key, laconic self—intelligent, perceptive and articulate about the making of his most decorated accomplishment. Scott is also candid about his film's historical "looseness"—if *Gladiator* isn't entirely accurate, well, it sure knows how to entertain. And so does Scott for 155 minutes.

How do you reimagine Rome in its day? "The Making of *Gladiator*" (twenty-five minutes) will show you how. That this mini-doc was formulated from standard electronics press kit interviews is what most dates this otherwise-pioneering set. But that Reed face-shifting stuff is sure creepy. The Learning Channel special "Gladiator Games: The Roman Bloodsport" (fifty minutes) is excellent; no, all that blood and guts on the screen is not made up—people really did wear skirts and get eaten by lions. Yikes. And "Hans Zimmer: Scoring *Gladiator*" (twenty minutes) is a strong look at Zimmer's stunning score and gives this often underrated composer a long overdue appreciation.

Rumors of a "director's cut" of *Gladiator* making its way to DVD continue to persist, charges Scott shoots down directly in the set's liner essay. But judging by the eleven deleted scenes presented here (totaling sixteen minutes), the notion of some sort of lost epic seems a bit unlikely. Some nicely expanded character moments make them worth watching, but there's nothing essential. Four additional deleted scenes are presented as a collection of storyboards, a gallery of which also includes eight more sequences that did make it into the final film. Add in another eight still galleries, ranging from conceptual art to extensive production and publicity photos, and yes, you will be entertained.

Additional extras include the unique "Journal of the Shooting of *Gladiator*," featuring over 120 pages of text excerpted from the diary young star Spencer Treat Clark kept during production. There are also plenty of cast and crew filmographies, production notes, and a gaggle of theatrical trailers and TV spots to finish off this trendsetting special edition.

The Presentation Scott will never let you down when it comes to painting a pretty picture, and *Gladiator* is no exception. It is what DVD dreams are made of. This 2.35:1 anamorphic widescreen transfer is still one of the best: incredibly vibrant colors, magnificent detail and rich, deep blacks. Unusual for an early DVD release, the transfer does not suffer from an overly digital appearance, with smooth, filmlike images and no edginess or processed color. But as good as *Gladiator* looks, it sounds even better. It's sonic verisimilitude is positively terrifying—turn this one up *loud*. The included Dolby Digital Surround EX and DTS 6.1 ES Discrete soundtracks can shatter glass, and *Gladiator* continues to be one of the most popular demo discs. A highly engaging, incredibly aggressive 360-degree soundfield pummels the senses. Zimmer's evocative score somehow meshes seamlessly with all the *sturm und drang* of the sound design. But don't worry, you will still hear to maximum effect every last word that Crowe whispers.

The Godfather Collection

DISTRIBUTOR: Paramount Home Entertainment
DVD RELEASE: October 9, 2001
THEATRICAL RELEASE: March 1972/December 1974/December 1990
RUNNING TIME: 725 Minutes
MPAA RATING: R

Would you want to invite the Corleone family over for dinner? Sure, they are well dressed, polite and esteemed connoisseurs of fine pasta and red wine, but they can also be a bit, um, temperamental, and what if they don't like dessert? You may find a horse's head in your bed the next morning. Yet audiences worldwide did more than invite the Corleones into their homes, they lovingly embraced a clan thoroughly evil, and unapologetically so. Wrapped up in misguided loyalties, passionate betrayals and epic violence, *The Godfather Collection* is the Corleone saga, the rise and fall of the screen's most prominent mob family, and considered by critics and audiences alike to be one of the greatest triumphs in cinema history.

Based on the novel by Mario Puzo, Francis Ford Coppola's *The Godfather* revolutionized American cinema. This 1971 film showed us just how powerful, ornate and elegant filmmaking could be. It once and for all vindicated the auteur theory, which says that a film is a director's medium. And it proved just how transformative mainstream filmmaking could be when the collaborative processes are firing on all cylinders and filtered through a single, unifying sensibility.

The Godfather and its sequel, 1974's *The Godfather Part II,* are quintessential 1970s movies. Both were also Best Picture Oscar winners (*Part II* is the first sequel in history to earn such an honor). Coppola managed a daring feat: keeping the world of the Corleones completely insulated. We never see the civilian victims of their violent crimes or the families left devastated by the trail of corruption they leave behind. Instead, we share in their triumphs, tragedies and ambitions, solely on their terms—Coppola refused to critique or satirize from the outside. This led many to lambast the film as a glamorization of a very real and pervasive evil. Because while the moral codes we adhere to are often complex and here to are often complex and

> "Just when I thought that I was out, they pull me back in."
>
> —Michael Corleone

contradictory, the mob adheres to only one: "Don't ever take sides against the family."

More than fifteen years passed before 1990s *The Godfather III,* still the black sheep of the Corleone family trilogy. Coppola constantly refers to this trilogy as being "one film, a sequel and an epilogue." (Coppola's original title for his saga? *The Death of Michael Corleone.*) It is a minor distinction but an essential one, and absent from most negative responses to the film. *Part III* is certainly the most cryptic of the three, and some of Coppola's choices are questionable. Is Sofia Coppola underacting or merely being natural? Why stage a lengthy opera sequence as a climax to the film? But it is impossible not to admire Coppola's unwavering dedication and sheer ambition. And *Part III* is truly a film whose appeal has grown as the bittersweet aftertaste of disappointment has faded.

Strip away the grandeur, majesty, bravura and bloody violence, and *The Godfather* saga may be just a simple family melodrama. But it is also symbolic of an America in transition, and a portrayal of the lust for the American dream taken to nightmarish extremes. Coppola stages Puzo's soap-opera-meets-dime-store-gangster storylines with the ferocious intensity and serious authority of a manic, fevered social theorist. That any saga this potentially dark, morose and seemingly oft-putting could remain so compulsively watchable is some kind of cinematic miracle. When you throw together good filmmakers, an extraordinary story and enough money in your budget to pay for all of it, Hollywood movies really can be both popular *and* great.

The Goodies The epic saga of the Corleones is available only on DVD as a trilogy, in this five-disc *Godfather Collection*. But for once it does not seem like a marketing gimmick; watching all three films in tandem only enhances our enjoyment and deepens our appreciation for Coppola's achievement. The auteur's three screen-specific audio commentaries are only one highlight of this groundbreaking set. He has reams and reams of marvelous material to explore and is, both as a filmmaker and a speaker, a masterful storyteller. The best moments of these commentaries are when he momentarily loses his composure—his tirades throughout *Part III,* especially in defense of Sofia, are by turns hilarious, sad, defiant and cynical. But a warning: at 545 minutes, even a speaker as engaging as Coppola is hard-pressed to keep up the pace. These commentaries are best digested in smaller helpings.

"The Godfather Family: An Inside Look" is the key documentary in this set (laserdisc fans will likely remember it from the box set released in 1990). Running seventy-five-minutes, it probably should have been reedited; eight featurettes, exclusively produced for this DVD set, go a long way to flesh out some of the material breezed over throughout "An Inside Look," but even such a disjointed experience is well worth the effort. Highlights include "Francis Coppola's Notebook" and "Puzo and Coppola on Screenwriting," with the film-maker offering candid thoughts on Puzo's original novel and his often hard-won victories during the development process, plus loving tributes to "The Music of *The Godfather*" and "Gordon Willis on Cinematography."

In 1977, Coppola and editor Barry Malkin created a special version of *The Godfather* and *The Godfather Part II* for television. Reassembled in chronological order and adding some previously excised material, this version is not presented here (nor has it ever been released on DVD). Instead, over a dozen deleted and additional scenes are presented as a separate supplement, "*The Godfather* Chronology," which also provides a text list to the excised material. These scenes, over an hour total, are fascinating if wildly varying in quality, as is some never-before-seen additional material from *The Godfather Part III*, including a bizarre alternate opening that really sets the mind reeling.

Rounding out the collection is "*The Godfather* Family Tree," which is an extensive collection of character, cast and filmmaker biographies, two still galleries, various theatrical trailers; and "Acclaim and Response," an amusing collection of awards show excerpts, including Coppola's *Godfather Part II* Oscar acceptance speech. (And if you are a Sopranos fan, keep hunting for that easter egg . . . it is worth the effort.)

The Presentation Gordon Willis's work on all three films in *The Godfather* trilogy is considered seminal, so hugely influential that it continues to be scrutinized at film schools and anniversary screenings around the world, frame by frame. *The Godfather Collection* has a lot to live up to if it hopes to do justice to such masterworks of visual design. Each film is presented here in 1.66:1 anamorphic widescreen; the results are not, alas, definitive, but good enough. The lush browns and yellows of *Part II* fare the poorest; the film looks appropriately aged but too soft and lacking in detail. The original is actually slightly sharper with purer blacks and less flat contrast. Befitting its youth, *Part III* fares the best; it is soaked in color and overall richer and more three-dimensional. The prints are generally clean but some dirt and blemishes mar the first two installments.

Each film has also been remixed in Dolby Digital 5.1 and can't quite surmount the technological deficiencies of the time. Despite its epic scope, *The Godfather* trilogy is one of great intimacy; these sound tracks excel when they are at their most subtle. These mixes largely sound monaural, with the most prominent elements directed front and center. Fine detail is audible, especially the operatic scores with their booming orchestrations. Even whispered dialogue is sharp and clear, and what surround effects there are, especially in *Part III,* are effective. Altogether, *The Godfather Collection* is an offer you can't refuse.

Goldfinger

DISTRIBUTOR: MGM Home Entertainment
DVD RELEASE: October 19, 1999
THEATRICAL RELEASE: October 1964
RUNNING TIME: 98 Minutes
MPAA RATING: PG

In 1964, the year of *Goldfinger,* the world could not get enough of James Bond. For a society adrift in confusion—political, cultural, sexual—he represented a new optimism, decidedly British but a symbol of the mass globalization of western values. He was wealthy, sexual, violent, an efficient killer, and unapologetically so. And with his arsenal of gadgets, guns and girls, he brought a moral sophistication to the sexual revolution, both progressive and modern but with a healthy sense of tradition. With popular culture changing so rapidly, it was inevitable that Bond would become more than a constant. He would become an icon.

> **"World domination. Same old dream."**
>
> —James Bond to Dr. No

The first two big-screen James Bond adventures, *Dr. No* and *From Russia with Love,* effectively primed the world for the Bond-mania that was to follow. *Goldfinger* remains the prototypical 007 film. No subsequent Bond movie has matched it for sheer style, suave sophistication and cheeky cool. Firmly establishing himself as *the* James Bond, Sean Connery imbued the character with a duality that perfectly captured the spirit of Ian Fleming's original creation: a man with the giddy rush of a schoolboy who knew he could make the girls blush, but who was still a tad afraid he might get caught. His brazen conquests captured the world's affections and only added more fuel to the fires of sexual liberation, inspiring a sea change in fashion, attitude and morality. Capturing the zeitgeist of the time would never be this much fun again.

But *Goldfinger* works just as well on its own as a top-notch spy thriller. "It's laughs, it's excitement, suspense, pretty girls, adventure!" raved director Guy Hamilton. Some critics were not impressed by the juvenile antics, but Hamilton and Connery brought an elegance and sense of refinement to Fleming's sexual spy games, smoothing out the rough edges and throwing in just enough wry humor and wink-wink cheekiness to reassure us that, yes, it was, after all, just an elaborate put-on.

Subsequent Bonds have tried to top *Goldfinger* with bigger stunts, bigger action, bigger effects. None have bettered it. And with the best Bond villain ever, Shirley Bassey's definitive title tune and the world's most famous car, *Goldfinger*'s aim will always be true. This is the one Bond you can't afford to live—or die—without.

The Goodies The Bond series has been a perennial favorite on home video, and in 1999 MGM Home Entertainment finally brought 007 into the digital age with The Bond Collection. Three sets of staggered releases mixed and matched Bonds past and present, each a souped-up, first-class affair, with stunning menus, nifty transfers and dossiers full of commentaries, documentaries and rare archival materials. And they didn't skimp on *Goldfinger,* which is one of the best of the bunch.

The first of three featurettes, "The Bond Phenomenon" is the perfect entry point into the world of 007. The rapturous reception afforded *Goldfinger* back in 1964 was, in many parts of the world, on par with Beatlemania. The thirty-minute "The Making of *Goldfin-*

ger," produced in 1995, is hosted by Patrick Macnee and delves further into Bond's most iconic adventure. It is notable for featuring the last interview Connery has given about his tenure as 007. And the film's "Original Promotional Featurette" is a great piece of 1960s fluff nostalgia.

Two audio commentaries delve deeper into *Goldfinger*. Director Hamilton delivers a solo, screen-specific track in the first, while the second is a finely edited amalgam of *Goldfinger* collaborators: famed production designer Ken Adam, stunt coordinator Peter Lamont, composer John Barry and members of the special-effects team. Host John Cork of the Ian Fleming Foundation gives us a complete tour of *Goldfinger,* from conception to production to blockbuster release. All manner of tasty tidbits will whet the appetite of Bond fanatics everywhere, and the group commentary also includes the last comprehensive interviews given by the late, great Barry and Adams.

The *Goldfinger* DVD also contains one of the most elaborate still galleries ever produced, loaded with hundreds of images divided into twenty-two different sections. From publicity and production photos to never-before-seen conceptual designs and artwork, even the film's vast merchandising and ad campaigns are dissected in depth.

Various odds and ends complete the set. Given Connery's reluctance to talk about Bond in recent years, the assorted vintage radio interviews included are a real find. Other valuable gems include the film's orignal theatrical trailer and nearly twenty-five minutes of TV and radio spots.

The Presentation While the older Bond films can't hope to match the slickness of today's 007, their vintage charm is in many ways even more appealing. *Goldfinger* was a relatively low-priced affair; it was only after the film's phenomenal profits that 007 was able to command blockbuster budgets. So it is perhaps expected that *Goldfinger*'s transfer is actually the weakest aspect of its DVD release.

With a source print in fine shape, *Goldfinger* looks fairly smooth and silky. Rich golden hues, deep blacks and sharp contrast initially impress. But the presentation suffers from a common ailment of early DVD transfers: edge enhancement. The loud, prominent ringing around any remotely contrasted object is an eyesore. Figures standing in front of brightly lit skies appear to be glowing, while any detailed exterior suffers from jagginess. The film's original mono track is also included with no remix provided. The source elements have been cleaned up but can't overcome the lack of envelopment. Both the transfer and the soundtrack have their attractive qualities, but *Goldfinger* deserves a proper restoration.

Additional Versions *Goldfinger* was initially released on DVD in a bare-bones edition, sans extras, with the same transfer and mono soundtrack. It remains out of print.

The Gold Rush

DISTRIBUTOR: Warner Home Video
DVD RELEASE: July 1, 2003
THEATRICAL RELEASE: June 1925/January 1942
RUNNING TIME: 82 and 72 Minutes
MPAA RATING: Not Rated

In 1914, while rummaging through a prop room, Charlie Chaplin first put together the Tramp costume. The character proved instantly, insanely popular, and with it Chaplin turned pratfalls, absentmindedness and just plain dumb luck into an art form, fusing the best slapstick elements of the Keystone era with a sweet idealism and romantic longing that redefined silent comedy. Chaplin has been cited as a major influence on the most important filmmakers of the twentieth century. Groucho Marx proclaimed him "the funniest man on Earth." For Buster Keaton, Chaplin was "the greatest comedy director who ever lived." Woody Allen gushed, "It would be hard to say anyone in my generation was not influenced by Chaplin." Despite a hard-won career spanning forty years and twice as many movies, he suffered his share of detractors, who often labeled his unabashedly sentimental and oftentimes overtly political escapades as mere pathos; his rival Keaton consistently won greater praise as the better director and actor of the two. But screen comedy began—and some would say ended—with Charlie Chaplin.

Picking the greatest Chaplin film is like being forced to choose the best Rembrandt or a favorite Beatles song. So perhaps the best introduction is to start with Chaplin's own favorite among his works, *The Gold Rush*. It contains some of the funniest scenes ever committed to celluloid. Charlie as a chicken pursued by a hungry, hallucinating prospector; Charlie dancing with bread rolls; Charlie eating a boot; or the most consistently hysterical eight minutes of film ever seen, the classic sequence of a cabin balancing on the edge of a precipice. Chaplin, with *The Gold Rush,* proved himself not only a master mimic but also a master craftsman; his sustained lunacy and unrivaled comedic timing is matched only by his irreplaceable skill as a filmmaker and the sheer glee in which he executes his complex, mammoth set pieces. If you can't laugh at Chaplin and *The Gold Rush,* then you should get yourself to a doctor because you may be missing a gene.

> "On the way to the wardrobe, I thought I would dress in baggy pants, big shoes, a cane and a derby hat . . . I had no idea of the character. But the moment I was dressed, the clothes and the make-up made me feel the person he was. I began to know him, and by the time I walked on to the stage he was fully born."
>
> —Charlie Chaplin, from *My Autobiography*

The Goodies As part of Warner Home Video's extensive Chaplin Collection, *The Gold Rush* received a lavish two-disc treatment that not only serves as the perfect entry point for those new to Chaplin but also constitutes the most definitive presentation yet of this seminal classic.

Noted Chaplin biographer David Robinson contributes a new introduction, fully illustrated with stills, that provides the necessary background on the essential place *The Gold Rush* holds in the Chaplin oeuvre. Included are the film's original 1925 version that runs eighty-two minutes, and the 1942 reissue that Chaplin himself trimmed to seventy-two minutes. This rerelease version is the only one for which the Chaplin Film Company retained copyright, and in addition to a new music accompaniment and narration by Chaplin, it was assembled from footage shot with an alternate camera, which results in very slight if notable differences in camera angle and composition. The reissue remains controversial even among Chaplin devotees, many of whom regard the original as definitive despite the Chaplin-approved alternative. Examining both is fascinating and predates today's controversial trend of revisionist filmmaking by decades.

The twenty-four-minute documentary "Chaplin Today—*The Gold Rush*," directed by Serge Le Peron with Idrissa Ouedraogom, is brisk but comprehensive. And two impressive still galleries are some of the best yet assembled for a DVD: an overview of various poster and ad concepts and a remarkably comprehensive collection of over 250 rare publicity and production images, many released for the first time by the Chaplin estate. A collection of theatrical trailers rounds out the set.

The Presentation Many of today's generation's first impression of Chaplin comes from watching terrible, decaying prints projected at the wrong speeds and with inappropriate, rinky-dink soundtracks. On television, essential details are lost to poor transfers and low broadcast standards. In July 2003, Warner Home Video unleashed the first four titles in a twenty-film retrospective collection of Chaplin classics that at last restored the auteur's work to its former brilliance. *The Gold Rush* was one of these initial releases, and it received a glowing restoration that is truly remarkable. Both the 1925 and 1946 versions are included in their original 1.33:1 aspect ratios and each is remixed in Dolby Digital 5.1. They look and sound stunning. Source elements have been painstakingly restored to remove as much dirt, grain, grime and print defects, and pop, crackle and hiss, as possible. Chaplin's often-glorious black-and-white imagery is at last given its due, with a clarity and sharpness never before seen. Of course, neither the transfers nor the 5.1 remix can fully surmount the limited technologies of the time, but Warner has certainly come darn close with the Chaplin Collection.

Alternate Versions and Recommendations Many of Chaplin's best films have languished in the public domain, suffering numerous mediocre releases on VHS, laserdisc and DVD. The Warner collection, restored with the official sanction and cooperation of the Chaplin estate, towers head and shoulders above the rest. Initial titles released by the studio include *City Lights, Modern Times, The Kid, The Great Dictator* and Chaplin's vastly underrated meditation on lost fame, *Limelight*.

Halloween (25th Anniversary Edition)
DISTRIBUTOR: Anchor Bay Entertainment
DVD RELEASE: August 5, 2003
THEATRICAL RELEASE: September 1978
RUNNING TIME: 90 Minutes
MPAA RATING: R

The most financially successful independent motion picture of all time, John Carpenter's highly influential *Halloween* is the kind of horror movie that creeps out at you from behind the bushes and taps you on the shoulder, sending a long, ice-cold chill down your spine. And like its star boogeyman, Michael Myers, it is a film whose legacy just will not die. With its cheap budget, simple premise and highly imitable conventions—girl, monster, knife, blood—*Halloween* begat one of the most incredible phenomena in recent motion picture history: the slasher movie. Yet Carpenter's stylish scarefest is so much better than its imitators as to be almost incomparable. It has been rightfully called the most terrifying motion picture since *Psycho;* if you don't want to be scared, don't see *Halloween*.

What sets apart Carpenter's admittedly simplistic modern fable— Myers returns home on the eve of Halloween, fifteen years after brutally murdering his sister, to wreak even more havoc on a trio of baby-sitters—is that its minimalist brilliance was impossible *not* to copy. Carpenter and coscenarist Debra Hill's skeleton-thin narrative was the perfect film at the perfect time, tapping into 1970s America's growing fear of random, faceless, unmotivated violence. Myers's "The Shape" remains a terrifying cinematic creation because of his very blankness—the white mask (actually a painted visage of William Shatner!), black eyes and almost robotic walk suggest a pathology at work but never explain it. Just smart enough to be truly dangerous but lacking the intelligence to allow for reason, Myers is the archetypal boogeyman, evil personified in human form and blown up to mythic proportions.

> "It's Halloween. I guess everyone's entitled to one good scare."
>
> —Sheriff Leigh Brackett, to Laurie Strode

Halloween is truly one of the most expertly constructed modern horror movies. All a cut above are the film's sharp cinematography (by future Oscar nominee Dean Cundey), energetic performances by a cast of then unknowns (including a fresh-faced Jamie Lee Curtis, making her motion picture debut and still the genre's honorary "scream queen") and Hill's fine ear for teenage "girl talk," which effectively counterbalances Carpenter's sometimes nihilistic worldview and his unrelenting need to scare the audience, occasionally at the expense of logic.

The spooky haunted house interiors, cat-and-mouse games and "Gotcha!" scares are the cinematic equivalent of a game of peekaboo. Carpenter's sometimes sluggish pacing can tax our patience to the breaking point because he stretches the suspense to such a degree that we *almost* want him to kill his next victim just to get it over with. But Carpenter is an intuitive filmmaker who understands it is not the blood and violence that gets the audience off, but the buildup. It is this innate respect for craft—and Carpenter's absolutely relentless glee in playing the audience like a piano—that has earned *Halloween* its place as a horror classic. It is the one American franchise horror film of the past three decades to rightly earn comparisons to Hitchcock.

The Goodies You just can't keep a good masked maniac down. Almost as endless as *Halloween*'s inferior sequels are the number of DVD editions of the classic that have been released over the past five years—and all by independent distributor Anchor Bay Entertainment. The first was a bare-bones version in the fall of 1997 that was dreadful; it was quickly discontinued and is not even worth buying at budget price. It was followed by three subsequent releases in August 2000: a limited edition two-disc set, the first disc containing the film's theatrical cut, a featurette and stills, the second disc reserved solely for the film's "Television Cut," which includes twelve minutes of material shot by Carpenter for the film's 1981 network television premiere; plus separate single-disc versions of the limited edition, dubbed The Special Edition and The Expanded Television Version. Finally, in August 2003 came this 25th Anniversary Edition, which was intended to be definitive . . . well, almost.

The majority of the supplements on the 25th Anniversary Edition are new to DVD. The eighty-nine-minute documentary "*Halloween*: A Cut Above the Rest" seems to want to outdo all of the myriad of TV specials and featurettes that have glutted the market over the past several years; it is certainly the most comprehensive. While Curtis appears only via old electronic press kit footage shot during the publicity tour for *H20,* the majority of the cast and crew return for new interviews, including Carpenter, Hill, Cundey, warring producers Irwin Yablans, Joseph Wolf and Moustapha Akkad (the "grandfather of *Halloween*"), and even "The Shape" himself, Nick Castle. But the biggest find for collectors? The inclusion of nearly ten minutes of production footage shot on location by a British television crew. Cult icon Donald Pleasance appears and is typically curmudgeonly. (It is easy to see why Carpenter was both "in awe of him and afraid of him.") While the length is sometimes punishing—only the most diehard *Halloween* fan will care about some of the finer details—it is an excellent document of an independent film that succeeded like no studio-produced horror film ever had.

Anchor Bay has also licensed the audio commentary from the 1995 Criterion Collection laserdisc (long out of print), which features Carpenter, Hill and Curtis. Its freshness can be attributed to the fact that it was recorded long before Carpenter, Hill and Curtis had grown tired of talking about *Halloween*. Much of the material covered is inevitably redundant given the new documentary, but it has a spark and energy that is appealing, especially because of Curtis, who is modest and appealing here.

An additional ten-minute featurette "On Location—25 Years Later" will appeal only to those obsessed with visiting the sites of past mass murders; there is also a still gallery that is a bit slim (and doesn't include many of the images on the previous *Halloween* special editions), a trailer, TV and radio spots, and all the film's complete screenplay and a pair of screensavers downloadable for your PC. The big omission is the film's "Television Cut," with that version's additional scenes not even provided as a supplement. While Carpenter has publicly disparaged the footage, calling it an unnecessary concession to network censorship, it has become a much beloved part of *Halloween* lore and should have been included here for the fans.

The Presentation Remastered yet again, this time in high definition—in a process Anchor Bay has dubbed DiviMax—*Halloween* is presented here in 2.35:1 anamorphic widescreen and looks sharper and more detailed than ever before. Despite the film's exceedingly dark look, grain has been so reduced as to be almost imperceptible. The print is just about immaculate, with strong blacks and excellent contrast. However, the film's color timing has been slightly altered to compensate for Cundey's extensive use of filters; it is a decision that has angered the purists, lessening the rich oranges and blues that have proved so identifiable with the film's style. The trade-off? A sense of three-dimensionality and clarity that still makes this version of *Halloween* as sharp as a kitchen knife.

The Dolby Digital 5.1 remix included on the 25th Anniversary Edition sounds identical to the versions on the previous Anchor Bay DVDs. Some sounds have been rerecorded—most obviously lightning and other atmospheric effects—which can sound gimmicky and distracting. Otherwise, it sounds like a cleaned-up, slightly more expansive mono track, which suits Carpenter's classic, minimalist score

PRINCE OF DARKNESS: A CONVERSATION WITH JOHN CARPENTER

In 1978, the horror classic *Halloween* heralded the arrival of a vital new talent, director John Carpenter. Over the course of a filmmaking career that has spanned three decades, this University of Southern California grad has written, produced, edited, scored and directed some of the most successful genre films of all time, from the cult classics *Escape from New York*, *The Fog* and *They Live* to the big-budget successes *Starman*, *Big Trouble in Little China* and his classic remake of *The Thing*. Tough, iconoclastic and steadfastly independent, Carpenter continues to produce challenging genre pictures and remains a filmmaker at the forefront of DVD technology.

You have long been one of the most ardent supporters of the special edition, from the days of laserdisc and now with DVD. What is it about the medium that so appeals to you?
DVDs are extraordinary. I collected movies first on videotape, then on laserdisc, and then suddenly the DVD format was presented. The potential with DVD—because of its size, of course—is with the quality of the image and if somebody takes a great deal of care with it, it's extraordinary. Plus the extras are fun, and it makes us all film students.

How do you feel about the fact that more people will be seeing your movies on DVD than in theaters? Is that something that worries you as a filmmaker who is so committed to the theatrical experience and shooting your films in widescreen?
Things change so profoundly and quickly in the business. The movie business, to start with—everything is primed by this theatrical release, almost invariably. You see the bestsellers on the DVD list are movies that were pretty successful in their first run. It's necessary to have the theatrical experience, which is still the best. But even that's going to change. I just went to a demonstration of these digital projectors, and my God! It's a new age. It's pretty astonishing.

Was that the first time you'd ever seen a movie digitally projected?
Yeah. It wasn't a movie—it was a big comparison of old films and

new films, of black and white—they transferred between 35mm and digital projection. It was also very difficult—*Road to Perdition* is a difficult movie to watch, and because of its darkness—how does the digital handle contrast? Is it really as good as film? It's close.

One of the many exciting aspects of digital projection is the lack of any degradation of the film element from repeated exhibition, which afflicts even the best prints and movie houses.

That's another thing. It's astonishing. The movement within the gauge—I saw one comparison I couldn't believe. You watch a film image and it moves—it goes back and forth as the image goes through the projector—but it's rock steady with digital.

We have to take a deep breath and see what happens. Are theaters going to equip themselves? That's another problem. I know things are changing and I know people see a lot of things on TV. I'm delighted that some of these films that were neglected or forgotten are now being watched. That can't be bad.

Are there any of your films you think have been particularly

reevaluated or rediscovered because of DVD?

Most of them. A lot of them get appreciated later, which is always very nice.

You once said something interesting when you were discussing the blockbuster success of *Halloween*, that most of your films were either ahead of their time or behind the times. Do you consider DVD a great equalizer?

It is. That's a really good way to put it. It brings films down on an equal level, which is really where they should be. When you go out to a movie theater, there's a lot of hype going on and a lot of Internet hype, there's a lot of advertising and marketing going on, and a lot of bullshit comes about. DVD is a great democratic thing—everything is equal. I like that.

You've been very honest when talking about your films, what worked and what didn't, when you contribute an audio commentary. Do you think there's ever a danger in baring it all, that perhaps it might take away from the "great equalization" that DVD is capable of? In a sense, you can again cloud preconceptions of your own movie.

Yeah. I know what you're saying. I don't know that you should *ever* talk about a film. In the old days—the guys who taught me—didn't used to talk about them this way, but it's a new era. I don't see anything wrong with it. What's it going to hurt?

Have you seen a change in people's interests in making movies? Is DVD bringing out a sort of latent interest in moviemaking, or has it always been there and we only now have a format to spur it?

I think it's general. The technological advances in the past ten or twenty years are bringing out opportunities for people to make movies in a way that wasn't available way back when, because the equipment is now much less expensive. You can make a movie on digital—that's great. That really democratizes everything. That can't be bad. Everybody who wants to try can have a shot at making something. Does it take a little magic away? Sure. And movies are a lot less magical than they were. Basically something comes along and you say, "Wow. That's incredible." You don't think you're going to see a lot of people making their version of *Finding Nemo*—that's a little beyond them. That had its magical abilities.

But just in terms of straight narrative, it's no longer the wonderful act of going to the movies—the specialness is gone. But that's okay. The more the culture and everybody becomes accustomed to filmmaking techniques, they don't buy as much bullshit.

Have you seen any change in terms of distribution? It seems like making a movie is fairly easy, but getting it released is difficult. Has DVD helped in the funding of any of your films, especially the more risky or possibly less commercial ones?

Well, it's certainly a component, and it's certainly a big call when you have successful DVDs. People want to make money—that's what the business is about. It helps.

Does the fact that you can now include deleted scenes on a DVD help your job editorially?

It's irrelevant, in a way. You're not going to cut a really great scene with an actor. If the only reasons you cut things are for time and pace and maybe for censorship purposes, then to have them to be able to show is fun.

On the special edition of *The Fog*, you mentioned that there were numerous deleted scenes, yet you chose not to include them on the DVD.

Because we reshot some of it. We fixed what the problems were. To string together what we originally did—it was too complicated. It wouldn't have made any sense. I didn't want them on there. It probably would have been all right. They weren't as good of quality—they just weren't up to it.

Yet, on *Escape from New York*, you revealed, for the first time, the long-rumored opening prologue cut from the film.

We have that new opening scene on it. The film's half-assed focus group—I realized they weren't with the movie until that sequence was over with—they didn't know what was going on. One person said to me, "Once we get into it, it's really good." It was like an unnecessary scene. I took it off and showed it to some other people and they got it immediately. I realized it doesn't matter how he got caught, his back-story—we don't care. That was when I was young and stupid. Now I'm old and stupid.

What are your feelings on test screenings in general? Is that something you still participate in?

I don't like them, but they're necessary. You need to see how an audience reacts.

Do you have final cut on your movies or are there still struggles with that?

It varies. It depends. I could be a director for hire—I could do somebody else's projects, which is fine. I don't mind doing that. If it's my own, I don't mind doing that, either. And it's always a struggle for control. There are different ways of doing it. It's not necessary to have final cut. You can shoot a movie in a certain way where it can't be fucked with. I don't care. It doesn't matter anymore. I try to keep as much control as possible. If I don't have it, I don't worry about it.

You have long been a proponent of shooting your films in wide-screen, specifically 2.35:1. What do you feel when you see all of your carefully constructed compositions panned and scanned on video?

I hate it, but that's a whole customer thing. It's hard to educate the viewer that is the way to see it. They don't want little black spaces on their screen. I don't get it.

You are one of the few filmmakers that has seen just about all of **your films, whether hits or not, get the special edition treatment. Would there ever be a situation where you would say, "I don't want to do a DVD version of this"?**

Nah. What have I got to hide? O

well. Wisely, Anchor Bay has included the original mono soundtrack to satisfy everyone.

Additional Recommendations Even *Halloween* completists will have a tough time slogging through all seven of its sequels. The best of the lot is likely 1998's *Halloween H20,* Curtis's triumphant return to the character she made famous. The inferior but still entertaining *Halloween II* also benefits from the presence of Curtis, as well as cinematographer Cundey, working from a script by Carpenter and Hill. And for an indication of just how influential *Halloween* ultimately was, check out its disciples: *Friday the 13th,* Wes Craven's *A Nightmare on Elm Street,* and the blockbuster *Scream* series.

A Hard Day's Night

DISTRIBUTOR: Buena Vista Home Entertainment
DVD RELEASE: September 24, 2002
THEATRICAL RELEASE: August 1964
RUNNING TIME: 88 Minutes
MPAA RATING: G

A *Hard Day's Night* may seem painfully silly to contemporary audiences, a generation of tweens infatuated with prepackaged Mc-Celebrities and rappers who'd rather kill you than sell you their record. However, the further we get from the era of the Beatles, the more we risk forgetting there was a time before MTV, before the Internet, before *Entertainment Tonight,* before everybody knew everything. And in 1964, nobody had ever seen anything like *A Hard Day's Night*.

From its opening shot of the band gleefully evading a group of rampaging teenage girls to the closing concert, *A Hard Day's Night* is delightful and cheeky and designed to run with three wheels off the tracks. The film chronicles the band's Marx Brothers–inspired exploits during the thirty six hours leading up to a television appearance. Although they're shuttled from train to car to dressing room to stage, the boys are not prisoners of their fame. Never for a moment is the audience asked to pity our poor lads and marvel at how they sally forth despite the searing, unforgiving limelight. *A Hard Day's Night* is irrational musical exuberance made cinematic.

The film was directed by Richard Lester, a Philadelphia-born expatriate approved by the Beatles on the strength of his Oscar-nominated 1959 short, *The Running, Jumping and Standing Still Film* starring Peter Sellers. Lester lent *A Hard Day's Night* a free-wheeling, mischievous energy that highlights the band's personality, not their acting ability. None of the actors were rigidly blocked: if they moved, the cameramen were instructed to follow them. Blown takes were used whenever appropriate, including George Harrison stumbling while being chased in the opening scene. Alun Owen's quick-witted script (in which the name of the band is never uttered) had the frisky foursome look down upon all manner of authority figure, including the humorless fusspot on the train who asks them to turn down their radio. "I fought the war for your sort," the old man says. "I bet you're sorry you won," Ringo replies.

> REPORTER: "Are you a mod or a rocker?"
>
> RINGO STARR: "No, I'm a mocker."

Today some musical artists fall all over themselves trying to create an identity based on family tragedy and inner-city suffering; in contrast, the early Beatles were the embodiment of unadulterated musical joy. And the film made their joy into our joy, and left us with an enduring classic that forever changed how audiences hear and evaluate music and film. As for Lester, years after *A Hard Day's*

Night, MTV sent him a parchment scroll proclaiming him "The Father of Music Television." He demanded a blood test.

The Goodies Beatlemania meets DVD mania in Miramax's exhaustive special edition, a collection of supplements spread over two discs that seems endless. The first platter contains only one extra, a thirty-six-minute documentary called "Things They Said Today." Almost every surviving member of the cast and crew is interviewed (including director Lester and Beatles producer Sir George Martin), and the result is a tight and informative overview of the film, its origins and its aftermath.

The rest of the extras are crammed onto the second disc. There is certainly a lot of material to wade through, which is a windfall for Beatles fans, although the supplements are confusingly presented. (Still, bless Miramax for making such an enormous effort and providing a digital document so thorough, especially forty years after the fact.) The supplement disc is essentially a truckload of interviews, split into sections and given cheeky, sometimes obtuse titles. Some of the more interesting items? "Listen to the Music Playing in Your Head," a revealing interview with Beatles producer Martin. "Such a Clean Old Man" is a fine tribute to Wilfrid Brambell, who plays Paul's grandfather. (Brambell was known in England for his starring role in the sitcom *Steptoe and Son,* later redone in America as *Sanford and Son* starring Redd Foxx). The minutiae includes a short piece called "I've Lost My Little Girl," which features actress Isla Blair discussing a scene with Paul that was cut from the film.

With even the biggest DVD releases, ROM-based extras tend to be mere afterthoughts, if any are included at all. Not here. We get the original screenplay presented in a full-featured but easy-to-use viewer with direct scene access, an extensive, souped-up version of the film's official website, and tons of excellent discography and biographical information on the Beatles. Other gems include the original movie program, a gaggle of publicity stills and the famous *LIFE* magazine spread heralding the film's arrival.

The Presentation Considering that *A Hard Day's Night* is forty years old, Miramax has done a yeoman's job of creating a very nice transfer minted from the original 35mm negative. For budgetary reasons, the film was shot in black-and-white, so the most obvious potential trouble spot is the condition of the print. Luckily, there are only a few blemishes worth noting, and grain, while evident, is very slight. Blacks are quite terrific, contrast and sharpness good, and detail far better than expected. And there is no edge enhancement or pixelization present. Considering the film's low-budget origins and advanced age, the final product looks outstanding.

Also new is a very sharp Dolby Digital 5.1 remix, one that purists may find problematic but that certainly any Beatle enthusiast will be very pleased with. The original film was presented in mono, which means the 5.1 mix attempts to create something out of nothing. The result can seem processed, as if the mix is trying too hard. Luckily, where it counts, it works. Dialogue can be harsh at times, partly attributable to the original sound recording. Plus, it doesn't help that characters speak quickly and in thick accents. However, on the whole, dialogue is clean with no discernable hiss and no pops or other audio anomalies. Now for the most important consideration: the songs. They sound terrific. The front speakers predominate, which is appropriate—forcing the surrounds to be responsible for heavy musical lifting would be unfortunate. So sit back and enjoy, because the songs are as timeless as ever.

Harry Potter and the Sorcerer's Stone

DISTRIBUTOR: Warner Home Video
DVD RELEASE: May 28, 2002
THEATRICAL RELEASE: November 2001
RUNNING TIME: 152 Minutes
MPAA RATING: PG

After months of endless hype and a marketing machine cranked up to overdrive, the long-awaited film adaptation of *Harry Potter and the Sorcerer's Stone* finally debuted in November 2001 to enthusiastic critical notices and nearly $1 billion dollars in worldwide receipts. J. K. Rowling's unstoppable publishing phenomenon was the equivalent of Beatlemania for the preteen set: was there any kid in the world who had not read every Harry Potter book cover to cover? So how to please the legion of near-hysterical Potter fans while still creating a movie that could stand upright, on its own two magical feet? No need to worry. Not since *Pokémon* had a movie so captivated the hearts and minds of its young patrons. *Harry* was an unqualified hit.

Impeccably produced, *Sorcerer's Stone* was an operation of massive proportions. After an exhaustive worldwide search and some 2,500 screen tests, young Henry Radcliff was chosen for the title role, and makes a fine and sturdy Harry. The topflight supporting cast, including Richard Harris, John Hurt, Maggie Smith and Robbie Coltrane, give the adults something to watch and chew up the scenery with the necessary aplomb. Even the special effects are integrated well within the milieu (except for a few robotic all-CGI creations). Despite these faults, Harry Potter works his magic as effortlessly on the big screen as on the page.

> **"It does not do to dwell in dreams, Harry, and forget to live."**
>
> **—Dumbledore**

Yet as visually dazzling as it may be, director Chris (*Mrs. Doubtfire, Stepmom*) Columbus's $100 million adaptation is still an oddly guarded and even perfunctory take that relentlessly treads the straight and narrow. Fans were delighted that Columbus so slavishly stuck to Rowling's original text, but such devotion often feels like a crushing obligation rather than the license for the audacious cinematic flights of fancy required to truly let Harry soar. Clocking in at an over-long 152 minutes, the movie has been changed very little from the source novel. The consquent predictability, and the film's sluggish pace, dull the excitement, and the big action set pieces feel rote and uninspired, with little surprise in store for anyone even remotely familiar with the novel.

But why nitpick? *Harry Potter and the Sorcerer's Stone* is still enchanting and an encouraging reminder that movies made for children can inspire, illuminate and educate without being preachy or heavy-handed. With ugliness routinely sold to kids in movies, music and video games, Rowling's tale of magical lands, wands and wizardry is instantly timeless. And with all seven of Rowling's novels set for adapatation, that is a fine thing indeed.

The Goodies Clearly designed for the young at heart and quick of finger, *Harry Potter and the Sorcerer's Stone* is undoubtedly the most interactive DVD yet created—and the most frustrating (if you are over the age of twelve). In order to keep the viewer immersed inside Harry's world, Warner Home Video has structured this set like a giant interactive game, which is short on in-depth making-of features but will fascinate its target audience. Who says adults should have all the fun?

Aside from the perfunctory eighteen-minute featurette "Capturing the Stone," offering interviews with the principal filmmakers, and some well-presented deleted scenes, there is little here to entice the adult viewer. In order to unlock the disc's many secrets, users are required to navigate through complex menus, picking up objects along the way to solve Potter-related puzzles. There are some highlights amid the endless menus—a "360-degree" guided tour of the film's sets is a DVD first and a technological marvel, and some of the games are highly engaging even for us grown-ups. Industrious kids with a lot of patience will likely wring hours of enjoyment out of all of this razzmatazz. (The only surprising omission? Turn off your player or eject the disc, and all that hard work is lost, as there is no way to save one's progress throughout the game.)

Very special mention should be made of the disc's web interactivity and excellent ROM features. Pop the disc into your PC (with Internet access) and let the disc take you to a very extensive online interactive portal. Sign up for "Owl Email," get sorted by the "Sorting Hat," share Potter trading cards, or converse with other Potter fans via chat forums. Unlike the sometimes-clunky set-top extras, dulled by slow access time, this is one of the best integrations of web features yet created for a DVD and is, in many ways, superior to the DVD-Video portion of the set.

The Presentation *Harry Potter and the Sorcerer's Stone* is a bold blend of traditional special effects and cutting-edge CGI, splashed across gargantuan sets. It is also a dark and hazy film, to give it the appropriate air of mystery and magic. Many of the best scenes, such as those set in the vast interiors of Hogwarts School, look gorgeous, filled with vibrant blues and oranges, and juxtapose perfectly with the "real-world" exteriors, which are purposely flat and undistinguished. The transfer has a nice, filmlike look that is a bit soft, but otherwise free of digital artifacts or intrusive video processing. And make sure you pick up the widescreen edition—Harry deserves the full grandeur only the entire 2.35:1 frame can provide.

Harry and the ghosts of Hogwarts also rumble to life in Dolby Digital 5.1 Surround EX, tweaked for maximum home theater impact. No expense has been spared to create a soundtrack as tantalizing and engrossing as the visuals. Highlights are the more elaborate action scenes, such as the "Quidditch Match" and the scary climax. While surround use is subdued during the quietest passages, there are moments of excellent transparency that create a fully enveloping 360-degree soundfield. John Williams's Academy Award–nominated score is also forcefully rendered and nicely spread out across all channels.

Additional Recommendations For the rabid Potter fan in your household, consider the Harry-like thrills of *Chitty Chitty Bang Bang,* Disney's delightful *Bedknobs & Broomsticks* and the *Escape from Witch Mountain* films, and the underrated, Steven Spielberg-produced mystery-thriller, *Young Sherlock Holmes,* written by Columbus. And it goes without saying, all of the Harry Potter films that follow this one have lavish DVD editions.

It's a Wonderful Life

DISTRIBUTOR: Artisan Home Entertainment

DVD RELEASE: August 18, 1998

THEATRICAL RELEASE: December 1946

RUNNING TIME: 132 Minutes

MPAA RATING: G

So *It's a Wonderful Life* is the sappiest movie of all time. Does it matter? We are all suckers for it—who can make it through the end of this movie without going through at least a box of tissues?

Frank Capra probably made better films than *It's a Wonderful Life*—*It Happened One Night* (1934), *You Can't Take It With You* (1938), *Mr. Smith Goes to Washington* (1939), to name a few—but *Life* is the one that resonates the most. It is also one of those perennial favorites that were bona fide flops when first released. (Other inductees of this elite club? *A Christmas Story, Chitty Chitty Bang Bang, The Wizard of Oz*.) It was endless television airings that allowed audiences to rediscover and cherish what has since become required family viewing around the holidays. *It's a Wonderful Life* is more than a movie. It is an institution.

Some may call *It's a Wonderful Life* vanilla, but what an exquisite flavor of vanilla it is! No one but Capra could have infused a film with so much bright-eyed optimism. And in Jimmy Stewart's George Bailey he found the perfect protagonist. Stewart's aw-shucks naiveté, shuffling feet and radiant grin are the very embodiment of decency. Stewart even found a way to make nobility and honor *sexy*. Watch his witty and romantic banter with the criminally underrated Donna Reed—never has coy restraint been this erotic. Reed is delicious as the schoolgirl-turned-devoted-wife; she manages to take a thankless role and give her character depth, dimension and integrity. And guiding it all is Capra's steady hand, never heavy but always reverential. The film may run a

> "One man's life touches so many others. When he's not there, it leaves an awfully big hole."
>
> —Clarence the angel

bit long at 132 minutes, but here is one weepie that earns every single one of our tears.

Some may never be able to look past the simple emotions and lack of irony in *It's a Wonderful Life,* and its tremendous attributes as a motion picture have been overshadowed by its ubiquitous presence on television. But *It's a Wonderful Life* is a movie you don't argue with. You just surrender. And don't worry if you can't help but break into sobs at the end . . . it is a secret you share with the entire world.

The Goodies What is there left to say about *It's a Wonderful Life*? Judging by this DVD, a great deal. Two excellent documentaries are included on the disc's flipside. "The Making of *It's a Wonderful Life*" was previously issued on laserdisc and is narrated by Tom Bosley. The film's surprisingly difficult gestation period is documented in fine detail with a combination of interviews with the late Capra and Stewart, and stills and clips. Given the film's age, it is not surprising that there is no trace of behind-the-scenes footage, and the quality of the transfer is sometimes poor, but it matters little as the drama shines through. Frank Capra Jr. has also created a loving tribute to his late father, "A Personal Remembrance," which is often poignant and very candid. Anyone expecting Capra Sr.'s dark side to be revealed will be in for a disappointment, but the struggle to bring *Life* to the screen required a fortitude, stamina and perseverance that is, well, very George Bailey–like.

Also included is the film's vintage theatrical trailer.

The Presentation *It's a Wonderful Life* has suffered for so long from television broadcasts of inferior quality and abysmal public domain video releases that it is easy to forget what a good-looking movie it really is. For this THX-certified, wonderfully restored new transfer, Artisan Home Entertainment has minted a new print of *It's a Wonderful Life* and shined it up like a new penny. The sharp black-and-white photography has a crispness and depth rare for a film over fifty years old. The print is in fine shape, with deep and consistent blacks and generally excellent detail. A few weak patches remain, with some occasional dirt and blemishes, but they are minor. The film's original mono soundtrack has also been restored, although due to the lack of the film's original source elements, it has been remixed here in only 2.0 stereo. However, it sounds more natural and clearer than ever before. Dialogue is still a bit thin and a slight hiss remains, but it is a great improvement over all past video versions and television broadcasts. Somewhere, an angel got his wings for this fine, fine effort.

Additional Versions *It's a Wonderful Life* long ago fell into the public domain, which resulted in a glut of poor video releases and rip-offs. The definitive DVD version remains, so far, this Artisan release. The ultimate irony? Due to a clerical error not unlike that suffered by George Bailey, Capra never received a dime in royalties from any television airings or video sales.

Additional Recommendations Can't get enough of Frank Capra? Many of his best have received the special edition treatment: *Lost Horizon, You Can't Take it With You, Meet John Doe* and *Mr. Deeds Goes to Town.*

JAWS

DISTRIBUTOR: Universal Studios Home Video
DVD RELEASE: July 11, 2000
THEATRICAL RELEASE: June 1975
RUNNING TIME: 121 Minutes
MPAA RATING: PG

Prerelease buzz pegged *JAWS* as the biggest boondoggle in Hollywood history. A production plagued by endless delays and mounting bad press, even then-unknown Steven Spielberg predicted it might be the end to his once-promising career. But leave it to a mechanical shark named Bruce to get the last laugh. Audiences turned *JAWS* into one of the biggest box office successes of all time, ushering in the era of the Hollywood blockbuster and guaranteeing that a trip to the beach would never be the same again. *JAWS* was the first

presold film phenomenon, a triumph of marketing magic that
was, for once, actually selling a
truly great film. And it worked.
Audiences ate it up, a few even
threw it back up, and all came back for more.

> "We're gonna need a bigger boat . . ."
>
> —Police Chief Martin Brody

A flop in hardback, Peter Benchley's tale of a great white shark that terrified the residents of a small coastal town became a runaway publishing phenomenon in paperback. It was the perfect "beach read," a pulpy page-turner dismissed by critics but tailor-made for the big screen. Rare for an adaptation, Spielberg's lean-and-mean retelling actually improved upon the book, eliminating needless, soapy subplots and, in a move of Hitchcockian brilliance, turned the shark into the most terrifying screen creation you never saw. What became a failure of technology became a triumph of craftsmanship, a lesson that, alas, few heed in this day and age of ready-made computer-generated special effects.

The arduous production of *JAWS* is now the stuff of Hollywood legend, but it guaranteed the film's effectiveness. The film's fifty-five shooting days ballooned into 153, and "Bruce," the mechanical shark, failed to cooperate. *JAWS* "went from a Japanese Saturday-matinee horror flick to more of a Hitchcock, the less-you-see-the-more-you-get thriller," marveled Spielberg. And the big rubber fish *is* pretty phony-looking when it does finally appear. But it is a testament to the young auteur's innate ability to excite the eye that by the time the film reaches its thoroughly ludicrous climax, we are so immersed in the narrative that it hardly matters. Even today, Spielberg's shark-fest still hasn't been equaled for sheer primal terror and visceral impact. *JAWS* is grand entertainment and Hollywood at its best.

The Goodies Since its first home video release on VHS in the late 1970s, *JAWS* has been repackaged and repurposed in a number of permutations, most notably a deluxe laserdisc box set released to great acclaim in 1995. That release was a landmark, both the first home video release of a Spielberg film to benefit from the inclusion of any sort of supplemental material and also the first of the auteur's collaborations with documentarian Laurent Bouzereau, who has since worked with Spielberg on all his subsequent DVD releases. For this 25th Anniversary DVD Edition, Universal has culled material from the laserdisc box set and also produced supplements exclusive to this release.

Originally seen in two-hour form on laserdisc, "In the Grip of *JAWS*" has been pared down to a leaner sixty minutes and retitled "Spotlight on Location: The Making of *JAWS*." The experiment offers mixed dividends: some of the detail and depth of its longer cousin are lost, but so is the longer version's sluggish pacing—what was once leaden is now brisk and more entertaining. "When I think about *JAWS*," Spielberg quips, "I think about courage . . . and stupidity!" The troubled production makes for terrific drama—whatever could possibly go wrong did, and the tales of broken-down sharks, strained egos and the irascible Robert Shaw are fascinating and often hilarious. Featured recollections include all of the film's principals: Spielberg, Benchley, producers Daryl Zanuck and Carl Brown, and cast members Roy Scheider, Richard Dreyfuss and Lorraine Gary. Also ready for the time capsule is rarely seen still and location footage—"Alright, there's a shark in the water. He's been killing people. Legs have been bitten off and there is blood all over the place," yells an assistant director. "Now, action!" Even in truncated form, "Spotlight on Location: The Making of *JAWS*" remains a seminal retrospective, a document of both a great film and a landmark of modern Hollywood.

Per Spielberg's much-publicized reticence toward the audio commentary, no such track is included. However, some additional extras take up the slack. An intriguing assortment of deleted scenes, many of which routinely show up in television airings of the film, help illustrate that less is often more, and what is *not* needed to tell a story effectively. There is also a clutch of amusing outtakes, including some priceless moments with the ornery Shaw. And while a still gallery with over fifty rare publicity and production photographs impresses, the remaining text-based extras do not, including some pithy shark facts and a simplistic trivia game. But the ROM-based materials are better than average: the web link to the *JAWS* anniversary web portal is worth visiting, featuring a wealth of additional photographs, production notes and downloadable goodies.

The Presentation To celebrate the film's twenty-fifth anniversary, Universal finally gave this classic a much-needed restoration. Using the original negative, the studio minted a new high-definition master. The result is often wonderful. Although lacking the sharpness and clarity of today's modern blockbusters, the film's 1970's stylistic tendencies actually heighten its effectiveness—shot in an almost documentary style, *JAWS* exhibits the more subdued colors and handheld camera work that lend it a you-are-there feeling more glossy thrillers lack. DVD still can't compensate for all of the era's technical limitations, however; many of the antiquated special effects, including primitive matting and rotoscoping techniques, result in inconsistencies to the print and some noticeable film grain. Nevertheless, *JAWS* looks terrific.

Universal has also extended its restoration efforts to the film's soundtrack, which has been remixed in 5.1 surround. (Separate Dolby Digital and DTS editions are available.) For a film originally produced in mono in 1975, the remaster is impressive. John Williams's famous score is powerfully rendered. His classic five-note motif for the shark is unmistakable, and with even a half-decent subwoofer, will certainly shake up the living room. The rest of the soundtrack also now has a more pronounced fullness and sense of depth, especially across the front soundstage, with nicely rendered stereo effects and improved dialogue reproduction.

Alas, in a controversial move, Spielberg and Universal decided to alter the film's original, Oscar-winning mono soundtrack by rerecording and inserting new sounds and incidental effects. Newly replaced are gunshots, breaking glass and other physical effects. For purists—many of who know by heart every single line of dialogue—these changes will be jarring and all too readily apparent, although for the average viewer they will likely remain unnoticed. Regardless, Universal has elected not to include the film's original mono soundtrack, a regrettable decision that remains the sore spot for an otherwise very fine DVD release.

Additional Versions Universal Studios Home Video has released four editions of *JAWS* on DVD: two each in 2.35:1 anamorphic widescreen or 4:3 pan-and-scan, containing either Dolby Digital or DTS soundtrack options. Supplements remain identical on all versions.

Additional Recommendations Often called "*JAWS* on land," Spielberg's acclaimed telefilm *Duel* predated this box office smash and is essential viewing for any serious fan of the director. Also see a trio of *JAWS*-inspired, waterlogged thrillers, each loaded with extras: the inferior if enjoyable sequel *JAWS 2, Piranha* (the best of the numerous *Jaws* rip-offs) and the rather terrible if campy CGI shark-fest *Deep Blue Sea*.

Jurassic Park

DISTRIBUTOR: Universal Studios Home Video
DVD RELEASE: October 10, 2000
THEATRICAL RELEASE: June 1993
RUNNING TIME: 127 Minutes
MPAA RATING: PG-13

J*urassic Park* is pure entertainment. That it was conceived, without remorse, as a cinematic thrill ride has never been questioned; what has been questioned is how guilty we should feel for buying a ticket. Michael Crichton's novel was a runaway bestseller and, like Steven Spielberg's relentless blockbusters, impervious to critical opinion. It is like a tub of buttered popcorn and a giant box of red licorice. If it tastes so good, why bother counting the calories?

We don't watch *Jurassic Park* to be challenged. We watch *Jurassic Park* to see how Spielberg is going to stage the next miracle of dino-action. Along with James Cameron's *Terminator 2, Jurassic Park* was responsible for ushering in the era of the computer-generated image, delighting audiences the world over with sights never before imagined possible on a movie screen. Spielberg's dinos are not the jerky go-motion of your father's Ray Harryhausen films;

those long-ago epics may trump *Jurassic Park* for quaint, campy thrills, but the living, breathing creations that chomp and stomp all over Crichton's wafer-thin characters were the first real stars of the computer generation.

That the formidable cast of *Jurassic Park* would be overlooked amid all the PG-13–friendly dino-carnage was perhaps a foregone conclusion, which is a shame, given members like Sam Neill, Laura Dern, Sir Richard Attenborough and, most memorably, Jeff Goldblum. Spielberg stretches the first hour of the film so close to the breaking point that by the time we reach the film's *pièce de resistance,* the infamous "T-Rex Attack," we have lost all patience. We are just as hungry as the dinos for a human buffet. But *Jurassic Park* is as much of an adventure flick as it is a horror movie; Spielberg has no peer in staging intricate, breathless action set pieces that constantly surprise—what is so continuously thrilling about *Jurassic Park* is not just watching screaming people evading rampaging monsters, but seeing how our heroes will escape their latest jam, whether it be freeing themselves from a car stuck in a tree, climbing an electrical fence or, in one of the film's most bravura sequences, outsmarting two velociraptors in a kitchen.

> "Yeah, but when the Pirates of the Caribbean breaks down, the pirates don't eat the people."
>
> —Ian Malcolm

Jurassic Park will always be best remembered as a landmark in the history of cinematic special effects, which is also its albatross. The CGI thrills that once amazed audiences now appear dated. (Those big brachiosaurs sure look phony when we first see them.) But Spielberg's ingenuity pulls it all together. Despite its dated digital showmanship, *Jurassic Park* still makes us think we see lots more of its dinosaurs than we actually do. And perhaps that is enough. The thrill of watching it today is witnessing how, for one brief, shining moment, art and artifice combined to make us believe once again in cinema's limitless potential.

The Goodies That the *Jurassic Park* DVD contains little that is actually new may feel like a bit of a cheat; Universal Studios Home Video likely knew that a blockbuster this highly anticipated didn't need any bells and whistles to sell it—it was a presold commodity out of the box. But even old features can sparkle when shined up on DVD.

Viewers already familiar with the one-hour television special "The Making of *Jurassic Park*" will experience déjà vu. It is included here in its entirety, but it is so good its inclusion seems mandatory. James Earl Jones narrates, and typical of the increased budgets usually afforded television productions, it was shot on film and remains far more polished than even the best DVD documentaries to date. *Jurassic Park*'s narrative qualities remain secondary to its success; that it redefined the art of motion picture special effects is what constitutes its legacy, and for that very reason this documentary remains vital. Witness Spielberg, mouth agape, watching the first full-motion CGI creations bound across a computer monitor. It is a landmark moment in film history and essential viewing. But fans of the film will also be treated to a thorough and comprehensive making-of, and a highly entertaining one at that.

New to the DVD are four additional short vignettes that run less than fifteen minutes total and serve more as one raw lump of archival footage than as stand-alone pieces. "Phil Tippet Animatics" offers some charming stop-motion footage of the crowd-pleasing "Raptors in the Kitchen" sequence; "Foley Artists" gives a glimpse at the process of compiling the film's multilayered sound effects; "Early Pre-Production Meeting" feels truncated; and "Location Scouting" is so short it is practically an outtake. None of these segments can compare to the documentary, which is the true star of the piece. Additional storyboards and a wealth of stills provide a fairly comprehensive overview of the conceptualization and execution of the film's many dinosaurs.

Recognizing the film's immense and enduring appeal to teens and preteens, the included "Dinosaur Encyclopedia" may seem like a throwaway but is great fun for the kids. Entirely text-based, it combines nicely drawn illustrations with a timeline, and, for once, is a kid-directed DVD extra that is both educational and entertaining.

Universal has also released *The Jurassic Park Trilogy,* a four-DVD set that includes the Dolby Digital versions of all three Jurassic Park films. The additional material on the fourth bonus disc is similar to the four additional featurettes just mentioned namely, just a few minutes of outtakes and on-set video footage (the material on *Jurassic Park* totals less than twenty minutes) plus the film's original electronic press kit (EPK), aka an extended commercial. The price for this material is high—the two sequels are largely inferior, and the presentation of the bonus disc cheaply done. Skippable for all but the most diehard *Jurassic Park* completist.

The Presentation Any film as highly anticipated as was *Jurassic Park* on DVD was bound to come up for intense scrutiny from technophiles. Its transfer was much picked apart upon release, but although imperfect, it still ranks as mighty impressive. An improvement even over the laserdisc, the new THX-certified transfer was minted from a newly remastered high-definition master and possesses great depth and clarity. *Jurassic Park* is often a very dark film, and even most daylight sequences suffer from an overcast look that appears flat on video. But here colors are quite rich and vibrant, especially the midnight blues in the "T-Rex Attack" sequence.

And the soundtrack roars to life. The first motion picture to be exhibited theatrically in DTS, Universal has released separate Dolby Digital and DTS editions (each available in anamorphic widescreen or full-screen versions) with the edge going to the DTS. While all of the featurettes (see "The Goodies" section) are dropped from the DTS version, the improved dexterity of the soundtrack may make up for it. *Jurassic Park* is what home theater was made for; put on the legendary "T-Rex Attack" sequence, crank it up and watch the pets bounce off the couch.

Additional Recommendations Want to know where it all started? Dinosaur fans and effects buffs need look no further than the pioneering work of animation legend Ray Harryhausen. Many of his best classics have received the special edition treatment, including *The Sinbad Collection* and *20 Million Miles from Earth* from Columbia TriStar Home Entertainment, and *Clash of the Titans, The Beast from 20,000 Fathoms* and *The Valley of Gwangi* from Warner

Home Video. And don't miss BBC Video's excellent *Walking with Dinosaurs* documentary, given the deluxe two-disc treatment on DVD.

Lawrence of Arabia

DISTRIBUTOR: Columbia/TriStar Home Entertainment
DVD RELEASE: April 3, 2001
THEATRICAL RELEASE: December 1962
RUNNING TIME: 228 Minutes
MPAA RATING: PG

T. E. Lawrence (Peter O'Toole) was lumbering, lanky, almost clumsy, of ambiguous sexuality and with a chiseled beauty and eloquent speaking manner that made him seem perpetually bemused; he also projected an intense charisma and persuasive power that rivaled the greatest military leaders of the twentieth century. Yet he was the most unconventional of men, a reluctant hero who, by appealing to the worst instincts of selfishness, was instrumental in enlisting desert tribes to rally against the Turks in the First World War from 1914 to 1917. Or, some argued, he did it completely by accident, indifferent to the political wars raging around him. Was he insane, a savior or both?

David Lean's *Lawrence of Arabia* just might be the biggest movie ever made. Like its protagonist, it invites as many interpretations as questions and is impossible to fully describe. Its visual style and Lean's notorious perfectionism are legendary: every shot is a work of art, a masterpiece of form, construction, composition and style. Some called its making as mad as Lawrence himself.

> GENERAL MURRAY: "I can't make out whether you're a bloody madman or just half-witted."
>
> T. E. LAWRENCE: "I have the same problem, sir."

But its insanity remains one of the most influential of all time—it is hard to imagine any respectable ten-best list that would not include it. It is simply one of the greats, a timeless classic that reminds us why we go to the movies—to dream, to soar, to see the best part of ourselves magnified on a screen three times wide as it is tall. *Lawrence of Arabia* has few peers.

Released in December 1962, *Lawrence of Arabia* was one of the last movies of Hollywood's classical period, when films epic in their grandeur and massive in scope were commonplace. But with *Lawrence* Lean didn't use his giant canvas to make up for narrative inadequacies as a Cecil B. DeMille or D. W. Griffith might have; instead he commanded vast resources to illustrate and complement his themes. It is more than just a biography, an adventure movie, a picturesque travelogue of arid desert vistas, or a quirky, unusual love story. It is, most elegantly and with great refinement, a clear study of a complex man, presented without judgment and uncluttered by preconceptions.

Lawrence of Arabia is certainly a mammoth trek—it runs 228 minutes with a short intermission—and much of its silver-screen grandeur is impossible to re-create in the home environment, even on DVD. But Lean's extraordinary achievement is one that demands repeated viewings, a motion picture so multifaceted, so majestic, so full of pure moviemaking passion that it transcends whatever dimensions try to contain it.

The Goodies *Lawrence of Arabia* has never seen a home video release quite like this one, a deluxe two-disc set whose elegance is clear from its packaging: a smooth, cloth-covered collectible box that resembles nothing so much as a lost hardback book.

Laurent Bouzereau's hour-long "The Making of *Lawrence of Arabia*" is the stand-out supplement. Compiling rare and new interview footage with O'Toole, Omar Sharif, Anthony Quinn, Alec Guiness, and, most fascinating of all, excerpts from a 1989 discussion with Lean himself, Bouzereau is able to craft a documentary that is like a minimovie itself, compulsively watchable and flush with drama. It delves into the exhaustive restoration process required after the film almost slipped into extinction (the original camera negatives were in their final stages of decay until the rescue team, led by Robert Harris, brought them back from the brink). It was an undertaking almost as vast as the making of the film itself.

"A Conversation with Steven Spielberg" is a benign if passionate collection of anecdotes about the king of modern cinema's adoration and brief interaction with Lean. Spielberg was partially responsible for bankrolling *Lawrence*'s restoration, and the most moving moment of the documentary is Spielberg's poignant recollection of finally seeing a restored print of the film that so inspired him. A bevy of vintage featurettes are also included, and if they are largely promotional, they are a wonderful time capsule and filled with priceless archival footage of Lean and cast and crew. A short peek at the film's New York premiere is also quaintly charming, and other extras include talent files, trailers, an extensive advertising gallery and a welcome rarity, a bibliography with recommended reading for T. E. Lawrence buffs.

ROM-enabled viewers can also access the copious "Archives of Arabia." This is a unique use of PC-enhanced content, allowing the user to view the film in three separate windows: one with the finished film scene, another a text window with facts, background and biographical information, and a third with showcase photos and continuity stills. The "Journey with Lawrence" is an interactive timeline that provides more historical detail on T. E. Lawrence's real-life adventures and the territories in which they occurred. Both the enhanced viewing mode and the timeline are exemplary.

The Presentation *Lawrence of Arabia* is a film that demanded a top-flight restoration and got it, but its DVD debut is alternately glorious and frustrating—just like its title character. This 2.20:1 anamorphic widescreen transfer can look grand—deep blacks, rich colors (although even Harris has publicly criticized this release for improper color timing) and a clean new print. (There are a few defects, including splice marks and dropped frames, as even the mighty *Lawrence* is not immune to the ravages of time.) But what haunts *Lawrence* is a surprising amount of edge halos easily noticeable around any sharply contrasted object, which gives the transfer a very digital appearance. It is harsh when it should be smooth. But *Lawrence* is such a must, these flaws are forgiven.

Dolby Digital 5.1 and 2.0 surround tracks are included, each wonderful, although the 5.1 has the edge. Some dialogue and effects cues suffer from the limitations of the original mono source elements; however, the sense of envelopment is pronounced and this is a fine example of how a decades old film can be digitally remixed but still sound natural. Any shortcomings are overcome by the warm and pleasing sound, nice use of direction effects and Maurice Jarre's evocative score, which is spread out across the entire soundfield. *Lawrence of Arabia* is true cinematic royalty; if not quite given the royal treatment here, it's good enough.

Additional Versions Columbia TriStar Home Entertainment has also released *Lawrence of Arabia* as part of their Superbit line of no-frills, bare-bones DVDs, which include no supplements in order to allot maximum bit space for picture and sound. The Superbit two-disc version includes a remastered transfer, which Harris supervised. It is superior to this special edition, but lacks any extras. The best of both worlds? Finances permitting, you will want to own them both.

The Lord of the Rings: The Fellowship of the Ring (Extended Edition)

DISTRIBUTOR: New Line Home Entertainment

DVD RELEASE: December 17, 2002

THEATRICAL RELEASE: December 2001

RUNNING TIME: 248 Minutes

MPAA RATING: PG-13

That a creature as small in stature as a Hobbit can change the course of history is one of the many themes in J. R. R. Tolkien's masterful story of *The Lord of the Rings*. It is also a universal metaphor for the human condition. Against great odds, enormous obstacles and great physical hardship, and despite ridicule and derision, we sometimes attempt the impossible. And persevere, to create magic out of thin air and raise mountains from the ground. But just as often we fail. Many of the greatest of human achievements have disappeared in the mists of time, forgotten, or rediscovered only long after the fact. But sometimes the planets align and, through an intangible alchemy, everything comes together to create that indescribable, unfathomable force known as *perfection*. Such is Peter Jackson's epic telling of *The Lord of the Rings*.

The saga Tolkien created in his four novels—*The Fellowship of the Ring, The Two Towers, Return of the King* and the trilogy's prequel, *The Hobbit*—has long been considered unfilmable: too long, too sprawling, too many characters, too many subplots. And how to create a workable series of movies that would play as well to newcomers as to the faithful? That Jackson assigned himself such an impossible task was creative lunacy. That he managed to pull it off is sheer cinematic genius.

> "It is a strange fate that we should suffer so much fear and doubt over so small a thing."
>
> —Boromir

The Lord of the Rings trilogy ranks as one of the greatest gambles in cinema history. New Line entrusted Jackson, a New Zealand native whose only previous big-budget studio picture was the flop horror-comedy *The Frighteners,* with a budget exceeding $150 million and a shooting schedule that spanned eighteen months. It was an enormous risk, but a gambit that in hindsight seems the perfect match. Jackson's best films have always combined the fantastical with the everyday, from the zany, anarchist *Dead Alive* to the film that truly announced him as a major new talent, the intense true-crime drama *Heavenly Creatures*. *Rings* now feels predestined, the epic Jackson was born to make, the perfect marriage of filmmaker and material. It may be the trilogy's only weakness that, taken as three separate, individual films, none is entirely satisfying on its own. Each is an act in an overall narrative and feels episodic, but watched as a complete whole, the entire trilogy spans nearly twelve hours. That Jackson took to reinserting an additional forty minutes of material excised from the 139-minute theatrical cut of *Fellowship* for this DVD only makes the time commitment more daunting. That *Fellowship* is singled out here is not to say it is superior to either *The Two*

Towers or *Return of the King* (considered by many to be the best of the three); rather, it is simply the best place to start. It is the beginning of an incredible adventure. So stop reading, and start watching.

The Goodies On November 12, 2002, New Line Home Entertainment released *The Lord of the Rings: The Fellowship of the Ring—Special DVD Extended Edition*. It was the day that the format truly came of age, when the efforts of the filmmaker, the studio and the documentarian coalesced to produce a work perfect in its conception, execution and presentation. Such lavish praise may sound hyperbolic, yet the Extended Edition is a genuine triumph, a set staggering in its breadth of scope and depth of content. Jackson has made movie history with *The Lord of the Rings,* and, along with New Line and the production team of Jeff Kurtti and Michael Pellerin, sanctified the DVD format. With a combined twenty-two-odd hours of supplemental content, this DVD set could be considered overkill. Yet there is not a single minute wasted or without purpose.

To construct the Extended Edition, Jackson, New Line, and Kurtti and Pellerin spent months assembling both the new cut of the film and an amazing array of extras—a mammoth undertaking from all perspectives, and any fan not satiated by this set is simply being ungrateful.

The set includes four screen-specific audio commentaries with a staggering thirty-two participants. Each track has been carefully constructed and edited to focus on a specific aspect of the production, from the filmmaker commentary with Jackson, Fran Walsh and Phillippa Boyens to the extended discussions with the design team, the cast and the production crew. Many group commentaries quickly break down into rambling monologues, chaotic free-for-alls or inane giggle-fests, but not here. There is an almost ruthless dedication to ensuring that each track remains focused and free from padding. With a total run time of nearly sixteen hours, these commentaries alone rival the special features of the best special editions on the market.

However, as engaging as an audio commentary can be, it still can't replicate the experience of a great documentary. So New Line and the

Kurtti/Pellerin team created one that runs six hours, here called "The Appendices." But even more incredible than its run time is its almost complete lack of redundancy with the commentaries. Jackson allowed the documentary team almost unprecedented access throughout all stages of the production. The result is a thoroughly effective amalgam of a video diary, the traditional talking head interview and interactive elements such as multi-angle studies and effects progressions. This overwhelming amount of information is wisely divided up into "chapters," each of which works just as well on its own. Over forty minutes are devoted to the fantastical world J. R. R. Tolkien created and its impact on modern myth. The preproduction process and the arduous task of imagining Middle-Earth takes up nearly an hour and a half. Another ninety minutes takes place on the set, with over half of the material culled from the hundreds of hours of video recorded during production. Another ninety minutes is devoted to post-production and the film's release. A ten-minute coda supplies the required emotional epilogue such a thoroughly exhausting journey requires. "The Appendices" is a staggering achievement, not just for the DVD format, but the documentary medium itself.

Another hour of interactive vignettes include special effects and editorial demonstrations, an "Interactive Atlas of Middle-Earth," and extensive previsualizations and animatics. And the set's still gallery encompasses over 2,000 stills—from publicity photos and storyboards to conceptual art and ad materials. Staggering. (Treasure seekers will also be heartened to discover a couple of easter eggs hidden in the set—see if you can find them.)

The Presentation It is unimaginable that a set containing supplements constructed with such dedication would deliver anything less than a reference-quality transfer and soundtrack, and sure enough, everything impresses: the seamless integration of the additional footage, the pristine print, the rapturous colors, the breathless sense of depth and detail, the complete lack of any digital processing trickery or compression artifacts, and the sense of sheer three-dimensionality that makes every frame suitable for framing. The Extended Edition is a work of art.

TO MIDDLE-EARTH AND BACK: A CONVERSATION WITH JEFF KURTTI AND MICHAEL PELLERIN

The team of Kurtti/Pellerin—Jeff and Michael, respectively—has produced many of the most highly acclaimed and biggest selling special editions of all time. Their early work on laserdisc with the Walt Disney Studios pioneered many of the hallmarks of supplemental content. After making the successful transition to DVD, they continued to break barriers and set records, crafting such landmark special editions as *The Fantasia Anthology, The Ultimate Toy Box* and *TRON*. Then in 2001 they made DVD history with New Line's four-disc *Lord of the Rings: The Fellowship of the Ring* collection, a set so extensive and comprehensive that it has been widely cited as the greatest DVD ever made. The team has, collectively, been the recipient of over twenty-five honors and awards. Kurtti is also the author of twelve books, including *Since the World Began: Walt Disney World's First Twenty-Five Years* and *The Great Musical Treasury Book*.

They say all documentarians are pack rats, and judging by *The Lord of the Rings,* you've done a lot of packing. What was it that drew you both to the form and a career in the industry?

Michael Pellerin: When I was a kid, I would collect everything. I'd tape the show, I'd cut out the articles—I still keep binders on movies I like. For a kid out there like I was, you're either going to become a director or a documentary maker or a writer. And pay attention to that because it means something. It's not just your parents giving you a hard time for that box of junk in your room. It is actually a sign that you have a calling.

Jeff Kurtti: Within a few hours my life was changed by a movie. I saw *Mary Poppins* when I was five years old and it changed the course of what I was interested in during my life.

I'd like my next career to be a teacher. Some people say to me, "Well, what do you think you're doing now?" And I never thought about it that way. What's teaching but getting people involved with things they don't know about and getting them excited about it? That is what we do, and one of the great things about DVD. You really are enhancing people's understanding, and not just of how a movie was made. *The Lord of the Rings* touches on many things—literary, cinematic, geographic, historical, personal.

DVD has certainly struck a chord in a way laserdisc did not, but what is the appeal of supplemental content? Why are we so fascinated by the filmmaking process?

MP: People have always been interested in seeing how movies are made for the simple reason that people have always been fascinated by watching other people do things. Movies are basically a whole bunch of people who throw a whole bunch of years in their lives all together into one thing. And that a whole bunch of other people are going to go and sit down and watch together.

JK: On an anthropological level, there's nothing that fascinates a human being more than another human being. That's very basic. Then you factor in human beings who create something that you've watched as a separate form of entertainment, and that makes it doubly, triply fascinating. And there are certain peo-ple—a large proportion—who love to be fooled and then to be shown how they've been fooled. "Oh, *that's* how that works!" That's part of magic. People always love to know what's behind that curtain that made that show so great.

Your work always has a very strong element of storytelling to it, but you have also embraced DVD's more interactive elements. What influences your approach to a particular title?

MP: As a documentarian, you have to immerse yourself in the culture of whatever it is you are communicating to other people. You have to go there. You have to live it. Therefore, it will inform what needs to be told. You will follow the pattern set by the movie. If the movie is very original and unique and interesting and you bring those stories to life, you're going to have material that is going to be completely unique to that movie. If, however, the movie was just *Police Academy 9,* you might have a harder time making things seem original.

JK: For instance, when we did *Inspector Gadget 2* it wasn't a film that bore scrutiny in terms of a two-hour, in-depth documentary. It was a direct-to-video sequel: What does it require? Well, it's about gadgets. What was interesting? The gadgetry of filmmaking. What did that lend itself to? To a particular editorial style that was zippy, funny, fun, but still not stupid. It was still informative. The filmmakers did such great documentation while they were shooting in Australia that you could literally break down some of the gadget effects and make little videos out of them.

Tell me about the beginnings of the *Lord of the Rings* project. It was a huge leap for the format, both in form and content.

MP: People are used to film. They're used to the temporal journey you go on when you switch a program on. It starts and then at some point it ends. Interestingly enough, over time, I've seen this voyage become less interactive and more of just a story. When we first put together the material for *Fellowship*, we realized we had over ten or eleven hours of documentary. Just documentary.

I said, "Great—we can have half that." Yet no matter how good this programming is, I don't want anybody to have to sit down for six hours, so all of a sudden it became, "Let's make this compartmentalized like a week-long series and make it so the viewer can do that or if they go insane." Peter [Jackson] really wanted that.

How responsive was the cast to your requests for such extensive participation?

MP: Elijah Wood was shooting other films, and his agent kept saying he was busy, and when I got in touch with him, he was on a plane that night. And he was here for three days. And he got Sean Astin and Andy Serkis by saying, "Hey guys, we have to do this together," that this film is about relationships. Viggo Mortensen— he showed up with presents and artwork and personal photos. Every time I'm with Viggo, we'll talk for days before and after and leave long messages on the phone about ideas. And this is a guy who doesn't like to do interviews. He's more of a loner. He's raising his son and fishing and painting and taking photos and writing poetry—that's where his heart lies. But there was a photo book that Peter gave out as a scrapbook to those people on the set like a yearbook, and Viggo said that this was the equivalent of that book. It's from the heart.

Lord of the Rings, **the DVD, is filled with all of the DVD bells and whistles fans expect but is also almost classical in its storytelling approach. And the one through-line across DVD and laserdisc has been the commentary and documentary, which are both the most similar to traditional narratives. Why do you think these two forms in particular have endured?**

JK: The reason they keep coming back is because the documentary is probably the broadest based and the strongest supplemental content. It appeals to the most people.

To a large degree, people still really don't give a crap about set-top games. If you want a game, go buy a game. The question is: are you going to have cake or are you going to have frosting? You have, sadly, a lot of people in the DVD production world who are much more fascinated by frosting than a good, well-made cake. It's a lack of confidence in what a documentary is: good, solid, elemental storytelling. It's not about how flashy the package is or how good the presentation is or whether you have enough swish-pans to keep people interested.

Even with such a generous amount of time and perhaps one of the largest budgets, if not the largest budget, ever for a DVD, do you feel like you were able to tell the whole story of *Lord of the Rings*?

MP: There is a whole DVD for *Lord of the Rings* that could never be seen. First of all, most movies—especially movies with big budgets—have many political issues. And that's the case with *Rings,* of course. Some of the things that happened on and off set were somewhat incriminating.

JK: You also have stuff that's better suited to people's autobiographies!

Has the mainstream success of the DVD format forced you to pull more punches beyond your own personal barometer of what is appropriate?

JK: When we were doing *Beauty and the Beast,* there's a hard story at the core of its making, which is that Howard Ashman died. This had an enormous effect on everyone in the film. It's there in the middle of the documentary. One of the key creators and collaborators is suddenly gone before he can enjoy the success of his film, and it's told with enormous forthrightness and great emotion. It's not cut out. It's not sacrificed because it's a mass-market sensibility. They say [in the documentary that] Howard Ashman died of AIDS.

Lord of the Rings has without a doubt raised the bar for what is expected. Is that necessarily a good thing?

JK: It depends on the movie. Nobody expects a four-disc set of *The Ghost and Mr. Chicken*. I'd make it, but the world doesn't need it. There are certain films that dictate the need to have this kind of attentive, reverent, authoritative, encompassing attention paid to it because that's what audiences have demanded. Has it raised the bar? I sure hope so. It would only mean great things for DVD consumers.

MP: What I hope for DVD is that this raising of the bar means that producers can make DVDs as good as they can be.

Is there a danger that consumers have begun to expect too much, because they are being overfed?

JK: It's not quantity. "I'm pissed because they're not doing four discs each on the *Indiana Jones* movies." No. They should do as well with *Indiana Jones* as they did with our four-disc set.

MP: I remember people getting upset when I said we had to cut half of our twelve hours of material. But I wanted it to be crystalline. I'd rather have one good hour than fourteen hours of boredom. If it's going to be fourteen hours, you make sure it comes out of a hundred hours and that you're giving people the crème de la crème. It lets people focus on the things we want them to focus on instead of just droning out.

JK: I just hope the quality goes up. Make good shows. *Lord of the Rings* was done with the filmmakers, the studio, the DVD producers, as a team working together. I had an office right below Barrie Osbourne's office and a production team there. They absorbed us in. They made the DVD as important as anything else going on.

MP: That's where I hope the DVD world goes. I want great films to give birth to great DVDs. ◯

Such beauty is not solely reserved for the transfer. *The Fellowship of the Ring* is one of the great DVD soundtracks, thrilling in its sound design and offering a sonic experience that elevates the medium. Jackson and his team of sound designers set out to fully immerse the viewer in the world of Tolkien and succeeded. Included are DTS ES 6.1 and Dolby Digital Surround EX mixes. While the DTS track gets the nod with a more transparent, engaging soundfield, your enjoyment of *Fellowship* is only limited by the quality of your home theater. Low bass rumbles, Howard Shore's majestic score sings, the lively effects emanate from all channels, and the sense of reality and fullness in even the most subtle of sounds is stunning. *The Fellowship of the Ring* is a landmark.

Additional Versions New Line Home Entertainment has released each installment in the Rings trilogy in three versions: anamorphic widescreen and full-screen two-disc sets of each episode's theatrical cut, plus a four-disc set of the extended versions available only in anamorphic widescreen. The two-disc sets all feature unique supplements that don't overlap with any of the material on the four-disc sets. However, all the two-disc set extras are of the promotional or publicity variety, including TV specials, music videos, short films and trailers, and TV spots. The extended versions are well worth the greater financial investment.

The Mack

DISTRIBUTOR: New Line Home Entertainment
DVD RELEASE: December 3, 2002
THEATRICAL RELEASE: May 1973
RUNNING TIME: 110 Minutes
MPAA RATING: R

Mainstream cinema has a long, tragic history of ignoring, silencing or misrepresenting the minority voice. To watch any Hollywood movie made before 1970 is to bear witness to a world inhabited by only bourgeois, heterosexual white people; those of "color" almost exclusively occupy positions of subservience—housekeepers, traveling minstrels or slaves. And those films that did attempt to tackle racial injustice, such as *To Kill a Mockingbird* (1962) or *Guess Who's Coming to Dinner?* (1969) still told their stories through the eyes of white protagonists or were so heavy-handed as to nearly crumble under the weight of their message-movie clichés. It was not until the early 1970s that the modern American cinema at last began to mirror the civil unrest that had been simmering for years, freeing itself from the shackles of a studio system that deemed stories about minorities unworthy or uncommercial. And leading the revolution was the blaxploitation genre.

The Mack's crude technique has caused it to be somewhat over-looked in evaluations of the blaxploitation cycle; it is not the most immediately identifiable of the genre but it was the first. The script by Robert J. Poole infused the most timeworn and hoary B-movie clichés with the high melodrama of white gangster classics, told with a gritty aesthetic ignited by graphic violence and incendiary politics. After five years of incarceration, Goldie (Max Julien), aka "The Mack," gets out of prison and decides to become Pimp of the Year. But like the Corleones of *The Godfather* series, *The Mack* is told en-tirely from the vantage point of its protagonist, who is as much an ideologue as a criminal. "Anyone can control a woman's body," he says. "The key is to controlling her mind." Goldie will ultimately face a crisis of conscience—to stay in or get out of the life—and what is at stake is not just his soul, but also the very future of his race. The potent, allegorical storyline is enlivened by tight direction from Michael Campus, Julien's seminal gangsta portrayal, the freestyle comic riffing of a young Richard Pryor as Slim and a classic score by Willie Hutch.

If the violence in *The Mack* now seems both tame and irrespons-ible, the film's legacy has rendered any debate about it moot. The film and the blaxploitation phenomenon it inspired were pioneering because they, for the first time, presented a minority character who was no longer reactionary but proactive. When Goldie, attired in full pimp gear, grabs his gun and opens fire, it is hard not to cheer him on, not in support of wanton destruction and lawlessness, but as a clarion call for the end of thousands of years of discrimination, oppression and injustice.

Despite being less well known than some of the his fellow, more iconoclastic blaxploitation counterparts, Julien paved the way for the major stars of the movement, including Richard Roundtree (*Shaft*) and Pam Grier (*Foxy Brown, Coffy*). But *The Mack* remains even more relevant because Julien created an archetype so intoxicating he crossed all racial and social boundaries. White boys in the suburbs weren't afraid of the "urban black gangsta with a gun," they wanted to *be* him. Julien's speech, dress, demeanor and attitude continues to influence every major hip-hop artist on MTV, regardless of race and class, from Eminem to Snoop Dogg to the Beastie Boys to Tupac. But Goldie could eat all of them for breakfast; he is the ground zero for the cross-pollination of suburban white America and urban culture. And still one helluva cool pimp.

The Goodies While a good number of blaxploitation classics have been released on DVD, including the *Shaft* series, *Foxy Brown, Dolemite* and *Blacula,* all are put to shame by the treatment New Line Home Entertainment has given *The Mack*. Produced by the team at Automat Pictures, this collection of extras regards the film as the pioneering achievement it is—a landmark in American cinema whose influence continues to be criminally underrated.

The thirty-eight-minute documentary "Mackin' It Up" is truly stunning—typical of Automat's work, it is less a formal study of the vagaries of production than a comprehensive and insightful examination of the film's historical relevance and place in the pop culture pantheon. A deft mix of new interviews with Julien, Campus and Hutch, film historians Todd Boyd and Jesse Chies, and filmmakers Albert and Allen Hughes makes an inarguable case for a reevaluation of *The Mack*. Julien is almost gleefully confrontational when he comments on the continued hypocrisy in critical evaluations of the blaxploitation genre, asking, "Would anyone claim that *The Godfather* shouldn't have been made because it took the mob as its subject matter?"

A stellar audio commentary finds Campus joined by producer Harvey Bernhard and the cast, including Julien, Dick Anthony Williams, Annazette Chase, Don Gordon and George Murdock. It is the perfect complement to the documentary with no redundancy, going far more in-depth into the quick-and-dirty low-budget shoot. No punches are pulled, including the reduction of Pryor's screen time given his insatiable cocaine addiction at the time, and Campus rightfully lauds his own visual style, a mix of stylized violence and beat-based editing that has been so co-opted by MTV he should be on the network's board of directors.

Due to lost or damaged archival materials, no other extras are included, not even trailers or any other promotional materials or stills. But the documentary and commentary are more than enough to compensate.

The Presentation Shot on 16mm, *The Mack* is a gritty, unpolished little gem, which doesn't make for a great transfer but it is an effective one. It is a testament to New Line that the print is in such great shape—only a few minor blemishes and defects and only minimal grain. Colors are predictably dated but still robust for a film of this type and vintage and generally clean and smooth. The lack of any edge enhancement also makes for a very filmlike if appropriately rough-and-tough transfer.

The Mack may sound like a 1970s porno movie, but that only adds to the fun of the Dolby Digital and DTS 5.1 surround tracks included here. It may seem futile or even inappropriate to attempt a modern remix of such material, but the groovy score by Hutch requires strong bass, which the DTS track especially delivers forcefully. Surround use is slim, which does not offer much in the way of envelopment, but compared to all past video versions, the clarity of the dialogue and overall robust frequency response is a startling surprise. The film's original mono mix is also included for those who would rather simulate the sound of an old 8-track.

Magnolia

DISTRIBUTOR: New Line Home Entertainment

DVD RELEASE: August 29, 2000

THEATRICAL RELEASE: December 1999

RUNNING TIME: 188 Minutes

MPAA RATING: R

What happens when people finally get everything they dream about, but they're still dreaming? Such is the dilemma faced by the characters in *Magnolia,* Paul Thomas Anderson's sprawling, epic mosaic of crossed paths, coincidence and divine intervention. Anderson previously directed *Boogie Nights,* his second film (after 1992's little-seen *Hard Eight*), and another sprawling mosaic that chronicled the rise and fall of the 1970s porn industry. He was heralded as the arrival of a blazing new talent, and Anderson, flush with success and granted the rare final cut for *Magnolia,* set out to make the most of the opportunity. *Magnolia* may be messy, unfocused and overlong at 188 minutes, but it proved that Anderson was one of the most audacious and courageous American filmmakers of his generation.

> "Now that I've met you, would you object to never seeing me again?"
>
> —Claudia Wilson Gator

Anderson's sense of narrative disconnect can be challenging, even frustrating. Channeling the spirit of Robert Altman (*Short Cuts, Nashville*), he constructs *Magnolia* as a series of interlocking stories that take place over one long day in Los Angeles. His characters are sad, desperate, defiant, lonely, ambitious and yearning for connection. They will, through chance, accident and fate, cross paths, zigzag through time and space and double back on themselves. Anderson is not content with a single theme: the fear of death, abandonment, resentment, betrayal and unfulfilled desire will cross all barriers of class, privilege and geography. (Only race seems to be of little interest to Anderson; all of his main characters are Caucasian.)

An ensemble cast could get lost in a film this expansive, but Anderson is also an actor's director and wrings strong performances from Julianne Moore (whose lengthy tirades are hilarious), the late Jason Robards (in his final film appearance), Philip Seymour Hoffman, Melora Walters and, most surprisingly, Tom Cruise, who Anderson reinvents as T. J. Mackey, a cynical, deceptive "self-help guru" who specializes in helping lonesome losers seduce women. But the greatest character in *Magnolia* is never seen on the screen. It is the voice of Aimee Mann, who performed the film's haunting songs and served as Anderson's inspiration while writing the script. From the Oscar-nominated "Save Me" to her gorgeous interpretation of the Three Dog Night classic "One," her songs are *Magnolia*'s true heart and voice.

Anderson has been labeled a hack, a wannabe, and a thief who pillages from the best of 1970s cinema. But *Magnolia* is brimming with life, passion and unique, quirky characters. Unlike most of his peers, who wallow in postmodern irony and self-referential humor to avoid intimacy and emotional honesty, Anderson revels in erasing the artifice. Anderson's aggressive, constantly roving camerawork is so reminiscent of Martin Scorsese's work it gives some credence to those who say he lacks originality. His penchant for overlong soliloquies can be pretentious, and sometimes his characters are hard to identify with, but his mastery over film reassures us that we are nonetheless in the hands of a capable, supremely confident storyteller. He stretches almost every scene to the breaking point, and sometimes he confounds our expectations, but we never for a minute doubt that he knows where he is taking us. Anderson is an unapologetically romantic filmmaker, as in love with love and his characters as he is with the history, lexicon and language of film. By the time Anderson pulls the ultimate existential joke on us—a narrative twist at the film's climax that we were prepared for if unaware of all along—we willingly suspend disbelief and just let Anderson's divine rain wash over us. *Magnolia* is an audacious, thrilling, one-of-a-kind motion picture.

The Goodies Anderson allowed documentarian Mark Rance and his team complete access throughout all stages of the making of *Mag-*

nolia. The result is "That Moment," perhaps the greatest behind-the-scenes documentary ever produced for a DVD. It is *that* good. Film-making, especially Anderson's brand of orchestrated improvisation, is a nebulous process that has never been captured quite so elegantly as it has here. We track the often hyper Anderson throughout the entire production, from the early development and pitch to preproduction, filming, postproduction and release. It is a you-are-there video diary whose immediacy and honesty raises it to the level of art. An absolute must, not just for Anderson fans, but any serious student of the cinema.

This two-disc set's remaining extras are not extensive, but "That Moment" is enough. Additional material includes Anderson's terrific music video for Mann's "Save Me," a hilarious, unexpurgated Frank T. J. Mackey "Instructional Video" and "Seduce & Destroy" in-fomercial, and a few theatrical trailers and TV spots. And don't forget to check out the color bars in the "Set Up" section on the first disc, as you'll find an amusing set of bloopers.

The Presentation *Magnolia* looks like an exotic flower in full bloom. Presented in its theatrical aspect ratio of 2.40:1 and anamor-phically encoded, Robert Elswit's evocative photography is so alive and vibrant it is mesmerizing, like a painting come to life. The film is chiaroscuro in style—much of it is either very bright or very dark, which can prove taxing for even the best DVD transfer. But the challenge is handled beautifully here, with deep blacks and a smooth, very detailed and filmlike look. The Dolby Digital 5.1 surround track is almost as ambitious; Anderson loves to play with sound, especially soft ambiance and the warm textures of Mann's compositions. Surround use is low key as to not intrude on the intended sense of intimate drama and pathos. A little front-heavy, but an otherwise sharp and smart soundtrack.

Additional Recommendations More P. T. Anderson films available on DVD include special editions of all three of his other films: *Hard Eight* (aka *Sydney*), and two-disc sets of *Boogie Nights* and *Punch-Drunk Love,* starring Adam Sandler.

M*A*S*H

DISTRIBUTOR: Fox Home Entertainment
DVD RELEASE: January 8, 2002
THEATRICAL RELEASE: January 1970
RUNNING TIME: 116 Minutes
MPAA RATING: R

In 1970, the protest film took over the American box office. While the Vietnam War was still raging, television beamed nightly broadcasts of the bloody consequences of our occupation in South Korea. The youth of America, growing increasingly angry at the rising death toll, fueled a growing antiauthoritarian movement that threatened to explode. Hollywood, always quick to capitalize—and exploit—the zeitgeist, unleashed a wave of war-themed films. Mike Nichols's seriocomic *Catch-22* was pegged as the sure-fire blockbuster, while the more conservative and traditional *Patton* took home the Oscars. But Robert Altman's unorthodox *M*A*S*H* became the runaway hit of the year, eschewing a traditional narrative in favor of nonstop insanity, slapstick and ribald sexual antics. It was the irreverent underdog that hit the box office bull's-eye, and the most influential comedy of the 1970s.

Smart and biting, *M*A*S*H* may not be Altman's finest film but it is certainly his funniest. It is primal scream comedy, a bold act of defiant protest that punches its fist in the air while it kicks you in the groin. It is also the most subversive studio picture ever made. At the insistence of Twentieth Century Fox, Altman was not allowed to make any direct reference to the Vietnam War. But Vietnam infuses every single frame of *M*A*S*H*. Frustration, rage, pain and anger empower every moment; it is this fury, so expertly channeled, that separates *M*A*S*H* from the other, more overt antiwar films of the period, most notably *Catch-22*. *M*A*S*H* bit the hand that fed it, and bit hard.

> "This isn't a hospital! It's an insane asylum!"
>
> —Margaret "Hot Lips" Houlihan

The brilliance of *M*A*S*H* is that it is never didactic, obvious or heavy-handed. To brand it a polemic is to deny just how much fun it really is. This is smart-mouthed filmmaking at its best, with one of the best comedy ensembles of all time. Look at the effortless camaraderie between Donald Sutherland and Elliott Gould, or Robert Duvall's hilarious holier-than-thou hypocrisy. And there is a method to their madness. Some critics called *M*A*S*H* lowbrow, or juvenile, but that is precisely Altman's point. The *only* way to survive an insane world is to act even more insane. Plotting intricate schemes to see just what "Hot Lips" Houlihan looks like naked is the *only* way for these characters to reaffirm their humanity. These doctors and nurses, hands bloodied and hearts bruised, can remain conscious of the world around them only if they gleefully, shamelessly and without guilt, revel in the simplest pleasures in life.

M*A*S*H was a social event of early 1970s cinema. Like the antiestablishment movies before it—*Dr. Strangelove, The Graduate, Rebel Without a Cause*—mere attendance was a rebellious act, the ticket stub an emblem of what side of the fence you stood on. It ushered in a new era of bratty, middle-finger-in-the-air comedy that gave anarchy a good name and offered a healthy alternative to civil disobedience. It has been cited as a major influence on comedy both big and small, from television's *Saturday Night Live* to *National Lampoon's Animal House* to *There's Something About Mary*. It is both mercilessly funny and the most socially conscious big-studio comedy of all time. And, sadly, as relevant today as it was over thirty years ago.

The Goodies Part of Fox Home Entertainment's Five Star Collection, *M*A*S*H* is filled with an exemplary set of extras. Four documentaries are included. Originally produced for American Movie Classics, the "Backstory *M*A*S*H*" TV special is the glossiest, and features interviews with Altman and most of the cast and crew. But more thorough is the forty-minute "Enlisted: The Story of *M*A*S*H*," which goes into greater detail on the film's social importance and lasting cinematic impact. "*M*A*S*H*: Comedy Under Fire" runs forty-four minutes and takes a more sociological approach. Veterans of the Korean Mobile Army Surgical Hospital analyze the historical accuracy of the film's dialogue and situations, and the interviews with the survivors are surprisingly poignant. Yet another TV special, the Fox Movie Channel's thirty-minute "*M*A*S*H* Reunion" rounds up most of the main principals, including Sutherland, Gould and Sally Kellerman, for an affectionate and witty tribute to Altman, who received Fox's first "Legacy Award."

Altman also contributes a new screen-specific audio commentary, but it is a great tribute to the many documentaries that there is little left to say. Still, Altman continues to be one of America's great cinematic mavericks, and his edge has not been dulled by age. He is irascible, unsparing, ornery and often hilarious.

Rounding out this fine set is a still gallery, the film's theatrical trailer, and a few marginal easter eggs, including a Spanish trailer and the ability to change the background audio of the menus.

The Presentation Altman and director of photography Harold Stine strived for a neodocumentary, gritty feel for *M*A*S*H,* which is reproduced here nicely. The print is grainy on purpose, and Altman utilized a variety of filters and other photographic tricks to desaturate colors, darken scenes and otherwise distort our sense of perception. Aside from a few contrast problems and occasionally excessive fluctuations of the print, this is a clean, filmlike transfer that accurately reproduces the intended effect. Likewise the soundtrack, which has been upgraded from mono to stereo. The film is largely dialogue driven, but the majority of the hiss and overly abrasive high end has been minimized. It sounds dated but appropriate to the material.

Additional Recommendations For more Altman on DVD, some of his finest include special editions of *McCabe & Mrs. Miller, The Long Goodbye, Dr. T & the Women, Gosford Park, The Player* and his Oscar-winning masterpiece *Nashville.* Long a proponent of DVD, Altman has recorded new audio commentaries for each, and many, including *The Player* and *Gosford Park,* feature additional making-of material and behind-the-scenes footage.

The Matrix

DISTRIBUTOR: Warner Home Video

DVD RELEASE: November 25, 1999

THEATRICAL RELEASE: May 1999

RUNNING TIME: 136 Minutes

MPAA RATING: R

She jumped in the air and the camera swirled around her. At that moment, everything from big-budget moviemaking to clothing design changed. While many late-1990s science fiction films such as *Dark City* and *Strange Days* embraced the same grim, urban aesthetic, *The Matrix* absorbed it, internalized it, then expanded on it. The film also stretched the boundaries of computer-generated imagery—literally. Characters run along walls before delivering a kick. Bullets visibly ripple through the air, moving slow enough for their intended targets to move out of the way. Neo (Keanu Reeves) and Trinity (Carrie-Anne Moss), wearing black trench coats and black sunglasses, shoot their way through an office lobby leaving heroic amounts of shattered concrete and dead bodies. When it was over, audiences had a new benchmark for what constituted cool.

But the writing and directing team of Larry and Andy Wachowski were not content to just drape everyone in black and call it style. Nor were they content to rely on their extraordinary visual sense. *The Matrix* depends on obvious religious parallels (Neo has been interpreted to be a spiritual stand-in for everyone from Christ to Buddha) to give it a familiar, universal feel and a philosophical bent. But, like the outlet embedded in the back of Neo's head, the real power of *The Matrix* is its ability to plug into the psyche of its target audience: young males. The idea that our world is an elaborate simulation meant to divert us from the knowledge that our bodies are being enslaved and harvested for their energy by sentient computers is, at once, heady, ridiculous and supremely clever. And it played right into the hearts and minds of a generation of adolescent males who question authority, listen to techno music and play video games. Much as *Crouching Tiger, Hidden Dragon* introduced mainstream

American audiences to the Chinese martial arts film, *The Matrix* introduced them to the kinetic visuals of Japanimation, John Woo–inspired violence and the Cyberpunk ethos pioneered in the novels of William Gibson.

Arguably, the film's biggest achievement was to make Keanu Reeves watchable. He plays it mostly stoic here, while his oddly angular, dramatic poses work for the material. Carrie-Anne Moss is feisty, sinewy and smart, but not so beautiful as to seem out of reach to legions of cybergeeks who clutched the film to their hearts. And, as the man holding the Looking Glass, Laurence Fishburne, with his low, matter-of-fact line readings, is the perfect mentor. While the Wachowski brothers get most of the credit for the film's success, composer Don Davis's hardworking score, Bill Pope's noir-inflected cinematography and Yuen Wo Ping's balletic, gravity-defying fight choreography are essential.

> **"Whoa."**
>
> —Neo, upon discovering his new powers.

Ultimately, *The Matrix* embodies a delicious paradox: it uses state-of-the-art technology to tell the story of mankind's near destruction brought about by our reliance on state-of-the-art technology. In the dark ages of the late 1990s, with society reaching a point of no return in its dependence upon the Internet, cell phones and global positioning systems, *The Matrix* asked moviegoers to think about the implications. And never underestimate the power of black leather.

The Goodies *The Matrix* contains special-effects sequences of a creativity and quality that audiences had never before experienced. Not content to let the magicians keep their secrets, fans have been aching for the illusion-shattering information that DVD goodies were created to provide. To satisfy these fan longings, *The Matrix* DVD contains two icon-based supplements, meaning symbols pop up at specific intervals providing access to additional features. Enjoyment of these extras depends upon whether you like special features laid out simply in menu form, or you don't mind hunting for them.

Laced throughout the menus' structure are "Red Pills," which, when found and activated, take you to a featurette that further explores the all-encompassing world the Wachowski brothers created. For instance, "What Is Bullet Time?" is a technical yet fascinating five-minute look at how the "bullet time" effect was accomplished. That so much thought, effort and money could go into a seven-second effect will make you feel guilty for not watching this at least once. Another "Red Pill" featurette, "What Is the Concept?", is an eleven-minute comparison of storyboards to final scenes. The second icon-based supplement is "White Rabbit." If activated, an icon in the shape of a rabbit will flash on screen at certain points during the film. There are nine of these "White Rabbits" sprinkled throughout the movie. Select one and you're taken to a short featurette on the making of that particular scene.

The primary documentary is "Making the Matrix," which contains copious amounts of behind-the-scenes footage and interviews with all the cast members as well as the reclusive Wachowski brothers. There are also two audio commentaries, the first from special-effects supervisor John Gaeta, editor Zach Staenberg and actress Carrie-Anne Moss, the other with composer Don Davis. His comments and his score are contained on an isolated track, and Davis speaks only when there is no music.

Pop the disc in your PC and even more wonders can be yours: read the screenplay, explore dozens of storyboards or delve into essays inspired by the film.

In November 2001, two years after *The Matrix*'s blockbuster DVD release (it remains one of the bestselling discs of all time), Warner Home Video released *The Matrix Revisited,* a separate single-disc DVD with even more extras. The heart of this set is an excellent 123-minute documentary, cleverly titled "The Matrix Revisited." Culled from over one hundred hours of on-set and behind-the-scenes footage, it is a virtual video diary, interspersed with new interviews taken during the simultaneous making of the film's two sequels, *The Matrix Reloaded* and *The Matrix Revolutions*.

The set also includes a wealth of additional short featurettes, including "True Followers," which introduces us to *Matrix* fanatics who live, breathe and dream Neo; breakdowns of many of the film's key action scenes; additional trailers and easter eggs; and the requisite previews (now dated) of the sequels.

While both *The Matrix* and *The Matrix Revisited* are available separately, Warner subsequently released both as a two-pack, which is essentially the equivalent of one full-fledged, two-disc special edition. It is the best choice for the true *Matrix* fan.

The Presentation Within months of its release, the visual style of *The Matrix* became de rigueur shorthand for macho posturing and trench coat cool. As such, it deserved Warner Home Video's best effort. The resulting 2.35:1 anamorphic widescreen transfer is generally excellent, especially considering the film contains many dimly lit interiors and dark surfaces. Although film grain is evident, resulting in some compression artifacting, the dark shades of the color palette are rendered extremely well. The daylight scenes are bright, clear and free of any overtly digital appearance. The scenes where Neo stands in front of a completely white background are rendered perfectly; however, there is an occasional print flaw, which is disconcerting for such a recent release.

The Dolby Digital 5.1 surround audio is excellent and continues to play in demo showrooms all over the world. The film is a dense and dynamic mix of dialogue, music and effects, all of which are reproduced with great clarity. Surrounds can be quite active, especially the "bullet time" sequences. The low end is given quite a workout, resulting in an excellent, floor-rattling bass. Those with the appropriate audio/visual gear should send the kids to the baby-sitter's, turn down the lights, crank up the volume and follow Neo down the Rabbit Hole.

Memento

DISTRIBUTOR: Columbia TriStar Home Entertainment

DVD RELEASE: May 21, 2002

THEATRICAL RELEASE: May 2001

RUNNING TIME: 113 Minutes

MPAA RATING: R

Leonard Shelby has a "condition." He'll be the first one to tell you. He'll be the second one to tell you. He'll even be the third one to tell you. But whether this condition makes sufferers behave the way Leonard does in director Christopher Nolan's *Memento* is a question for the experts. Factual inconsistencies aside, his condition does make for one trippy, challenging and mesmerizing movie.

Told in a convoluted, flashback-filled narrative, Leonard witnesses the death of his wife and subsequently develops short-term memory loss. He can remember everything about his life before his wife's murder, but every memory afterward disappears within moments. Since he can no longer file away the events of his life in his head, he writes notes and sticks them in his pockets.

> LEONARD: "I am Leonard Shelby. I am from San Francisco."
>
> TEDDY: "That's who you were. That's not what you've become."

He takes Polaroids and adds captions. He even turns himself into an illustrated man, tattooing upon his every limb "the facts," immutable truths about the man who raped and murdered his wife. The man he has sworn to find and kill.

But Nolan isn't content to merely tell the story of a man with no short-term memory trying to avenge his wife's murder. In a daring and completely rewarding gamble, the story is told backward. The ending comes first, followed by the scene that, in real time, came before it. It's a clever conceit that's not just high-concept trickery. Nolan has created a masterful approximation of life the way Leonard experiences it. We don't just live in Leonard's world. We live in Leonard's head. When he looks at a Polaroid with the caption "Don't believe his lies," neither he nor we know why he wrote it. And when we find out, it's dramatically satisfying and helps him (and us) solve the mystery.

Leonard's condition is juxtaposed with the saga of Sammy Jankis (Stephen Tobolowsky), a case from Leonard's former life as an insurance investigator. Jankis suffered the same short-term memory affliction as Leonard, who refused to pay out on Jankis's insurance claim because Sammy's condition was considered psychological, not physical. The identity of Sammy Jankis is just another clever way Nolan (working from an original story written by his brother Jonathan) uses memory to deceive not only the audience but also the characters. Memory is untrustworthy and can be clouded by emotions, faded by distance, and manipulated by perception and prejudice.

Guy Pearce is dead-on as Leonard. He shows sinewy determination while still allowing the edges to fray as he tries to piece together who murdered his wife. The ever-reliable Joe Pantoliano keeps viewers off balance; he seems smarmy enough to hurt Leonard, yet friendly enough to be helpful. Nolan, who never sacrifices the story for the storytelling, saves his best trick for last. In a film that begins with the end, how interesting can the actual end of the movie be? *Memento*'s final revelations justify the journey. Leonard is trapped in an endless loop, as the audience realizes something he never will: nothing can lie like the facts.

The Goodies This Limited Edition of *Memento* generated a good amount of fan controversy due to its complicated menu structure and generally ungainly navigational system. The supplement disc is laid out like a psych exam, with the viewer having to answer multiple-choice questions that (occasionally) result in being taken to a particular supplement. (There is also a full list of the extras accessible from the Main Menu by choosing the clock and answering "E" to all the multiple-choice questions.) And in fact, it is too clever by half. Any DVD that thwarts a viewer's attempt to access items they paid for is not to be praised. It's a shame Nolan (whose brother helped design the disc) made it all so hard to figure out, because there are plenty of interesting supplements for those hearty enough to hunt for them.

The first disc contains an audio commentary by Nolan. Gossip lovers stay away, because his remarks are a bit dry; he focuses exclusively on the development and creation of such an odd cinematic puzzle. His thoughts on story construction are fascinating and illustrate that while traditional three-act structure will always be dominant in commercial filmmaking, filmmakers can take chances and get away with it. Also available is the entire director's script (complete with notations in the margins). As the film's audio plays, script pages turn at the appropriate moments.

The primary supplement on disc two is "Anatomy of a Scene," a twenty-five-minute Sundance Channel documentary that quickly touches on all aspects of *Memento*'s production. The major behind-the-scenes players are interviewed, along with actor Joe Pantoliano. Elsewhere, there are plenty of production stills, storyboards and poster concepts. And be sure to read *Memento Mori,* the Jonathan Nolan short story from which the film was adapted.

Finally, there are a number of easter eggs, many which take quite a bit of patience (and smarts) to solve. But the payoff? A true DVD original: the ability to play the film backward, which is surprisingly entertaining. Talk about trippy.

The Presentation High marks go to this splendid 2.35:1 anamorphic widescreen. The picture is exceedingly crisp and bright with a very smooth and filmlike appearance. Although the movie takes place in some dingy locales, the colors are fully saturated and very stable, with no bleeding or smearing. Blacks are smooth and pixel-free with top-notch shadow detail. Overall detail is so impressive that new information about the plot can be gleaned by use of your DVD player's pause button to scan Leonard's mountainous paperwork.

DTS and Dolby Digital 5.1 options both offer an enveloping aural experience. The front speakers and the surrounds are given a creative workout, considering this is a dialogue-driven movie—and all of the dialogue is exceptionally clear. Ringing phones and various ambient noises deepen the soundscape effectively. David Julyan's multilayered score also benefits from this excellent mix.

Metropolis (Restored Authorized Edition)

DISTRIBUTOR: Kino International

DVD RELEASE: February 18, 2003

THEATRICAL RELEASE: March 1927

RUNNING TIME: 124 Minutes

MPAA RATING: PG

Fritz Lang's *Metropolis* is widely considered to be the most influential science-fiction film of all time, and also challenges D. W. Griffith's *Birth of a Nation* and the finest achievements of Buster Keaton and Charlie Chaplin as the best silent film ever made. It is a visionary epic that created a universe so unique it has been completely absorbed into the cultural consciousness. *Metropolis* has influenced the way we think of the future, our world and ourselves.

Lang's story echoes all of the great autocratic tales of our time, most notably George Orwell's *1984,* and was eerily prescient of twentieth-century totalitarianism. Metropolis is a city cut in two: above live the privileged, below the slaves. It is run by a capitalist dictator, Joh Fredersen (Alfred Abel). His son Freder (Bustav Froehlich) discovers the world below when he meets the

> FREDER FREDERSEN: "It was their hands that built this city of ours, Father. But where do the hands belong in your scheme?"
>
> JOHHAN FREDERSEN: "In their proper place—the depths."

beautiful Maria (Brigitte Helm) after she brings up a group of workers' children from the depths. Employing the services of the demented Rotwang (Rudolf Klein-Rogge), who knows all of Metropolis's secrets, Freder rallies a revolution to overthrow his father and the oppressive regime.

Due to extensive postproduction cutting, demanded by censors who objected to the more controversial elements of the story, *Metropolis* suffers from many gaps in logic. The narrative feels scattershot and poorly constructed. But it contains images of such beauty and power, even the censors could not dull Lang's vision; it is a great testament to *Metropolis* that seventy-five years later and in abridged form, it remains relevant. In his book *Fritz Lang: The Nature of the Beast,* author Patrick McGilligan describes a tyrannical director who would rival the villainous demagogue of his own film. Commanding over 25,000 extras, the conditions were punishing: freezing water, angry mob scenes that resulted in injury, outrageous stunts that risked death. Actors functioned as props to ensure Lang's need for perfection, his colleagues were treated with cruelty, and few were allowed into the inner circle of a man growing mad with obsession. Production eventually stretched to a year, and postproduction proceeded no more smoothly. And at the end of it all, Lang emerged with a masterpiece. *Metropolis* has informed many science-fiction masterpieces that followed: Robert Wise's *The Day the Earth Stood Still* (1951), *Alphaville* (1965), *Blade Runner* (1982), and *Gattaca* (1997). Its famous art deco production design was also given its greatest homage in *Batman* (1989), where Anton Furst's widely praised and heavily Lang-inspired art direction is often credited with elevating what would have otherwise been a standard comic book film into one of the most influential and successful movies of the 1980s.

The Goodies A lavish two-disc set, this 75th anniversary edition of *Metropolis* includes a new audio commentary by film historian Enno Patalas. It is the weakest aspect of this set: Patalas, while knowledgeable, offers little more than a simple narration of the events on the screen. But Patalas's documentary, "The *Metropolis* Case," is excellent. This forty-five-minute retrospective is comprehensive; it is surprising just how much material, including vintage interviews with Lang and his collaborators and extensive stills, have survived intact since 1927. The story of Lang's rise in Hollywood is fascinating, and the effects, while antiquated today, are sophisticated and inventive, and it is fascinating to dissect how they were conceptualized and created. We also learn of the eventual fate of *Metropolis* and the details of its extensive recutting.

A short nine-minute featurette, "The Restoration," examines the efforts of restoration supervisor Martin Koerber and includes split-screen, before-and-after comparisons. Additional notes on Lang and the film's production can be found in the included booklet. There is also a still gallery with many shots from lost scenes, as well as cast and crew biographies and a well-researched "Facts & Dates" timeline. ·

The Presentation Lang's intended version of *Metropolis,* which ran 153 minutes, was rarely seen. His original cut was heavily censored by distributors and exhibitors within days of its premiere, the reasons for which were never fully explained and have long since been lost in the mists of time. In 1984 a reconstructed version, taken from newly discovered European prints, was completed with the additions of color tinting and a modern pop score produced by Giorgio Moroder. Then in 2001, in honor of the film's seventy-fifth anniversary, Kino International announced a definitive restoration of the "Munich Version," which would eventually run 124 minutes, the closest yet to the epic length of Lang's original. This new *Metropolis* was restored from the original camera negative; each of the film's 1,257 shots were scanned in at high resolution and cleaned up with the latest digital technology.

Presented here in its original 1.37:1 theatrical aspect ratio, *Metropolis* looks better than one would ever think possible. The digital restoration is almost completely free of even minor blemishes and scratches—usually only modern films receive a presentation this good. Blacks are deep and contrast excellent, the proper grayscale restored. Lang's visionary world is now detailed and textured, with a sense of real depth and presence. Gottfried Huppertz's original score has also been remastered in Dolby Digital 5.1. Some age-related defects are still apparent, including a compressed sound with muted high end and flat low bass. But his score is nicely spread out across the soundstage; surround is present but not intrusive, and the track is free from any excessive digital gimmicks.

Additional Versions Both Alpha Video and Madacy Entertainment have released DVD editions of *Metropolis,* both featuring a 115-minute cut. The Kino version is far superior.

Mildred Pierce

DISTRIBUTOR: Warner Home Video

DVD RELEASE: March 21, 2000

THEATRICAL RELEASE: September 1948

RUNNING TIME: 111 Minutes

MPAA RATING: Not Rated

In *Mommie Dearest,* the most notorious of all Hollywood tell-all bios, Christina Crawford enacted the most famous character assassination in history. By documenting a life of torment at the hands of the woman she described as an overbearing, alcoholic hellion bent on self-destruction, Christina got in the last word she so desperately desired. Few paid much attention to the fact that Christina had no real proof to back up her claims of child abuse; in one fell swoop, Joan Crawford's reputation was destroyed, Christina's book shot to the top of the bestseller lists and the subsequent movie adaptation became an instant camp classic. The damage was instantaneous and irrevocable. Her alleged skill with wire hangers will be remembered long after Joan's Oscar wins are forgotten.

But who was the real Joan Crawford? Her movies are all we have left to savor, and in *Mildred Pierce,* she found the role of her career. After a string of flops had led the head of Metro Golden Mayer to label Crawford "box office poison," *Pierce* represented the comeback she so desperately needed. Hunger infuses every frame of her performance; Crawford does not so much channel Mildred as she inhabits her. "I'll do anything," Mildred/Crawford says at one point, and with those three simple words, the line between character and actress became irrevocably blurred. And with *Pierce,* Joan at last won her Oscar.

But more than just a showcase for Crawford, both actress and movie star, *Mildred Pierce* is one of the great film noirs: dramatic, suspenseful, funny, well acted and brilliantly executed. Based on the novel by James M. Cain, Ranald MacDougall's adaptation is an incisive character study and a cunning mystery. Director Michael Curtiz is able to wring top-flight performances out of not only Crawford but also a suitably oily Jack Carson as Pierce's fait accompli and Ann

Blyth as her on-screen daughter Vida, still one of the best bad girls in noir. Director of photography Ernest Haller's moody black-and-white compositions effectively set the stage for the gripping melodrama and mis-

> "Personally, I think alligators have the right idea. They eat their young."
>
> —Ida Corwin

placed passions, and the climax is a humdinger that brings the story full circle. And back to Crawford. "Mommie Dearest" will always be what her tombstone reads, but her true monument is *Mildred Pierce*.

The Goodies *Mildred Pierce*'s DVD may not, at first glance, appear to contain much in the way of extensive supplements, only a ninety-minute documentary, "Joan Crawford: The Ultimate Movie Star." But what a documentary it is! Originally produced for Turner Classic Movies, this perceptive look at the life of Crawford is still one of the best documentaries ever made about a Hollywood legend.

Crawford's meteoric rise was not an easy one. Born Lucille le Sueur to an impoverished Oklahoma family, Crawford first emerged as a day player in a series of walk-ons in forgettable films, then rode the Hollywood pendulum from "queen of the movies" to "box office poison" in less than a decade. The later stages of her career were mired by tragedy and heartbreak; in 1951's *Whatever Happened to Baby Jane?* she teamed with her arch-rival Bette Davis and was re-born as a campy, put-upon victim-monster, frequently with ax in hand and eyebrow arched. Relegated to a series of campy William Castle flicks, her career slide culminated in the disastrous *Trog,* her final screen appearance. Then *Mommie Dearest*.

"The Ultimate Movie Star" shines a light on the dark underbelly, not just of Crawford, but of Hollywood. Many who worked with Crawford contributed new interviews, among them Vincent Sherman, Anita Page, Douglas Fairbanks Jr., Virginia Grey, Andreckna Lee, Betsy Palmer, Cliff Robertson and Diane Baker, plus Crawford historians Karen Swenson and playwright Charles Busch and even Christina herself, still biting and bitter. As narrated by Anjelica Huston, it is a deft mix of sharply edited remembrances and rare and never-before-seen archival footage. The early passages are a joy to watch, a visual travelogue of a great actress riding a career trajectory that seemed predestined until the inevitable fall from studio grace. Then comes Crawford's victory in *Mildred Pierce*; only the final passages are difficult to watch, but Crawford had an indefatigable spirit. Her eagerness to appease her fans—even when swinging a hatchet or tempting a half-man/half-beast with a giant bone—only makes her more endearing and has assured her a place not only as a Hollywood icon, but also as a cult hero of audiences who weren't even alive when Crawford was actively making movies.

Rounding out the set is a fun gallery of theatrical trailers for other hits (and misses) during Crawford's tenure at Warner.

The Presentation Presented in a sparkling new transfer properly framed at the film's original 1.37:1 aspect ratio, Haller's excellent black-and-white cinematography is at last given its proper due. The source print has been nicely cleaned up and is often mesmerizing in its clarity, with none of the fading and instability that often mars a film of this vintage. Detail is excellent and the picture is sharp but not edgy or artificial-looking. While the film's original mono soundtrack is not as revelatory as the transfer, and no remix is offered, it is clear of defects and sounds warm and natural.

Monty Python and the Holy Grail

DISTRIBUTOR: Columbia TriStar Home Entertainment
DVD RELEASE: October 23, 2001
THEATRICAL RELEASE: May 1975
RUNNING TIME: 89 Minutes
MPAA RATING: Not Rated

The roots of the Monty Python comedy troupe can be traced back to 1963, when five students at Cambridge University—John Cleese, Eric Idle, Michael Palin, Terry Jones and the late Graham Chapman—joined the "The Footlights," a celebrated performing society. Terry Gilliam, an American cartoonist for the humor magazine *Help!* would subsequently meet the quartet during a stopover on the U.S. tour for

"The Footlights Revue." In 1967 Idle, Palin, Jones and Gilliam wrote and starred in the English TV series *Do Not Adjust Your Set,* while Cleese and Chapman teamed up for the popular satire *The Magic Christian.* They all came together the following year to create *Monty Python's Flying Circus,* a wildly successful British comedy series and a staple in American syndication. The troupe quickly built a small but devout cult following, and subsequently teamed up for five films. They remain the most successful and widely imitated British comedy team in history.

> "You don't frighten us, English pig dogs! Go and boil your bottoms, sons of a silly person! I blow my nose at you, so-called 'Arthur King,' you and all you silly English K-nig-hts!"
>
> —French soldier

Monty Python and the Holy Grail, the troupe's first film, may be their most inspired and inventive movie, as well as their silliest. There are those who simply cannot stand the Pythons' relentlessly cheeky, vulgar and self-conscious brand of humor ("Piss off!"), finding it lowbrow, distasteful or just plain stupid. Yet their episodic, sketch-based comedy continues to be hugely influential; it is unlikely the lunacy of *SCTV, Saturday Night Live* or the Farrelley brothers (*There's Something About Mary*) would have been possible without the Pythons. And it is also more political, even subversive, than its detractors claim; the Pythons were first to attack many of Britain's most revered institutions, including the royal family, organized religion and just about every single historical icon of mention.

Much of the best humor in *Monty Python and the Holy Grail* isn't strictly outrageous, regardless of how many surreal and rapid-fire gags the troupe throws at us: animated sequences fuse into musical numbers, killer rabbits make way for a nymphomaniac all-female revue, gorilla page-turners live harmoniously with benevolent shrubberies. There at first appears to be little method to the Pythons' unique brand of madness, but it is music that fuses the Pythons' disparate styles together. *Holy Grail* ebbs and flows like a symphony. The individual sketches, if hit or miss, work as both self-contained vignettes and a cohesive whole. I believe the secret to the success of Python is in their absolute ruthlessness at the writing stage; the five members would often spend up to a year collaborating on a single script. They were the rare comedy team able to find the proper balance in their parts, their respective strengths fine-tuned in service of the group. They were able to make the hard work of comedy appear effortless, the most calculated gag seemingly off-the-cuff. The giddy rush of their schoolboy humor is some of the best slapstick ever put on screen.

The Goodies The insanity of Monty Python has come to DVD and no one is safe. This two-disc set is gargantuan, as ridiculous and zany as their most outlandish skits. Even the menus are a lulu (you can choose the "Hard of Hearing" option to have the navigation options read to you) and there are so many throwaway gags and hidden easter eggs scattered throughout that you might miss all the great stuff in between.

The two new audio commentaries are actually *serious*. Gilliam and Jones share the first one (carried over from Criterion laserdisc), while Palin, Cleese and Idle romp through the second. Gilliam dominates his track but all are candid and informative. Sometimes the humor is so dry and raw you don't know whether anyone is kidding or not—the tales from the production are more akin to war stories than warm and fuzzy memories of making a movie. And most of the Python members hadn't seen this movie—or one another—in years, which lends both tracks the feel of a high school reunion.

In the spirit of the branching features made famous by such DVDs as *The Matrix,* the *Python* DVD offers the "Killer Rabbit" feature. When a cute little bunny appears on the bottom right of the screen, just click and you'll be treated to some of Gilliam's conceptual sketches or other droll insights.

The second platter of this two-disc set is stuffed full. "Quest for the *Holy Grail* Locations" is a splendid forty-five-minute documentary that reminds us that not everyone in Britain loved the Pythons' brand of satire—many castles in England refused to let the troupe film within their gates. Likewise, *BBC Film Night* is a location report originally broadcast in 1974 where a poor sap tries to get some straight answers out of the Pythons. His embarrassment, our hilarity.

"Old Rubbish" is an extensive still gallery with production photos, posters and a number of theatrical trailers. And in typically cheeky Python style, there's a collection of pompous, cranky and just plain nasty diatribes against *Holy Grail* and the Pythons. An extensive cast section includes some nifty "Unshot Footage," including a stop-action version of the "Knights of the Round Table" sequence with a cast of LEGOs, plus a tongue-in-cheek featurette with vintage travel footage, and some unused Gilliam storyboards.

More great touches include cute subtitle options: read the screenplay as the movie plays, or enjoy *Holy Grail* with excerpts from William Shakespeare's *Henry IV*. Wrap your brain around that one.

The Presentation *Monty Python and the Holy Grail* has never been a great-looking movie, with a rather drab, dreary and murky visual style. Presented here in an expanded cut that runs only forty-five seconds longer—leave it to the Pythons to lampoon even the very concept of a DVD special edition—this 1.85:1 anamorphic widescreen transfer has been digitally remastered, but that can only do so much. The print still suffers from wear and tear, including noticeable dirt and scratches. Detail is relatively mediocre and color reproduction decidedly average (bleed is a problem, as are inconsistent fleshtones.) Only Gilliam's animation sequences look good, with an overall sharper and more detailed appearance. But part of the fun of any Monty Python movie is its playful lack of pretension, so such shoddiness, in some ways, enhances the experience.

The new Dolby Digital 5.1 surround track is also a valiant effort but can't do much to improve upon the film's limited monaural source elements. Surround use is sporadic and uneven, and the score sounds abrasive and shrill. However, even though the original mono track is also included, the remix is preferrable due to better consistency, cleaned-up elements and expanded frequency response.

Additional Recommendations DVD is a feast for Monty Python fans. All of the troupe's best work is available in a series of fine special editions, including *Life of Brian, The Meaning of Life, Live at the Hollywood Bowl* and the excellent fourteen-disc *Monty Python's Flying Circus Complete Collection*.

IT'S THE FILM THAT COUNTS: A CONVERSATION WITH SIR ALAN PARKER

Once one of London's most talented advertising copy editors, Alan Parker got his start as a filmmaker in the 1960s editing and directing a string of influential commercials and short films. He would make his motion picture directing debut in 1976 with the kid musical *Bugsy Malone,* starring Jodie Foster, and quickly established himself as one of England's most diverse and passionate filmmakers. Never one to shy away from even the most controversial of issues, his many accomplishments include the Oscar-winning *Midnight Express* (1976), *Fame* (1980), *Pink Floyd The Wall* (1982), *Birdy* (1984), *Angel Heart* (1987), *Mississippi Burning* (1988), *The Commitments* (1991) and *Evita* (1996), for which Madonna won a Golden Globe for her performance as the title character. His most recent films have been no less incendiary: the controversial *The Life of David Gale* (2003) and an acclaimed adaptation of *Angela's Ashes* (1999), which received three British Academy of Film and Television Award (BAFTA) nominations. In 2002, he earned Britain's most prestigious honor—a knighthood in the United Kingdom's annual New Year's Honours List.

You have long been intimately involved with the production of the special editions of your films, both on laserdisc and now DVD. What is the appeal for you, as a filmmaker, about documenting your work in this format?

With the advent and popularity of DVD, it's great for a filmmaker that you can closely replicate how it was meant to look in the movie theaters. Videotape technology was very crude, and it was often painful to see your films shown that way. With DVD you can now grade the film pretty closely to the original film—indeed, it could be argued that a filmmaker can grade the film *better* on DVD, because of the advances in technology, than when grading it on film in the laboratory.

And the beauty of DVD is that *all* your films can now be seen by an entirely different audience—one that didn't originally experience them in the movie theaters, but can see them afresh. Not only afresh, but looking and sounding as they *should* be. Suddenly our work is there for all to see—forever more, not just as a jaundiced film review, or a scratched print in a film archive, but available to all, and looking and sounding great, to enjoy and evaluate for themselves. That's a wonderful advance in the history of film.

Has the impact of DVD altered how you approach the actual process of making a movie?

Well, to be completely honest, I have to say that making the film itself is as much of a handful for any filmmaker, so any *other* presence on set, particularly a documentary camera crew, can often be an aggravation. For years, film studios had a laissez-faire attitude to this, sending down to the set video camera crews for basic interviews and perfunctory shots of the filming, what is known as the EPK, electronic press kit. These are not proper documentaries and so shouldn't be praised or encouraged. However, the DVD is probably going to be the "final record" of how and why a film is made and so it's a good idea that making-of documentaries are included on the DVD, as long as they are made with style and integrity.

How did you go about selecting your DVD producer and deciding how you are going to approach the project?

I probably don't have the answer you want. There is only one "producer" of the DVD and that is the person or persons who produced the *actual film*. I think that too many people are usurping the "producer" credit, giving an inflated credit to the person assembling the bonus materials—a person totally not involved in the creation of the actual film—and that it denigrates the actual film's producer credit. I know that many filmmakers often feel mugged by these people.

So with that answer, you probably have gathered that I don't seek out the people who have created a whole business out of attaching themselves to other people's movies like barnacles to a ship. I control the materials that go on the DVD of my films. For my films that were made before we had this in our contracts, before these technologies were invented, it is more difficult, and you hope that you can affect the content by reeling in the DVD cowboys stealing our work.

You have begun to include deleted scenes on many of your DVDs . . . What is the process you

go through in selecting what deleted materials are going to "make the cut"?

There are two schools of thought about this. If you are a "final cut" director, there are probably not the "great scenes the studio wouldn't let me include" available. By definition—if you have the "final cut"—if a scene has been deleted, it's probably because it wasn't good enough for dramatic or technical reasons. So why would you want anyone to see it? This to me seems an odd masochism on the part of directors, although I can see some scatological interest from the DVD nuts.

[But] because "deleted scenes" are much enjoyed by DVD buyers, I've started to include scenes that I liked but that didn't make the cut, because of pacing or length issues on the final movie. Frankly, when I see people include scenes on their DVDs that should never see the light of day, it makes me cringe. However, I think the advent of DVD makes you more mindful of which box the editors put the deleted scenes in, and which warehouse you sent them to, just in case they might be needed. Until DVD came along, deleted materials and outtakes were just junked by the studios. Sadly, it was cheaper to incinerate the outtakes than to store them. Also, because the DVD is worked on these days immediately after the first cut of the film has been finished, any extra materials are at hand.

You have yet to redo any of your past films as a "director's cut." What are your feelings about this growing phenomenon?

I was fortunate in that I had the "final cut" on my films from way back, so my films, for good or ill, are the way I wanted them to be. I can't blame any studio. Consequently, there is no such thing as the "director's cut" of my films. It is mostly a marketing tool rather than a beneficial experience.

I tease my friend Ridley Scott, who has a couple of "director's cut" movies out, that I am amazed he allowed the studios to cut his film in the first place. A "director's cut" often means the "long version" with the inclusion of all those tedious, self-indulgent, boring bits the studio and the audience didn't want to see in the first place.

Also controversial are many of the technological innovations

that DVDs allow, such as multiple angles, Internet connectivity, etc. Are there any of these types of features that you would like to explore in the future?

I'm a bit of a Luddite here. I've personally always held the opinion that the movie is the movie. The angle or ending should be the one chosen by the filmmaker. Movies are not a multiple-choice SAT exam. Picasso ought not to have his Blue Period paintings painted pink, nor should anyone interfere with his or our imagery. This is a backward step in art. To the people who like this multiple-choice stuff, I say: Make your own art; don't vicariously interfere with the work of others.

DVD supplemental features are becoming so ubiquitous and extensive that consumers now have more access than ever before to the nuts and bolts of making a movie. Do you feel there might be a limit—that there could be any possible danger in revealing too much of the magic, so to speak?

Absolutely. The most vain film people in the film business are the digital special effects people. Every time I see those grandstanding know-it-alls boasting about what they did and how important they are, it makes my blood boil. They constantly let the rabbit out of the hat, continually giving away the mystery of film to anyone who wants to point a documentary camera at them in their cubicles. It is the cubicles that are the giveaways to this process. These computer nerds never go near a film set. They never see or experience the beauty or the madness. They never "smell the napalm in the morning." They are boring nerds who have no contact with anyone to do with the creative process of actually making a film at the sharp end, and so the moment anyone turns up with a camera in their office they rattle off their self-serving opinions.

Due to ever-shrinking theatrical-to-video windows, DVD has virtually replaced the second-run theater. Have you found that because of this new ancillary market, it has opened up new avenues to get riskier or less mainstream projects financed and distributed?

I wish this were the case. This was one of the great hopes of the DVD explosion. I see no evidence that it has helped get riskier, less mainstream projects off the ground. A lot of people had hoped that the cinema of DVD would be the cinema of independent film. This hasn't happened.

The studios are pleased because they have an enormously important additional revenue stream—principally from their blockbusters. The enormous disappointment of the DVD revolution is that it almost always replicates the interest of film in the "action" or "special effects" type movies—the very movies that command most of the screens in the multiplexes. The great hope had been that the audience that had deserted the movie theaters—older and better educated, aged twenty to sixty—which is five times the size of the teen and preteen audience that are currently being targeted by film studios on DVD—would enjoy a more diverse and intelligent cinema at home with this wonderful new technology. Perhaps a more thoughtful cinema, perhaps a cinema from other cultures in differ-ent languages. This hasn't been the case. The studios say that their core DVD audience is mostly young males, who want to slow down and be informed of the special effect scenes of the films they've already seen in the cinemas. It's a terrible waste of a wonderful medium. The art of cinema has been confused with a video game.

Ultimately, what do you think the biggest impact of the DVD format has been on the film medium?
I come back to my main point. For me, the most important reason to own a DVD is the film itself—beautifully graded by the filmmakers and with sound that pretty well replicates the original studio mix. The stuff that comes with it . . . the "bonus bits and bobs"—well, it brings a lot of people pleasure, but for the filmmaker it's always the film itself that counts. So my favorite DVDs are my favorite films. ○

Moulin Rouge!

DISTRIBUTOR: Fox Home Entertainment
DVD RELEASE: September 12, 2001
THEATRICAL RELEASE: May 2001
RUNNING TIME: 126 Minutes
MPAA RATING: PG-13

M*oulin Rouge!* is a movie musical unlike any other. When it hit theaters in May 2002 amid an avalanche of intense hype, it was hailed as the first sure-fire blockbuster musical since *Grease* (1978). Australian-born auteur Baz Luhrmann's third film, it had hip young stars (Nicole Kidman and Ewan McGregor), a soundtrack bursting with classic songs and a visual style so kinetic it made MTV look old-fashioned. But many of those hoping for a return to the style and form of the classic musical left the theater not merely disappointed but furious. Luhrmann broke every convention, churning the most beloved tenets of the genre through a pop-culture blender that turned *Rouge!* into the first motion picture megamix.

The first thirty minutes of *Moulin Rouge!* are so intense a nausea bag may be needed. Song, dance and image are combined with such force that one scarcely has time to wonder what it all means. But Luhrmann was doing more than just working in the increasingly popular form of postmodern pastiche; he was challenging every established notion of style versus substance. In *Moulin Rouge!,* style *is* substance. Reaction was intensely polarized. Those who loved it did so with a passion and fervor that transformed it into an instant cult classic on the level of a *Rocky Horror Picture Show.* But some hated it with a fervor so poisonous it branded Luhrmann a heretic.

Moulin Rouge! is neither as cold and calculated as its detractors claim, nor the epic of romantic abandon its fiercest admirers would have you believe. It is too carefully constructed and overproduced to truly soar. Luhrmann's relentless razzle-dazzle oftentimes lacks coherence—Cole Porter mingles with Nirvana with no apparent significance to plot, theme or place—but there *is* a story buried somewhere beneath all the hard-sell artifice. In its heart, *Rouge!* is a surprisingly traditional tale of love, loss and tragedy. Putting up a brave fight against the din, McGregor and Kidman make a charming romantic pair, but it is tough being a prop in Luhrmann's cinematic amusement park. Spectacle often towers over intimacy, and the frenetic editing—which does slow down in the second act—requires a second or third viewing to take it all in. *Moulin Rouge!,* while spectacular, simply doesn't know when to quit.

Despite the buzz, *Moulin Rouge!* enjoyed only a moderate run at the box office, although it found its true home on DVD. Oscar also did not shine too brightly on *Rouge!* Nominated for seven Academy Awards including Best Picture and Best Actress (for Kidman), the film walked away with only three awards, all in technical categories, and Luhrmann was snubbed for a Best Director nomination. Many felt the movie was ahead of its time; *Chicago,* released the following year, received all of the box office and acclaim denied *Rouge!,* including a Best Picture statuette. (The biggest irony? Due to an Academy technicality, *Rouge!* was ineligible for the Best Song and Best Score categories, which were supposed to be a lock.)

> "The greatest thing you'll ever learn . . . is just to love, and be loved in return."
>
> —Christian to Satine

The Goodies *Moulin Rouge!* the DVD is an overwhelming experience. The packaging promises hours of supplemental material and delivers. Even the film's fiercest detractors have to concede that this is a mightily impressive two-disc set as substantial as it is stylish. And in a nice complement to the film itself, the user can experience the supplements in both a linear and interactive fashion. A dual navigation system allows for access to much of the material through both a traditional menu structure and an enhanced viewing mode that integrates the extras into the film itself. Luhrmann had an intensive level of involvement in the creation of the *Moulin Rouge!* DVD, which results in a highly eclectic assortment of supplements. Film is a director's media, and as Luhrmann proves here, so is DVD.

Two audio commentaries were recorded, featuring Luhrmann and his wife, Oscar-winning costume designer Catherine Martin, plus writer Craig Pearce and director of photography Doug Alpine. These commentaries can be activated independently or in tandem with the enhanced viewing mode, which features multiple video-based making-of segments. The experience is disjointed but perfectly suits the material. And the passion of Luhrmann and his team for *Rouge!* is so great, it may warm a few cold hearts toward his arch visual style. The level of their achievement was amazing—what a spectacle! *Rouge!* is a masterpiece of conception, design, sound and vision—it is almost impossible to take it all in.

A copious amount of additional material is provided, including twelve minutes of deleted and alternate scenes and four extended dance numbers trimmed from the final cut, which are presented in their entirety. These scenes highlight the excitement of pure song and dance when they are freed from excessive cutting and stylization—a lesson Luhrmann may have been well advised to adhere to when editing *Rouge!*—but they also lack the intense energy of his far more aggressive final cut. See which version you prefer. Plenty of further extras burst from the seams of this two-disc set: nifty "previsualizations" of key segments; plenty of cast and crew interviews; extensive still galleries that cover all phases of the production, including costumes, locations and the effects; plus three music videos, trailers and more advertising materials. There are also nearly a dozen easter eggs, most of them insignificant but all fun.

The Presentation *Moulin Rouge!* looks smashing. Released in separate anamorphic widescreen and full-screen versions, both THX certified, the widescreen is imperative to fully appreciate the scope of Luhrmann's vision. The intricate sets, costumes and cinematography are fabulous, and reproduced here in a highly detailed, nicely three-dimensional transfer. The gorgeous, rich colors are eye-popping and the level of detail and depth reference quality. The Dolby Digital and DTS 5.1 soundtracks are also amazing. Luhrmann's barrage is endless—music, dialogue and effects emanate from all channels. Can you count how many songs and snippets are integrated into the space of just the opening *Moulin Rouge!* number? Overall dynamics are top-notch, with very expansive frequency response and a thoroughly enveloping 360-degree soundfield. *Voulez-vous coucher avec moi?*

Additional Recommendations As the concluding chapter in Luhrmann's self-proclaimed *Red Curtain Trilogy*—1992's *Strictly Ballroom* being the first, 1996's *Romeo + Juliet* the middle—*Moulin Rouge!* is the capper of an ambitious achievement. Fittingly, nearly a year after the DVD release of *Moulin Rouge!* came the four-disc *Red Curtain Trilogy* box set. Included are all three films, plus a bonus disc of additional material. It may be overkill, but for Luhrmann connoisseurs, essential.

National Lampoon's Animal House

DISTRIBUTOR: Universal Studios Home Video

DVD RELEASE: August 26, 2003

THEATRICAL RELEASE: June 1978

RUNNING TIME: 109 Minutes

MPAA RATING: R

On the list of things every teenage boy must complete before graduating into adulthood, watching *National Lampoon's Animal House* falls somewhere between raiding your parents' liquor cabinet and sniffing women's panties. It may not be important, but somehow, it is essential.

The beauty of *Animal House* is that everyone who watches it feels as if it was made just for them—it endures because every character is an archetype. Every fat nerd believes *Animal House* is the story of Flounder (Stephen Furst). Every suave, sarcastic ladies' man believes *Animal House* is the story of Otter (Tim Matheson). And every seventh-year party animal thinks that *Animal House* is his life story—and that he invented the toga party.

But if anything defines the gleefully stupid, futile and lovably rebellious spirit of *Animal House,* it is John Belushi. He is the spark of insanity that ignited the film and ensured its place in the pantheon of comedy classics. With a wonderfully animated face and eyebrows so mobile he seems able to will them fully around his head, he turns Bluto into a beer-swilling buffoon with a grade-point average of 0.0 and a sweatshirt that reads "College." Every move he makes, from impersonating a zit to smashing Stephen Bishop's guitar against a wall, has the perfect touch of anarchy that defined post-Watergate, pre-Reagan screen comedy.

Animal House was directed by John Landis, who, in 1970s films like *The Blues Brothers* and *Kentucky Fried Movie,* honed an unappreciated style of controlled insanity that is always madcap but never rudderless. Here the frame is filled with cute and funny touches that reward repeated

> **"Christ! Seven years of college down the drain."**
>
> —John "Bluto" Blutarsky

viewings and play like a live-action parody ripped right from the pages of *National Lampoon* magazine—*Animal House* remains the only film that truly earned such pre-title honors. Even writers Chris Miller, Doug Kenney and Harold Ramis would admit that the rest of the story, if not the entire story, is irrelevant as long as it is believable enough and universal enough to hang 110 minutes of college-themed jokes on. But thank goodness for that.

It is true that *Animal House* is no longer as raunchy and ribald as it was back in 1978; today it would be downgraded to playfully wacky, especially considering the fun you can have with a flute while at band camp. Yet if *Animal House* may have lost a bit of its anarchist's edge and subversive politics, it retains something more important and longer-lasting: a broad, good-natured sense of humor. After twenty-five years, *Animal House* is still the next best thing to attending college.

The Goodies Considering the amount of *Animal House*-related trivia available on the Internet, Universal Studios Home Video's Double Secret Probation Edition of the film is, at best, interesting. Exhaustive would have been a little better, but it is still a blast.

The key supplement is a very fine forty-five-minute documentary "The Yearbook: An Animal House Reunion." Much like Barry Levinson's 1982 comedy *Diner, Animal House* was a breeding ground for future stars, including Matheson, Furst, Kevin Bacon, Tom Hulce and Karen Allen. And, according to producer Ivan Reitman, the film was not greenlit until Donald Sutherland signed on as pot-smoking Professor Jennings. All the key surviving players are interviewed (with the exception of Hulce), and their recollections are warm and generous and include plenty of gossip. The doc also includes some priceless vintage behind-the-scenes footage, including Landis palling around with Belushi and other moments of surprising candor and poignancy.

The other big extra is "Where Are They Now? A Delta Alumni Update." Here the actors reprise their characters as narrator Landis finds out how they're faring in postcollegiate life. For instance, we find Otter (again played by Tim Matheson) is a Beverly Hills gynecologist and Hoover (again played by James Widdoes) is an attorney in Baltimore. Witty and fun. "Animated Anecdotes" is a subtitle track that imparts bits of trivia about the film (for instance: to impersonate a zit, Belushi filled his mouth with mashed potatoes). While not as fact-filled as the subtitled tidbits found on the DVDs for, say, the *Star Trek* films, it's still entertaining and interesting.

Rounding out the DVD are fairly lengthy production notes and cast and filmmaker bios as well as the film's theatrical trailer.

The Presentation For the twenty-fifth anniversary of *National Lampoon's Animal House,* Universal Studios Home Video went the extra mile with a digitally remastered picture in, at long last, the film's original 1.85:1 theatrical aspect ratio. The results are the best the film has ever looked, and came under fire from Landis himself, who revealed that he had the film grunged back up a bit because the remaster looked "too good." Daytime interiors and exteriors look the best, with nice detail and contrast. Colors are still a bit underwhelming, but consistent with other low-budget films of the 1970s. Landis was right not to give *Animal House* too much digital sparkle—it looks here like a great 1970s slob comedy, far better than it has ever looked before but not too good. Bluto would be proud.

Universal has remixed the film's original mono soundtrack (which is also retained here) in Dolby Digital 5.1. Purists may prefer the 2.0, but the remix is the better choice with a soundfield that fills out the film in the appropriate places, namely the party scenes and the great performance sequences. Dialogue emanates mostly from the center speaker, although there are some welcome directional effects. Not all the of the dialogue sounds clean, but it's nothing for the average viewer to be concerned about. Fidelity is generally limited in both mixes, although the Dolby has more bells and whistles available to make up for it. The songs, including "Shout" and "Louie, Louie," still sound a bit dated but are so much fun to listen to that it is hard to complain.

Additional Versions Universal Studios Home Video has released *National Lampoon's Animal House* in three versions. The first was a dismal full-frame, movie-only version best forgotten. They then reissued the film in a Collector's Edition that sported a remastered transfer and included "The Yearbook" documentary but no 5.1 remix. Both of these editions have been discontinued, replaced by this far superior Double Secret Probation Edition.

Night of the Living Dead (Millennium Edition)

DISTRIBUTOR: Elite Entertainment
DVD RELEASE: March 12, 2002
THEATRICAL RELEASE: October 1968
RUNNING TIME: 96 Minutes
MPAA RATING: Not Rated

George A. Romero's *Night of the Living Dead* unfolds with the gritty immediacy of a newsreel. A tale of a band of survivors, trapped in a farmhouse, who must work together to defeat a world overrun by zombies, *Dead*'s unflinching realism is matched only by its complete lack of sentimentality. Romero's vision of a world literally tearing itself apart

> "They're coming for you . . . there's one now!"
> —Johnny, to sister Barbra

is Darwinism taken to the extreme. All of our most sacred institutions have been destroyed: religion offers no salvation, community no sanctuary, government no protection. Those who were once our friends, our neighbors, our protectors, have turned against us, ready to tear us limb from limb. There will be no heroes, only survivors. And victory, even when hard won, will be short lived.

Night of the Living Dead has been called a black comedy, a nihilistic call to anarchy and the ultimate zombie movie. It was the first horror film of the Vietnam era, a masterpiece of modern paranoia that revolutionized the genre. It remains a landmark, not only for its depiction of graphic violence but also for its sheer relentlessness—never had such horrific subject matter been depicted in a manner so realistic and aggressive. Ravaged by nightly broadcasts of the atrocities in Vietnam, moviegoers settling in for a night of innocuous B-movie fun came out shell-shocked and assaulted. And critics, hoping to dismiss it as mere crass exploitation, could not deny Romero's intelligent handling of the material and its thinly veiled political implications.

Perhaps *Night of the Living Dead*'s greatest achievement was bringing a social conscience to the horror genre. The microcosm Romero created—man against zombie, man against man, man against his own worst instincts—confronted, head on, not just Vietnam but racial intolerance, capitalism and wanton vigilantism. It set the tone for political filmmaking in the decades that followed; Romero's stark use of black-and-white photography, gritty realism and a downbeat ending continues to be cited as an influence on filmmakers as diverse as Francis Ford Coppola, William Friedkin and Martin Scorsese.

If time has dulled some of the impact of *Night of the Living Dead,* it remains a testament to the fiercely independent and original vision of Romero, who directed the film on a shoestring budget and outside of the Hollywood establishment, calling in favors and using friends as crew. It was the first film of its kind to break out of the grind house circuit and insinuate itself into the cultural vernacular, and helped open the avenues of independent distribution. *Night of the Living Dead* proved that daring, original and uncompromised visions, produced outside of the established system, could attract mainstream audiences and seriously threaten the status quo. And it is still one hell of a scary movie.

The Goodies *Night of the Living Dead* was produced on a budget of only $200,000 and remains one of the most financially successful and influential independent motion pictures ever made. But despite this enormous success, it slipped into the public domain in the 1980s, resulting in countless, largely inferior video releases. For this Millennium Edition—far superior to all that have come before—Elite Entertainment worked intimately with Romero to produce a special edition that would pay appropriate tribute to the steadfastly independent auteur and his most well-known achievement. Rare is the special edition that feels this personal.

There are two screen-specific audio commentaries, with Romero, producer Russell Streiner and cast Bill Heinzman, Judith O'Dea, Keith Wayne, Kyra Schon and Vince Survinski. *Night of the Living Dead* was a benchmark: highly controversial, graphic, with an unconventional structure and a multiracial cast. Romero scrounged up the money for his labor of love from relatives and private investors, which created a familylike atmosphere that lasted all throughout production. As much as the story divided the characters, the film's low-budget, highly collaborative environment united cast and crew. All involved claim to have been aware that something special was happening, and the group track may be the more entertaining of the two, if less in-depth on the technical aspects than is Romero's solo.

Additional video interviews—with the late Duane Jones, one of the first African Americans to headline a major mainstream American picture, and Judy Ridley—achieve a rare level of poignancy. Unlike the blaxploitation heroes of the era, Jones never got his due; *Night* remains his final cinematic epitaph, and this is a fitting tribute.

Adding to the intimate, personal feel of the Millennium Edition are extensive "Personal Scrapbooks" and additional still galleries. Romero's influence on the independent film scene is examined in an extensive series of notes detailing the auteur's beginnings as part of The Latent Image, a successful commercial production house, along with outtakes from the short film *Derelict,* and additional commercials.

Rounding out the array of materials is an amusing short parody, *Night of the Living Bread,* additional clips and stills from Romero's "lost" film, *There's Always Vanilla,* the film's complete screenplay and treatment presented as a series of text screens, and the theatrical trailer. And contributing a new two-page liner essay is a frequent collaborator of Romero's, Stephen King.

The Presentation *Night of the Living Dead* has often been called "amateurish." Erratic distribution resulted in most audiences seeing the film in poor second- and third-generation prints; when the film slipped into the public domain, a flood of inferior video releases did little to inspire a reevaluation. Enter Elite Entertainment, who rescued *Night of the Living Dead* with the Millennium Edition.

Presented here in its original 1.33:1 aspect ratio from a new print minted from the original negative, the film's considerable craft and ingenuity can at last be fully appreciated. Under the auspices of the THX certification program, virtually all of the film's so-called faults have been greatly reduced or eliminated completely. Deep blacks and excellent contrast reveal details never before seen; the subtle tones, gradations and fine textures of Romero's own photography—director was also cinematographer here—are no longer obscured by murkiness or excessive grain. The film is still stark and gripping with the immediacy of a newsreel, but so smooth and filmlike that it will astonish longtime fans.

Elite has also produced a new Dolby Digital 5.1 remix that is sure to be controversial among purists. While an excellent remix for a film of this vintage—Elite went back to the original audio elements to create a new mix as opposed to using digital processing to add reverb and other faux-surround enhancements—it does substantially change the overall feel and texture of the experience. The presence of active surrounds lends a more cinematic feel to the film, in contrast to the immediacy of a mono mix. Wisely, Elite has also included the original mono track, all cleaned up and boasting greatly increased heft, depth and presence. Dialogue is at last free from excessive harshness and crackle, and low bass is more supple and full-bodied. In both sound and vision, *Night of the Living Dead* has been reborn.

Once Upon a Time in the West

DISTRIBUTOR: Paramount Home Entertainment
DVD RELEASE: November 18, 2003
THEATRICAL RELEASE: May 1969
RUNNING TIME: 165 Minutes
MPAA RATING: R

Of the five Italian-made westerns Sergio Leone directed—*A Fistful of Dollars* (1966), *For a Few Dollars More* (1967), *The Good, The Bad, and the Ugly* (1968), all with Clint Eastwood, and *Duck, You Sucker!* (1972)—*Once Upon a Time in the West* (1969) is his masterpiece. It is one of the all-time great westerns: ambitious, lyrical, impeccably shot, perfectly cast and evocatively scored by Leone's frequent composer, Ennio Morricone. Although heavily influenced by such classics as John Ford's *The Searchers* (1956) and the Italian sensibilities of Leone and his coscenarists Sergio Donati and Dario Argento, *Once Upon a Time in the West* was a pioneering achievement, the first western to successfully weave the reverential aesthetic of classical Hollywood narrative ("once upon a time") and the neodocumentary, realistic attitudes of late-1960s modernist cinema ("in the West"). Leone created a fairy tale that brutally chronicled the end of the wild frontier, as progress brought with it civilization and the eradication of the archetypical outlaw. *Once Upon a Time in the West,* like all of Leone's westerns, dramatized the transition when recorded history emerged and the mythical age disappeared into our collective cultural consciousness. And its considerable critical and commercial success paved the way for the revisionist "anti-westerns" that proved popular over twenty years later, including the Oscar-winning *Dances with Wolves* (1989) and Eastwood's *Unforgiven* (1992).

Symbols of encroaching civilization are littered throughout the film: the laying down of railroad tracks that stretch like tentacles

> **"People scare better when they're dyin'."**
>
> —Frank

toward the Pacific Ocean; Jill McBain (Claudia Cardinale), an ex-whore, avenging her murdered husband and becoming an entrepreneur; and the building of the community of Sweetwater, soon to become a boomtown. But while Leone, in his Eastwood westerns, explored the struggles of the antihero to continue his wanton ways amid two colliding ideologies, in *West,* Leone bears full witness to the death of "an ancient race," as Frank (Henry Fonda) defines it to "The Man" (Charles Bronson). When Bronson rides off into the sunset at the end of *West,* it completes the metaphorical journey Leone began in *A Fistful of Dollars,* when Eastwood first enters the screen on his donkey, as near a deity as the genre allows. These two men with no name share more than their anonymity; both carry with them a ruthlessness, simplistic moral code, distrust of authority, little interest in romance and no capacity for remorse or sentimentality. But whereas Eastwood is able to return to his lawless ways at the end of *The Good, the Bad, and the Ugly* (the final chapter in Leone's "The Man with No Name" trilogy), for Bronson at the end of *West,* the frontier no longer exists; the only place for him to ride off into is to the annals of western folklore itself.

Once Upon a Time in the West was widely hailed for being the first western to feature a female (Cardinale) as its de facto main character, and it was also be the first time Leone gave top billing to one of his actresses. But now the compliment seems backhanded; at the time, Leone said of the use of Jill as the protagonist, "You had there the end of the world: the birth of matriarchy and the beginning of a world without balls." Leone is more successful when manipulating audience expectations by casting against type. Henry Fonda, as the despicable Frank (who has murdered Jill's husband and fails to have "The Man" assassinated in the film's bravura, classic opening sequence), has the face of an angel, while Bronson, as "The Man," would look far more comfortable wearing all black and twirling a mustache. The phrase "The good, the bad, and the ugly" is applicable to the triangle formed by the three main male characters: "The

Man" (the good), Frank (the bad), and the warrior Cheyenne (Jason Robards, the ugly). But Leone is not literal; "ugly" refers not to appearance but to lack of purity. Frank and "The Man" may be opposites but both are without ambiguity. Cheyenne, like all of the devalued characters in Leone's westerns, is simply flawed: he has emotions, is fallible and constantly on the run from the law, is funny and cares about women and children. Leone suggests that because the "good" and the "bad" are "pureblooded," unlike "the ugly," they understand right and wrong and are free from the corruption of a civilized world and its laws. They are gods, Cheyenne a mere mortal.

Leone was even more audacious in his visual style. *Once Upon a Time in the West* is certainly one of the most ornate and artful of westerns; Leone was not afraid to suddenly cut from grand, deep-focus vistas to extreme close-ups, a brave approach that allows us the time to be fascinated by the amazing faces that populate his world. Leone also had impeccable taste in using color, setting and composition to tell his story and build tension—he used every last inch of the frame, filling it with vivid details. His visual style is as overwhelming in its grandeur and vast expanse as it is intimate and subtle. A frequent Leone collaborator, Ennio Morricone provides a majestic score that may be his finest for the director; it shifts seamlessly between the dramatic, ethereal, comedic and suspenseful, and also ebbs and flows in volume as the themes and motifs for the various characters intertwine. And most important, despite the period details of the score, Morrison always maintains its appropriate mythic quality. It is the very essence of *Once Upon a Time in the West,* and the essence of Leone.

The Goodies Long one of Paramount's most requested titles, *Once Upon a Time in the* West has gotten a masterful two-disc special edition. An impressive lineup of major filmmakers pays tribute to the late Leone: John Milius, John Carpenter and Alex Cox, Christopher Frayling (author of *Sergio Leone: Something to Do with Death*), historian Sheldon Hall and star Cardinale. Each has been interviewed for the excellent seventy-minute documentary (divided into five "chapters"), excerpts from which have also been assembled into a full-length audio commentary. Vintage interviews with Leone and Fonda are deftly edited into the documentary, which is magnificent; it traces Leone's rise as the most well-known and highly acclaimed Italian auteur in history, as well as his reluctance to take on another western so soon after completing his "Man with No Name" trilogy with Eastwood. The film's extensive production is also examined in great depth, as is its lasting impact and influence.

An additional six-minute featurette, "Railroad: Revolutionizing the West," is a quick and informative piece on the beginnings of the railroad and the transition it wrought. Two still galleries with over one hundred images include extensive location and production stills, as well as rare photos of a deleted scene with Bronson. Rounding out the set are the film's theatrical trailer and some brief filmographies.

The Presentation Paramount has crafted a gorgeous restoration of *Once Upon a Time in the West*. For a thirty-five-year-old film, it looks stunning. The film's gritty realism is retained, but the print is free from all of the usual blemishes that mar source material of this vintage, including scratches, dirt, dust and speckles. Leone was famous for his widescreen compositions and intense close-ups, and the level of detail present in this 2.35:1 anamorphic transfer is startling. The crags of the great Western expanses and the cracks in Frank's grizzled face are equally exquisite. The new Dolby Digital 5.1 remix does not have as much to work with as the transfer, as the original audio elements have invariably dated. But it is a clean presentation, with very distinct dialogue reproduction and Morricone's expert score lush and full-bodied.

Additional Recommendations Another great Sergio Leone classic to get the two-disc special edition treatment is *Once Upon a Time in America,* his searing epic of mob-torn 1920s America, starring Robert De Niro. More great westerns on DVD including Clint Eastwood's Best Picture winner *Unforgiven,* also available in a two-disc set with commentary and a documentary, and Leone's "Man with No Name" trilogy, available from MGM Home Entertainment although shamefully devoid of major supplements.

One Flew Over the Cuckoo's Nest

DISTRIBUTOR: Warner Home Video

DVD RELEASE: September 19, 2002

THEATRICAL RELEASE: November 1975

RUNNING TIME: 133 Minutes

MPAA RATING: R

Milos Forman's *One Flew Over the Cuckoo's Nest* was a ray of hope for a nation on the verge of losing its will to fight. One of the most celebrated American films of the 1970s, it premiered at the Chicago Film Festival in 1975 to rapturous applause. News quickly spread that the film was one of the greats; long lines formed at the box office, with many viewers going back for repeat viewings. The film's protagonist, R. P. McMurphy (Jack Nicholson), a disenfranchised, rebellious delinquent who is wrongly institutionalized at a mental health facility run by the tyrannical Nurse Ratched (Louise Fletcher), became an emblematic antihero for a generation that feared democracy was slipping through its fingers. The most embraced and remembered scenes fit the growing antiauthoritarian sentiments of the time: McMurphy's defiant stands against Ratched, the fishing trip escape, comedic poker games and a rousing inmate rebellion. But *Cuckoo's Nest* was more than just a ribald antiestablishment comedy. It was a deeply political film, directed by a European, that tore at the very fabric of America's moral hypocrisy.

> "I must be crazy to be in a loony bin like this."
>
> —R. P. McMurphy

Based on Ken Kesey's 1962 bestselling novel, *Cuckoo's Nest* is not really about mental illness; Forman and his screenwriters, Lawrence Hauben and Bo Goldman, purposely downplayed the wide-ranging issues Kesey approached in his novel, streamlining and cutting away to focus on McMurphy's liberating influence on the inmates. The characters that surround McMurphy are played broadly as lovable crazies. Ratched is portrayed as a gross caricature, so sterilized and self-righteous she is the overbearing mother gone berserk.

(Fletcher is so good because she completely sublimates all of the emotions her character refuses to process, but with just enough humanity to avoid being monstrous.) And Nicholson's Oscar-winning performance holds *Cuckoo's Nest* together. He is Hollywood's greatest rebel, able to convey the widest range of emotions with the simple lift of an eyelid or a twist of the lip. Nicholson has to walk an emotional tightrope and does so flawlessly. He is a man on the brink, teetering between the easy laughs and harmless pranks of the first half of the picture and the growing realization that he may not escape. The scene where McMurphy realizes he may have made the wrong choice, nearly three-fourths of the way into the picture, is a small masterpiece and may be the finest piece of Nicholson's acting ever committed to celluloid.

One Flew Over the Cuckoo's Nest was the first film in over twenty years to win all five of the top Academy Awards (Best Picture, Director, Actor, Actress and Screenplay). Some found it odd that Forman, born in Czechoslovakia in 1932, directed one of the great critiques of American morality. But who better than the leader of the Czech new wave—his early films include *Loves of a Blonde* (1965) and *The Fireman's Ball* (1968)—to so cleverly use humor and irony to dissect an America on the verge of institutional autocracy? Murphy's final victory is not a hollow one. He may have lost the battle but his spirit has won the war. *One Flew Over the Cuckoo's Nest* was a watershed of American cinema and still has the power to instill hope and courage in a world sorely in need of both.

The Goodies This two-disc set includes a very fine audio commentary by Forman and producers Michael Douglas and Saul Zaentz. Douglas, who wandered around stunned at the film's rapturous world premiere in 1975, talks with great passion and pride of his first earned producer's credit. Forman has lost none of his edge, eloquent about what he, as an observer of American manners and mores, felt important to draw out of Kesey's original novel. The track can be a bit choppy Forman was recorded previously for the 1996 laserdisc and spliced in, but this is a great commentary.

The forty-five-minute documentary "The Making of *One Flew*

Over the Cuckoo's Nest" is also excellent. (Like the commentary, it has also been trimmed from its original ninety-minute form as seen on the laserdisc. Due to legal clearance issues, the interviews with many real-life mental health professionals have been excised.) The lack of on-set production footage does force the interviews to carry most of the weight, with Forman, Douglas and Zaentz again appearing, along with most of the main cast, although not Nicholson. The doc is breezier than the commentary, focusing more on the acting and development of the screenplay, as well as the incredible reception the film received. Fletcher is especially poignant when recalling her Oscar acceptance speech, which she also delivered in sign language as a tribute to her parents, who were hearing impaired.

Rounding out this edition are eight deleted scenes that are surprisingly strong but, given the film's already considerable runtime, were wisely cut. A theatrical trailer and extensive awards list complete the package.

The Presentation Newly remastered in 1.85:1 anamorphic widescreen, this transfer is a clear step up from the VHS and laserdisc editions as well as the previous, movie-only DVD release. *Cuckoo's Nest* is still a very flat, colorless film. The white walls of the asylum are the dominant color—only some splashes of red and the occasional exterior brighten up the mood. But the print is very stable with minimal defects; detail is substantial and blacks pure. Likewise, the film's sound design is direct and plain. The Dolby Digital 5.1 remix here has little to do, so is wisely focused on the dialogue, which is well placed in the center channel. Only Jack Nitzche's brooding musical score is directed to the rear channels, which makes for a subtle, engaging experience that is appropriate to the material.

Additional Versions After the highly acclaimed 1996 laserdisc release, Warner Home Video released *One Flew Over the Cuckoo's Nest* on DVD in 1998 as a lackluster, movie-only edition. It was devoid of extras and had a good, if marginal, transfer. It is now discontinued; however, its cover is very similar to the one that adorns this far-superior two-disc set, so pay close attention to the packaging before purchasing.

Peeping Tom

DISTRIBUTOR: The Criterion Collection
DVD RELEASE: November 16, 1999
THEATRICAL RELEASE: April 1960
RUNNING TIME: 101 Minutes
MPAA RATING: Not Rated

Upon its initial release in 1960, Michael Powell's *Peeping Tom* was not reviewed, it was condemned. It was called amoral, sadistic and an insult to British cinema. Despite a career as a filmmaker that spanned thirty years and many highly acclaimed achievements—*The 49th Parallel* (1941), *The Life and Death of Colonel Blimp* (1943), *Black Narcissus* (1947), *The Red Shoes* (1948) and *The Tales of Hoffman* (1951)—Powell was suddenly a pariah in his own country and deemed unbankable by the studios. *Peeping Tom* flopped and was swiftly pulled from theaters; a highly censored version played briefly in American grindhouses in 1962, but it would not be until 1979, largely due to the efforts of Martin Scorsese, that Powell's lost masterpiece was restored and rereleased to impress American and foreign critics. At last, Powell's fascinating, challenging film was vindicated.

> "The only really satisfactory way to dispose of *Peeping Tom* would be to shovel it up and flush it swiftly down the nearest sewer. Even then the stench would remain."
>
> —Critic Derek Hill, in the *British Tribune*

While the horror film had been mass produced by the studio system for over forty years prior to *Peeping Tom*'s release, the tale of a voyeur, Mark Lewis (Carl Boehm), who murders a string of beautiful young women, films their deaths and—most troubling for critics and censors—achieves sexual gratification from his acts, was one of the first of a new wave of psychological character studies that were more interested in the condition of the insane than in the heinous acts they commit. But unlike Alfred Hitchcock's *Psycho* (also released in 1960) and its more commercial breathen, Powell's unflinching, perceptive look at murder, voyeurism, sexual frustration and child abuse proved just too unsettling for the public to handle: the controversy prevented critics from separating *Peeping Tom*'s subject matter from the virtues of the film itself.

Powell implicates us as much as Mark. He equates our own desire to witness Mark's crimes with Mark's voyeurism, so we are, by extension, peeping toms ourselves. Mark is, like Powell, a filmmaker, and like us, a spectator. In his hands the camera is a lethal weapon and the only tool he has to achieve sexual gratification (importantly, Mark never rapes his victims—only watches their horrified faces in the throes of death). Such themes were troubling enough for audiences of the time, but Powell goes further, refusing to paint Mark as a villain, inviting us to empathize with a killer. This approach was revolutionary and further predated the psycho-films from the 1970s onward that explored madness and murder from the eyes of the killer, not the victims or the heroic avenger.

Powell challenges us throughout; he will not condemn Mark for his crimes and asks us to like him, even root for him. We come to learn that Mark's father, known only as Professor Lewis (played by Powell himself, in a further act of postmodern character/filmmaker cross-identification), performed sick medical experiments on his son when he was a child. Powell places the blame for Mark's psychosis firmly at the feet of his upbringing, illustrating that killers are not born, they are made. This became the modus operandi for all serial killer films that followed, most notably the 1992 Oscar winner for Best Picture, Jonathan Demme's *The Silence of the Lambs*. Powell's finale—Mark and his images become one through his own suicide—prove a haunting epitaph for the prepsychological cinematic horror cycle. *Peeping Tom,* along with *Psycho,* remains the most influential—and most underrated—horror film of the twentieth century.

The Goodies The main supplement on this very fine Criterion Collection special edition of *Peeping Tom* is the BBC documentary "A Very British Psycho." It excels as one of the better documentaries produced about a film that doesn't actually document the film's making at all. Rather, it is the story of screenwriter Leo Marks (Mark Lewis?), whose own life paralleled that of his protagonist in fascinating if potentially troubling ways. Marks was not, thankfully, a serial killer; however, his work as a codemaster during World War II mirrors the emotional double life of his lead character: doing monstrous things while masking the insanity of one's actions. It is a chilling examination of a truth all too absolute but rarely, if ever, confronted—that real life must always inform art. "A Very British Psycho" is required viewing.

Film historian Laura Mulvey also contributes a screen-specific audio commentary, although compared to the documentary, it is dry and straightforward. But still, it is an informative listen, especially for Powell buffs.

Other extras include a short still gallery and the film's intriguing theatrical trailer.

The Presentation Lovingly restored from a pristine new 35mm print, *Peeping Tom* is a beauty to behold. This anamorphic 1.66:1 widescreen transfer—achieved by slight windowboxing of the frame on all sides—boasts stunning color reproduction. Powell's garish, sleazy milieu is now appropriately lurid. Detail is terrific, with even the finest textures in the darkest scenes apparent. There is a still a bit of grain to the image, but there are no compression artifacts nor any excessive edge enhancement or other digital processing. The restored mono soundtrack is in keeping with Criterion's mission statement, which is to present a film in the manner as closest to the original theatrical exhibition as possible. Here, the elements have been cleaned up nicely, with no major aural defects and a pleasing, warm sound. Otherwise, this is an undistinguished mono track and appropriate to the material.

Pink Flamingos/Female Trouble

DISTRIBUTOR: New Line Home Entertainment

DVD RELEASE: October 2, 2001

THEATRICAL RELEASE: March 1972/October 1975

RUNNING TIME: 93 and 97 Minutes

MPAA RATING: Not Rated

An early John Waters movie is like one of those gruesome, color-faded, 16mm, highway safety films from the 1970s. Except without the car crashes. And with more incest. And more dancing anuses. And more sex with chickens. Indeed, Waters has become synonymous with the bizarre, disgusting and no-budget. Yet his early movies managed to stop short of moral irresponsibility, and creatively, they were never train wrecks. In fact, when considering Waters's oeuvre, it can be argued that the more polished the production, the less memorable the film (with the notable exception of 1988's *Hairspray,* which became a Tony Award–winning musical). Waters is at his best when he is at his cheapest and filthiest.

It was in the 1970s, far removed from a Hollywood too eager to tell filmmakers what they couldn't do, that the Baltimore native vented his cinematic spleen by writing campy screenplays about outrageous characters, then casting his friends and making them stick syringes into their vaginas and eat dog shit. But with Waters, there was always that knowing wink, as if he had more on

> **"Mama, nobody sends you a turd and expects to live. Nobody!"**
>
> —Crackers, to Babs Johnson

his mind than just pointing a camera at his troupe of bad actors and making them indulge his deviant fantasies.

Waters's interest in fame-baiting criminality (including his fascination with Charles Manson) took cinematic root in 1975's *Female Trouble*. Divine (the obese female impersonator and high school friend of Waters) plays Dawn Davenport, who embarks on a life of crime after her parents fail to get her cha-cha shoes for Christmas. Soon she falls under the sway of two fascist beauty salon owners

(David Lochary and Mary Vivian Pearce) who brainwash her into be-lieving "crime is beauty." Dawn then becomes a sort of performance-art criminal, whose crowning achievement is being put to death in the electric chair.

Pink Flamingos (1972) is about the quest to be named The Filth-iest People Alive. And in John Waters's Baltimore, there are plenty of nominees. Divine plays Babs Johnson, who lives in a trailer park with her son Crackers (Danny Mills), their friend Cotton (Mary Vi-vian Pearce) and Babs's egg-obsessed mother (Edith Massey) who sleeps in a crib. Babs's biggest competition for Filthiest People Alive are Connie and Raymond Marble (Mink Stole and David Lochary). They kidnap women, throw them in their basement and impregnate them. When the women give birth, the children are sold to lesbian couples.

Of course, those are just the basics. With John Waters, the devil is always in the details. Some say *Pink Flamingos* and *Female Trouble* are so underground, they should just stay buried. They are extremely raw in subject matter and technique, the cinematic equivalent of find-ing a dead body in a ditch and poking it with a stick. The perform-ances are terrible and at that point in his career, Waters clearly could not direct. And yet we wouldn't want it any other way. Even more bizarre then the Egg Lady asking, "How could a person be an egg, Cotton? How could a person be an egg?" is the idea of the line being uttered by a trained actress.

The filthy one-upmanship that cemented Waters's reputation has since been co-opted and turned into acceptable mainstream enter-tainments like *There's Something About Mary* and the *American Pie* series. But what makes Waters so one of a kind is that he gives us the real thing: Divine actually ate dog feces. Cameron Diaz did not ac-tually put semen in her hair in *There's Something About Mary.* And if Divine is willing to eat dog shit for his art, then the least we can do is laugh.

The Goodies When New Line Cinema rereleased *Pink Flamingos* theatrically in 1997, it tacked on fifteen minutes of bonus footage (introduced by Waters) after the closing credits. Those scenes are included on the DVD. While none of the cut scenes deserves to be in the finished film, *Pink Flamingos* completists will be thrilled. The supplement ends with Waters introducing the film's original theatrical trailer, which includes no footage from the movie. Instead, it consists of priceless audience interviews and film critic blurbs.

Both *Pink Flamingos* and *Female Trouble* also include scene specific audio commentary by Waters. For a man who disgusts people for a living, Waters is an intelligent speaker and popular college lecturer. Both commentaries contain his detailed recollections on the making of the films. Along with plenty of entertaining anecdotes, he remembers where scenes were shot, where he found the various actors and what he was trying to say thematically. Many fans will find themselves rewatching both films with the commentary tracks, because they are often far more hilarious and good-natured than are the movies.

The Presentation New Line has made the best of a bad situation with an admirable and generally successful attempt to get *Pink Flamingos* and *Female Trouble* into shape for their DVD debuts. The results are as good as bad can get. DVD viewers expecting glorious Technicolor vistas or full-blown digital restorations should disabuse themselves of that notion here. Although *Female Trouble* looks better than *Pink Flamingos,* both movies feature faded colors that lack vibrancy but at least don't smear or bleed. Blacks are fair while contrast and shadow detail are below average but tolerable. The overall picture is soft, with a persistent, though not distracting, layer of grain. On the upside, there are no edge enhancements or compression problems. And both films are presented in a widescreen aspect ratio of 1.85:1, which has been altered from the original 1.37:1. Purists will mind, but others may actually applaud seeing less of Waters's vision.

New Line has also included new Dolby 2.0 surround remixes and the original mono. Frankly, it's six of one, half a dozen of the other. Both mixes contain poorly recorded dialogue presented at various volume levels, although amazingly, most is quite understandable. There is some hiss but nothing distracting, and overall frequency response is limited. To be fair, the original source recordings are poor

SHOCK VALUE: A CONVERSATION WITH JOHN WATERS

Born in 1946, John Waters has been called the "prince of puke" and "the most irresponsible filmmaker of all time." He began by making amateur movies in his hometown of Baltimore, Maryland, and quickly attracted a stable of local counterculture performers, most infamously Harris Glenn Milstead, a 300-pound cross-dresser who billed himself as "Divine." His ensuing assault of pop-culture satire, awash in gleeful, graphic tastelessness, skewered the bourgeois middle-class values with which he was raised. Such notorious works as *Monde Trash*, *Female Trouble* and the infamous *Pink Flamingos*—which climaxed with Divine eating real dog shit—turned the burgeoning auteur into the darling of the avant-garde and the midnight movie circuit. Crossing over to the mainstream with his biggest hit, *Hairspray*—which was, shockingly, rated PG-13—he continues to explore his decidedly deranged worldview without having lost any of his manic energy or gleefully anarchic spirit. He has also written two collections of es-

says, *Shock Value* (1980) and *Crackpot* (1986).

New Line recently released a seven-disc John Waters Collection, which even featured your face stamped on the cover, almost as if you were a brand. How important do you think DVD has become to preserving your legacy?

DVDs are, of course, incredibly important. To me, DVDs are the new hardback books. When you used to go into someone's house, you could look at their books and see what they were like. Now you look at their DVD collection. No one realized that DVD was going to hit it so perfectly about making people want to collect them—even if they don't watch them.

The audio commentaries you have recorded for your films are hilarious. Do you go in having done any sort of preparation or is it entirely off-the-cuff?

I have done all of them with Mark Rance. We go in and we talk about the film and then we stop, and then we start talking and then we stop. It's all about editing to make a good track. I have never once listened to the commentaries on my films. People tell me they're good. I'm flattered. I do them all the time. I like doing them. But I used to make the joke that Barbra Streisand is the only director who actually sits and listens to her own commentary as she watches her own movies.

Another thing I've learned is that I really have to milk my anecdote bank because I did *Pink Flamingos* for Criterion, and they won't sell you that commentary. [Editor's Note: Waters originally recorded an audio commentary for the Criterion laserdisc of *Pink Flamingos,* which Criterion would not subsequently license to New Line for the DVD release; Waters was forced to rerecord it.] So you have to do the whole commentary all over again, so you have to think up all new anecdotes. It's like movie star school—a quiz. If you can each time do anecdotes and have people buy them for the fourth time—you have to think up new stories you didn't come up with before.

Do you enjoy listening to other filmmaker's commentaries?
I like bad commentaries where there are long silences, and then, "I fucked her." I saw a *New Yorker* cartoon and it was an actor's com-

mentary and it was like, "Watch this part! I'm really good here!" I had a whole thing about how craft service should do it, where basically they say, "That bitch didn't have food." The makeup person says, "You should see what she looks like at five a.m.!" The editor, "This guy—you should have seen the footage I had to work with here!" They only ask the director and the stars. They should ask other people.

You were a bit ahead of your time in terms of the whole revisionist cinema thing. With *Pink Flamingos,* you put some deleted scenes on after the movie was over . . .
I like doing that because that was the only movie where I really had that. I hadn't seen that footage for twenty years, and somebody finally synched it up and I looked at it. Once the movie comes out, it's in your mind the way it's released that even in the short term, you forget some of the footage. But twenty-some years later—and I remember I didn't even know what an "assemblage" was back then—but the assemblage of *Pink Flamingos* was almost two-and-a-half hours long. And I learned from that not to overshoot. But to see some of those plot points—I

didn't want to cut them back in because I cut them out for a reason—but to see them separate as a "best of," I thought fans would like to see different scenes and different looks for Divine and stuff.

Have you ever wanted to go back and reedit any of your films?
Oh, always, but you can't. They'd all be ten minutes long. *Monde Trash* was ninety minutes—it should have been ten. You always see thing you don't like. Especially in my early films, where I was just learning it by doing it—that's the way they are.

I've corrected things—like in *Pink Flamingos,* I've fixed sound glitches or blings on a microphone. Yes, I've corrected them and no one's ever howled to bring them back, believe me. *Pink Flamingos* is way more politically incorrect today than it ever was—except for the lesbians buying babies, which is now completely normal. It was thought of as a really shocking thing then, and now it's very, very accepted.

Was it shocking to see *Pink Flamingos* the fully remastered treatment for DVD?
I was just amazed at how good they could do it, how much better they made them look. It's amazing to me that you can correct mistakes or technical ignorance that you had at the time you were making the movie. There was dialogue I could never even understand in the movie. (laughs) You're [not only] missing the smell of pot in the air and the occasional person vomiting, you're missing the communal experience of screaming and yelling together.

Is it fair to say that DVD has replaced the revival house and the drive-in, for better or for worse?
With this, everybody can see it. I think it's better, in a way. Kids don't know about that experience. But they have their own midnight movie. They smoke pot in their own house while their parents are out and watch a movie. I think it's the same thing—it's just a different time and a different way of seeing it. But in a way, it's much better, because now in East Bumfuck, Mississippi, someone can order it on the Internet, not get busted. I don't have to get a censorship case in courts and anybody can see it. What's so great is that young people are really paying attention and understanding sex-

ploitation movies and movies that my generation never saw.

It's an entire new industry. It seems to give many of these films a brand-new life and makes every film look historic. Even the worst movie that no one remembers suddenly feels important when they add all these extras. It's funny, I think. But in a way, that's maybe saying that no film needs to be a failure. If you can get enough outtakes or blooper reels—enough information about it—all films are successes. And maybe that's what DVD has done.

Do you think the success of DVD has fostered an era where audiences can deconstruct movies to such a degree as to be detrimental?

You could never do that when movies were at their peak, because you have it at your home—the magic trick is that you're allowed to look. You were in a movie theater—you couldn't rewind or watch it over. You're taking away all the smoke and mirrors by watching it. But I understand looking for mistakes looking for ways in. When I was growing up, the only way you found out the Top Ten movies was in *Variety*—certainly not in your hometown paper or on the radio. The film business has become very much of interest to the general public. It completely wasn't when I grew up.

Do you still have the same sort of trouble with the MPAA today as you did back then?

I have the same problems. When we finally rereleased *Pink Flamingos*, we wanted an NC-17, and we got one. To me, I think the MPAA is fair. What's not fair is that theaters won't play NC-17 movies, that companies won't distribute them. There's nothing wrong with NC-17. That's not the MPAA's fault. But, to me, the only trouble I had was that the difference between PG-13 and R was much, much harder. R—if it's a comedy, you can get away with a lot. If it's a real turn-on, you can't. But if it's really sexy . . . I've fought censorship my whole life, certainly.

Does the advent of DVD make your job any easier? At least you can get the nasty stuff on disc . . .

Unfortunately, you can't say that when you're negotiating a contract. If you say that, your movie will fall through these days. Believe me. That's what they fear you want to do. When you promise you're going to do an R, they want an R. They don't want you to come back and recut—that costs a lot of money every time you do it. You have to remix, you have to do all that. They don't want that. They want the same movie.

I remember a time, long before DVD, when I made the drive to a revival theater to see *Pink Flamingos* in Chicago. Going to see a "cult" movie still felt like a political act. But now you can just go and rent them at Blockbuster . . .

Well, you can't rent them at Blockbuster because Blockbuster doesn't carry NC-17 or unrated movies. I want to be sure you mention that: They are the new legion of decency, censor-board chain that they are. I've said this in lectures, though, and people have come up to me and said, "They say that, but we carry them in our store." That's ludicrous, I think. And when *Pink Flamingos* came out, they offered me to appear at Blockbuster. I said, "Absolutely not. If you change your rule, I'll go to every one in the country." They'll deny that, but they're lying because they did say that.

You can't get some of these movies everywhere. And at the same time, the good part is that you lived in a suburb outside Chicago—what about all the other places in the country where you could have never gone and seen *Pink Flamingos*? There were many, many—like in ninety-seven percent of the country, you couldn't have seen it.

You've been called the ultimate cult movie director. Do you get any sort of satisfaction knowing that DVD is now bringing your work to a whole new generation, that your influence is now assured?

William Castle was my idol as a kid. William Castle, Walt Disney—all their films, even if you hated them, were a genre. And I think I have done that. You can hate every one of my movies and think they're terrible, but you have to give me the fact that no one copies them. That they are "John Waters movies" sort of says something. Maybe it's a good warning. To some, it probably is. ○

and no amount of twenty-first century tinkering could yield significant results. Still, eating dog doo-doo never sounded so good.

Additional Recommendations New Line has also released a special John Waters Collection DVD box set. It includes all three of the Waters two-packs (*Pink Flamingos/Female Trouble, Hairspray/Pecker* and *Desperate Living/Polyester*) plus a bonus seventh disc of rare odds and ends, arranged as a Waters timeline. There are a few notable interview snippets with Divine and much of the cast of *Flamingos* and *Female Trouble*. But it is likely only Waters completists will want to invest in the whole set. Other Waters favorites on DVD include *Cry-Baby,* from Universal Studios Home Video, and special editions of two of his post-*Hairspray* epics, *Cecil B. Demented* and *Serial Mom,* starring Kathleen Turner.

Pirates of the Caribbean: The Curse of the Black Pearl

DISTRIBUTOR: Buena Vista Home Entertainment

DVD RELEASE: December 2, 2003

THEATRICAL RELEASE: July 2003

RUNNING TIME: 143 Minutes

MPAA RATING: PG-13

Taking in over $600 million in worldwide box office booty, *Pirates of the Caribbean: The Curse of the Black Pearl* was the ultimate synergy of new millennium corporate Hollywood: not a movie but a merger, a crass, manipulative exercise that brought the era of marketing cross-pollination to a new level of refinement. *Pirates of the Caribbean* was not just another movie engineered to be turned into a thrill ride, it already was a thrill ride, and an E-Ticket at that. If Hollywood had long ago stopped feeling guilty for plundering bookstores, syndicated television schedules and its own vast library of classics for "original" ideas to adapt, remake and reimagine, now it was cannibalizing its own theme park attractions and regurgitating them with a bit of polish and a lot of spit. But what a tasty treat: if

Hollywood was going to serve up as delicious a dessert as this, then the least we could do was eat it.

By any reasonable measure, a film "adapted" from a theme park ride should be a sure recipe for disaster. It does not help when the ride in question is as cheesy as the venerable Disney World attraction Pirates of the Caribbean. Much beloved it may be, but plastic pirates chasing mechanical wenches in circles, complete with annoying songs, do not exactly inspire confidence for a strong narrative. But out of a cynical concept came an inspired conceit: these cursed, undead *Pirates* shift in and out of the shadowy moonlight, which reveals them as the rotting skeletal E. C. Comics monsters they have become. Such supernatural skullduggery grants *The Curse of the Black Pearl* license for flights of fancy that take our modern age's obsession with irony and artifice to a new level. *Pirates* is a masterful pastiche: its hodgepodge of genre clichés and conventions offers nothing new—dashing hero, damsel in distress, cackling one-eyed jacks, hidden treasure—but we are not watching a modern pirate movie filled with fresh ideas. Instead it is a loving ode to our memories of riding a junky old amusement park ride that was itself a funhouse reflection of our own antiquated movie memories. That the ghosts that haunt *Pirates of the Caribbean* are of fictional pirates past is apt: *Curse* curses us with the sight of reality twice removed. And as directed by Gore (*The Ring*) Verbinski with a savvy, able precision, *Pirates* expertly and seamlessly filters this sensibility throughout its breathless 143-minute run time.

> WILL TURNER: "You ignored the rules of engagement. In a fair fight, I'd kill you."
>
> JACK SPARROW: "That's not much incentive for me to fight fair, then, is it?"

But *The Curse of the Black Pearl*'s ace in the hole is the casting of Johnny Depp as the mangy Captain Jack Sparrow. Think Queer Eye for the Pirate Guy—Depp daringly channels the spirit of Keith Richards and C-3PO, turning Sparrow into a fumbling, mumbling wiseacre that is neither high camp nor low condescension, but a creation unique in the annals of the genre. If proper leads Orlando

Bloom and Keira Knightley are beautiful but bland, Depp infuses the movie with a tacky grace that is sublime, gliding in and out of scenes and stealing every single one. He is the pirate movie's answer to James Bond and Freddy Krueger rolled into one. And he raises his eyebrow just enough to let us know that he is in on the joke.

As smart and sly as Depp, *Pirates of the Caribbean: The Curse of the Black Pearl* is the first post-postmodern Hollywood epic and just about the most perfect realization of cinema as thrill ride as is imaginable.

The Goodies At the risk of overdoing a pirate-y metaphor, this two-disc set is equivalent to a treasure chest of chocolate gold coins: shiny on the outside, sweet on the inside, and about as good for your health as a day at the Disneyland commissary.

The three audio commentaries are an embarrassment of riches and a heck of a lot of fun Verbinski joins Depp for an informal, sprightly chat on staging such a mammoth production and Depp's chance to fulfill a childhood dream of becoming a pirate. Next Knightley and costar Jack Davenport generate big laughs, riffing in such a rapid-fire fashion that there is never a dull moment, although an audio interview with producer Jerry Bruckheimer is spliced in to take up any perceived slack. And last is a fascinating full-length discussion with the screenwriting team of Stuart Beattie, Ted Elliott, and Terry Rossio and Jay Wolpert, who prove that adapting a theme park ride is no easy task nor a laughing matter, especially when Disney is fronting the $100-million plus price tag.

Disc two offers more booty. The sharp thirty-seven-minute documentary "An Epic at Sea: The Making of *Pirates of the Caribbean*" excels, with tons of production footage including clever time-lapse photography of the film's gargantuan sets being constructed and plenty of cast and crew interviews. Over an hour of additional video footage includes "Fly on the Set," a twenty-minute assemblage of DV-cam footage deconstructing five key days on the set; twenty-six minutes of "Diaries" that gives us an intimate look at the art of trying to keep a straight face in a pirate movie from three perspectives: the actor, the producer and the ship itself; eighteen minutes of deleted scenes (nearly twenty in all) that only serve to drag an overlong film out even further and another three minutes of outtakes that prove Depp is as much a cut-up on the set as on the screen.

Thar Pirates also be interactive: "Below Decks: An Interactive History of Pirates" is a complex interactive map filled with gems, including video snippets of cast, crew and pirate historians waxing philosophical on the seafaring life, historical anecdotes and even a haunting mini-travelogue of "A Prisoner's Last Tale." The "Moonlight Serenade Scene Progression" uses the DVD format's multi-angle capabilities to break down the film's complex use of blue screen and CGI to accomplish its supernatural effects, while the vast "Image Gallery" offers an army of conceptual artwork, production photographs and advertising materials.

And no DVD for a movie made from a thrill ride would be complete without a look at the theme park attraction that started it all; the "Disneyland: From The Pirates of the Caribbean to The World of Tomorrow" episode of the television series "Walt Disney's Wonderful World of Color" originally aired on January 21, 1968, and the eighteen-minute excerpt here is retro-fantastic. The set's PC-enhanced extras are also some of the best yet created: another featurette on the ride, "Dead Men Tell No Tales: The History of the Attraction"; a "Virtual Reality Viewer" that promotes a newly-retooled version of the Pirates of the Caribbean adventure that Disney World launched after the movie's blockbuster success; a cutting-edge "Moonlight Becomes Ye Effects Studios," which allows users to input their own photos and turn themselves into pirates; highly intuitive and user-friendly script and storyboard viewers; and another extensive still gallery with even more text and photos.

The Presentation *Pirates of the Caribbean* is a very slick, good-looking movie, transferred here for maximum effect. The expansive 2.35:1 anamorphic widescreen dimensions are essential: Verbinski has fast become one of Hollywood's most underrated visual stylists, and his strong use of rich, contrasting colors (*The Curse of the Black Pearl* is full of striking midnight blues and lush golden ambers) gives

Pirates a look both modern and timeless. If a bit of edginess distracts—the image can suffer from an overly digital look—the deep blacks and strong detail make up for it. Even better are the Dolby Digital and DTS soundtracks. *Pirates* is alive with cannon fire and swordplay, and emboldened by Klaus Badelt's earnest score; all of these elements are aggressively spread out across the entire soundstage and the effect is highly enveloping. The deep, rumbling bass is also a stunner and even better realized by the DTS track. *Pirates of the Caribbean: The Curse of the Black Pearl* looks and sounds like the epitome of the gangbusters Hollywood epic.

Platoon

DISTRIBUTOR: MGM Home Entertainment
DVD RELEASE: June 5, 2001
THEATRICAL RELEASE: December 1986
RUNNING TIME: 120 Minutes
MPAA RATING: R

Vietnam has informed every one of Oliver Stone's films, even those that did not deal directly with the conflict. Stone, long one of American cinema's most incendiary and controversial filmmakers, fought as a soldier in the conflict, and *Platoon* marked the end of a twenty-five-year odyssey to bring the story of what he felt, saw and experienced to the big screen. It was not a project many wanted to make. It is not an overtly political film in the vein of Michael Cimino's *The Deer Hunter* (1981) or Hal Ashby's *Coming Home* (1978), both multiple Oscar winners, nor is it a fantasy, a glossy message movie or a heroic tale filled with nobility, courage and honor. It is a bloody, searing recollection of young men sent off to a war no one wanted to fight, to die for a country that greeted their return with hatred and bile.

> "I love this place at night. The stars . . . there's no right or wrong in them. They're just there."
>
> —Sergeant Elias Grodin

Platoon is narrated by Private Chris Taylor (Charlie Sheen), a stand-in for Stone. He is white, middle class, humble and patriotic. The first scenes we see of combat are horrific, bloody and utterly realistic. There are no heroes in war, only survivors. Taylor is soon torn by a power play between Elias (Willem Dafoe), who he comes to idolize, and Sergeant Barnes (Tom Berenger) who, having seen more combat than any of the other men, is perceived to be invincible, and slowly slipping into madness. The enemy is, at first, never seen, or only barely, shrouded in darkness and fog. But then we get to the pivotal, unforgettable scene in the Vietnamese village. It is chaos, and the true loyalties of Taylor, Elias, Barnes and the soldiers are tested. They kill the enemy, the innocents mistaken for the enemy, and one another. It is a vision of hell.

Platoon strips away the comforts and conventions we expect from a traditional war movie. We are not granted the easy identification with a traditional hero, nor told what is right and wrong. Even the battle scenes crush down the syntax of the war movie—we no longer have any sense of where the enemy is, what side the endless rain of gunfire and bombs is coming from. It is utter chaos. It is not exhilarating or exciting. And we are not "rooting" for our side to win. Only at the climax, when Chris makes the decision he was destined to face, does Stone's message become clear. But it is not preachy or heavy-handed. *Platoon* is the most restrained film Stone has ever made, and his best. It is not antiwar, anti-American, or even anti-Vietnam. It is simply a memory of one man's loss of innocence. And the loss of innocence of an entire nation.

The Goodies Charlie Kiselyak's fifty-three-minute documentary "A Tour of the Inferno: Revisiting *Platoon*" is a showstopper. Stone is an articulate, often mesmerizing speaker, intense and direct. The experience of making *Platoon* was a deeply personal and emotional one for him, which bled into the production. Kiselyak has also rounded up nearly the entire cast and crew, including Sheen, Dafoe, Berenger, Johnny Depp and more. Collaborators talk eloquently of the passion they all felt, not only to make a great film but also to rally around Stone and bring his dream project to life. An unforgettable documentary.

There are also two audio commentaries—one by Stone, the other by military advisor Dale Dye. Stone is again fascinating—both egotistical and his harshest critic. There is little redundancy with the documentary, and genuine moments of poignancy are reached as Stone quietly recalls the many real horrors he experienced. Dye is similarly involving and his own memories are as haunting despite his hard demeanor. This is one of the few "technical" types of commentaries that is a must-listen.

Additional extras include two very strong still galleries with production photographs, publicity photos and rare material from Stone's personal collection, as well as the film's theatrical trailer and three TV spots.

The Presentation *Platoon* has been released numerous times on VHS, laserdisc and DVD, but for this excellent two-disc set, director of photography Robert Richardson went back to the original source elements to create the definitive version. It is presented here accurately in 1.85:1 anamorphic widescreen. Most of the changes are subtle, if important. Fine alterations in hue now bring out the many lush greens and blues. Contrast is less harsh, which gives the transfer a much more filmlike appearance. And detail, especially in the darkest scenes, is far better realized. The Dolby Digital 5.1 surround track is often immersive, if inconsistent. Surround use is engaged primarily during the combat scenes, which deliver a sonic wallop. The film's you-are-there verisimilitude results in dialogue that is sometimes obscured and far from polished and clean, but otherwise this is a fine soundtrack.

Additional Versions *Platoon* has been released twice before on DVD: a 1999 Polygram release (now discontinued) and MGM's single-disc edition, still on the market. Both were without extras.

Additional Recommendations Oliver Stone is well represented on DVD. Warner Home Video has released a lavish, ten-disc Oliver Stone Collection that includes *Wall Street, Talk Radio, Born on the Fourth of July, JFK, The Doors, Any Given Sunday, Heaven & Earth,*

U-Turn, Natural Born Killers, and *Nixon,* and a bonus disc with another Kiselyak documentary, "Oliver Stone's America."

The Princess Bride

DISTRIBUTOR: MGM Home Entertainment
DVD RELEASE: September, 2001
THEATRICAL RELEASE: September 1987
RUNNING TIME: 98 Minutes
MPAA RATING: PG

Rob Reiner's *The Princess Bride* defies classification. Is it a children's fairy tale or an adult satire? A period romance? A swashbuckling adventure? A silly spoof? That it was a box office disappointment upon first release is not surprising. Few knew what to make of it, the studio didn't know how to market it, and critics just shrugged their shoulders. But, as with so many

> **"This is true love. You think this happens every day?"**
>
> **—Westley**

of the most beloved modern favorites, a small and extremely passionate cadre of fans kept the film alive. A huge hit on video and one of the most popular and often-aired movies on cable, *The Princess Bride* has become a true cult phenomenon.

Reiner frames his tale—which is just as much about movies as it is about fantasy and magic—in the present day, not only to allow a point of entry for the audience but also to show us that his film is a warm, nostalgic ode to our movie memories of the past. An old man (Peter Falk) reads a fairy tale to his sick grandson (Fred Savage), who is initially reluctant to listen to such an antiquated story. But as the tale unfolds, the grandson, and by extension we the audience, warm to this corny tale of romance, nobility and valor. Buttercup (a pre-Penn Robin Wright) is a young maiden confused by her growing attraction to the farm boy Westley (Cary Elwes). He, feeling unworthy of her love, leaves to claim his fortune and return a prince. Five years pass, and Buttercup is chosen as a bride for the dastardly Prince of Florin (Chris Sarandon). Despite the potential of a loveless marriage, Buttercup, still smarting over the loss of Westley, blithely accepts. But then an unlikely band of rogues, led by Vizzini (Wallace Shawn), Fezzik (Andre the Giant) and Inigo Montoya (Mandy Patinkin) kidnaps the future princess. It will not be a surprise that Westley returns and finds the princess, and that they make their escape through a series of high-flying, romantic adventures to live happily ever after.

The Princess Bride is a marvelous fantasy. It combines modern wit and style with the best conventions of old-fashioned adventure moviemaking. Much of the magic comes from the chemistry generated by the terrific ensemble. Wright and Elwes are gorgeous to look at—have ever a prince and princess been so flawless?—but also wonderful actors. (Perhaps their offscreen relationship seeped in during filming?) Sarandon makes a fine, swarthy villain, and the kidnappers—Shawn, Patinkin and the lovable Andre the Giant—are the funniest, scrappiest band of bumblers since the Three Musketeers. And *The Princess Bride* is filled with priceless cameos, including Reiner regulars Christopher Guest as the noble Prince Rugen, the late Peter Cook as a pompous cardinal and—almost unrecognizable under heavy makeup—Billy Crystal and Carol Kane as the hilarious wizard Miracle Max and his wife Valerie.

It is too bad that *The Princess Bride* came near the end of Reiner's prolific early period as a director. It was one of a glorious string of successes—*This is Spinal Tap* (1984), *The Sure Thing* (1985), *Stand By Me* (1986) and his biggest hit, *When Harry Met Sally . . .* (1989). Reiner's later films have been marred by poor choices and middling results; of his post-1980s work, only *A Few Good Men* (1992) rises above a string of misfires, including *North* (1994), *Ghosts of Mississippi* (1996), *The Story of Us* (1999) and *Alex & Emma* (2003). *The Princess Bride* remains his most magical achievement.

The Goodies MGM Home Entertainment has created a whimsical special edition for *The Princess Bride*. Reiner and legendary scribe William Goldman each contribute an audio commentary, and Goldman's is actually the more intriguing. The road from script to screen was a rocky one for *Bride*; Goldman's unabashed, old-fashioned leanings were at first deemed too antiquated, and frequent meetings with Reiner resulted in a long gestation and development process. Reiner has some jovial anecdotes about certain elements of *The Princess Bride*'s rocky road to the silver screen, but Goldman's old-school Hollywood perspective on moviemaking processes lends his discussion a bit more weight and significance. It might be too much to call it a miniature film school, but he definitely relays some important information about the business.

Next is a documentary and two shorter featurettes. "As You Wish" is a loving and sweet thirty-minute retrospective that touches on some of the stories Reiner discusses in his commentary and benefits greatly from newly shot interviews with all of the cast and crew, including Elwes, Wright, Crystal, Patinkin and more. The two eight-minute featurettes were shot during production and are of the fluffy, electronic press kit variety. Also included is some short Hi-8 footage shot by Elwes during the production with a charming and intimate you-are-there feel.

An extensive photo gallery encompasses nearly one hundred stills, including a variety of color and black-and-white production and publicity photos. There is also a collection of theatrical trailers and TV spots.

The Presentation *The Princess Bride* is a lush and misty-looking epic, all the better to stir romantic longing and memories of movies past. This 1.85:1 anamorphic widescreen transfer, remastered especially for the DVD release, is appropriately a bit soft. But colors are rich and pure, and detail, if slightly obscured by the heavy use of filters, is ample. Blacks are also rock solid, and there is no apparent edge enhancement or compression artifacts. Mark Knopfler's dated and cheesy synth score has not aged well, but this Dolby Digital 5.1 remix is nicely done. Surround use is somewhat sedate but consistently engaging. Dialogue is warmly reproduced and the effects have a rich, lush sound.

Additional Versions MGM Home Entertainment's original 2000 movie-only release of *The Princess Bride* remains on the market at a reduced price. However, it suffers from an inferior non-anamorphic transfer, which does not make it a bargain even at a discount.

The Producers

DISTRIBUTOR: MGM Home Entertainment
DVD RELEASE: December 3, 2002
THEATRICAL RELEASE: March 1968
RUNNING TIME: 90 Minutes
MPAA RATING: PG

Beginning his career in the early 1950s as a staff writer on *Your Show of Shows,* starring Sid Caesar and Imogene Coca, Mel Brooks created some of the series's most enduring characters and quickly earned a reputation as one of the top comedy writers in the business. Seeking more public recognition, he teamed up with Carl Reiner for a popular stand-up act, directed the prize-winning animated short *The Critic,* and then cowrote, with *The Graduate*'s Buck Henry, the 1960s spy spoof series *Get Smart.* But it was not until 1968's *The Producers* that Brooks finally had the breakthrough success he was craving; the film was an enormous hit, earned multiple Oscar nominations including Best Picture, and snagged him a statuette for Best Original Screenplay.

The Producers has a great premise. Hack Broadway producers Max Bialystock (Zero Mostel) and Leo Bloom (Gene Wilder) are so desperate for money that they hatch a seemingly foolproof scheme: they'll find backers for a show they know will flop so they can pocket the investment money. So these two Jewish producers create a musical called *Springtime for Hitler: A Gay Romp with Adolf and Eva in Berchtesgarten.* Brooks has always been one to cross the boundaries of good taste if it means getting a laugh, from the infamous "flatulence scene" in *Blazing Saddles* to the nonstop mocking of religious doctrine in *History of the World Part I.* In *The Producers,* he is lampooning the lengths to which anyone will go (whether in the theater, or by extension, Hollywood) to make a buck and, more important, achieve fame and respect.

Some find Brooks's do-anything-for-a-laugh brand of humor too lowbrow, but *The Producers* is still one of the most consistently laugh-out-loud hilarious comedies ever made. Mostel and especially Wilder are absolutely inspired as Bialystock and Bloom. They bring a camaraderie and unbridled energy to their pathetic characters. Some read their affection as homoerotic, but it is more paternal; the father of the pair (Bialystock) will teach the son (Bloom) the manipulative and shameless ways of the world.

MAX BIALYSTOCK: "How can you take the last penny out of a poor man's hand?"

THE LANDLORD: "I have to. I'm a landlord."

The climax is one of the great bonding scenes in movie history. And Brooks lets Wilder play it to the hilt—the more hysterical he gets the more we laugh—and the combination of such over-the-top but sweet-natured lunacy and the burlesque of *Springtime for Hitler* makes for a winning chemistry.

It is a shame Brooks chose to forgo writing more original scripts in the latter half of his career, instead turning to uninspired spoofs and movie parodies, like the forgettable *Dracula: Dead and Loving It, Robin Hood: Men in Tights* and the overrated *Spaceballs*. Because *The Producers* is the epitome of over-the-top comedic silliness. It is no more politically correct today than it was in 1968 and has enough jokes to fill ten other comedies combined. It is Brooks's best, most fully realized work.

The Goodies *The Producers* may not benefit from the most generous array of supplements ever assembled for a DVD, but with comedy one of the more underrepresented genres on the format, it ends up being one of the best DVDs of its kind.

The real gem of this set is the sixty-minute documentary "The Making of *The Producers*," produced, written and directed by Laurent Bouzereau. (No, the title is not inspired, but its execution is.) Structured like a two-act Broadway play, complete with curtain call, the documentary makes it a pure joy to revisit this landmark comedy. Most of the key cast and crew return to recount the often arduous task of making people laugh. Anyone who thinks the funny business is an easy business hasn't heard Brooks describe the process of successfully staging *Springtime for Hitler*. Wilder, Kenneth Mars, Andreas Voutsinas and Lee Meredith join most of the crew in recalling Brooks's unflagging energy and providing a sweet curtain call for the late Zero Mostel. While the intermission dance number with Meredith doesn't click, "The Making of *The Producers*" is an otherwise snappy, jazzy sixty minutes that feels like six.

Also unearthed are a number of rare or never-before-seen archival finds, including the "Playhouse Outtake" deleted scene long sought after by fans, and Paul Mazurzky reading "A Statement from Peter Sellars." The actor dropped out of the film on the eve of the first day of shooting but eventually praised the film. Other extras include an animated sketch gallery, another gallery with nearly fifty publicity and rare production stills, and the film's badly dated theatrical trailer.

The Presentation Suffering for years on video in poor, washed-out pan-and-scan transfers, here *The Producers* can be seen in its original 1.85:1 theatrical aspect ratio. (A 4:3 full-screen version is also included on the flipside of the disc.) Nicely restored with little grain and fuzziness, the film now looks colorful, bold and sharp. Underrated as a technical achievement, the show-within-a-show is a marvel of staging, choreography and design, its cinematic grandeur at last opened up to widescreen dimensions. The included Dolby Digital 5.1 surround remix is not so special; with limited material to work with (the film's original mono soundtrack is also included), any sense of envelopment is sparse, but the basics of the soundtrack—dialogue, music and score—come through cleanly and clearly.

Psycho

DISTRIBUTOR: Universal Studios Home Video

DVD RELEASE: May 27, 1998

THEATRICAL RELEASE: March 1960

RUNNING TIME: 109 Minutes

MPAA RATING: R

They say a boy's best friend is his mother, but there has never been a mother quite like Mama Bates in *Psycho*. Alfred Hitchcock's landmark thriller remains his most popular, well-known and oft-imitated film. It is, save perhaps for *The Birds* (1962), his only out-and-out horror movie and the granddaddy of the modern slasher. Decades of imitators regurgitated its basic elements (naked girl, long knife, fake blood) but with none of Hitch's mastery of suspense and keen understanding of how to completely unnerve the audience. Time may have diluted some of its shocks and surprises—does anyone not know the film's then-revolutionary twist ending?—but *Psycho* is still a thoroughly terrifying, emotionally paralyzing experience.

Hitchcock begins *Psycho* with a typically Hitchcockian conceit: the innocent turned criminal, caught in a web of guilt and deceit, who must eventually be punished. Marion Crane (Janet Leigh), a "typical bourgeois woman" according to Hitch, steals $40,000, makes a series of foolish choices, and ends up at the Bates Motel. Hitchcock then uses our identifi-

> "We all go a little mad sometimes."
>
> —Norman Bates

cation with Marion to deliver a sucker punch—has a heroine ever been murdered halfway through a major American motion pic-ture?—yet still won't let us off the hook. Working off of scribe Joseph Stefano's excellent screenplay (based on his novel), he lets us live in Marion's world and experience what she sees and feels, so that by the time she meets Norman, we have come to see her as a real person, not a victim. Which makes her death not just shocking, but tragic. And Hitch is extremely clever (and deliciously manipulative) by clearly linking Marion's repressed guilt with that of Norman's.

They are two halves of the same whole: when they meet, it is not accident but destiny—the doomed have come home at last. And there is never a cleansing shower in hell.

There would certainly be no *Psycho* without Hitchcock, but it would not be a classic without Anthony Perkins. His performance is one of the most complete inhabitations of a character in screen history; it is impossible to imagine a more perfect fit of an actor and a role. (Perkins became so identified with Norman in the public's mind that, like a boy trapped under the thumb of his dominating mother, he could not escape being typecast.) He makes Norman immensely likable but drops subtle clues throughout as to the extent of his madness. When the mystery is finally solved and the madman revealed, we don't feel cheated or angry at being manipulated but revel in the pleasure of its inevitability—we realize Hitchcock and Perkins had tipped us off all along.

Psycho has all the hallmarks of a cheap exploitation film. It was shot quickly on the back lots of Universal Studios, in black-and-white, and with a budget of only $800,000 (inexpensive even by 1960 standards). And it was marketed like a cheap potboiler, complete with a brilliant carny-trick trailer (featuring Hitch taking us on guided tour of the Bates house). But *Psycho* strictly adheres to the basic tenet of all great horror movies: it is not what we see but what we think we see that is always the most terrifying. The film's legendary shower scene is a masterpiece of audience manipulation and misdirection. A rapid montage of shocking juxtapositions, the knife is never seen striking flesh; there is blood—only a little—but no gore. The scene has been analyzed and dissected frame by frame for decades, yet still people insist they saw more than they actually did. By the time we get to the climax and Vera Miles's audience-paralyzing tour of the Bates house, Hitchcock has kept us so completely off balance we don't know what to expect next. In *Psycho,* Hitchcock didn't just create one of the scariest movies of all time, he raised the B-movie to the level of art.

The Goodies *Psycho* has received a bloody good special edition courtesy of Universal Studios Home Video. In sharp contrast to its subject matter, the sixty-minute "The Making of *Psycho*" is sentimental and poignant. With the passing of both Hitch and Perkins, documentarian Laurent Bouzereau reassembled most of the film's surviving cast and crew, including Leigh, Stefano, assistant director Hilton Green and Hitch's daughter, Patricia Hitchcock O'Connell. Stefano is frank about the struggles in working with Hitchcock and bringing the material to the screen under the strict censorship guidelines of the production code. (The most controversial shot? Leigh flushing a toilet.) Leigh also candidly rebukes the accusation that Hitchcock was a technical director with little regard for the actor, and her memories of shooting the shower sequence are deftly intercut with storyboards and rarely seen stills. And all contribute fond, highly emotional remembrances of Perkins, in a role that so typecast him he was never able to surpass it. A superior documentary.

A rare deleted scene, too controversial to get past the censors in 1960, now seems tame but remains a fascinating example of shifting tastes and mores. The highly influential shower sequence is presented with and without music, further illustrating Hermann's essential contributions to *Psycho*'s impact. There is also a top-notch still gallery with over 250 images, including storyboards and production drawings by Hitch to construct many of the film's best-known sequences, a series of publicity and production photos, and a wealth of ad materials including abandoned concepts. A separate gallery features more promotional materials including newsreels and the film's famous trailer. And in a great touch, Hermann's score is presented nearly in its entirety as underscore, over both the menus and the still-based supplemental features.

The Presentation Presented in its original 1.85:1 matted theatrical aspect ratio but not anamorphically encoded, *Psycho* is still in need of a major restoration. It is not a bad transfer: blacks are generally pure and consistent, and the print, while somewhat grainy, boasts solid detail. But there are frequent scratches and obvious patches of dirt, darker scenes can be murky and there is some edginess that gives the image an artificial feel. The film's original mono soundtrack is reproduced here with no remix; source materials have been cleaned up and don't suffer from such defects as hiss or dropouts, but the track still sounds dated. Mother could have used a touch of work . . .

Additional Recommendations *Psycho* begat three sequels: 1983's *Psycho II, Psycho III* (1986) and the direct-to-cable *Psycho IV: The Beginning* (1992), all starring Perkins. All but *The Beginning* have been released on DVD. For more Hitchcock horror, recommended are top-flight special editions of such classics as *The Birds* (1962), *The Trouble with Harry,* the disturbing *Frenzy* (1972), *Strangers on a Train* (1945) and the audacious *Rope* (1958), each of which includes a new in-depth documentary by Bouzereau. The famous auteur's excellent anthology series *Alfred Hitchcock Presents* (1960–1963) is also available in a box set of Hitch classics from Universal Studios Home Entertainment.

Pulp Fiction

DISTRIBUTOR: Buena Vista Home Entertainment
DVD RELEASE: August 20, 2002
THEATRICAL RELEASE: October 1994
RUNNING TIME: 154 Minutes
MPAA RATING: R

P*ulp Fiction,* Quentin Tarantino's best film, is arguably the most important motion picture of the 1990s. It won the grand prize at Cannes, the Palme d'Or, then went on to gross $100 million at the domestic box office, top every critic's ten best list and earn six Academy Award nominations including Best Picture (and a Best Original Screenplay trophy for Tarantino and co-screenwriter Roger Avary). Tarantino, the ultimate movie geek made good, wrote his first film, *Reservoir Dogs* (1992) while working at a video store. It became a runaway cult hit and paved the way for the more ambitious *Fiction*. Both films reveal the sensibility of a kid let loose inside a candy store. In *Fiction*, he begged and borrowed not just from the cinema, but also from television, music, art and the dime-store paperbacks that give his most famous film its title.

Screenwriter Joe Eszterhas—he wrote *Basic Instinct* and *Showgirls*—called Tarantino's filmmaking "masturbatory," but in *Pulp Fiction* all of the mise-en-scene means something. Tarantino is nothing if not methodical. His characters speak in whimsical half-phrases and long soliloquies, but not a single word is wasted; every line is carefully constructed to reveal character, hint at theme or set up a payoff. His ear for the natural way people talk, infused with a heightened theatricality and peppered by nonstop pop-culture references, is the still the most oft-imitated dialogue style in today's cinema. Equally famous is his circular story structure, which doubles back onto itself and is inherently self-referential; if it didn't quite create a whole new language for the medium, then it did significantly expand its lexicon. *Pulp Fiction*'s popular success gave the independent scene a whole new sandbox to play in, the pleasures of toying with chronology, structure and audience expectation influencing films as diverse as *The Usual Suspects, Memento* and *The Sixth Sense,* and the entire oeuvre of New Jersey native Kevin Smith.

> "That's a pretty fucking good milkshake. I don't know if it's worth $5, but it's pretty fucking good."
> —Vincent Vega

Pulp Fiction has been roundly criticized for being violent and bloody, which it is. But while Tarantino is more visceral and graphic than Alfred Hitchcock, he hasn't forgotten the lessons taught by the masters. Tarantino cleverly uses cutaways, long shots and reversals to trick us into thinking we see more gore than we actually do. And his gallows sense of humor turns even the most repugnant scenes into hilarious, pitch-black comedy. After hitmen Jules and Vincent (Samuel L. Jackson and John Travolta) inadvertently kill a passenger in the backseat of their car, their matter-of-fact-ness is what makes it so funny. Tarantino purees other scenes in his pop-culture blender and out comes everything from light romantic comedy (the sweet-natured dialogue scenes between Butch (Bruce Willis) and Fabienne (Maria de Medeiros) to retro-musical (the famous "Jackrabbit Slim's" dance number with Travolta and Uma Thurman).

Pulp Fiction is a pop-culture milestone, a movie now impervious to dissenting opinion. Like all the classics, love it or hate it, you cannot forget it. And its unconventional structure assures that every time you see it, you won't be able to remember what comes next. Tarantino remarked that he intended his film to be like those old pulp magazines, disposable entertainments that were cheap, fast and compulsively readable. What he intended to be a throwaway instead became indispensable.

The Goodies He has been called the ultimate film geek, but Quentin Tarantino took a considerable while to fully embrace DVD. At last released as a two-disc special edition in August 2002, this terrific set for *Pulp Fiction* was well worth the wait.

The biggest surprise: Tarantino actually turned *down* an opportunity to talk and there is no audio commentary. But just about everything else is here. An enhanced "Trivia Track" is a stream of subtitles with a barrage of information, from the deep to the dumbfounding, that is almost the equivalent of a Tarantino commentary. The "Soundtrack Chapters" may promise more than it delivers; it is not an isolated score, but rather a unique navigation tool that allows you to directly access the film's key songs, complete with dialogue and sound effects intact.

Disc two presents the majority of the supplements. The thirty-minute "*Pulp Fiction*: The Facts," is a sharp chronicle of not just *Fiction* but Tarantino's road to Miramax and the funding of the film. "Behind-The-Scenes Montages" provides a better look at the actual production. Two Hi-8 video montages show Tarantino at work directing two key sequences, "Jack Rabbit Slim's" (4:44) and "Butch Hits Marsellus" (6:02), while the "Production Design Featurette" runs six minutes and is primarily an interview with production designer David Wasco and set decorator Sandy Reynolds-Wasco. Tarantino's interview for *The Charlie Rose Show* is also included in its entirety and runs sixty minutes.

More supplements include a very thorough still gallery that packages the requisite publicity and production photos with extensive text reviews, essays and articles. The five deleted scenes all come with rather bizarre introductions by Tarantino, who himself admits that they were wisely excised from the final film. Then there are further excerpts from a *Siskel & Ebert* episode, the "Tarantino Generation," plus interview footage with famed documentarian Michael Moore recorded at the Independent Spirit Awards, and Tarantino's legendary, rowdy Palme d'Or acceptance speech at Cannes.

A cut above is the fine assortment of ROM extras. "The Screenplay Viewer" allows you to leaf through the shooting script of the film with direct scene access, while "Jack Rabbit Slim's Trivia Contest" is a surprisingly challenging pop quiz that asks just how tasty your burger really is. And the "Open Mic Commentary" is great, silly fun, where you can record your own audio commentary for select scenes in the film.

The Presentation Originally released on DVD in a lackluster movie-only, nonanamorphic edition, Buena Vista Home Entertainment reissued *Pulp Fiction* with this very strong 2.35:1 anamorphic widescreen transfer. Andrzej Sekula's cinematography is often as lurid and rich as the dime-store paperbacks of *Pulp Fiction*'s title. Hues are reproduced with great vibrancy, especially the deep reds and sun-drenched exteriors. Detail is generally above average, and blacks very deep. The one drawback is some noticeable edginess that gives the film an artificial appearance. Even better are the Dolby Digital and DTS 5.1 soundtracks, which pack a shotgun's worth of punch. *Pulp Fiction* was a moderately budgeted movie and sounds far better here than expected. Surround use is active if reserved only for the effects; however, Tarantino's relentless use of songs is inspired and helps open up the soundstage. Dialogue is accurately reproduced, essential for a film with one of the best screenplays of the past couple of decades.

Additional Recommendations All of Quentin Tarantino's films have been released on DVD, most as two-disc special editions, including *Reservoir Dogs* (1992), *Jackie Brown* (1997), each of which contain a wealth of extras that rival the depth of *Fiction,* and *Kill Bill Vol. 1 and Vol. 2* (2003 and 2004).

Rebecca

DISTRIBUTOR: The Criterion Collection

DVD RELEASE: November 20, 2001

THEATRICAL RELEASE: March 1940

RUNNING TIME: 130 Minutes

MPAA RATING: Not Rated

You could put any film by Alfred Hitchcock on the list of great thrillers, but *Rebecca* is the oddest bedfellow. It is an uneven film: part mystery, part thriller, part romance, and one of the few by Hitchcock that, if not overtly melodramatic, flirts with the gothic and sentimental. Which is what makes it so fascinating; in a career as close to perfection as is imaginable (has any filmmaker ever made so many memorable films?) it is the ugly duckling, intriguing because of its lack of polish and lack of cohesion. That it would become Hitch's only film to win the Oscar for Best Picture is some kind of surreal vindication.

> "Last night I dreamed I went to Manderlay again . . ."
>
> —Mrs. de Winter

At the heart of *Rebecca* is a mystery that will never be solved, a woman we will never meet. Hitchcock's film is about doubles, reversals and haunted reflections. There are two Mrs. de Winters, both wives to George Fortescu Maximillian de Winter (Laurence Olivier), a wealthy entrepreneur. Rebecca, the first wife, died in a boating accident a year prior to the film's start; the film's protagonist (Joan Fontaine), whose name is never revealed, has newly arrived in Monte Carlo and soon becomes the second Mrs. de Winter. She believes her dreams have come true, and the newlyweds return to Manderlay, husband Maxim's large country estate in Cornwall. There, the second Mrs. de Winter meets the housekeeper Mrs. Danvers (Judith Anderson) and begins to sense that all is not as it seems. Something is haunting Manderlay, and Maxim. Only when the mystery surrounding Rebecca's violent death are revealed can the second Mrs. de Winter be truly set free from the shackles of following Maxim's first wife.

One of the magical qualities of any Hitchcock film is that it will allude to so much but reveal very little. He is at his most elliptical in *Rebecca*. The film has been criticized as a victim of the stringent censorship of the time, preventing Hitchcock from fully expressing the film's themes and hidden relationships and draining it of the high tension we have come to expect of his best thrillers. The scenes between Fontaine and her employer (Edythe van Hopp) in the beginning passages of the film hint at a lesbian relationship, which is never further explored. Furthering the lesbian subtext is the true nature of Mrs. Danvers's obsession with Rebecca, which is never clarified (although possibly to the film's benefit), and the shift in focus from Fontaine to Olivier in the last third is abrupt. But *Rebecca* continues to haunt because all of its puzzle pieces don't quite fit. It hints at meanings that, like its title character, are never fully portrayed. Which makes it Hitchcock's most cryptic, unique thriller.

The Goodies The Criterion Collection has produced an absolutely lavish two-disc set for *Rebecca* that is one of the most in-depth and comprehensive ever created for a film of its era. Film scholar Leonard Leff's audio commentary traces Hitchcock's career leading up to *Rebecca* (his first major Hollywood production), the film's long shoot and its subsequent box office and Oscar success. It is both analytical and colloquial, but not dry and scholarly. An additional audio track features Franz Waxman's haunting score and the film's effects isolated in mono.

Criterion has arranged the rest of the supplements in three parts and in a manner as intriguing as the film's narrative. "Dreams" traces the more literary elements of the film: "Dreaming of Manderlay" is an investigation of the inspiration for the film's creepy fictional manor, and "Locations Research" is a collection of photos of potential candidates for the mansion; "Picturization of a Celebrated Novel" compares Daphne du Maurier's novel and the final screenplay, while "We Intend to Make *Rebecca*" concentrates on producer David O. Selznick's intentions to stay true to du Maurier; "The Search for 'I' " compiles text correspondence between Selznick and Hitchcock on the casting; and "Screen Tests for 'I'," "Lighting and

Makeup Tests" and "Costume Tests" compile rare video footage shot during preproduction.

"Fruition" moves on to the production. Three sets of stills—"Memos from DOS," "A Curious Slanting Hand" and "Set Stills; Picture No. 110, *Rebecca*"—examine everything from Fontaine's handwriting to wardrobe and makeup tests. Fascinating is footage from various test screenings that considerably shaped the final cut of *Rebecca* in "How Did You Like the Picture," and a deleted scene is also included, accompanied by another Selznick memo insisting the sequence be cut.

"Ballyhoo" chronicles the film's positive reception and ultimate Oscar victory. "Passion! Frustration! Mystery!" is an amusing array of publicity materials, including the theatrical and reissue trailers, silent newsreel footage of the Oscar win, and the eight-minute, audio-only "Hitchcock on *Rebecca*," a rare vintage interview with the auteur. Leff also conducted phone interviews with Fontaine and Anderson in 1986 that are presented here in their entirety and are mesmerizing. Even more audio material includes three full-length radio adaptations of *Rebecca*, the best of which is Orson Welles's 1938 Mercury Theater version starring Margaret Sullivan, while a 1950 Lux Radio Theater presentation has Olivier returning to the role of Maximillian.

An excellent twenty-two-page booklet completes the stunning set, with notes by historians Robin Wood and George Turner.

The Presentation *Rebecca* looks magnificent. Criterion has struck a near-pristine new print that is sparkling. George Barnes's photography is luminous, with deep blacks, lovely, subtle shades of gray and a richly detailed, very filmlike appearance. Criterion has also restored the film's original mono source elements, which still suffer from a dated sound but no major defects such as hiss, distortion or dropouts. *Rebecca* is a haunting masterpiece that looks positively regal here.

Additional Versions Anchor Bay Entertainment has also released a movie-only version of *Rebecca* that suffers greatly by comparison. It remains in print, but the transfer is sub par and there are no extras. The Criterion version is vastly superior.

The Red Shoes

DISTRIBUTOR: The Criterion Collection
DVD RELEASE: May 25, 1999
THEATRICAL RELEASE: April 1946
RUNNING TIME: 133 Minutes
MPAA RATING: Not Rated

An oddity in an era of great renown for the British film industry, *The Red Shoes* was a bust in its home country but went on to break box office records in the United States. It won three Academy Awards in 1946 including Best Foreign Film, earned rapturous acclaim from critics worldwide as the start of a new form of musical, bridged the gap between avid moviegoers and highbrow artists who previously scorned motion pictures *and* inspired a generation of young girls to become dancers. That the British public was immune to its charms seems strange in hindsight but was the only blemish in an otherwise Cinderella-like success story. But then *The Red Shoes* was no ordinary fairy tale.

In 1935 Emeric Pressburger, a recent expatriate from Germany living in England, wrote a surrealist tale, loosely inspired by the Hans Christian Andersen classic, about Vicky (Moira Shearer), who dreams of being a dancer, is discovered by Boris Lermontov (Anton Walbrook), performs to great success and meets with an ultimately tragic fate. Pressburger was unable to attract interest in his unusual, genre-busting musical; it would be a decade until he resurrected the project as an ideal vehicle for his partner Michael Powell, who had become a darling of the British cinema after such hits as *One of Our Aircraft Is Missing* (1942), *The Life and Death of Colonel Blimp* (1943) and *I Know Where I'm Going* (1945). Powell, who had long enjoyed combining two seemingly opposing forms, proved to be the ideal director for *The Red Shoes*. Pressburger's screenplay was a marriage of realism/fantasy and whimsy/grim fatalism that had never before been attempted, as much a meditation on art and the musical form as it was a story inspired by the straight-ahead melodrama of the Bubsy Berkeley extravaganzas popularized during the era. It was the right

BORIS LERMONTOV: "What do you want from life, to live?"
VICTORIA POSE: "To dance."

film for the right time, tapping into the growing dissatisfaction of audiences with the increasingly banal, pure fantasies Hollywood was churning out, despite the growing realities of World War II.

The Red Shoes revolutionized the musical by bridging a highbrow art form—ballet—with a lowbrow medium that had not yet achieved legitimacy, the popular Hollywood musical. Its dance sequences, especially the amazing ten-minute "The Ballet of the Red Shoes" that forms the centerpiece of the film, are as delightful as its second half is bleak. Moira's discovery at the hands of Boris echoes the story of Pygmalion. She eventually falls in love with composer Julian (Marius Goring), but her love of all three—Julian, Boris, the dance—can never truly coexist.

Some critics found Pressburger and Powell's mix of fantasy and realism too inconsistent—Moira appears to be a magical princess in flowing gown and tiara, about to live out her fairy tale, which does not prepare us for what is to come. Jack Cardiff's highly stylized photography also leads us to believe that we are watching a movie about the magic of dance rather than a traditional narrative that does not call attention to its own artifice. The film's concluding scenes are indeed hard to watch, as Vicky's world collapses around her. Some were outraged at what they perceived to be Powell and Pressburger's nihilism and refusal to let the audience have a happy ending. But it is this emotional frisson that won *The Red Shoes* such a passionate response and continues to make the musical the most ornate, intelligent film of its kind ever made.

The Goodies After the disastrous reception of Powell's *Peeping Tom* in 1960, the filmmaker was all but blacklisted in his home country. It wasn't until the subsequent two decades, with great help from Francis Ford Coppola and Martin Scorsese, that the auteur enjoyed a rebirth. *The Red Shoes* was the first of Powell's films to receive a lavish restoration and theatrical rerelease. The film's legacy continues to reverberate generations later, cited as a major influence on filmmakers as diverse as Baz Luhrmann (*Moulin Rouge!*), Lars Von Trier (the highly similar *Dancer in the Dark*) and McG (who reportedly studied the formalism of *The Red Shoes* in constructing the balletic action of the *Charlie's Angels* films). To give this classic its proper due, The Criterion Collection originally released *The Red Shoes* on laserdisc in the early 1990s and then reissued it on DVD in the spring of 1999. It is an unusual release, with a collection of supplements that is by turns strange and surreal, but like *The Red Shoes* itself, it is often magical.

The main supplements are almost all audio-based, which at first seems strange for a film so renowned for its visuals. But what a fine commentary we get here: film historian Ian Christies hosts a wonderful collection of observations from Shearer, Goring, Cardiff, composer Brian Easdale and Scorsese himself. All aspects of the production are covered, from conception to filming. Created from the storyboards of artist Hein Heckroth, *The Red Shoes Sketches* is an animated short film that uses the multi-angle function and original underscore to present different versions of final scenes—a wholly unique and invigorating way to dissect the film's one-of-a-kind visual style. Even more inventively, actor Jeremy Irons contributes a second audio track, reading excerpts from Pressburger's screenplay and selected sections of the original Hans Christian Andersen fairy tale.

Scorsese contributes his own collection of memorabilia, along with an extensive still gallery with additional production stills and publicity materials. The Powell and Pressburger interactive filmography with film clips and stills is far more extensive than the pithy type usually found on a DVD; and a liner essay in the included full-color booklet rounds out the package.

The Presentation It cannot be denied that *The Red Shoes* is a visual masterpiece, and this is as gorgeous a transfer as you are likely to see. By presenting the film in its original 1.37:1 theatrical aspect ratio, Criterion has done full justice to the vision of Powell and Cardiff. Colors are rich, clean and bold—images literally dance off of the screen. The print, marred only by a slight grain and a few instances of dirt and dropouts, is wonderfully filmlike. Criterion has been able to restore the film to such a degree that it appears nearly three-dimensional and worth studying frame by frame. The restored mono soundtrack, however, is a bit of a disappointment, if only because this is a film that cries out for a surround remix. One must respect Criterion's refusal to "upgrade" vintage films with gimmicky digital processing and other tricks but *The Red Shoes* would have been the film for which to make an exception with at least an optional surround remix. Otherwise, this is a sharp mono track with a fairly warm sound and clear, clean dialogue reproduction.

The Right Stuff

DISTRIBUTOR: Warner Home Video
DVD RELEASE: June 10, 2003
THEATRICAL RELEASE: September 1983
RUNNING TIME: 193 Minutes
MPAA RATING: PG

Upon its release in 1983, Philip Kaufman's *The Right Stuff* was greeted with a sense of excitement and hope so intense it was more befitting a moon landing than a motion picture. Critics hailed it as a new American masterpiece, the film that would fully capture the best of Tom Wolfe's bestselling 1979 book about the early days of the space program and the private lives of its most famous astronauts, the "Mercury Seven." But despite eight Academy Award nominations including Best Picture (it won four, all technical), it was a box office flop; its failure to "punch a hole in the sky" is still one of the more curious in recent American cinematic history.

At the heart of Kaufman's film is Chuck Yeager (Sam Shepherd), widely considered the greatest test pilot in history. He is a man of deeds, not words. His belief in the nobility of flight, of adventure, of progress, outweighed any risk to his own safety and, to many, exceeded the bounds of common sense. His principles fueled the space program's public relations machine. For the United States government, appalled at being upstaged by the Russians' Sputnik, it was a matter of national urgency to "sell" the American people on the necessity of the program, no matter what the costs, financial or human.

The Right Stuff honors Yeager and the Mercury Seven, but there is a satire rumbling underneath the soaring romanticism and seemingly straitlaced patriotism; the film's many humorous scenes came under fire from detractors who did not want to see the space program's policies and overriding purpose questioned. Kaufman is unflinching in his critique of a machine that was transformed from a noble military program into a public relations coup. Reporters at the early space flights were turned away; by the end of the Mercury program, launches would routinely preempt all television broadcasts. But Yeager's ultimate victory—breaking the sound barrier—would be more than a just a "stunt." It was the preamble to the space program's ultimate victory, the 1969 moon landing.

> "I, for one, do not intend to go to sleep by the light of a Communist moon."
>
> —Vice President Lyndon Johnson

The Right Stuff is a film of astonishing authenticity, and now, in the shadow of the *Challenger* and *Columbia* disasters, an all-too-real reminder of the human costs of space exploration. Wolfe lived with *Mercury 7* astronauts, absorbed their culture and lingo, and realized the inherent contradiction of their existence—despite loving families and the comforts of home and heart, they were only truly alive for those brief, magical moments up there in the heavens, looking down far below at their now infinitesimally small world. Only by accepting their own insignificance could the pilots achieve transcendence. But the most wrenching scenes of *The Right Stuff* depict the struggles played out on the home front, as wives and families deal with the reality that every time a pilot tests a new plane, he has a one in four chance of dying. (A wife, just having arrived, asks how her husband can get his photo on the wall. The answer? He has to die.)

The Right Stuff is her monument, and a reminder that the courage of the heroes up there was equaled by that of those left behind.

The Goodies The journey of *The Right Stuff* from page to screen was not an easy one. Kaufman chose not to tell his story as a straightforward, "factual" account of the birth of NASA. The film's original scripter, William Goldman, publicly complained about "nightmarish" meetings with Kaufman, and bowed out of the project. The film's final screenplay bore Kaufman's name only. Wolfe, however, was pleased with the final product, as is evidenced in the wealth of supplemental features offered on this two-disc set. It is a story as exciting and dramatic as *The Right Stuff* itself.

Rather than a single, full-length audio commentary, Warner Home Video has produced an intriguing conceit: two commentaries for select scenes only, assembled from audio interviews with the cast (including Jeff Goldblum, Veronica Cartwright, Scott Glenn, Ed Harris, Dennis Quaid and Barbara Hershey) and the filmmakers (Kaufman, producers Irwin Winkler and Robert Chartoff, and cinematographer Caleb Deschanel). Likely the disparate nature of the recorded comments necessitated this unique approach, but it works wonderfully. There is no wasted space, quality replacing quantity. Kaufman and especially the cast are quite articulate about all aspects of the production.

The eighty-six-minute PBS documentary *John Glenn: American Hero* and the newly produced fifteen-minute featurette "The Real Men of *The Right Stuff*" provide the necessary historical background, while two exclusive featurettes, "Realizing the Right Stuff" and "T-20 Years and Counting," delve into the making of the film. Analyzed are the film's casting, lengthy production shoot, the amazing special effects—despite the absence of computer-generated effects, never has space travel felt so real—and, fascinatingly, the initially muted reaction to the film. *The Right Stuff* is truly a movie that was rediscovered on home video, but it is not fair to merely label it a "cult classic"—it is far too big for that. Which makes it all the more essential a DVD experience.

Other extras include ten minutes of additional scenes that are largely superfluous, an "Interactive Timeline to Space" that includes video highlights from fourteen important dates in history, and the film's theatrical trailer.

The Presentation *The Right Stuff* is a film of true majesty and one of the underrated visual achievements of the 1980s. Deschanel's Oscar-nominated cinematography simply soars here in this newly remastered, 1.85:1 anamorphic widescreen transfer. This restoration is superb—a pristine print with rock solid blacks and lush, vivid colors. The cool blues and crisp whites of space are eye-popping. Detail is often extraordinary, with a smooth, very filmlike appearance. And despite the movie's epic run time and extended static shots, compression artifacting is not a problem.

Also a winner is the Dolby Digital 5.1 remix. Surround use is highly aggressive, with wonderful pans all across the soundfield. The illusion is almost transparent, making the viewer feel as if they are up there with the astronauts; even Bill Conti's Oscar-winning score sounds as if it is another character, so expertly is it integrated into the mix. Exquisite.

Additional Versions Warner Home Video originally released *The Right Stuff* in 1999 as a "flipper," the movie spread across both sides of a DVD-14. The set also suffered from a poor transfer and lacked any supplemental features. It is now discontinued.

Rocky

DISTRIBUTOR: MGM Home Entertainment
DVD RELEASE: April 24, 2001
THEATRICAL RELEASE: November 1976
RUNNING TIME: 119 Minutes
MPAA RATING: PG

It's fitting that a movie about a no-name boxer, written by a no-name actor, would come out of nowhere to earn ten Oscar nominations. And in 1976, a year when the Best Picture Oscar nominees included *All the President's Men, Network* and *Taxi Driver,* it was *Rocky* that stole the coveted statuette as well as the hearts of the world.

When it came to making the film, *Rocky* was a noun and an adjective. In the early-1970s, Sylvester Stallone was a working actor, but his earlier appearances (*The Lords of Flatbush* and Woody Allen's *Bananas*) would only take on importance in the wake of *Rocky*'s success. After pitching the *Rocky* story to producers Irwin Winkler and Robert Chartoff, Stallone agreed to write the script for free in exchange for playing the lead role. So, with a budget of only $1 million and a shooting schedule of a paltry twenty-eight days, *Rocky* began filming on location in Philadelphia.

The story was a bundle of sports-movie clichés, but it didn't rely on those clichés to excite the audience. In the hands of Stallone's honest, unsparing script, clichés become universal truths. And universal truths become the foundation upon which to build the real story of Rocky: a man who not only learns to achieve but also realizes that the attempt is more important than the outcome. The fact that Rocky finds love, in the person of shy, pet-store employee Adrian (Talia Shire), is a cliché. The fact that he earns it by learning to respect himself is not. It's a character turn that is subtle, well earned and believable. At the beginning of the film, Rocky is a "ham-and-egger," a club fighter who'll take on anyone for a $50 purse. He lives in a disgusting apartment and works as an enforcer for a loan shark. Rocky Balboa is going nowhere slowly. But his fortunes change when heavyweight champ Apollo Creed (Carl Weathers) arranges a Bicentennial title fight that involves picking a nobody and giving him a shot at the champ. That nobody is Rocky.

> "Nobody's ever gone the distance with Creed. And if I can go that distance, seein' that bell ring and I'm still standing . . . I'm gonna know for the first time in my life that I wasn't just another bum from the neighborhood."
>
> —Rocky Balboa

Rocky accepts the challenge, but is consumed with self-doubt. His love for Adrian allows him to slowly, grudgingly come to believe he deserves this chance at success and happiness. That Rocky loses the title fight but wins his self-respect is an ending that today's studios, obsessed with opening weekend grosses and simple, neat conclusions, certainly would reject.

Stallone gets most of the credit for the success of the film, but the script would not have fulfilled its promise without director John Avildsen. His street-level approach is not afraid to be simple. Many set-ups are rudimentary lock-off shots, which became a necessity in a truncated schedule that did not allow time for multiple angles. Also, at the end of a scene, he's not afraid to linger where most directors would cut away. At times, Rocky sits motionless, assessing his fate, and these quiet moments allow us to share Rocky's doubts and insecurities.

The film includes a number of outstanding supporting performances: Shire avoids the ugly-duckling pitfalls of her character and truly makes Adrian her own. Burgess Meredith is hard-headed and heartbreaking as Rocky's manager. The scene where he visits Rocky's apartment, hat in hand, to ask if he can be his manager is a classic. And Burt Young is at once brutish and pathetic as Adrian's brother.

After *Rocky,* Stallone starred in four increasingly ridiculous sequels and the Rambo series, which only added to his thick-headed persona. Although history threatens to remember Stallone more for his bad films than his good, it cannot be forgotten that Rocky Balboa is one of the great screen creations and *Rocky* is a great film.

The Goodies *Rocky* finally gets the digital respect it deserves as MGM provides an instructive array of supplements. First is a terrific scene-specific audio commentary from director Avildsen, producers Winkler and Chartoff and actors Young and Shire. Many of the participants were recorded separately and edited together onto one track. However, the result is absolutely seamless and full of interesting tidbits.

While a Stallone audio commentary is not in the offing, we get a surprisingly fascinating "Video Commentary," a twenty-eight-minute interview with the man behind *Rocky,* interspersed with clips. Stallone tells his story honestly, succinctly and with good humor, making the video commentary well worth a look.

Next are three worthwhile featurettes: "Behind the Scenes with Director John Avildsen" includes priceless 8mm footage of Stallone and Carl Weathers in fight training, and there are two tribute pieces, one to the great Burgess Meredith and the other to noted cinematographer James Crabe.

Finally, there is a collection of trailers for all the *Rocky* movies and a pleasant easter egg that features Rocky having a conversation with his creator, Sylvester Stallone.

The Presentation For *Rocky*'s twenty-fifth anniversary, MGM produced a new anamorphic transfer in the film's original aspect ratio of 1.85:1. The results, while acceptable, should have been better. Casual DVD viewers will be quite pleased, although more discerning fans will be mildly disappointed. Problems include print flaws, overall softness, light edge enhancements and grain. Much of this can be attributed to the original source material, a low-budget affair that often utilized very little lighting. Detail and contrast are good, while colors look a bit tired, although some of that is intentional and works to the film's advantage. Blacks and shadow detail are fair, while the climactic fight looks admirably crisp.

MGM has included the film's original mono soundtrack as well as the same Dolby Digital 5.1 remix from the previous DVD release. Although spreading the wealth among five speakers sounds intriguing, there's actually very little to go around. The film is mostly dialogue, with some crowd effects and music. Still, MGM did a nice job expanding the soundscape without making it sound gimmicky. The surrounds kick in occasionally, as when Rocky passes by a group of street singers. The crowd during the title fight also sounds fuller. Dialogue is always understandable, if not crystal clear.

Additional Versions MGM Home Entertainment initially released *Rocky* as a bare-bones, movie-only edition marred by a weak transfer. It has been discontinued and replaced by the 25th Anniversary Edition.

AUTOMAT FOR THE PEOPLE: A CONVERSATION WITH JEFFREY SCHWARZ

What started out as a one-man operation huddled around a kitchen table has quickly become one of the industry's top DVD production outfits. In 1999, Jeffrey Schwarz, with his lead producing partner Laura Nix, founded Automat Pictures, which is now a brand that studios and fans ask for by name. With an impressive resume that boasts over 100 titles, from the biggest blockbusters to the most eclectic cult classics, Automat has earned its reputation as the most original, daring and progressive house in the business.

With the DVD industry so competitive, most producers working today haven't been able to develop a recognizable and consistent style and approach. Yet Automat has been quickly able to establish itself as edgy, pioneering and diverse. Has this been by design or accident?

It's such a small world—there are some companies that specialize in certain genres but we have never really been typecast. When I first got started, I got a call from MGM and said, "We're doing *Spinal Tap* and we hear you're really good with comedies." I was like, "What are you talking about?" I think somebody called them and said, "Oh, this guy did *Something About Mary* and you should hire him because he's good at comedies." And now I'm getting calls for horror movies because we have done a lot of horror. But we have also done *When Harry Met Sally* and *The Princess Bride,* so you really cannot peg us down.

Automat has developed a very strong reputation as the house to go to when you want to do a genre or "cult" movie right.

When I was ten years old, I was obsessed with Universal horror monsters and I had no way to see those movies. This was pre-videos, pre-VHS. I would basically scan the *TV Guide* every week trying to find out when *Dracula* was on. Now kids today can buy the box set of Universal horror monsters and they'll get the movie, which is this incredible thing to have, but not only that, they'll get all of this extra stuff. If I had that when I was ten years old, I'd be in hog heaven.

Do you think the fact that most studio marketing data shows that the prime DVD audience is eighteen- to thirty-five-year-old males has helped play a role in your success?

When DVD first started, the genres that all the studios were dipping into for first releases were horror and sci-fi because they knew early on that this was going to be the audience that would be most supportive. Whatever market research they did was correct. And fans of these genres are really loyal and really devoted and really obsessive. I feel it's a different breed of audience. People who go out to watch a Julia Roberts movie aren't going to have that real personal connection to these movies.

How important a role does passion play in what you do? It seems as if you innately understand the prime demographic without even breaking a sweat.

The fact [that] I got to do a doc about *Friday the 13th* boggles my mind. I think it's an honor and I do not want to fuck it up. I think most producers feel the same way. If you asked me to make a documentary on *The Texas Chainsaw Massacre* tomorrow, I could just show up and start doing it without having to do any kind of research or anything. I'm a fan, too, and I can get into that headspace of what a fan might want on their DVDs. I make the DVDs I would want to buy. Hopefully that lends it an authenticity perhaps lacking in other, more impersonal fare.

Automat has also made a strong name for itself as a production house that will take chances and create featurettes that are more original and certainly out of the norm. How open have the studios been to some of your riskier ideas?

I'm really kind of surprised—studios come to us for ideas, because we are creative and we can come up with unique ideas that have not been done. For *Final Destination 2*, we did the "Terror Gauge" featurette, which is something that had never been done. We pitched this to the studio and they were very skeptical at first. We were able to convince them that [it] did have an element of showmanship to it, but it was actual science. So we made the piece and it turned out really well. And the thing that they were skeptical about is now in every single advertisement for the DVD—it's on TV sports, it's on the web ads.

That is a marketing choice that was made by the studio to push that aspect of the DVD, but that was a choice we proposed to them.

But basically we have to tell them what we think will help them sell more discs. That is what it comes down to. They pay the bills and they want to sell DVDs and we want to help them sell DVDs. That is what we do. I'm not under any illusions about that. It ain't art. If it is successful as a documentary, that is great. But I am realistic about the fact that studios look at it as a marketing tool.

On the technological side of things, do you feel like you need to shake up the standard ways of doing things with DVD?
I think the studios all want to give the impression that they are on the cutting edge of technology. You can do all kinds of bells and whistles, but if no one's going to watch it, or if it's too complicated or it seems like you're doing something just for the sake of doing it, people aren't really going to care.

Do you think your success with all types of films has trickled down into your budgets, especially on smaller cult titles that

studios before would not pay much attention to?
No. Actually, that is not true, because our budgets are dependent on the scope and size of the movies. Obviously for *Charlie's Angels: Full Throttle,* we're going to get a more generous budget than we're going to get for *The Tick.* All studios and movies are different. Some studios just get it. The people who usually hire us aren't people who make films or make documentaries. They are marketing people. They do not necessarily know the real-world cost of things. We're always having to fight for more money. Home video marketing is not a world that is familiar with those kinds of things. That is why you see a lot of very cheap, cheesy-looking DVD extras that we take great pains not to fall into. We have to do stuff on a budget, but we do not want it to look like it cost us $1.29 to do. Our work has to speak for itself.

What influence do you think legal has had on the way you approach DVD?
I think every producer has to learn to think like a studio lawyer. I learn new things every day about legal that I had no idea about. We had to clear a lot of the actors who

appear in the documentaries because they are not necessarily cleared for DVD. We have to clear screen tests; we have to clear all third-party materials we use. And that is why it is impossible for me to do things alone without a support staff. That is why I think a lot of the studios like us, because we're a team. We're not defensive about the legal ramifications of what we do. We feel like it is part of our job to do that. So we do.

How important do you think the future of connectivity and web interaction is in terms of DVD?

I do not know and I really do not care. (laughs) People are always going to watch movies. The DVD interactivity thing—I cannot get into consumers' mindsets. I feel like they might enjoy knowing it's there, but they might not necessarily use it. Interactivity is how your brain perceives a movie and how it affects you emotionally. That is the interactivity I'm interested in.

What are the biggest changes you've seen in the DVD industry over the past five years?

When a movie can make more in the first week of its DVD release than it makes in its entire theatrical run, that changes things. What

I've seen is that the penetration has reached the point where everyone you know has a DVD player and little eight-year-old kids are watching DVD extras and know how to push buttons and everything, and it changes the way people watch movies.

Everybody has a DVD player in their computer. When I started producing five years ago, I did not have a DVD player. I did not even know what it was. It's become such an incredible revenue stream for studios. The movie is just a trailer for the DVD, and that is a significant development. Every studio knows it, and you see just as much advertisement for the DVD release of a movie that you do for the actual theatrical release. And they are showing DVD trailers in movie theaters. When records turned into CDs—it's the same model.

Some have wondered if perhaps the clamoring for DVD and extras features is just a fad.

If you have a VHS player in your house and a bunch of crappy old tapes, you're not cool. People feel like they need to keep up. I do not think people are going to get nostalgic for VHS. Artisan can have a title like *The Running Man,* which is basically worthless on VHS—nobody wants it and nobody's going to go out and buy a new copy—but they can contract us to make a souped-up special edition of this, to be a generous, mediocre '80s action movie and everybody's going to want to buy it. It's like finding millions of dollars under the couch. That is essentially what they've discovered. It is basically a license to print money. As far as that aspect of the business, that is significantly changed.

I even think studios are starting to greenlight movies based on the fact that they'll look cool on DVD. *The League of Extraordinary Gentlemen*, *X-Men* and movies like that—those are DVD-ready movies. It's interesting—the kind of movies studios make are the ones they feel will have a long life on DVD, that they can release more than once, and that they can make events out of.

Where do you see DVD in five years?

I think that something else will come along and I'm going to have to sell all my damned DVDs on eBay, just like I did with my records and my VHS. Buyer beware! But people do not really have a right to complain when something better comes along because that is the nature of technology. And you will always still have to have a theatrical release. You can have a straight-to-DVD title, but it's never going to have the same recognition or excitement that a theatrical movie does, even if you only release it for a week.

This behind-the-scenes thing is nothing new. It's just having it all in one place that you can access easily—it might morph into something else. It all comes down to economics. [If] the studios figure they can make just as much money putting out a DVD without extras than with extras, they'll stop doing it. But they've found that they do sell more DVDs with them than without. It also enables them to release something more than once. It's not like they have a real vested interest in chronicling films or their studio history—they do not care about that. They want to be able to release a movie then release it again and release it again. The extras are the way to do that.

I think it is going to be the fans that speak the loudest. If the fans stop buying this stuff, then that is when enough will be enough. ○

The Rocky Horror Picture Show

DISTRIBUTOR: Fox Home Entertainment

DVD RELEASE: October 3, 2000

THEATRICAL RELEASE: September 1975

RUNNING TIME: 98 and 100 Minutes

MPAA RATING: R

The ultimate cult film, *The Rocky Horror Picture Show* is the movie that defined the term. It is the one and only film you absolutely *cannot* talk about without mentioning its legion of fans, a group so passionate, dedicated and just plain obsessed that they transformed an undistinguished little musical into a campy spectacular, the ultimate pre-postmodern multimedia event. There was no such thing as the audience participation movie before *The Rocky Horror Picture Show*; it was truly revolutionary—what should have been a movie no one remembered instead became a movie no one would ever forget.

Watching *Rocky Horror* at home can never compare to experiencing it in a theater with a crowd doing its damnedest to upstage what is on the screen. But what you *do* get when you sit down to watch this zany musical in the comfort of your own home is the luxury to appreciate just how good of a motion picture it really is. The music is great, the songs are im-

> "So come up to the lab and see what's on the slab. I see you shiver in antici . . . pation!"
>
> —Dr. Frank-N-Furter

possible not to sing along with and the wonderfully wacky story is assembled out of the best parts of every bad sci-fi, horror, crazy-scientist-assembles-ultimate-beefcake movie ever made. You'll even spot a few soon-to-be-famous stars and one Oscar winner (Susan Sarandon, Barry Bostwick, Meat Loaf, Tim Curry), who seem so jazzed to be in a movie at all that they appear to forget they are breaking all the rules and getting away with it. And you can at last relive again and again—in private—a rite of passage every human on the planet should make: singing "Sweet Transvestite" in your underwear, volume at full blast.

It is a shame that Curry's portrayal of Dr. Frank-N-Furter was so indelible it forever fused the actor to the character in the minds of the public, as it likely cost him a wider choice of roles. But he is a marvel and the very soul of *Rocky Horror*. How does one even begin to approach a bisexual alien cross-dresser with a hunger for world domination, and transform him into a creature so devastatingly human that there isn't a dry eye in the house at the end of his curtain call? Curry's creation shares the crown with Divine as the greatest drag queen ever seen on screen. And would even Sharon Stone in *Basic Instinct* dare say "Touch me—I want to be dirty!" with such schoolgirl abandon?

The Rocky Horror Picture Show has been dismissed as a freak show, which it is, but the freaks are us. The film is a milestone in progressive cinema. It broke taboos and explored sexual no-no's that even today's supposedly liberated filmmakers are still afraid to touch—pansexuality, gender politics, blatant hedonism and repression as an ultimate weapon. It is an orgiastic, bona fide rock 'n' roll musical that, more than anything, celebrates the right to be who we are, make love with who we want, and revel in our most secret passions and desires free of judgment. And in this world of prefabricated cult classics and off-the-shelf rebellion, it is reassuring to know that every Friday and Saturday at midnight, in theaters across the world, teenagers are still doing the "Time Warp." Don't dream it, be it.

The Goodies About the only thing missing from this frank-n-fabulous DVD is that it doesn't come with two hundred fully made-up *Rocky Horror* freaks who want to watch the movie with you. There are the cute bells and whistles—an alternate audio track that screams "Asshole!" on cue—but it is hard to replicate the experience of the *Picture Show* without a group of scantily clad vampire girls and leather-heavy half-naked men dancing, singing and clapping along, every note, word and turn of phrase memorized and fetishized. Still, this kick-ass two-disc set sure tries.

We are treated to *three* versions of the film. The U.S. version will be most familiar, as it is the theatrical cut; the U.K. version adds an extra song, "Superheroes," at the climax, and the third is a mesmerizing, hidden "Conceptual" version, that, of all things, was inspired by *The Wizard of Oz*. For the film's first twenty minutes or so, everything is in black-and-white—until Dr. Frank-N-Furter makes his grand entrance. You might think this is a bit much, but it actually works surprisingly well and makes the film feel even more timeless. (How to find the "Conceptual" version? Go to the main menu, scroll down to "Scene Selections," then click left. You should see a pair of lips. Give them a click and let the monochrome flow!) And in a perfect fit for the ultimate audience participation movie, access the "Multi-View Theater Experience." Click the lips when they appear and you'll jump to a live stage performance of the same sequence, with "Participation Prompts" that offer the appropriate instructions (throw rice, yell, sing along, etc.) at the appropriate time.

Also included on the first disc are two alternate audio tracks. *Rocky Horror* creator Richard O'Brien and actress Patricia Quinn contribute an audio commentary that creates the illusion of sitting in a British parlor, laughing and smoking cigarettes with Riff Raff and Magenta. Sure, much of their discussion is tangential and too full of in-jokes—diehard fanatics will appreciate it the most—but it is still mighty entertaining. And the "Audience Participation Track" is best listened to at midnight. Just like in the theater, much of what these *Rocky Horror* devotees are yelling about is pretty indecipherable, but every once in a while they deliver a gem that makes this one worth a listen, especially if you're drunk or in an otherwise altered state.

Disc two is even more brimming with the odd and the outlandish. The "Rocky Horror Double Feature Video Show" runs thirty-five minutes and is a bit slim for such a landmark cult movie. More polished and entertaining is "*Rocky* on VH-1," an assortment of excerpts from the music station's infamous *Behind the Music* and *Where Are They Now?* shows. Due to clearance issues, we don't get full episodes, just raw, uncut interview material with each participant, including O'Brien, Sarandon, Curry and Bostwick. It may be a bit disjointed, but there is a ton of well-known and not-so-well-known *Rocky* tidbits that make for a great snack. Best moment? O'Brien doing an acoustic version of "Time Warp" while strolling around the film's memorable castle location.

Wait, there's more: deleted footage including two musical numbers ("Once in a While" and "Superheroes"), eleven alternate takes of various sequences, an alternate credit roll, the "misprint ending" that was accidentally attached to a handful of prints, aVH-1's *Pop-Up Video* version of Meatloaf's "Hot Patootee," a still gallery, karaoke versions of "Sweet Transvestite" and "Toucha Toucha Touch Me," and some theatrical trailers. We even get some ROM extras including a terrific *Rocky Horror* phenomenon timeline—from theater stage to Hollywood and back again—plus the bizarrely entertaining "Riff Raff's Story Lab" (aka *Rocky Horror* Mad Libs) and a "Masochistic Trivia Challenge." Oh, Brad! Oh, Janet!

The Presentation *The Rocky Horror Picture Show* is presented in a THX-certified, 1.66:1 anamorphic widescreen transfer and it looks better than it ever has. The film was made on the cheap and it still shows, but color reproduction is luscious—especially those rich, red lips. Gone are all those pinkish faces and weird flesh tones that made the old VHS and laserdisc versions distracting. The low-grade stock means the film still looks soft and the print is not quite pristine, but there are no major defects to be found. *Rocky Horror* still looks like the fun little amateur revue it is. God bless it.

The new Dolby Digital 5.1 upgrade can't quite rescue *Rocky Horror* from the drive-in, but that is what makes it so charming. Surround effects are sporadic and rather obvious, and most of the soundtrack still emanates largely from the front speakers. But the film's classic tunes are nicely spread out in stereo, and the elements have been cleaned up to near-pristine quality. And purists can still stick with the original mono track, so you can dance to "Time Warp" whichever damned way you want.

Additional Versions Fox Home Entertainment also released *The Rocky Horror Picture Show* as a single-disc edition that dropped the second platter of extras; it remains in print.

Additional Recommendations Want more kooky musicals on DVD? Try *Can't Stop the Music,* the inane Village People song and dance show, the manic ridiculousness of the notorious flop *Xanadu* or the ultimate party disc, Paul Verhoeven's *Showgirls*. Sadly, all of these are lacking in extras, but for more full-featured special editions that also were directly influenced by *Rocky Horror*, try Alan Parker's surrealist rock classic *Pink Floyd The Wall*, Brian De Palma's *Phantom of the Paradise* and the ultimate acid trip, The Who's *Tommy*.

The Royal Tenenbaums

DISTRIBUTOR: The Criterion Collection
DVD RELEASE: July 9, 2002
THEATRICAL RELEASE: October 2001
RUNNING TIME: 110 Minutes
MPAA RATING: R

The Royal Tenenbaums is a *New Yorker* cartoon, etched on stained glass. It's a brittle, precious fable that takes place in a city that could be New York and involves a family that could be yours. However, it's not and it's not. In fact, there is no family quite like the Tenenbaums. As explained in a prologue narrated by Alec Baldwin, Royal and Etheline Tenenbaum (Gene Hackman and Anjelica Huston) gave birth to two children and adopted a third. Chas Tenenbaum (Ben Stiller) was a business prodigy who recently lost his wife in a plane crash and now spends his nights running fire drills with his two identically clothed sons. Richie Tenenbaum (Luke Wilson) was a tennis pro who suffered a legendary meltdown during a televised match and now sails the oceans in search of . . . something. Adopted daughter Margot (Gwyneth Paltrow) was a gifted playwright who now spends six hours a day in the bathtub, smoking, watching TV and avoiding her husband, an older intellectual named Raleigh St. Clair (Bill Murray). The fourth member of the Tenenbaum childhood triangle (inaccuracy intended) is next-door neighbor Eli Cash (Owen Wilson), an author of bad western novels.

All three Tenenbaum kids were child prodigies, destined for fame, fortune and swanky dinners in restaurants where rich people hold their teacups with one pinky raised. However, although gifted as children, they're neurotic as adults. And director Wes Anderson (*Rushmore*) shows great

confidence in his ability to find a tone for the film and its performances, giving us a sense of the razor's edge of sanity upon which the Tenenbaum kids dance. And all the actors, especially Paltrow, play their parts as if their characters live underneath layers of emotional gauze.

For differing reasons, all three Tenenbaum children move back in with Etheline, where they're joined by their on-again, off-again father, who has been thrown out of the hotel he was living in and reappears with the claim that he's dying of cancer and has only six weeks to live. Talking his way back into Etheline's home, he sets up shop, complete with hospital bed and heart monitor equipment. Of course, Royal isn't dying of cancer, a ruse uncovered by Etheline's accountant Henry Sherman (Danny Glover), who recently proposed to her and is awaiting an answer. With the brood back together, Royal tries to "put things right" and reconnect with his family.

While all the Tenenbaums have their problems (especially Richie, whose love for his adopted sister, if not strictly incestuous, is close enough), everyone orbits around Royal's black hole of deviousness. A father who is better when he's absent (he once stole bonds out of Chas's safety deposit box), Royal is unrepentant in his conniving, and Hackman wisely plays him so. In fact, everybody is terrific in *The Royal Tenenbaums,* although Stiller is hard-pressed to find the emotional core to his character and take it seriously.

For all its considerable attributes, *The Royal Tenenbaums* is a droll and distant movie, and it's difficult to embrace its characters. The movie just won't let you in. Still, the film doesn't look down upon or make fun of this twisted family. Anderson and cowriter Owen Wilson want their characters to be happy or at least accept themselves as the architects of their own misery. In the end, the story of the Tenenbaums and the world in which they live is so fully realized and singular in style that you can't help but be intoxicated by it.

The Goodies In an interesting move, Disney turned over DVD responsibilities for *The Royal Tenenbaums* to Criterion. And, of course, as Criterion is the premiere producer of home video product, fans of the film could hope for no better. Beautifully drawn menus guide you through the wealth of interesting supplements.

Criterion put a majority of the extras on a second disc, a smart move that allows the film to stretch out on its own platter. The only extra on the first DVD is an audio commentary by Anderson, who is very conversational and helpful in explaining many of his stylistic choices. Quirky and unique, *The Royal Tenenbaums* is a very dense film so Anderson's insight and lack of pretension is welcome; he touches on just about every aspect of his creation from page to screen, sometimes in a tumbling rush of chatter. He is a great tour guide.

The second disc contains Criterion's typical array of comprehensive, far-flung features. "Scrapbook" is a wonderful arrangement of the visual shortcuts Anderson uses to convey character information, including book covers, murals and paintings. There is also a large photo gallery and a couple of easy-to-find easter eggs.

"With the Filmmaker: Portraits by Albert Maysles" is a terrific twenty-seven-minute special that follows Anderson as he makes just a few of the thousands of decisions, big and small, that every director must make. Wisely presented without narration, it's a great fly-on-the-wall look at the filmmaking process.

Along with two uninteresting cut scenes, there are on-set interviews with the cast. Not surprisingly, the best bites come from older actors Murray, Huston and the great Hackman.

Finally, there is the oddest supplement, "The Peter Bradley Show," a fourteen-minute parody of a Charlie Rose interview with five actors who barely appear in the movie. Bradley is only marginally prepared and the interviews go nowhere, which makes this extra all the funnier.

The Presentation Criterion presents *The Royal Tenenbaums* in the wide aspect ratio of 2.40:1. Anderson supervised the widescreen digital transfer and the color palette is extremely broad, although it does rely a lot on the browns and yellows of Etheline's home and the beautiful East Coast autumn. All colors are reproduced vibrantly, although some scenes are a bit too bright. However, most of the time saturation is spot-on, whether it be in the red jogging suits of Chas's sons or Henry Sherman's blue blazer. The transfer has a pleasing, filmlike appearance, with very little grain, accurate flesh tones and no print flaws. Blacks are solid and shadow detail is quite good as well. A colorful, eye-catching transfer.

Audio is available in two flavors: Dolby Digital 5.1 and DTS 5.1. Considering the film is dialogue driven, 5.1 is overkill. There isn't much going on, although what's there is rendered extremely well. Surrounds do very little here, and the left and right speakers are used to support the hardworking pop soundtrack and the rare instance of a sound effect. Dialogue comes mostly from the center speaker and is always very clear and distinct. Both the Dolby and DTS tracks are natural and appropriate to the material, with neither one particularly better than the other.

Saturday Night Fever

DISTRIBUTOR: Paramount Home Entertainment
DVD RELEASE: October 8, 2002
THEATRICAL RELEASE: December 1977
RUNNING TIME: 118 Minutes
MPAA RATING: R

Saturday Night Fever's most iconic image is also its albatross: John Travolta, arm raised skyward, adorned in gold chains and a white polyester suit. It came to symbolize the epitome of disco and all of its decadence; an era, pre-AIDS, when it was still fun to stay up all night, boogie until dawn and wake up not remembering what you did or who you were with the night before. But *Saturday Night Fever* is more than a mere disco movie, it is a film that transcended its time and penetrated the popular consciousness. It is tough, gritty, electric. It inspired a dance craze and sent white suit sales skyrocketing. And is proof that we should never, ever wear polyester again.

Tony Manero (Travolta) is nineteen, lives in Brooklyn, is the son to a deeply religious Italian family and works at the local paint shop. He, like many lower middle-class, blue-collar kids of his generation, is "nowhere, goin' no place." Cornered by his suffocating home life and a future of servitude selling paint cans, he spends his nights with his buddies at the Odyssey 2001, a nightclub where Tony and his gang rule. His boss puts it into perspective: "You can't fuck the future, Tony. It catches up with you and it fucks you, if you ain't planned for it." But when he is on the dance floor, he is the king.

Tony's life changes when he meets Stephanie (Karen Lynn-Gorney), a young dancer as sophisticated and worldly as Tony is uncultured and gruff. Her appraisal of him is direct and razor sharp: "You're a cliché." Tony does not disagree. For him, she represents a dilemma common to many young men of the late 1970s: a woman he wants, even loves but if he seduces and sleeps with her, he can no longer respect her, because then she will be like Annette (Donna Pescow) and all of the other girls at the Odyssey who worship him and would completely submit to his every whim and desire. Tony and friends cannot see women as equals, only receptacles. It is not until Tony makes his first, tentative steps toward his dream—to escape across the Brooklyn Bridge to Manhattan—that he embarks on the journey to becoming a man.

> **"So, are you as good in bed as you are on that dance floor?"**
>
> —Connie, to Tony Manero

John Badham's *Saturday Night Fever* is a smart and realistic little movie, filled with terrific dance sequences, great music and a star-marking performance by Travolta. His moves have become legendary; he is as graceful and fluid on the dance floor as were true legends like Fred Astaire and Gene Kelly, but with the fire and energy of a young Michael Jackson. But although *Fever* is a great dance movie and has a seminal soundtrack (the epic Bee Gees tunes like "Stayin' Alive" and "Jive Talkin' " have rightly become classics), and Travolta is terrific, that doesn't fully explain its enormous popularity. I suspect Tony Manero was so embraced as a cultural icon because, like all of us at that age, he was a dreamer. In the film's most poignant scene, he sits on a bench with Stephanie, staring at the Brooklyn Bridge. He knows every fact about it, down to how many steel girders and beams and pounds of concrete were needed to build it. And he clings to his dreams so desperately that it is impossible not to cheer his crowning moment on the dance floor. He may be goin' nowhere, doin' nothing. He may even be a cliché. But, if only for one moment, he was the king.

The Goodies *Saturday Night Fever* celebrated its silver anniversary in 2002, and Paramount Home Entertainment honored it with this fine special edition. It is a great, cheap date—you can boogie all night and not wake up with a hangover.

The extras are culled largely from the VH-1 special *Behind the Music: Saturday Night Fever,* one of the highest-rated programs in the series's history. Here we get twenty-nine minutes' worth of the best highlights, and it is a great, if glossy, look at the film. Travolta, Badham and most of the main cast, including Gorney, Pescow and Barry Miller, reflect on the film that catapulted them all to stardom. Other bonuses include rare behind-the-scenes movies and Travolta's choreographer Denny Terrio trying to prove he still has the moves. What before was useless trivia—Gene Siskel purchased Travolta's famous white suit for over $10,000 at auction—is now a part of pop-culture legend. And there was a dark side of the success. Ironically, the biggest victims of the "Disco Sucks" backlash were the Bee Gees, who were so identified with *Fever* they were forced to retreat to Europe for over a decade. So it is sweet music indeed to watch triumphant footage of the trio being inducted in the Rock 'N' Roll Hall of Fame in 1999.

Badham also supplies his own screen-specific audio commentary that balances nicely with the VH-1 highlights, filling in many of the gaps about the production. On a low-budget film with few expectations, Badham and his often beleaguered cast and crew showed great ingenuity in covering up the cracks, stringing up aluminum foil to spruce up the Odyssey 2001 and shooting around traffic. And *Fever*'s pop masterstroke would prove to be a fortuitous accident: The Bee Gees songs were a last-minute choice because they were so cheap.

Badham offers additional commentary on three deleted scenes, all dialogue exchanges. An oversight on this otherwise fine set is the lack of any theatrical trailers or archival material, or any clips from the hilarious PG-rated theatrical rerelease in 1978.

The Presentation *Saturday Night Fever* underwent an extensive restoration in honor of its twenty-fifth anniversary, and its transfer is electric. The film has a realistic, gritty look, and it isn't just the polyester that makes it so fabulously gaudy and 1970s. Excessive use of soft-focus filters gives the film a hazy sheen, and the colors, especially the reds, are slightly overpumped. But the new print is near-pristine and looks wonderful. The vibrant, disco-fueled nightclub scenes are vivid, and exteriors have a natural, filmlike look. Only some slight edge enhancement mars an otherwise sparkling restoration. The new Dolby Digital 5.1 remix is also a stunner, adding considerable heft and presence to the film's classic songs. The urban milieu now comes alive with a genuine sense of envelopment, and street sounds and other discrete effects are nicely spread across the rear channels. So throw on that white polyester suit and those gold chains, and get ready to boogie down.

Additional Recommendations *Saturday Night Fever* was followed up by an overproduced, woefully misguided sequel, *Staying Alive* (directed by Sylvester Stallone!), and a host of trendy imitators. But none captured *Fever*'s unique mix of gritty realism, electric dance and genuine idealism. Travolta's best musical bets are *Grease, Urban Cowboy,* the little-seen *Shout!,* and a true guilty pleasure, *Perfect,* costarring Jamie Lee Curtis. All but *Grease* contain no extras, although even that marginal special edition includes only a short featurette, leading one to hope Paramount will see fit to grant it the same treatment as *Saturday Night Fever.*

Scarface

DISTRIBUTOR: Universal Studios Home Video

DVD RELEASE: September 30, 2003

THEATRICAL RELEASE: December 1983

RUNNING TIME: 170 Minutes

MPAA RATING: R

To say that Brian De Palma's *Scarface* is loud, bloody, vulgar, excessive and operatic is to remind audiences why the film has endured since its 1983 release. However, what's largely forgotten is that *Scarface* is really the great American love story. It's about a man in love with his possibilities. Gordon Gekko, the uber-capitalist in Oliver Stone's other 1980's cautionary tale, *Wall Street* (Stone directed *Wall Street* and wrote *Scarface*), has nothing on Tony Montana, who comes over from Cuba with the 125,000 other émigrés that Castro let out of the country in 1980. Montana is a punk, but he's an ambitious one who sees in America what's impossible in Cuba. That anyone with a better idea and the sense of purpose and drive can succeed in America is not a new concept, although it is one that Montana takes to new and fast heights.

Montana is portrayed by Al Pacino in a performance that foreshadows hammy turns in films like *The Devil's Advocate* and *Scent of a Woman*. And while Pacino has taken some criticism for his flamboyance, the fact is, in *Scarface*, one must be excessive to tell a tale of excess. As he sticks his entire face into a mountain of cocaine and introduces a group of assassins to his "little friend," he shows us a man who totally, fatally believes his own press, a man of such bravado and fist-clenching fury that receding into the background to merely cash the checks is not an option. To the end, Montana displays not one ounce of remorse, nor does he ever question what he does. His only soft spot is for his sister (Mary Elizabeth Mastrantonio), who represents

> "All I have in this world is my balls and my word. And I don't break 'em for no one. You understand?"
>
> —Tony Montana

the only remaining bit of purity in his world. Even his marriage to Elvira (Michelle Pfeiffer) is loveless. In it for the drugs, she's almost immediately bored and he has nothing else to offer but the diminishing returns of his opulent lifestyle.

Montana's flameout is the inevitable by-product of his liftoff. Arriving in Florida, he's sent to Freedomtown, the Miami detention center housing the Cuban castoffs. In exchange for a green card, he murders a former Castro crony during a Freedomtown riot. Once on the street, he befriends Florida's cocaine czar Frank Lopez (Robert Loggia), who sees limitless amounts of untapped ruthlessness in Montana's unpolished but quick-witted style. As Montana climbs up through the ranks of the drug trade's best and brightest, he approaches the unavoidable descent upon which all cautionary tales rely.

Although the film is renowned for its copious amount of bloodshed, *Scarface* does not become brutally and satirically excessive until the last twenty minutes. With the exception of one character's early and unfortunate demise via chainsaw, director De Palma places the burden of excess upon Pacino's designer suit-enshrouded shoulders in the film's finale. Tony's rocket to the top has taken him so high, he's out of oxygen with nowhere to go but down, a logical extension of the film's buildup of bold stylistic strokes and Tony's increasing sense of paranoia.

About midway through *Scarface,* Tony sees the Goodyear blimp floating through the sky with the words "The World Is Yours" emblazoned across it. How that blimp mirrors Tony Montana: larger than life, higher than everyone else, full of hot air.

The Goodies Universal Studios Home Video put all the extras on a second disc, which allows room for all the major supplements from the previous release, as well as some new ones. Along with twenty-two minutes of deleted scenes, there is a sixty-minute documentary, split into three sections: "The Rebirth" (which explores why *Scarface* was remade and how the filmmakers decided on their modern approach), "Casting" (which explains how the major players were chosen) and "Creating" (about principal photography and the filmmaker's fight to avoid an X rating).

"*Scarface*: The TV Version" is a short but humorous piece about how the film was edited for network television broadcast. Along with the violence, the film contains well over one hundred instances of the word "fuck," the elimination of which became quite the challenge to Universal. The film was eventually shown on TV, where the line "Where'd you get that beauty scar, tough guy? Eatin' pussy?" became "Where'd you get that beauty scar, tough guy? Eatin' pineapple?"

Modern audiences will appreciate "Def Jam Presents: Origins of a Hip Hop Classic." Here we get a host of African American entertainers, from actor Mekhi Phifer to rappers Snoop Dog and Sean Combs, discussing the importance of *Scarface* to the hip hop community and their interpretations of the film.

The Presentation For the movie's twentieth anniversary, Universal Studios Home Video digitally remastered *Scarface* and the result is a huge improvement over the much-maligned 1998 DVD version. Presented in 2.35:1 anamorphic widescreen, the film shows very little of its twenty years. Colors are sharp, saturated and bright—essential in conveying the pastels of Miami and the bloody fate of Tony's victims. Detail and flesh tones are accurate, if not exemplary. Blacks are solid and dark, but shadow detail flags; there is some murkiness in scenes where blacks share the frame with brighter colors. Exterior night scenes suffer the most in this area, although exterior day scenes look terrific. There is a surprising and welcome lack of grain and print flaws, although edge enhancements are present in a few scenes. Still, given the age and the available source material, *Scarface* will never look better.

Audio is also an improvement over the original DVD's, but it's not the flamboyant mix one would hope for. Available in Dolby Digital 5.1 and DTS surround, most of the action comes from the center speakers. The dialogue is crisp and clear, although given the Cuban accents, a press of the subtitle button may be necessary. Giorgio Morodor's score, which stylistically doesn't really hold up, makes best use of the other front speakers. Panning and separation are only occasionally employed.

Singin' in the Rain

DISTRIBUTOR: Warner Home Video

DVD RELEASE: September 24, 2002

THEATRICAL RELEASE: March 1952

RUNNING TIME: 103 Minutes

MPAA RATING: G

To discover *Singin' in the Rain* is to discover the pure joy of song and dance itself. It is one of the genuine miracles of the cinema, a smart, funny, marvelously constructed masterpiece that feels as fresh and ebullient today as it did upon its release in 1952. It is doubtful that any Hollywood musical will leave you feeling as alive and optimistic as *Singin' in the Rain*—it is the cinematic equivalent of curling up in front of the fireplace on a rainy day with a pair of fuzzy slippers and a hot cup of cocoa.

Singin' in the Rain is a movie about moviemaking, and remains the most perceptive, informative and winning picture ever made about the industry. It spoofs numerous Hollywood contrivances and studio types with great class, wit and sophistication—but never to demean, only to celebrate. It is of course a romance (what musical isn't?) but also depicts the film industry undergoing a revolution, from silent to sound, as fabricated studio romances were becoming the dominant currency of fame and the influence of the tabloid paparazzi was growing by leaps and bounds. That *Singin' in the Rain* was able to so sharply, sweetly satirize is what makes it brilliant. Arthur Freed, the legendary producer at MGM, initiated the project as the ideal vehicle for screenwriters Betty Comden and Adolph Green. The missive from the studio was that the musical would consist only of recycled standards, including the title tune (surprisingly, only one new song was composed for the film, "Make 'Em Laugh"). Gene Kelly, who previously teamed with director Stanley Donen for 1949's *On the Town,* was joined

> "I'm laughing at clouds so dark up above, there's a song in my heart."
>
> —Donald "Donnie" Lockwood

by Debbie Reynolds and the late Donald O'Connor, and together they made movie magic. Each is at the top of their game—their flights of fancy are wondrous and breathtaking, and we literally gasp at them. It is a seemingly effortless display of energy, talent, craft and athletic ability. (That Reynolds and Kelly are also one of the sexiest romantic couplings in the history of the musical doesn't hurt, either.)

Then there is "Singin' in the Rain," which, along with "Over the Rainbow" from *The Wizard of Oz* (1939), ranks as one of the most uplifting musical sequences in history. It is amazing and perfectly constructed. Watch as the camera pans up at the precise moment a beaming Kelly sings "There's a smile on my face" in a startling close-up. It is impossible to watch this scene and not feel like your heart is being lifted up to the heavens. *Singin' in the Rain* is a movie you can watch over and over again and not get tired of. It may be the most joyous, lighthearted and just plain happy movie ever made.

The Goodies For the sixtieth anniversary of *Singin' in the Rain*, Warner Home Video produced an absolutely fabulous two-disc set. The audio commentary is delightful, with a verifiable parade of talent, including Reynolds (who also hosts the DVD), O'Connor, Cyd Charisse, Donen, screenwriters Comden and Green, film historian Rudy Behlmer and even filmmaker Baz Luhrmann (*Moulin Rouge!*). While it is a series of separate interviews expertly spliced together, it matters little with such a great lineup. There is also an extended branching feature, "Singin' Inspirations," that can be viewed separately or concurrently with the commentary, and features a wealth of textual information (presented as a subtitles stream) and additional behind-the-scenes featurettes that branch off at select points during the film. Each segment runs one to three minutes and features newsreel footage, cast and crew interviews, and more.

There are also two full-length documentaries on disc two. "What a Glorious Feeling" (thirty-six minutes) is again hosted by Reynolds and is somewhat limited in terms of new interview footage and behind-the-scenes material, but Reynolds eloquently narrates over a series of extensive stills that illustrate the complete history of the film, from conception to premiere. More unique is "Musicals, Great Musicals: The Arthur Freed Unit at MGM," a wonderful eighty-six-minute document that chronicles the rise of Freed and MGM's pre-eminence as the studio for classic musicals. It features some terrific clips, including some of Kelly's finest moments.

Also fascinating is a collection of Freed/Nacio Herb Brown songs presented in various versions, all audio-only, that traces the developing style of the classic duo. There is a rare outtake of "You Are My Lucky Star," a gem of a song excised from the final cut of *Singin' in the Rain,* and eighteen more alternate takes of twelve tunes from the film's soundtrack. Rounding out the collection are the film's theatrical trailer an awards list and a far-too-brief still gallery.

The Presentation Warner utilized its proprietary "ultra resolution" process to retain *Singin' in the Rain*'s original three-strip Technicolor, which caused some purists to complain that the film's original integrity would be compromised. It did result in a picture too clean, too smooth, too pure. But never mind the naysayers. This is one to swoon over, a transfer so breathtaking it ranks as one of the most beautiful you are ever likely to see on a DVD.

Color reproduction is staggering, with hues so rich, stable and clean they look painted on. It is that brilliant. Detail is amazing—it is impossible to believe this is a film now over fifty years old. Reports indicated that MGM's original negative of *Singin' in the Rain* was destroyed in a fire, but if this is what fire does to a film, perhaps they should burn more of them. (Okay, just kidding). What a revelation.

Warner has attempted a new Dolby Digital 5.1 remix, which tries its best but there is only so much that can be done with vintage mono source elements. Spatially, it is an exciting soundtrack, with active surrounds and a consistently engaging soundfield. However, despite an increase in frequency response—the highs now sing and low bass is surprisingly supple—the track can suffer from a processed feel. Some of the attempts at spreading the songs across the soundstage are also too obvious. But purists have no cause for consternation; the original mono mix is also included.

Additional Versions *Singin' in the Rain* was released once previously on DVD by MGM Home Entertainment. It contained few extras and a good, but not great, transfer. The film has also been released in no fewer than six(!) laserdisc editions and box sets.

The Sixth Sense

DISTRIBUTOR: Buena Vista Home Entertainment
DVD RELEASE: January 15, 2002
THEATRICAL RELEASE: August 1999
RUNNING TIME: 103 Minutes
MPAA RATING: PG-13

M. Night Shyamalan doesn't make films. He unmakes them. In each of his first three movies, he's taken a familiar genre, deconstructed and rebuilt it to the point where it's unrecognizable to the audience. That is his art: he doesn't adjust to the genre, the genre adjusts to him. It's what makes Shyamalan a singular and necessary filmmaker with an elegant, moody style unlike any other director's.

In his 2000 film *Unbreakable,* Bruce Willis plays the only survivor of a horrific train wreck. His emergence from the accident completely unscathed attracts the attention of Samuel L. Jackson, who suffers from an affliction that renders his bones brittle and easy to break. By film's end, Shyamalan has used his graceful, elliptical storytelling skills to give us a superhero origin story, complete with supervillian.

In 2002's *Signs,* Mel Gibson plays a lapsed Bucks County priest who discovers crop circles in his fields. He and his brother, played by Joaquin Phoenix, assume it's the work of pranksters until mounting evidence points to an alien invasion of Earth. While Steven Spielberg gave the alien-invasion genre a humanistic makeover in his 1977 masterpiece *Close Encounters of the Third Kind,* Shyamalan has added themes of faith and restoration that blended perfectly with his established style.

That style was established in *The Sixth Sense,* his 1999 breakout that became the tenth highest grossing domestic release of all time. The film is ostensibly a ghost story, but, as with his other movies,

Shyamalan has more on his mind. *The Sixth Sense* is about communication and the emotional and spiritual weight that lifts when you finally unburden yourself of things unsaid. Ten-year-old Cole (an amazing Haley Joel Osment) is unable to tell his mother (Oscar nominee Toni Collette) his secret—he can see ghosts—for fear of being labeled a freak. Child psychologist Malcolm Crowe (a melancholy Bruce Willis) can't get through to his wife (Olivia Williams), who has become distant since he was shot by a deranged patient (an unhinged and unrecognizable Donnie Wahlberg). And finally, there are the ghosts, who each have something to tell Cole before they can move on.

> "You ever feel the prickly things on the back of your neck? And the tiny hairs on your arm, you know, when they stand up? That's them."
>
> —Cole Sear

Although Shyamalan's sensitive script and stately directorial approach give the film depth and style, *The Sixth Sense* will be remembered mostly for its shock ending. And while the ending certainly added to the film's overall box office tally (since audiences clamored to see the film multiple times to add up the clues), if it had ended one scene earlier, it would have been, from an emotional standpoint, just as successful. In that scene, Cole and his mother sit in the car, while an accident has traffic at a standstill. Cole tells his mother he can see dead people, capping it with a message from her deceased mother. It's an amazing scene, smartly played without musical underscore, that really represents the emotional end of the film. The denouement became a mind-blowing coda that may or may not stand up to the strictest of scrutiny, but it did ensure the arrival of Shyamalan. And while he may run out of genres to reinvent, as long as there are stories to tell, his approach to telling them will be worth watching.

The Goodies Like other Vista Series releases, this is a two-disc affair, with supplements taking up the entire bonus DVD. In addition to some enlightening new extras, Buena Vista Home Entertainment has recycled all the extras from the previous Collector's Edition DVD (which wasn't worth collecting, after all). The older supplements are "Music and Sound Design" (about the importance of James Newton Howard's score), "Reaching an Audience" (the August 1999 release of the film), "Rules and Clues" (which helps answer the questions posed by the ending), some deleted scenes (four in all, each introduced by Shyamalan), and a publicity section with a theatrical trailer and two TV spots.

The new supplements include the thirty-nine-minute documentary "Reflections from the Set," which takes the viewer from Shyamalan's frustration with earlier drafts of the script to the film's blockbuster theatrical run. It's quite interesting, and bolstered by the participation of Shyamalan, who comes across as extremely intelligent and thoughtful.

"Between Two Worlds" is a thirty-seven-minute exploration of the afterlife and how movies interpret and express filmmakers' views of what lies beyond. Included are interviews with Shyamalan, William Peter Blatty (author of *The Exorcist*), and Bruce Joel Rubin (writer of the films *Jacob's Ladder* and *Ghost*). "Moving Pictures: The Storyboard Process" delves into how Shyamalan used storyboards to insure his vision. Finally, there are some goodies for those with DVD-ROM capabilities.

And it's all wrapped in a glossy foldout package, with a slip sleeve that includes a collectable storyboard sequence.

The Presentation Considering the film occupies one full disc in this Vista Series two-disc set, one would expect a top-notch transfer. And while the transfer is very good, it's not a marked improvement over the previous DVD release. The THX-certified 1.85:1 anamorphic widescreen presentation reproduces Shyamalan's somber color palette quite well. The film lives in a purposely dull world of blue and gray, with bursts of symbolically significant red being the only vibrant color. No matter what the hue, color reproduction is faithful to the source material. There is an odd bit of dirt that pops up on occasion, but otherwise the print is in good shape. Shadow detail shows some muddiness, although overall blacks recover nicely after a grainy start. Detail and sharpness are very good, and flesh tones are accurate. A very solid transfer, although one more pass would have given this mood piece the spit shine it deserves.

Audio is available in DTS and Dolby Digital 5.1 surround. Both options contain subtle aural shadings that honor the material. However, a more engaging, moodier soundscape was possible. Dialogue, directed toward the center speaker, is very clear and distinct, while Howard's atmospheric score is reproduced cleanly. Bass is rarely employed to much effect, while the highs evidenced in violin strings and the like are without fault. Surrounds kick in during the creepier moments, but overall surround utilization is low-to-medium.

Snow White and the Seven Dwarfs

DISTRIBUTOR: Buena Vista Home Entertainment
DVD RELEASE: October 9, 2001
THEATRICAL RELEASE: December 1937
RUNNING TIME: 83 Minutes
MPAA RATING: G

The first full-length animated feature film, *Snow White and the Seven Dwarfs* was an audacious, revolutionary milestone. Critics hailed it as a masterpiece (Sergei Eisenstein called it the "greatest movie ever made"), it broke box office records (*Snow White* remains the highest-grossing film in rerelease) and the Academy honored it with a special Oscar for Technical Achievement. But *Snow White* was more than a cultural force and an artistic breakthrough, it was transformative. Animated films, or "cartoons," had previously been relegated to children's entertainments—five-minute shorts filled with cute characters and simple gags, entertaining fluff to tide over the kiddies between the newsreels and the main feature. *Snow White* broke down those barriers, turning animation into a viable, long-form storytelling medium. The "cartoon" didn't just get longer, it got deeper.

> "Magic Mirror on the wall, who is the fairest of them all?"
>
> —The Wicked Queen

To realize his vision for *Snow White,* Walt Disney and his collaborators pioneered new techniques and technologies. The Technical Oscar was awarded for the invention of the "Multiplane Camera," a device that could create a far more realistic and three-dimensional style of movement by facilitating the photography of several layers of drawings simultaneously. It would became a standard tool in animation until the arrival of computer-assisted filmmaking. Walt also expanded the cel frame size itself, allowing for larger, more detailed and richer images. But all these technological innovations would mean nothing without a story, and in *Snow White,* Walt created a magical, timeless fable, starring seven of the most famous characters in movie history.

Is it wrong to point out that the most interesting characters are not Snow White and Prince Charming (who are rather boring and, at the risk of a bad pun, two-dimensional), but the Seven Dwarfs and the Wicked Queen? Perhaps dark and comedic characters are always more fanciful and intriguing. (Who do you remember most from *101 Dalmatians,* Roger Radcliff or Cruella de Ville?) Our heroes must hew to the straight and narrow; we know they are predestined to meet, fall in love and live happily ever after. But what of the dwarfs? They inhabit the world and accent it, but don't have to fill it. They can suffer real foibles, stumble and err and generally make fools of themselves. And the Wicked Queen gets all the best numbers. Through no fault of her own, Snow White may be the biggest drip of her own movie.

But what makes *Snow White and the Seven Dwarfs* such a giddy rush is realizing the sheer effort that went into producing it. There is something magical about the fact that it took a legion of animators over four years and millions of brushstrokes to create the film's visuals, which could never be replicated by even the greatest computer-generated illusions. Every corner of every frame of *Snow White* is alive with excitement and detail, a monument to the potential of human creativity and ingenuity. In *Snow White,* Walt wanted to create a classic story for the ages and make a quantum leap in technology. He succeeded beyond even his own wildest imagination.

The Goodies In 2001, Disney studios launched the Platinum Collection, a series of ten two-disc DVD releases, highlighting the studio's crown jewels of animation. The first was *Snow White and the Seven Dwarfs,* with future titles to follow at the rate of one a year (some of the others include *Aladdin, Beauty and the Beast, The Lion King* and *101 Dalmatians*). If *Snow White* is any indication, it is going to be a long, inexorable wait for all ten: *Snow White*'s DVD is a glorious, grand, wonderfully conceived and executed special edition. Walt would be proud.

With two full discs of material, navigating the world of *Snow White* can be tricky; Disney has employed the services of the Magic Mirror to be our guide. It is a cute conceit, and his irascible wit and endless quips are highly amusing. Those seeking a more traditional route can access all of the set's special features via a simpler, text-based index. It is the correct approach for a title that will appeal equally to children and adults, and whichever option you choose, the wealth of material will offer hours and hours of entertainment.

Roy Disney and a host of celebrity guest stars offer introductions to the extensive supplemental features, which are evenly split between age groups. The audio commentary is culled from vintage interview material with Walt himself and Disney animation historian John Canemaker. It is a wonderful track, full of insight, and Walt is, as always, an enchanting host. Kids will most likely be bored with it, but they can enjoy the marvelous sixty-minute documentary "The One That Started It All—The Making of *Snow White and the Seven Dwarfs,*" hosted by Angela Lansbury. A classy and reverential mix of vintage interviews with Walt, archival production footage, rare stills and new material with Canemaker, fellow Disney historian Paula Sigman and the Disney animation team, it is a fascinating chronicle of the conception of *Snow White,* the complete production process, its blockbuster release and phenomenal legacy. Disc one concludes with a genuine coup for the Disney Studios: Barbra Streisand, a devout *Snow White* fan, recorded a new version of "Someday My Prince Will Come" exclusively for the DVD release; it is presented here with a montage of stills and footage of Streisand in the recording studio.

Disc two offers five additional worlds to discover. "Wishing Well" chronicles the development of *Snow White* through interactive timelines and extensive still material including conceptual art and storyboards. "The Queen's Castle" includes more still-based art materials, which you can navigate via a 3-D interactive castlelike environment, exploring four different sections: "Camera and Tests," "Animation," "Voice Talent" and "Live Action Reference." "The Queen's Dungeon" looks at abandoned concepts and reconstructed sequences, as well as examines the restoration of *Snow White*. "The Dwarfs' Mine" includes ten minutes of deleted scenes, including alternate RKO opening and end sequences. "Disney Through the Decades" is a delightful interactive timeline—take a peek at the marketing campaigns for each of the *Snow White* rereleases, one a decade. Each is hosted by a different celebrity and includes the respective theatrical rerelease trailer. Finally, "The Dwarfs' Cottage" offers even more publicity and promotional materials, including premiere footage, vintage radio excerpts and even more still galleries with production photos, merchandising and posters.

A wealth of kid-friendly extras rounds out both discs: a "Heigh-Ho" karaoke sing-along, an interactive "Dopey's Wild Mine Ride" game and, accessible to ROM users, "The Princess Fashion Boutique" activity studio.

The Presentation If you've never seen *Snow White and the Seven Dwarfs* on DVD, you haven't seen it at all. It is a new benchmark in movie preservation. In 1993 the Disney Studios decided to bring *Snow White* into the digital realm. In a project that spanned a year, each and every frame of the film—over 18,000 in all—was painstakingly scanned and restored with the latest in digital technology. A new high-definition master was then created and improved even further, with additional grain reduction, color correction and dirt removal. The result is this amazing THX-certified transfer, presented in the film's original 1.37:1 theatrical aspect ratio. It is simply impossible to imagine that a film from 1937 could look this extraordinary. Colors are absolutely mesmerizing, detail stupendous and the illusion of three-dimensionality jaw dropping. *Snow White* is the first of its kind, the only film this old to look this new on DVD.

Disney also meticulously restored the film's original mono source elements and created a matrixed Dolby 5.1 surround track. The overall clarity of the mix is impeccable—Snow White's voice has never sounded so pure, rich and harmonious. Dialogue, both spoken and sung, is very distinct and warm, and the classical music arrangements are nicely spread across the front three speakers. However, due to the age of the material, surround use is subtle and sporadic and the rears sound slightly processed. However, it doesn't distract from an impeccable presentation.

Additional Recommendations Disney continues to raid its vaults for the best of the animated classics and has released so many fantastic titles the format is absolute nirvana for the Disney collector. Highlights include Platinum Collection editions of *The Lion King* and *Beauty and the Beast*; two-disc sets of *Alice in Wonderland, Sleeping Beauty* and *Peter Pan*; the classic *Dumbo*; the underrated *The Hunchback of Notre Dame* and *The Emperor's New Groove*; and the lavish *Walt Disney's Treasures* series, a collection of classic shorts, vintage material and episodes of the *Walt Disney Presents* television series, hosted by Walt himself.

The Sound of Music

DISTRIBUTOR: Fox Home Entertainment
DVD RELEASE: August 29, 2000
THEATRICAL RELEASE: December 1965
RUNNING TIME: 174 Minutes
MPAA RATING: G

Oddly for a movie called *The Sound of Music,* Robert Wise's masterpiece of sentiment and saccharine begins in total silence. We hear nothing as the camera pans across the vast mountains of Salzburg. Then the music slowly fades in, building to a crescendo. Julie Andrews appears, a mere speck at first, before bursting into the immortal "The hills are alive with the sound of music!" It is a glorious moment and the perfect introduction to the world of Wise. For he is one that knows as much about the joy of music as the pain of living without it.

The Sound of Music is one of the most beloved movie musicals of all time. Audiences around the world clutched it to their hearts, seeing it again and again, shattering all box office records in the process and turning it into the second highest-grossing film in rerelease (behind *Snow White and the Seven Dwarfs*). It is an unabashedly romantic, feel-good paean to wholesome values and the power of love, warmth and family. It has everything: picturesque locations, highly memorable songs, magnificent cinematography, engaging characters and a timeless message of tolerance and hope. *The Sound of Music* also saved Twentieth Century Fox from bankruptcy; the film's phenomenal grosses rivaled those of *Gone With the Wind* and restored the studio to solvency. Oscar, too, loved *The Sound of Music*. Long one of the Academy's "favorite things," the musical genre was at its peak when the film won the 1965 statuette for Best Picture. Sharing in the bounty was Wise, who took home his second trophy after his triumph four years earlier with *West Side Story.* (*Music* also earned honors for Adapted Score, Editing and Sound.)

> **"You have brought music back into my life. I had forgotten . . ."**
>
> —Captain Von Trapp

Critical reaction to *The Sound of Music,* however, was not unanimous, with many dismissing the film as schmaltzy and melodramatic. Pauline Kael described it in *The New Yorker* as a "tribute to freshness that is so mechanically engineered and so shrewdly calculated that the background music rises, the already soft focus blurs and melts, and, upon the instant, you can hear all those noses blowing in the theatre." Star Christopher Plummer dubbed the film "The Sound of Mucus," and even Andrews at times seems to be suffering from sugar shock. It is hard to watch *The Sound of Music* today without leaning in, waiting for the joke. That the film now routinely plays at midnight "Sing-A-Long" screenings, attended by drag queens and camp connoisseurs, seems only fitting. But its indefatigable spirit lives on. *The Sound of Music* has transcended its time and is a perennial classic, a glorious, grand, sweet and utterly silly masterpiece

The Goodies Fox Home Entertainment unleashed *The Sound of Music* on DVD in August 2000 in an excellent two-disc set brimming with extras. What continues to make the film so fascinating is the real-life story it is based on. The Von Trapp family, a clan so resilient they survived the rise of the Nazis, made the trek across Europe to become the most successful family singing act of their generation. Hollywood certainly polished off the rough edges, but the heart of their tale still infuses every frame of *The Sound of Music*.

The excellent eighty-seven-minute documentary "From Fact to Fiction: The Making of *The Sound of Music*" is an impeccably researched and impressively detailed account of the saga of the Von Trapps, from real life to screen. Wise, Andrews and Plummer are joined by many of those close to the Von Trapp family, who contribute new interviews that tell an incredible tale of struggle, heartbreak, hope and the power of music to uplift and inspire. Although originally produced for the 1994 laserdisc, the documentary has been reedited exclusively for the DVD and is a deft mix of interviews, archival material, stills and film clips.

Wise also delivers a screen-specific audio commentary that is superb. He, as always, is dignified and insightful, but due to the film's epic 175-minute length, the track is interspersed with select music cues from the score to compensate for a few long silences. Also included is the vintage fourteen-minute featurette "Salzburg: Sight and Sound," and nearly one hour of additional video and radio interviews with Wise, screenwriter Ernest Lehmann, Andrews, Plummer, and stage actress Peggy Wood. Equally impressive is a still gallery that is literally a book on DVD. Divided into nearly twenty subsections, the seemingly endless amount of rare archival material includes production notes, publicity photos, never-before-seen documents and more. Completing this wonderful collection are even more radio interviews with Wise and Andrews conducted for the film's 1973 theatrical rerelease, along with a gallery of trailers and TV and radio spots.

The Presentation It's unfortunate that given such a terrific collection of supplements, the transfer of the film itself is the weakest part of this package. It is not a poor presentation by any means—colors are wonderfully vivid, and the film's expansive panoramas are awash in lush greens, blues and striking primary reds. The print is sharp and clean, with some slight grain but nary a nick or blemish in sight. Alas, some excessive edge enhancement results in pronounced ringing, such as in the opening scene, where Andrews appears to be glowing, a noticeable edge outlining her head like a halo. Otherwise, *The Sound of Music* looks like the pretty wonderful thing it is.

The new Dolby Digital 5.1 remix is an undisputed winner. Frequency response is expansive and full-bodied, with subtle but effective uses of the rear channels. Dialogue also sounds crisp and clear. Best of all are the classic musical numbers, here more lush, alive and enveloping than ever before. The hills really are alive with the sound of music!

Additional Versions Fox Home Entertainment has also released *The Sound of Music* in a single-disc edition that drops the second disc of extras. The transfer and soundtrack remain the same.

Star Trek II: The Wrath of Khan (The Director's Edition)

DISTRIBUTOR: Paramount Home Entertainment

DVD RELEASE: August 6, 2002

THEATRICAL RELEASE: June 1982

RUNNING TIME: 116 Minutes

MPAA RATING: PG

Great science fiction is not about hardware, but humanity. The best of *Star Trek* understood this. Its creator, Gene Roddenberry, was an idealist. He dared to dream of a future where humans would put their best foot forward, that our destiny was not to destroy ourselves but to "seek out new life forms and civilizations." It was a leap of faith that continues to resonate—the *Star Trek* phenomenon has inspired one of the most devoted and diverse fan groups in pop culture history, one that crosses all barriers of gender, age and ethnicity. Trek

> **"Revenge is a dish best served cold."**
>
> —Khan

changed lives and stirred imaginations; Roddenberry not only opened our eyes to the endless possibilities of the genre but also inspired us to rethink our very potential as human beings. From technology to politics to philosophy, *Star Trek* boldly went where nothing had gone before.

The original *Star Trek* enjoyed a brief, marginally successful run as a network series from 1966 to 1969. Its cult grew through reruns, as the show proved far more popular in syndication than during its broadcast run. By 1980's *Star Trek: The Motion Picture,* meeting the expectations of a fan base that had grown exponentially weighed heavily even on Roddenberry's broad shoulders. Directed by Robert Wise, *The Motion Picture* was full of grand ideas and majestic imagery, but failed to spark the public's imagination. Despite big box office, fans left far from elated. It was not until 1982's *Star Trek II: The Wrath of Khan,* directed by Nicholas Meyer (*Time After Time, Volunteers*) that the series hit its stride on the big screen. It was a rousing, exciting, action-packed adventure that also didn't skimp on the grand human drama and big themes that exemplified the best small-screen *Trek.* The crew of the *Enterprise* was back and in top form.

Khan is a total blast. Widely regarded as the best in the series, it has a bit of everything—adventure, action, laughs, romance and thrills. It is the only *Trek* film that appeals as readily to the hardcore Trekkie as it does to the uninitiated. That we know the crew of the *Enterprise* so well—Kirk, Spock, Bones, Uhura, Scotty—is the series' greatest albatross. Character development is often discarded as the actors slip so comfortably into their established roles that there is little genuine urgency to their plight. But in *Khan,* at last these beloved characters are given a great story, one filled with universal themes of love, loss, death and acceptance. And the emotional climax, with the death of a major character, earns real tears. *Khan* is one of the only *Trek*s where more is at stake than just the future of the franchise.

But the best *Trek* adventures are only as good as their villains, and in *Khan,* boy do we get a great one. Ricardo Montalban made his first appearance in the original series episode "Space Speed," and here he returns in a commanding, fiery, rip-roaring performance that is not just the best in *Trek* history, but ranks as one of the greatest in the pantheon of science fiction. His verbal sparring with William Shatner's smug Captain Kirk is priceless—Montalban chews each line, savors it, then spits it back out with deadly venom. *The Wrath of Khan* has all of the requisite space battles, laser fights and wide-eyed *Trek* optimism. But it is also a grand commercial entertainment, a strong story well told with an unforgettable villain. What more can you ask for?

The Goodies Amid much consternation from diehard Trekkies, Paramount Home Entertainment originally released all of the *Star Trek* films except *The Motion Picture* as bare-bones, single-disc DVD releases. Later, the studio gave the fans what they wanted: new two-disc, feature-laden special editions of each film, all consistent in presentation, packaging and breadth of supplemental content.

The Wrath of Khan is presented on DVD here as The Director's Edition, running 116 minutes, reinstating four minutes of additional footage cut from the original theatrical release. Restored are significant dialogue exchanges and the introduction of a key subplot that heightens the emotional impact of Meyer's film and that makes the Director's Edition more than just a vanity project. (Purists need not fear: The previous single-disc, movie-only Paramount DVD release that contains the original 112-minute theatrical cut remains in print, although that cut is not included on this edition.)

A wealth of new extras highlights this set. Meyer contributes a wonderful, highly engaging screen-specific audio commentary. Articulate and intelligent, he guides us through the challenges involved in appeasing the demands of diehard fans while still entertaining a mass audience. A fine companion piece to the audio track is a text commentary by Michael Okuda, coauthor of *The Star Trek Encyclopedia*. Well-paced and highly informative, Okuda's track reveals the many references, character relationships and technical background that informed the making of *Khan*.

Disc two includes nearly two hours of video and still-based material. Three featurettes guide us through the film's development: "Genesis Effect" (examining the famous "Genesis" sequence, which was the first big-screen scene to utilize extensive computer-generated animation), "Designing *Khan*" (dissecting the film's production and costume design) and "Where No Man Has Gone Before" (an extensive breakdown of the special effects). "The Captain's Log" (twenty-four minutes) includes new interviews with Meyer, producer Harve Bennett, stars Shatner, Leonard Nimoy and the classy Montalban ("Yes, the chest is real"). Disappointing is the poor video and audio quality of some of interview material, but what it lacks in polish it makes up for in content. Vintage interview footage is also included of Shatner, Nimoy, Montalban and the late DeForest Kelley, along with another featurette, the twenty-minute "The *Star Trek* Universe— A Novel Approach," a look at the rise in *Trek*-inspired fiction with authors Julia Ecklar and Greg Cox. Additional extras include a set of storyboards for ten key action scenes and the film's original theatrical trailer.

The Presentation For this deluxe edition, Paramount reconstructed *The Wrath of Khan* from the best available source elements. This 2.35:1 anamorphic widescreen transfer looks very good, and the integration of the new footage is seamless. *Khan* remains a somewhat dark film, but colors, especially the rich reds and deep purples, are vivid and clean—a great improvement over the previous DVD, which was murky and noisy. Some of the antiquated effects techniques, especially any shots involving matte paintings, miniatures or composites, suffer from visible grain and some dirt, but otherwise this is a very detailed, sharp transfer.

Paramount has also remixed the soundtrack in Dolby Digital 5.1. Like the transfer, it is a noticeable improvement, delivering a considerable sense of depth and envelopment. Surround use is clever and consistent if subdued by the standards of today's biggest action spectacles. Some elements of the sound design sound dated—dialogue is especially flat—but *Khan* has never sounded so good.

Additional Recommendations DVD is a great place to be a Trekkie. Paramount has released the first six *Trek* films as two-disc special editions. Both *The Next Generation* and *Deep Space Nine* television series ran for seven seasons, all fourteen of which have been released in excellent box set collections loaded with extras. And for those still perplexed by the whole *Star Trek* phenomenon, don't miss the highly amusing documentary *Trekkies,* also available from Paramount Home Entertainment.

Star Wars Episode II: Attack of the Clones

DISTRIBUTOR: Fox Home Entertainment
DVD RELEASE: November 12, 2002
THEATRICAL RELEASE: May 2002
RUNNING TIME: 143 Minutes
MPAA RATING: PG

Star Wars Episode II: Attack of the Clones is likely the first film in history to receive glowing reviews just by the virtue of not being awful. The second (or fifth, depending on how you count) in George Lucas's never-ending space saga, *Clones* definitely had its work cut out for it from the very beginning. Despite boffo box office, *Star Wars Episode I: The Phantom Menace* underwhelmed fans and critics alike, so with *Clones,* Lucas needed to prove he was still one of Hollywood's A-list mythmakers, a filmmaker who hadn't lost his ability to fascinate the cultural mainstream.

It is true that Lucas was likely stuck in a no-win situation with *Episode I*; nothing could hope to match the charm and inventiveness of the original trilogy, yet fans expected nothing less than the second coming. Inflated expectations aside, *Menace* still disappointed due to unnecessarily convoluted plotting and an overreliance on special effects at the expense of characterization (not to mention the most annoying CGI character

> "I'm just a simple man, trying to make my way in the universe."
>
> —Jango Fett, as written by George Lucas

ever created, Jar Jar Binks, and a lifeless performance by moppet-haired Jake Lloyd as the boy who would be Vader, Anakin Sky-walker). Lucas (working this time with cowriter Jonathan Hale) wisely tones down the technically impressive clutter in the more streamlined and coherent *Episode II,* and the renewed focus on straightforward dramatic storytelling makes for a considerable improvement over the bloated *Phantom.*

Despite a long middle section that drags and plenty of insipid dialogue (never Lucas's strong suit), there is much that thrills in *Clones.* The effects wizards at Industrial Light & Magic have again created a dazzling, visually dense spectacle, every shot stuffed with fantastical creatures and computer-generated trickery. The action is also better integrated into the storyline; a chase through an asteroid field, a massive Jedi battle unmatched by anything in the previous trilogy and the now-infamous, ass-kickin' Yoda climax (although a mockery of the grace and beauty that so endeared the character to millions) at least deliver more action than three *Phantom Menace*s combined. This isn't vintage *Star Wars,* but at least it makes *Episode III* an exciting proposition again. And a digital Yoda on DVD is better than no Yoda at all.

The Goodies Amid much controversy, Lucas became one of the few high-profile moviemakers who chose not to fully embrace the DVD format. Not until a full year after the VHS release of *The Phantom Menace* did its DVD finally arrive. Reviews were generally enthusiastic, but Lucas continued to anger enthusiasts by pledging not to release the original *Star Wars* trilogy on the format until the completion of *Episode III.* As the long wait for Luke, Leia and Han continues, what is the *Star Wars* fan to do?

The Phantom Menace DVD was a very fine two-disc set, filled with plenty of extras, the most noteworthy being the excellent sixty-minute documentary "The Beginning . . ." But *Episode II* bests the already-impressive standard set by *Menace.* Three full-length documentaries are included: "From Puppets to Pixels," "The Pre-Visualization of Episode II," and "Films Are Not Released, They Escape." The *Star Wars* saga virtually invented the special-effects film, so each of these featurettes are predictably and appropriately geared toward this aspect of the production. Despite some complex concepts, each featurette is clear, concise and acceptable. But unlike the *Episode I* DVD, here Lucas doesn't skimp on the story: four additional featurettes explore the film's storyline, the boring romantic subplot (go make some popcorn), and best of all, the action scenes. Slick, well-edited and brimming with new interviews with all of the major cast and crew, the combined material exceeds two hours.

More nuts-and-bolts insight into the highly unusual experience of making a *Star Wars* epic, from script to screen, can be found in the screen-specific audio commentary with Lucas and his top artists, including coscreenwriter Hale, producer Rick McCallum and production designer Ben Burtt. It avoids redundancy with the featurettes, but many of the topics discussed require visuals; the featurettes remain the better choice except for the most devoted.

At a reported cost of over a million dollars, Lucas has gone back and fully completed eight deleted sequences cut from the finished film. Even if they are sometimes extraneous and thus wisely excised, the chance to see more of the beloved *Star Wars* universe beyond the final cut should prove irresistible to fans. *Clones* also contains a treasure trove of additional promotional material: an award-winning collection of twelve "web documentaries," an Industrial Light & Magic montage, a John Williams music video, extensive still galleries, and a wide assortment of teasers, trailers and TV spots round out the package. And continuing to push DVD technology to the next level, *Episode II* offers exclusive access to a secret web portal that contains more unique content, included additional production notes, stills, essays and, most impressive, further text and audio commentaries that could not fit on the disc.

The Presentation A true digital pioneer, Lucas continued to break boundaries with *Episode II,* the first full-length Hollywood motion picture to be shot entirely in High-Definition. Unlike traditional live-action films, movies shot in high definition require no film-to-tape telecine—the transfer stays entirely in the digital realm. While the practice is becoming increasingly common with computer-animated features, such as the *Toy Story* films, *Episode II* represents the first live-action feature-length motion picture released on DVD in purely digital form. The results are breathtaking!

What a flawless presentation: colors pop off the screen, almost unreal in their purity and clarity. The film offers a three-dimensional appearance with tremendous depth and detail. While some doubted that digitally shot material could produce true blacks, *Episode II* proves otherwise. Contrast is also excellent. If there are any drawbacks, *Clones* may be *too* sharp. Lacking the warm, natural appearance of film-based material, some of the darkest sequences lack definition and simply look murky. Some slight noise is also evident in the low-light, high-contrast sequences. But it is still hard to argue with how good *Episode II* looks. It is a stunner.

Attack of the Clones also rules with an earth-shaking 5.1 Dolby Digital Surround EX soundtrack. It is not hyperbole to say it is state of the art, perhaps the best aural presentation yet heard on a DVD. This is what home theater is all about: a highly aggressive, fully immersive sonic experience that remains unrivalled. The Lucasfilm team of sound designers, led by Academy Award–winner Gary Rydstrom, have created a wholly realistic, 360-degree soundfield that is consistently engaging and active. The subwoofer delivers such incredibly low frequencies it might rearrange the furniture. *Clones* attacks!

Additional Recommendations The largely lackluster *Phantom Menace* still makes for a decent time waster until the original, much beloved trilogy arrives. Other Lucas-produced or -directed hits that have received the special edition treatment: Ron Howard's sword and sorcery fantasy *Willow,* which also includes an audio commentary with Howard and Lucas; Francis Ford Coppola's underrated biopic *Tucker: A Man and His Dream*; and the little-seen if inventive CGI-addled mystery-thriller, *The Radioland Murders*.

FULL THROTTLE:
A CONVERSATION
WITH McG

Born Joseph McGinty Nichol, McG may be the ultimate movie brat. This self-professed child of the 1980s began his career directing a string of successful music videos and commercials, landing him multiple industry and MTV Awards, before graduating to the big leagues with the blockbuster *Charlie's Angels* and its sequel *Full Throttle*, which have grossed a combined half a billion dollars worldwide. Now making his mark in television production with the hit drama *The O.C.*, McG is one of the most successful, stylish and innovative filmmakers of his generation.

With both of the *Charlie's Angels* DVDs, you've proven yourself to be one of the most aggressive filmmakers around when it comes to pushing the limits of the format. How much is DVD on your mind when you begin a project?

I'm very excited about the DVD format, so I'm thinking about it from the first day of prep. I love when a guy like David Fincher takes it so seriously and does everything he can to make the DVD release that much more informative and interesting to the viewer. DVDs are my favorite medium because I go back and study my favorite films and listen to the commentary tracks. So I'm always thinking about how to take it higher and how to add more interesting materials, and I think it's really sort of the film school of this generation. Or at least a hell of a supplement.

Many have called your films "pop-culture blenders" and this aesthetic could be seen as carrying over to your approach to DVD.

Is that a good thing or a bad thing? Well, I'm a latchkey kid. I was raised on flat Pepsi and *Donahue*. Film and music are just really my two great passions in life, and I grew up watching movies and was exposed to many different sorts. My brother being a sort of rough-and-tumble guy, I got exposed to my favorite Marlon Brando pictures all the way through to the great action pictures of the '80s. And my sister was this huge fan of musicals and romantic classics, and my mom was showing me Bubsy Berkeley films. I had a very diverse upbringing in regard to what I was listening to and what I was looking at. And I was happy to sort of ingest and redefine that and hopefully develop something of a voice of my own.

That is certainly clear in your commentaries, which are so rapid-fire and dense. What sort of preparation, if any, do you do when preparing to record one?

I get a little nervous. Like anybody, I hate the sound of my own voice and you feel a little weird. You have so much on your mind when you make a movie, it's real easy to get in front of it and just start talking about it. At least it comes naturally for me.

On *Full Throttle,* you again brought in a new element with the Telestrator feature, which allowed you to draw on the screen.

I really dug it. I was familiar with what John Madden would do on Monday Night Football, and I said hey, that's a fun tool to have while we sit there and watch the film go down in real time. It's very interesting. It was a nice tool to encourage me to talk more frankly and openly about the things I liked and the things I was not so happy about.

You've often been called a "movie brat," in the sense that your style can be seen as having been clearly influenced by MTV music videos and possesses a very fast-cut edit style. How would you respond to criticisms that this kind of approach is style over substance?

Well here's the thing, I happen to think that an aggressive cutting pattern is correct for a movie like *Charlie's Angels*. But we try to find time to hold and develop shots that are one long, steady cam shot—again, the [Martin] Scorsese influence along with many others. The picture opens with a single shot that's, I think, north of two or maybe three minutes. And we had to hide cuts in there and have fun, sort of an Alfred Hitchcock *Rope* thing. But I also know that this is a pop-culture movie that's designed to have pace and keep all demographics entertained.

However, I promise you the next picture I make will be the most stark, the most architecturally photographed, the most purposeful and methodically shot picture you can imagine, because my favorite pictures are *The Graduate* and *Rushmore,* and these ultra-methodical pictures that create a proscenium and let the actors play out the action within that arch. That is what excites me most, and I look forward to showing some different moves.

Full Throttle was released on DVD in two versions, the PG-13 theatrical cut and unrated. One of the major criticisms of this trend toward "revisionist filmmaking"—which DVD has certainly accelerated—is that it contributes to the erosion of cohesive storytelling and a feeling that there is no longer one single version or defining vision for a film.

That's a very compelling point. I haven't given it a great deal of thought, and in this particular application I don't feel that the additional material altered the film in a great way. It's not as though it's an alternate ending or I had some mega-studio battle in regard to the direction I wanted to take the picture, that this is finally a director's cut. Frankly, this is a cut that just supercedes the PG-13 barriers. So in that respect I don't know if this unrated version qualifies as

one of those sort of controversial hot buttons.

But that's a hell of a question, because I kind of agree with you, as a filmmaker. I like locking into one version of a picture. I mean, do you want to see an alternate version of *Gone With the Wind*? Do you want to see an alternate version of *The Godfather*? It's like they're sacred cows that you enjoy every nuance [of], and it's sort of the fun of being a film fan, memorizing the lines and knowing what the cuts are and knowing the rhythm of the picture. I don't know if you always want to be hit with that kind of curveball. That's a hell of a point. What do you think?

I would argue that if it is a question of a film that was taken away from a director or where cuts or alterations were made for arbitrary reasons—such as *Blade Runner*—then most are in favor of a new version and DVD is a godsend. However, sometimes alternate cuts can become mere vanity projects or simply marketing driven with no regard for storytelling or historical relevance.

You know what? I think there are examples where they've messed it up. I know, for example, John Landis, and Landis redid *The Blues Brothers* [DVD]. That is a simple comedy, not an earth-changing film. I enjoyed the studio release much more than I enjoyed what was, I guess, the director's cut. It's a lot slower. It just didn't feel as punchy and as enjoyable. But I don't know, that's a fabulous question. And I would hate to think in any way I'm contributing to the downfall of the art form.

At least with DVD, you do know that any great cut material will eventually find a home and be seen.

You know, I must say in fairness that I have thought that way about a few things, and I know that some things we do are likely to end up on the cutting room floor. Then you put it in the back of your mind, "Well, there is DVD." And it's become such an extraordinarily well-received format that it really matters, and you can really count on people seeing this additional material on a DVD. The intention is to honor the fans and give them more, if they happen to enjoy your picture, to give them more to draw from. I think in a perfect world you'd always make the original theatrical release readily available, and if people are inter-

ested in the additional materials, God bless.

As the DVD format more and more races along the cutting edge, do you have any interest in pursuing its more interactive capabilities, such as presenting a film in multiple angles or allowing viewers to make their own edits or versions?

That's fantastic. It is very progressive thinking and the problem that took us out of pursuing that on this go-round was just a time-table. 'Cause I love exploring that idea and being able to watch the movie in a different way. Truthfully, I've thought about even doing something where you qualify a few people who are interested in doing it and making a lot of the dailies available so they could deliver a different cut of the picture. That's really going for it. Look, you got Final Cut Pro and everything on everybody's computers. Imagine if maybe we could just start with a couple scenes, where you go, "Here are the dailies; cut your own scene together." I don't know. Maybe that's stupid?

Not at all. I think it may be the next big paradigm shift in how

we watch movies. But it does have a dark side. Both *Charlie's Angels* films have seen multiple releases, which caused some fans to become very irritated at being asked to purchase different versions. Now, we have HD-DVD and other possible formats on the horizon. Where do you think the future lies?

You've got to be sensitive to the marketing needs of the studios. I'm very interested in vinyl, for example, but I bought everything that I had on vinyl on CD. When HD-DVD comes out, I suspect I'll be duplicating my DVD collection to a large degree. I'm always interested in exploring new sonic formats and new visual formats. So, in the event that they're able to make true progress, I suppose I'm all for it. O

Straw Dogs

DISTRIBUTOR: The Criterion Collection
DVD RELEASE: March 25, 2003
THEATRICAL RELEASE: December 1971
RUNNING TIME: 117 Minutes
MPAA RATING: R

Sometimes we go to the movies to laugh. Sometimes to cry. Sometimes to be scared. Then there are those movies that we go to simply to bear witness. Sam Peckinpah's *Straw Dogs* is such a movie. It is not entertainment but an artifact, a highly controversial and incendiary examination of man's propensity for violence. It depicts repugnant acts in unflinching detail and is often unpleasant to watch. But if movies are supposed to hold a mirror up to our society and show us who we are and why we do what we do, then *Straw Dogs* is one of the most important films of its kind ever made.

The crux of *Straw Dogs*'s dramatic arc rests on the prolonged rape of Amy Sumner (Susan George) at the hands of the strangers who have come to repair the summer home she is sharing with her husband, George (Dustin Hoffman). In the most outrageous scene in a film full of outrageous scenes, Amy does not initially tell George of the crime, because Peckinpah is as interested in the violence—emotional and physical—that the couple will do to each other as the violence that will be done to them by others. George, a self-professed pacifist, eventually discovers what has happened and metes out his own violent retribution. The protracted concluding scenes of *Straw Dogs* are some of the most intense, violent and brutal of any in a mainstream motion picture.

> "I'll have an answer, or I'll have blood!"
>
> —Tom Hedden

Straw Dogs has been praised and condemned in equal measure. It was unfairly lumped in with the 1970s vigilante boom, taking an uneasy place alongside such exploitation cheapies as *I Spit on Your Grave, Last House on the Left, The Hills Have Eyes* and *Death Wish*. But *Straw Dogs* is a fundamentally moral film. What caused the most consternation was that Peckinpah, no stranger to traversing political minefields, refused to make any obvious statements. His position and themes are clear in the film's text, presented without abstraction or bravura technique to soften the blow. Violence is inherent to the nature of man, as unavoidable and inevitable as death. We cannot eradicate it, only acknowledge its existence and react responsibly when afforded the choice to use it.

Many hate *Straw Dogs* and find no redeeming social value in its message whatsoever. Pauline Kael branded Peckinpah a fascist and took the film to task for what she and most critics saw as a disturbing message, writing, "The movie intends to demonstrate not merely that there is a point at which a man will fight but that he is a better man for it—a real man at last." That ideological warfare follows the film whenever it is shown, and it only reinforces Peckinpah's themes. *Straw Dogs* is a film that dares to present violence for what it is: ugly, repulsive and finite. It is not an incitement to violence or a plea for true pacificism, but finds the line between the two and stays just one millimeter off to the side. The right one.

The Goodies *Straw Dogs* is fascinating for the intense reactions it is still able to provoke. The fact that "names" such as Hoffman agreed to appear in the picture did nothing to quell audiences' moral outrage. And Peckinpah only helped to fan the flames of controversy during press for the film and subsequent interviews. All of this is prime fodder for a terrific DVD. *Straw Dogs* is the kind of incendiary motion picture tailor made for the intelligent, comprehensive treatment The Criterion Collection is famous for. It has delivered again with this excellent two-disc set.

Two alternate audio tracks are included: an audio commentary by film scholar Stephen Prince, who makes a strong case for the film while not shying away from the valid points its many detractors make, and an isolated music and effects track that is more peculiar. Jerry Fielding's score is a fine one, but this monoaural film does not benefit much from having its dated effects laid bare for examination. And they intrude on the score, making this a curious choice indeed.

The second disc of this set is highlighted by an excellent eighty-two-minute documentary produced for the BBC, "Sam Peckinpah: Man of Iron." Viewing it is best left for after you watch *Straw Dogs* (as it reveals almost the entire film). A cast of amazing luminaries contributes new interviews about their experiences working with the often irascible Peckinpah, including James Coburn, Kris Kristofferson, Jason Robards, R. G. Armstrong, screenwriters Jim Silke and Alan Sharp, and longtime confidants including Mort Sahl. Peckinpah was an addictive personality and waged a battle with the bottle that lasted up until his death in 1976, and the recollections of his fiery personality are by turns haunting and hilarious; Kristofferson sings songs, while Robards reads a poignant letter written before Peckinpah succumbed to cancer. A must-see.

A real find is the vintage 1971 twenty-six-minute featurette "On Location: Dustin Hoffman," with Hoffman speaking eloquently about the film's controversial themes and working with Peckinpah. Produced exclusively for this DVD are two more interviews, with George (twenty minutes) and producer Daniel Melnick (nineteen minutes), plus a newly-discovered eight-minute reel of behind-the-scenes footage.

Text and still-based material includes a "Correspondence" gallery featuring rare letters written by Peckinpah, and a stellar twenty-page full-color booklet that contains a reprint of a rare 1974 interview with Peckinpah.

The Presentation *Straw Dogs* is not a glamorous film, but it is not poorly made or photographed. Criterion struck a new interpositive from the original 35mm negative that looks amazing. This 1.85:1 anamorphic widescreen transfer rectifies most of the problems that marred all previous video incarnations. The majority of the print inconsistencies have been greatly improved or completely eradicated; blacks are now deep and consistent, and dirt, blemishes and scratches have been painstakingly removed. Detail and overall sharpness still fall far short of today's modern, glossy transfers but perfectly suit the film's intended documentarylike style. The film's original mono soundtrack is preserved here and it is fine given the age of the material. Some distortion is present, which is especially grating during the climax, and dialogue can sound muffled. Otherwise, it is clean and free of major defects and excessive hiss.

Additional Versions Anchor Bay Entertainment originally released *Straw Dogs* in a lackluster movie-only edition in 1998. It is now out of print.

The Stunt Man

DISTRIBUTOR: Anchor Bay Entertainment
DVD RELEASE: November 20, 2001
THEATRICAL RELEASE: June 1980
RUNNING TIME: 131 Minutes
MPAA RATING: R

The Stunt Man is a game of cinematic three-card monte. The three cards are reality, illusion and perception. The dealer is director Richard Rush. The player is Cameron (Steve Railsback), a Vietnam vet on the run from the police. The game itself is unwinnable; in every scene, not only are the cards reshuffled, but the cards themselves change. Cameron (and the audience that experiences the film through his eyes) sees and re-sees the motivations of each character based on whatever came before and whatever state of paranoia he happens to occupy. By the end, Cameron is resigned to live in a world not of his design or making, where if his friends, enemies and lovers didn't exist, he'd have to invent them to give his life purpose.

The Stunt Man is a complex and challenging film that is able to juggle multiple storylines and multiple themes. For those who've never seen it, the film seems impossible to describe and even more impossible to pull off in coherent fashion. When it's over, the viewer is confounded by the thematic implications and astonished that the film was able to accomplish such a magic trick.

As an audience, we never learn why Cameron is on the run until the third act, which is another way Rush keeps us off balance; if we learn of Cameron's crime too early, we may lose sympathy for him. The longer we're left wondering, the longer our feelings for him are in limbo.

Early in the film, Cameron's flight from justice takes him over an old bridge, where he seemingly causes a Duesenberg to plunge into the water, killing the driver. He continues to run, eventually stumbling onto the set of a World War I epic directed by the flamboyant, manipulative, possibly maniacal Eli Cross (Peter O'Toole). When the local sheriff (Alex Rocco) threatens to shut down the production for shooting on the bridge without a permit, not to mention manslaughter (the driver of the Duesenberg was one of the film's stunt men, filming a scene), Cross and Cameron make a deal: if Cameron pretends to be the dead stunt man, Eli will shield him from the police.

> **"If God could do the tricks that we can do, he'd be a happy man."**
>
> —Film director Eli Cross

With the deal struck, Cameron learns the tricks of the stunt trade, while also falling in love with Nina, the film's leading lady (Barbara Hershey). As beautifully choreographed by Rush, Cross floats in and out of frame on his specially designed crane, which feeds his messiah complex, as well as his desire to eavesdrop on everyone's business. And as Cameron and Nina begin sleeping together, Cameron finds his stunts are getting more dangerous. Eventually, Eli wants to reshoot the bridge scene, with Cameron driving the car into the water. Is Eli trying to kill him? Or is Cameron just being paranoid?

Rush has no answers—he's having too much fun asking the questions. As an audience, we experience the film solely through Cameron's eyes, so we're never sure if we're seeing reality, or reality as filtered through the mind of a confused Vietnam vet. It's an audacious conceit and one that could easily have stymied even the most attentive viewer, but Rush pulls it off. And he's helped by a cast and crew uniquely attuned to what he's trying to accomplish. Railsback must carry the conceit on his shoulders and he never waivers. As for O'-Toole, his Eli Cross is a riveting, zestful fusion of Zeus and Ming the Merciless. Moments before rolling on an emotional scene, Cross informs Nina that he "accidentally" showed her parents their daughter's nude scene, making her cry on cue.

The Stunt Man carries a heavy thematic burden, but Rush keeps things lighthearted and easy to digest. He's a master plate spinner: although he seems to have more plates than poles to spin them atop, nothing falls. It's extremely accomplished filmmaking and a wonderfully enjoyable film.

The Goodies Like The Criterion Collection, Anchor Bay produces some of the most exhaustive and interesting DVDs on offer. And with a limited edition pressing of only 100,000 copies, *The Stunt Man* is no exception. Fans of the film should be on the lookout, because it's well worth full price.

There is a terrific audio commentary from director Richard Rush and actors O'Toole, Railsback, Hershey, Alex Rocco, Sharon Farrell and Chuck Bail. Not everyone was recorded at the same time, but the result is seamless and always insightful. Viewers confused by the film will enjoy hearing Rush's interpretation of the more baffling plot and thematic elements.

Two deleted scenes are included. Neither warranted inclusion in the film, which of course, is the beauty of DVD: if it's not good enough for the final cut, it'll work as a DVD supplement worth promoting. Rounding out the festivities are three trailers and a collection of stills broken down into "Production Stills," "Behind-the-Scenes" and, best of the lot, "Original Production and Advertising Art." Those with DVD-ROM access can read the film's screenplay and browse script notes written by Rush that clear up some thematic mysteries.

The Limited Edition DVD contains a second disc featuring "The Sinister Saga of Making *The Stunt Man*." It's a 114-minute documentary about the torturous birth of this unique film. The documentary is written, directed and hosted by Rush, who is obviously less than objective. Still, he is extremely intelligent and wonderfully engaging. He is also quite comprehensive regarding the entire *Stunt Man* experience, from his love of the original book through his fights with a studio that didn't believe in or understand the final product. Look for interesting facts (Eli Cross was a pseudonym Rush used during his years directing exploitation films) and lots of insight into the filmmaking process.

The Presentation Anchor Bay presents *The Stunt Man* anamorphically encoded and in its original aspect ratio of 1.85:1. While the film has never looked better, without a complete digital overhaul it cannot overcome the deficiencies of the source material and the ravages of age. The primary culprits here are grain, digital noise and some edge enhancement. Aside from that, the film looks quite good. Colors are a tad muted, which is standard for films of this era. Blacks are dark and stable, with better-than-expected shadow detail. The picture is fairly sharp, with good detail and very good contrast. Flesh tones are accurate. Overall, the transfer is schizophrenic: most scenes look terrific, some look amazing, others look worn.

The audio comes complete with Dolby Digital Surround EX, DTS ES (which requires a DTS decoder) and Dolby surround 2.0 options. The EX and ES make great use of the front speakers, with decent directional effects involving helicopters, off-screen voices and battle sounds. The soundscape is surprisingly active, but the dialogue tends to sound a bit edgy with an occasional hard-to-discern line. During more complicated scenes, the EX and ES mixes tend to favor effects and music over dialogue. Those without fancy receivers will be glad to know the Dolby Digital 2.0 is very good and, in reproducing dialogue, actually better.

Sunset Boulevard

DISTRIBUTOR: Paramount Home Entertainment
DVD RELEASE: November 26, 2002
THEATRICAL RELEASE: August 1950
RUNNING TIME: 110 Minutes
MPAA RATING: Not Rated

Billy Wilder's *Sunset Boulevard* is the ultimate Hollywood ghost story. It is not a horror film per se, although it abounds in gothic imagery and its morbid, death-obsessed heroine recalls many of the twisted and psychologically bent protagonists of classic horror literature. And it is not about the supernatural, although in Hollywood, a town built on illusion and delusion, the recently departed will always live on, forever immortalized on celluloid. But in a tinsel town that creates has-beens before they have even arrived, and you are only as famous as your last picture. For aging screen "legend" Norma Desmond (Gloria Swanson), no price is too high for screen immortality. Even murder. She is, and will always be, ready for her close-up.

Still considered the most stinging indictment of Hollywood ever put on film, *Sunset Boulevard* has achieved a screen immortality of its own. It is the definitive movie of faded glamour and broken dreams. As much indebted to film noir as to horror, it is a frequently talky picture, in fact it's a film all *about* talk, about hyperbole and verbal deception and hack writers long on exposition but short on talent. Our hero, Joe Gillis (William Holden), comes to live with Desmond at first out of pity for the aging siren and her futile attempt at a comeback. But Gillis's pity turns to profit; he begins to see this feeble "sleepwalker," a "poor devil, still waving at a parade that has gone by," as his meal ticket.

> "I am big. It's the pictures that got small."
>
> —Norma Desmond

Norma, meanwhile, has fallen in love with Joe, although in the long tradition of tarnished noir heroes, he is in love with another writer his own age, Betty (Nancy Olson), who is unaware of how close to the edge of madness Norma is teetering. When Gillis rebuffs her advances, Norma begins to plot his murder. And Gillis will realize he has underestimated a woman he thought was none the wiser.

If *Sunset Boulevard* had only been a joke at the expense of Norma Desmond, it would not have endured for over fifty years. The script, by Charles Brackett, D. M. Marshman Jr. and Wilder, is witty, sharp and impeccably constructed, but it is Swanson's tour de force performance that turned Norma into a cinematic icon—a symbol for every star we have long since forgotten. Swanson, in one of the film's many stinging parallels, returned from self-imposed retirement to conquer Hollywood—she won an Oscar nomination for her performance here. In the beginning, we think *Sunset Boulevard* is about Gillis: at first we see Norma through his eyes, as a pathetic, narcissistic has-been Joe has "lowered himself" to associated with. But Norma will be only one in a long line of Hollywood women that he and the industry—and by association, we the moviegoers—have written off. Her script for her planned comeback vehicle *Salome* is dreadful, but she is the actor, not the writer. He is. And a failed one, who has never achieved fame or success of any measure. The studio ultimately rejects *his* script, the one that *he* spent months polishing, which reminds us that it is *she* who has lowered herself to be with *him*. The film's climax is filled with a sense of dread but, paradoxically, also a near-euphoric feeling of triumph. Norma returns to Hollywood, if not famous than at least infamous, while Joe lies dead in her pool, like a rat floating in a sewer. It is only at the end of the brilliant *Sunset Boulevard* that we realize we have been listening to the narration of a dead man.

The Goodies Creating meaningful and worthwhile supplemental content for classics whose participants have long since passed away continues to pose one of the greatest challenges for DVD producers and the studios. *Sunset Boulevard* is an example of how supplements, if done with passion, craft and class, can excel regardless of the age of a film. Ed Sikov, author of *On Sunset Boulevard: The Life and Times of Billy Wilder,* provides a new screen-specific audio commentary and succeeds at holding our interest for 110 minutes. Solo tracks with historians are often dry, but Sikov manages to be engaging, clear and concise. Fans of his book may find much that is familiar, but newcomers will discover a great deal that is informative. The twenty-eight-minute featurette "The Making of Sunset Boulevard" is a bit slim on original material—only Sikov, actress Nancy Olsen, producer A. C. Lyles, critic Andrew Sarris and Broadway's Norma Desmond, Glenn Close, offer new interviews. But it is more visually stimulating than the commentary, with a wealth of rare stills and, even better, rare script excerpts. Two shorter featurettes honor "Edith Head—The Paramount Years" (fourteen minutes), with biographer David Chierichetti, "The Music of *Sunset Boulevard*" (fifteen minutes), featuring a new interview with legendary composer Elmer Berstein.

Test audiences reacted so negatively to *Sunset Boulevard*'s original opening "Morgue Prologue" that it inspired guffaws and turned the film into an unintentional comedy. Wilder promptly cut it, and most of the footage was destroyed. Long the stuff of legend, the sequence has been reconstructed here in two versions. Excellent use is made of the DVD format's multi-angle capabilities, as the script version presents the sequence in text form, and the montage version arranges it as a montage of stills, narration and text.

Additional supplements include the amusing "Hollywood Location Map," which offers one- to two-minute video vignettes on six of the film's famous locations, three still galleries—"Production," "The Movie" and "Publicity"—and the film's theatrical trailer.

The Presentation The faded glamour of *Sunset Boulevard* has been cleaned up with an eerie verisimilitude. Presented in its original 1.37:1 aspect ratio, this is a near-immaculate print, with rich, pure blacks and excellent contrast. John F. Seitz's mesmerizing black-and-white photography is evocative and haunted, flush with never-before-seen detail—the interiors of Norma's decrepit mansion are dripping with texture—and is incredibly smooth and filmlike. Paramount has also restored *Sunset Boulevard*'s original mono track, which is now cleaner and more robust; the film's extensive dialogue and Holden's hard-boiled narration come through with great clarity and considerable heft. It is still mono, but more than adequate. *Sunset Boulevard* is at last ready for its own close-up.

Superman: The Movie

DISTRIBUTOR: Warner Home Video
DVD RELEASE: May 1, 2001
THEATRICAL RELEASE: December 1978
RUNNING TIME: 151 Minutes
MPAA RATING: PG

Late one summer evening in 1933, a young author named Jerome Siegel had a dream. Raised on a steady diet of Saturday matinee serials, pulp magazines and short-story anthologies, he imagined the ultimate superhero: an orphan from the planet Krypton who possessed amazing powers and would speak directly to a country eager to re-embrace heroism, nobility and truth after the struggles of the Great Depression. He called his creation Superman. He developed the idea after school with fellow classmate and amateur illustrator Joseph Shuster, and soon "The Man of Steel" was flying high in comic books the world over. By the end of the 1930s it had become a bona fide phenomenon—from comics to books to radio to TV. Seventy years later, Superman remains the most recognizable superhero in history.

> "Some people can read *War and Peace* and come away thinking it's a simple adventure story. Others can read the ingredients on a chewing gum wrapper and unlock the secrets of the universe."
>
> —Lex Luthor

The greatest strength of Richard Donner's *Superman: The Movie* is its respect for Siegel's character. Donner's motto throughout the making of the movie was "verisimilitude," his intention to make a fantasy that was so honest and true, "people had to believe it was real." He and screenwriter Tom Mankiewicz refused to make a campy update, like the *Batman* television series, or a dark reimaginging full of irony and despair. We love Superman because he is square-jawed, noble and honest (corny qualities even in 1978). *Superman: The Movie* understands this. It is a grand slice of classic Americana, a film about ideals and values and doing what is right. Superman doesn't just fight for truth, justice and the American way. He *is* America.

It is hard to imagine anyone in the role of Superman other than Christopher Reeve. More formidable than his physique is his charisma: who else would have been able to find the inherent strength, dignity and goodness in the character *and* pull off blue tights, a red cape and a spit curl? Also perfectly cast is Margot Kidder as Lois Lane. Their witty banter and playful flirting are funny and sexy. And Donner and Mankiewicz stuff *Superman* with memorable supporting characters and a great cast. Gene Hackman, an actor so perfect for the role you would think he was born bald, is the ideal Lex Luthor; ex-Little Rascal Jackie Cooper is an inspired Perry White, and Ned Beatty plays the ultimate dimwitted accomplice. Marlon Brando, who sent shockwaves through the industry by earning a then unheard-of $4 million for only a few minutes of screen time as Jor-El, lends an appropriate air of regality to the proceedings. The secret of *Superman: The Movie* is easy: everyone here has fun with Superman, but they don't make fun *of* Superman.

Originally planned for a major theatrical rerelease in 1999, *Superman: The Movie* underwent an extensive restoration, including the reinstatement of eight minutes of additional footage, supervised by Donner. It eventually played in only a few local theaters, so the first time most will see this restored version is on DVD. Several key sequences have been expanded, giving precious insight into Superman's backstory and his home planet of Krypton. Rare for an expanded cut, the additions do not disrupt the pacing or feel intrusive, but only enhance the story. And the film's landmark special effects have been cleaned up but not touched up—and still amaze. I am afraid that if you think you have already seen *Superman: The Movie,* you will have to see it again.

The Goodies One of the most requested titles in the Warner Brothers library, *Superman: The Movie* finally took flight on DVD in the spring of 2000. It was well worth the wait. The story of the making of *Superman* is legendary, a torturous production fraught with chaos, contention and clashing egos. The production was originally conceived as two movies to be shot back to back, but Donner was unceremoniously fired by producers Ilya and Alexander Salkind after completing the first film and much of the footage for 1981's *Superman II,* and eventually replaced by Richard Fleischer. Cast and crew quickly took sides in the growing war, and tensions reached the breaking point, not helped by the film's punishing shooting schedule and pioneering effects, which rarely worked. It was Reeve, not cast until the eve of principal photography, who finally unified the production and proved that, yes, a man really could fly.

This amazing story is told in an excellent ninety-minute documentary, divided into three acts: "Taking Flight: the Development of *Superman,*" "Making *Superman*: Filming the Legend," and "The Magic Behind the Cape." Donner, Mankiewicz, Reeve, Kidder, Hackman, editor Stuart Baird, composer John Williams and the effects team return to pay tribute to the film that catapulted them into the stratosphere. Donner's contentious interactions with the Salkinds and the studio are addressed matter-of-factly, time having dulled some of the edge but none of the heart. While the amount of behind-the-scenes footage is not extensive, what is here is revealing; the effects are fascinating to witness and often hilarious, especially when all does not go as planned. And priceless is the footage of the various costume concepts Reeve had to endure and the discussion of his ever-changing codpiece.

Donner and Mankiewicz also contribute a screen-specific audio commentary that delves into even more detail on the massive shoot, the casting and the endless feuds with the Salkinds. The development of the script was complex; two movies were eventually combined into one shoot (which is even more apparent watching the disjointed *Superman II* today), and Mankewicz was relegated to a "creative consultant" credit. This commentary is their vindication, a portrait of Hollywood at its worst and the comic-book movie at its best.

A wealth of additional supplements fills out an amazing special edition: two deleted scenes not incorporated into the expanded version of the film, screen tests with many of the major stars beaten out by Kidder for the role of Lois Lane (including Anne Archer, Stockard Channing and Lesley Ann Warren), a text-based production history, a selection of alternate music cues, and, best of all, Williams's breathtaking score isolated as its own music track in Dolby Digital 5.0

The Presentation As photographed by Oscar-winner Jeffrey Unsworth, *Superman: The Movie* is big, bold, bright and the perfect realization of comic-book style. For years, his work suffered from washed-out, murky video transfers, with nearly half of the expansive 2.35:1 frame cropped and the film's many effects shots riddled with dirt and grime. Not anymore. *Superman* soars! Meticulously restored, the Man of Steel's tights are now the proper shade of blue, a big red "S" blazing across his chest. The print is near-pristine, blacks rich and detail a revelation. Scenes that before appeared poorly shot or obscured by haze and softness are now clear, sharp and three-dimensional. A stunning piece of work.

The film's majestic soundtrack has also been remixed in Dolby Digital 5.1, complete with newly recorded sounds and, for the reinstated footage, rescored music cues. The soundtrack is much more expansive, with a lively presence to the surrounds and distinct separation across all channels. Sometimes, the balance between the dialogue, effects and Williams's tremendous score (rightfully a classic) feels a bit off—the effects can overwhelm the action, and the score can be a little too subdued. Otherwise, this is an exciting, enveloping presentation. Up, up and away!

Additional Recommendations While 1980's *Superman II* is an above-average sequel, both *Superman III* and *Superman IV: The Quest for Peace* remain two of the most misconceived follow-ups in Hollywood history. All four *Superman* films are available separately or as a four-disc box set, although none except the first include any extra features at all aside from theatrical trailers, and there are no additional supplements offered in the box set. And for the truly brave,

Anchor Bay Entertainment has released a two-disc special edition of *Supergirl,* easily one of the most misbegotten spinoffs of all time.

Taxi Driver

DISTRIBUTOR: Columbia TriStar Home Entertainment
DVD RELEASE: June 15, 1999
THEATRICAL RELEASE: February 1976
RUNNING TIME: 113 Minutes
MPAA RATING: R

As cities get more crowded, people get lonelier. And the technology of the twenty-first century only encourages that isolation. Inside, people surf the Internet, play video games and engage in other solitary pursuits that require locked doors and minds turned in on themselves. Outside, people walk the streets to the private bleating of an MP3 player or chat on a cell phone as the girl of their dreams, the bane of their existence or the answer to their prayers walks by. How would Travis Bickle, the lonely, alienated cab driver in Martin Scorsese's 1976 classic *Taxi Driver,* fare in such a world?

Bickle, as indelibly portrayed by Robert De Niro, is desperate for the tiniest shred of meaningful human contact, but hasn't the faintest idea how to achieve it. When we first meet Bickle, a Vietnam vet suffering from insomnia, he's just landed a job as a graveyard-shift cabbie. As he cruises the rain-slicked streets of New York, steam rising from every other manhole, the lives of others play out not in front of him, but behind him. Travis's interaction with humanity is available only through the limited scope of his rearview mirror, with the cab's partition a physical and emotional barrier.

As Bickle crisscrosses a crime-infested New York, his sense of isolation only increases. "All the animals come out at night," he says. "Whores, skunk pussies, buggers, queens, fairies, dopers, junkies . . . Someday a real rain will come and wash this scum off the streets." To Travis, those who won't invite him into the world, the world of normal, civilized men, become his enemies.

With a loneliness matched only by his growing hostility, Travis anoints himself a knight in shining armor to one girl who yearns to be liberated from the living dead who inhabit his New York. She is Betsy (Cybill Shepherd), a campaign worker for Senator Palantine, who is seeking his party's presidential nomination. Travis boldly asks her to coffee and she accepts, and during their lunch she describes Travis by quoting Kris Kristofferson: "He's a prophet and a pusher, partly truth, partly fiction. A walking contradiction." Travis does not

> **"Loneliness has followed me my whole life, everywhere. In bars, in cars, sidewalks, stores, everywhere. There's no escape. I'm God's lonely man."**
>
> —Travis Bickle

understand what Betsy means and replies, "I'm no pusher." For their next date, Travis takes Betsy to a porn film, which offends her, much to his confusion. Bickle responds by trying to assassinate Palantine, the man he feels is controlling her.

Travis's other project is Iris (Jodie Foster), a twelve-year-old prostitute under the control of Sport (Harvey Keitel). Travis wants to save Iris, not sleep with her, and she is his ultimate challenge. Whereas Betsy lives in an upper-middle-class world of politics, Iris is among the very filth he has come to despise.

When all the events of Travis's postwar life converge in an orgy of violence, savagely staged by Scorsese, it provides Bickle with his one, brief, glorious opportunity, not to save Iris, but to be considered Iris's savior.

Taxi Driver's dark, disturbing sense of urban isolation has been brought masterfully to life by Scorsese and De Niro, with Paul Schrader's unflinching script and Bernard Herrmann's dark, supple score playing crucial roles. Travis Bickle is one of cinema's most memorable characters. Maybe Bickle would be happier in the twenty-first century. In a video game, he can rescue the fair maiden a hundred times . . . and not have to pay the price in blood.

The Goodies Columbia TriStar Home Video has assembled a terrific set of supplements that honor this essential American film. The premiere extra is "Making *Taxi Driver*," a thorough seventy-one-minute documentary produced in 1999 by DVD documentarian Laurent Bouzereau. All the principals are interviewed: Schrader discusses his inspiration for writing the script and dissects the film's meaning; actors De Niro, Shepherd, Foster, Keitel, Albert Brooks, and Peter Boyle talk of their contributions; and director Scorsese deconstructs his technical approach. Everyone involved is articulate, intelligent and obviously grateful for the chance to work on the film.

"Photo Montage" is nine minutes of decent behind-the-scenes stills that run continuously as Bouzereau relates anecdotes that didn't make the final cut of his documentary. There is also a collection of storyboards from the climatic scene, with each storyboard preceeded by its matching frame in the film. An interesting supplement is Schrader's excellent original screenplay, which can be read straight through, or, with the touch of a button, the viewer can jump from the written scene to its corresponding scene in the film.

Rounding the set out are stills of the original lobby cards, filmographies of the major players and *Taxi Driver*'s theatrical trailer.

The Presentation Columbia TriStar Home Entertainment presents this seminal film in its original aspect ratio of 1.85:1, anamorphically encoded. It's an outstanding transfer, especially considering the film's age and the amount of night scenes that could easily have rendered the picture a muddy, pixelated mess. Colors are well saturated and look as vibrant as the original source material, with exterior colors looking especially vivid. The picture is sharp, with exceptional flesh tones and detail. Black levels and shadow detail, where the transfer was most likely to fail, are generally excellent, although some later scenes look a bit dim. Travis's journey through the Manhattan night, punctuated by red and blue neon, is rendered exquisitely. Most of the time, grain is either nonexistent or light, which is quite an achievement. More impressive is the lack of print flaws or edge enhancement. Fans of *Taxi Driver* should consider this Collector's Edition the gold standard in terms of video quality.

Less impressive but still very good is the Dolby Digital 2.0 surround soundtrack. Benefiting most from the mix is Herrmann's

Oscar-nominated score. Heavy brass and a single pleading sax combine beautifully, and the mix reproduces the highs and the lows accurately. Dialogue, which comes mostly from the center speaker, is generally clean, although certain lines sound rough. Background city noise is occasionally harsh; however, the original recording probably sounded exactly the same. Surrounds are intermittently utilized to acceptable effect. Otherwise, there are no pops, hisses or other aural anomalies. Considering the film was originally presented in mono, Columbia TriStar has done a terrific job of filling out the soundscape.

Additional Versions Columbia TriStar Home Entertainment originally released *Taxi Driver* on DVD in September 1997. That movie-only edition was quickly retired and replaced by this much-improved special edition.

The Terminator

DISTRIBUTOR: MGM Home Entertainment
DVD RELEASE: February 21, 2001
THEATRICAL RELEASE: October 1984
RUNNING TIME: 108 Minutes
MPAA RATING: R

In the role he was born to play, Arnold Schwarzenegger didn't just inhabit the Terminator, he became him. A cyborg sent from the future to kill the coming savior of mankind, the character was the perfect fit for Schwarzenegger's decidedly unique persona: big, intimidating, limited to monosyllables and—befitting a future governor—a person who knew how to get the job done. It is impossible to imagine anyone else in the role, so synonymous is Schwarzenegger with the character. Overnight, the Hungarian-born bodybuilder went from onetime Mr. Olympia to blockbuster action superstar.

> "I'll be back."
>
> —The Terminator

The Terminator began life as an orphan. The name Schwarzenegger had no box office clout, James Cameron was coming off the forgettable flop *Piranha II: The Spawning,* and the story teetered on the brink of B-movie pulp—a "tech noir" melding of sci-fi, action, love story and horror, a scrappy little heavy-metal comic book with no stars and little sequel potential. But Cameron was the best kind of guerilla filmmaker: dedicated, ambitious, exacting and relentless. Convincing Orion Pictures to front the meager $1.8 million budget, Cameron, Schwarzenegger, producer Gale Anne Hurd and a cast of unknowns-about-to-become-knowns, including Linda Hamilton, Michael Biehn and Lance Henriksen, pulled from every last reservoir of strength they had to create a modern sci-fi pop masterpiece. Literate, inventive, directed with flair by Cameron and with one of the most formidable villains ever seen, *The Terminator* became the cult phenomenon of 1984.

In making *The Terminator,* Cameron had to rely on classic, time-worn techniques of the pre-CGI era—models, matte paintings, miniatures and animatronics. The film is dated; many of the robotic effects are obviously phony, and the fashions are woefully of the 1980s. But the Terminator himself is a classic—Stan Winston's juggernaut is a masterpiece of metallic malevolence. And Cameron never sacrifices heart for mechanics; *The Terminator* has endured as a classic because it is ultimately a love story. Biehn's Kyle Reese is the most vulnerable of action heroes; his confrontations with the hulking Schwarzenegger are undeniably nerve-racking. And Hamilton ably pulls off an even more difficult task, plausibly convincing us that this onetime waitress could become the savior of the world. *The Terminator* transcends mere science fiction; a true cinematic original, it is the rare film that goes above and beyond the strictures of its genre to become a great piece of pop moviemaking.

The Goodies What's a *Terminator* fan to do? Perhaps no other film series in history has seen as many rereleases, box sets and endless reconfigurations on home video as this one. *Terminator 2: Judgment Day* has been published in over a dozen permutations on laserdisc and DVD. There is also the Cameron-less *T3: Rise of the Machines,* available in an extensive two-disc set. But if you can buy only one *Terminator,* make sure it is the best one: the original.

Required viewing for anyone interested in low-budget, balls-to-the-wall filmmaking, the sixty-minute documentary "Other Voices" chronicles in great detail the film's casting, production, strenuous reshoots, effects and subsequent release. Favored Cameron documentarian Van Ling has reunited the film's key collaborators for all-new interviews, including Cameron, Hurd, Winston and most of the cast and crew (Schwarzenegger and Hamilton appear via on-set interviews shot during the production of *T2*). With a minuscule budget, no major stars and a concept few thought was commercial, the making of *The Terminator* has much to teach today's filmmakers about what you can do with very little. "Other Voices" speaks directly and eloquently to the power of the independent voice: marry a great concept with passion and inspired execution, and success is assured. Well, getting a guy named Schwarzenegger to star in your movie sure helps, too.

While there's no audio commentary, MGM and Ling have included many additional supplements. The 1989 "*The Terminator*: A Retrospective" featurette is a nostalgic ten-mintue interview with Cameron and Schwarzenegger that is notable mostly for Cameron's bad fashion sense. Seven deleted scenes are included with optional commentary; much discussed among fans, most are fairly short dialogue exchanges that slightly flesh out the film's themes and characters. The arsenal of still galleries is comprehensive, boasting never-before-seen storyboards, production and publicity photos and ad concepts, plus the film's original treatment as a series of text screens and a clutch of theatrical trailers and TV spots.

The Presentation There once was a time Cameron could not command the best technical resources money could buy, yet *The Terminator* benefits greatly from these limitations. Gritty and raw, director of photography Adam Greenberg's harsh visual style lends the film a unique and effective sheen. Presented here in a 1.85:1 anamorphic widescreen transfer minted from the original negative, this film is slick and dirty. Colors are bold, with Greenberg's stylistic choices veering toward heavy blues and pumped-up contrast, which can result in slightly "blown-out" whites and an appropriately harsh look.

Even better is the newly created Dolby Digital Surround EX sound-track, which is a vast improvement over the film's original mono mix. While not quite the juggernaut of *T2*'s, the soundfield has been greatly expanded with aggressive surrounds and strong low bass. Brad Fiedel's neo-industrial score nicely spreads out across all channels and is forcefully rendered. This is the best *The Terminator* has ever looked or sounded.

Additional Recommendations The Cameron-helmed *Terminator 2: Judgment Day* outgrossed the original by over four-to-one, while the pulpy *Terminator 3: Rise of the Machines* lacked Cameron's finesse but did bring Schwarzenegger back for one more, pre-governor go-round. Of the myriad of *T2* DVD editions, the Extreme Edition features the best transfer plus a first-rate audio commentary by Cameron and coproducer Bill Wisher, as well as a unique high-definition version of the film, encoded on the set's second disc and accessible only to PC users. The ill-named Ultimate Edition contains a more substantial set of supplements than does the Extreme Edition, but its transfer suffers from inferior video and audio quality. But you can bet the Terminator will be back.

The Thing

DISTRIBUTOR: Universal Studios Home Video

DVD RELEASE: September 8, 1998

THEATRICAL RELEASE: June 1982

RUNNING TIME: 108 Minutes

MPAA RATING: R

What happened to cinematic paranoia? Back in the 1950s, audiences just couldn't get enough of mad scientists, alien invaders and government experiments run amok—potent allegories for the nation's Red Scare politics and fears of imminent nuclear disaster. But flash-forward to the early 1980s: with the Cold War about to end and Ronald Reagan in the White House, America just wasn't interested in bug-eyed aliens anymore. Witness the chilly reception of John

Carpenter's big-budget remake of Howard Hawk's classic slice of 1950s paranoia, *The Thing*.

Returning to the original Joseph Campbell short story *Who Goes There?*, Carpenter ditched most of what made Hawk's classic fun but ultimately cheesy. Working with his coscenarist, screenwriter Bill Lancaster, Carpenter conjured a creature that was a shape-shifter, a phantom from outer space that could look like anyone at any time. Who are your friends?

> **"Trust is a tough thing to come by these days."**
>
> —R. J. MacReady

Who can you trust? The film is unremittingly grim and oppressive, and the location chilly. A team of arctic researchers accidentally thaw out an odd-looking spaceship and unknowningly offer refuge to the alien visitor after it assimiliates the form of an Alaskan husky. Communication breaks down as the men, led by the take-charge, iconic MacReady (Kurt Russell), are unsure of who is human and who is the Thing and fall prey to the worst of human instincts. You can't blame a Thing for being without remorse and conscience. But can you blame a human?

The Thing was ideal material for Carpenter, a filmmaker of great craft but with little patience for pretension. He revels in the breakdown of spirit and communication. The ending, which some called inappropriately nihilistic, is cynical and calculated. But *The Thing* works so effectively because it preys on one of our most basic fears—our body in revolt against itself. It is also one of the most purely visceral and downright disgusting mainstream horror movies ever made. The awe-inspiring effects Carpenter unleashes—designed by makeup wunderkind Rob Bottin—pulsate, ooze and slither, so grotesque and imaginative they achieve a surreal blend of the horrific and beautiful. Not since *ALIEN* had an otherworldly menace been so breathtaking.

The Thing had the unfortunate luck of being released just a week after the arrival of another, far more cuddly alien, *E.T.*, and audiences and critics alike stayed away in droves. Carpenter was vilified for wallowing in graphic violence and failing to find the heart and humanity in his characters. But *The Thing* has become the prototypical example of a film rescued by home video. It is a bona fide cult phenomenon and now stands as one of Carpenter's most highly regarded and respected works. Its pioneering special effects and relentless sense of doom and paranoia still pack a wallop. Just don't watch it after you eat.

The Goodies One of the most requested special editions in the history of Universal Studios Home Video, *The Thing* was at last given the deluxe treatment in 1998 on both laserdisc and DVD. Because the DVD format was still in its infancy, the presentation of the supplements is a bit more linear and traditional. The menus are basic and straightforward, lacking in any interactive bells and whistles, but such directness is refreshing and the material is terrific.

The beauty of this set is the eighty-five-mintue documentary "Terror Takes Shape: The Making of *The Thing,*" which still stands as one of the best documentaries ever produced on a horror film. Featuring recollections from Carpenter, Bottin, director of photography Dean Cundey, Russell and most of the major cast and crew, making *The Thing* was an ordeal not quite as grotesque as the film itself but certainly as demanding. While actual on-set production material is sparse, "Terror Takes Shape" makes the most of its extensive interviews, chronicling the film's lengthy gestation, difficult arctic shoot and eventual box office bust. "Terror Takes Shape" is one of the few full-length modern docs to benefit from a clear and focused narrative arc. At nearly ninety minutes, it is a commitment, but one that pays off; its story is dramatic, involving and fascinating.

Carpenter and Russell contribute a wonderfully lively audio commentary; the pair have recorded tracks together for their other collaborations, including *Big Trouble in Little China* and *Escape from New York*. Jovial, sarcastic and hilarious, the mood here is as far removed from the frigid subject matter as is imaginable—Russell's riffing on all of the blood and guts is worth the price of admission.

Other goodies include an excerpt from the film's much sought-after alternate ending, some charming unused effects footage including a go-motion version of the titular creature, and a fairly extensive gallery of storyboards and stills. A genuine surprise is the inclusion of the film's complete score—a one-of-a-kind collaboration between Carpenter and Ennio Morricone, who adopted the austere electronics favored by the horror auteur. The track can actually be accessed as an alternate track over the documentary and is presented in its entirety.

The Presentation Presented in Carpenter's favored 2.35:1 widescreen, this is a strong transfer; the only disappointment is the lack of anamorphic encoding. Cundey's expert use of shadow and directional lighting creates a dark, eerie, downright scary-looking movie that demands to be studied and savored. Colors are crisp and blacks deep. Detail is also above average save for some slight edginess and an occasionally digital appearance. The remixed Dolby Digital 5.1 surround track is reflective of the more subdued remixes of the time, but still enveloping. Morricone's score is nicely wrapped around the listener, its minimal, bass-driven blips and beats moody and effective. Some minor discrete effects are also noticeable and creative if sporadic.

Additional Recommendations If you loved Carpenter's remake of *The Thing,* a must-see is Howard Hawk's brilliant, if far different, original, *The Thing from Another World,* available in a Sixtieth Anniversary Edition from Warner Home Video. Other extras-packed, sci-fi monster classics worth checking out include *Forbidden Planet, The Time Machine, War of the Worlds* and Robert Wise's highly influential *The Day the Earth Stood Still.*

The Third Man

DISTRIBUTOR: The Criterion Collection
DVD RELEASE: November 30, 1999
THEATRICAL RELEASE: February 1950
RUNNING TIME: 104 Minutes
MPAA RATING: PG-13

T*he Third Man* is about angles. The angles director Carol Reed employs to create a postwar Vienna that is somehow not what it seems. The angles that Major Calloway (Trevor Howard) uses to dismiss then exploit Holly Martins (Joseph Cotton), our naive American hero. But the ultimate angle is, of course, played by Harry Lime (Orson Welles), a man whose only allegiance is to himself. Lime is sly, condescending, mischievous and confident, and his mere presence on screen electrifies a film in which he doesn't even appear until the second hour.

> "Nobody thinks in terms of human beings. Governments don't. Why should we?"
>
> —Harry Lime

Two generations after its 1949 release, *The Third Man* now must live and die by its style, its story and its stars. Sixty years after the end of World War II, the backdrop of a bombed-out Vienna and its four-power governmental structure no longer provides familiarity and subtext to a modern audience. That *The Third Man* is the product of a world that doesn't quite exist anymore doesn't lessen its impact as an unforgettable cinema experience. It's an enduring, timeless piece of British film noir, bolstered not only by its director and star, but also writer Graham Greene's mastery of the noir form and Robert Krasker's black-and-white photography, which combines dramatic lines and deep shadows to create a nightmare-vision of Vienna from which the end of the world seems to radiate.

Holly Martins, an American writer of western novels, arrives in Vienna to take a job offered by his friend Harry Lime. Upon his arrival, he learns that Lime was killed in a traffic accident. Sensing something is awry, Martins begins to investigate Harry's death, while at the same time falling for Anna (Alida Valli), Harry's lover. Holly's investigation reveals not only the depths of human depravity, but also the depths of Vienna's sewer system, the location of the film's classic climax.

Cotton is perfectly cast as the naive American, with a wide-open face that slowly sinks into a punch-drunk realization of what his supercilious friend is actually doing in Vienna. Although never achieving the success in America that she ultimately achieved in Italy, Valli has the perfect femme fatale look and steel magnolia fortitude. But despite wonderful turns by Howard as Calloway, Ernst Deutsch as the oily Baron Kurtz and Bernard Lee as Sergeant Payne, the movie belongs to Welles. The entire first hour of the film centers around every character talking about, worrying about and reminiscing about Harry, so when he finally appears, it's one of cinema's grandest entrances. And while there are those who incorrectly believe Welles, creator of *Citizen Kane,* directed *The Third Man*'s two most famous sequences (the Ferris wheel confrontation and the sewer chase), he did contribute its most famous speech, a perfect encapsulation of Lime's prideful cynicism and gleeful amorality: "In Italy for thirty years under the Borgias they had warfare, terror, murder, bloodshed—they produced Michelangelo, Leonardo da Vinci and the Renaissance. In Switzerland they had brotherly love, five hundred years of democracy and peace, and what did they produce? The cuckoo clock!"

The Third Man was written by Graham Greene, a World War II spy himself. Anton Karas provided the zither score, which exists in mesmerizing counterpoint to the images on the screen. Famously, *The Third Man* is also a triumph of art over commerce: Reed fought with legendary producer David O. Selznick (*Gone With the Wind*) and won, getting permission to add everything that made the movie great: the zither score, Welles (instead of Noel Coward) as Harry Lime and the film's unforgettable final shot.

The Goodies As usual, Criterion has assembled an impressive array of extras. Firstly, there is a five-minute introduction by director Peter Bogdanovich, who discusses *The Third Man,* its creation and its importance. Writer Greene first composed it as prose, which he considered the best way for him to craft a motion picture script. Criterion has included that story, as read by actor Richard Clark. An interesting text-based preface by Greene, written in Boston in 1950, is also provided.

In 1950, Welles revived the Lime character in a radio serial called *The Lives of Harry Lime.* Some of the episodes were written by Welles himself and one of them, "A Ticket to Tangiers," is presented here with crystal clear audio. The other radio-themed supplement is a Lux Radio Theater dramatic reading of *The Third Man* from 1951. Cotton reprises his role as Holly, but Welles did not participate. Criterion has even included the commercial breaks, which are absolutely priceless. There is also amazing archival footage, including three minutes of zitherist Karas playing *The Third Man* theme at a London club and Viennese sewer policemen patrolling the Vienna sewers.

Next is a comparison of the U.S and U.K. cuts of the opening scene; America's more straightforward (read: simpler) version is read by Cotton while the morally ambiguous British version is read by director Carol Reel. And there is a restoration demonstration that provides side-by-side comparisons of the print before and after it was worked on by film restorationists. Finally, there are two trailers and a text-based "Production History" that includes some terrific behind-the-scenes photos.

The Presentation *The Third Man* is routinely named on the types of lists that end with the words, ". . . of all time." And for the film's fiftieth birthday in 1999, it fell to the estimable Criterion to restore and release an anniversary DVD edition. As usual, Criterion was up to the challenge, with a fine black-and-white transfer that is as good as the movie will ever look. According to Criterion, the film is presented in its original aspect ratio of 1.33:1 and struck from a new digital transfer created from the restored 35mm fine-grain master positive, made from the original nitrate camera negative. Criterion made 22,000 digital enhancements to clean up the picture, which otherwise would have looked very disappointing. The only knock to it is the regular appearance of very soft flickering. Otherwise, grain is minimal and shadow detail is quite good with deep, rich blacks. Criterion digitally restored the audio from the original optical track negative, and the Dolby Digital mono presentation is excellent for what it is. Dialogue is always clear, although occasionally there is the tiniest hint of muddiness. The zither score sounds amazing and whatever effects there are (footsteps on cobblestone, gunshots) are rendered very well for a film of that time.

KINETIC ENERGY: A CONVERSATION WITH MICHAEL BAY

Much to the dismay of his often fervent detractors, Michael Bay is one of the most successful filmmakers working today. His resume includes some of the biggest blockbusters of the past decade: *The Rock, Armageddon, Pearl Harbor, Bad Boys* and its even more successful sequel, *Bad Boys II*. While his kinetic, highly attenuated style has caused many to brand him the epitome of Hollywood excess, Bay continues to have the last laugh. In 2003, he launched his own production company, Platinum Dunes, specializing in low-budget genre pieces designed to give first-time filmmakers their shot. The payback? The company's first release, a remake of the seminal cult hit *The Texas Chainsaw Massacre*, grossed nearly $30 million in its first weekend of release.

You've gone from directing music videos and commercials to some of the biggest blockbusters of the past ten years. Now you have moved into low-budget produc-tion with Platinum Dunes. What was the impetus to make the change?

It's bizarre. We started this company named after one of my first student films, and the idea was to help bring young directors in and give them a shot. I had this idea—how are we going to start this company? How are we going to sell this title?

I took something from the original *Texas Chainsaw* movie: "In the annals of American history, one of the most gripping crimes happened in August 1973." Picture yourself in a big audience with a big screen, eerie music and the screen goes black and there is an amazing sound of a woman running, terrified, up these creaky stairs and into a closet in front of the screen where she's panting. Then you hear male footsteps come up, and he has something metal in his hand. Then he comes in front of the screen and then there is dead silence for four seconds and then BAM! He hits the door and the audience screams then laughs because they can't believe they were surprised by the sound. Then he bangs the door and a chainsaw comes on.

Was it tough to sell the concept of a remake of a notorious cult classic as your company's first venture?

I was shooting a Mercedes commercial, and we sold the movie worldwide in three days. We got all our foreign money, then we had all the studios, and Bob Shaye [of New Line Cinema] picked up on it right away.

I heard the Weinstein brothers were pissed because we offered them to buy the movie for Dimension. "So what do you want, Michael?" "We want you to buy the movie. Do you want it?" (laughs)

Many of your recent films, as both a director and a producer, have come shrouded in even more secrecy than is usual for Hollywood. Very limited test screenings, very little prerelease, on-set publicity, no Internet coverage . . .

Piracy. I am a maniac for that stuff. The finished print of this movie was finished months before. Even though it's a big studio, these things get out. People get paid. I have a rule where none of my movies leave my office. I never give the studio the movie. I give them pieces of the movie because

if one of my movies got out two weeks before it came out . . .

How do you feel about these non-traditional forms of distribution, such as DVD, digital satellite and, eventually, video-on-demand and Internet downloading?

Texas Chainsaw is not one of those effects-laden movies where you want the big sound and whatever. It could work on a camcorder. It's always great to have the movie experience, but as a distribution tool, we have created our own worst nightmare.

You have been very vocal in the past, speaking out in what some perceived as an attack on DVD and studio support of digital prerecorded formats and distribution.

I've been in the [Director's Guild of America] saying that DVD is going to kill us one day. It's going to bite us in the ass because we have this digital world. With videotapes, there is always a way to stop it. It's going to take a big bite because if you can't get a good ancillary market—we just have to figure out a way to control it.

Do you think the theatrical experience is dying because of the

success of DVD? Is the era of the drive-in gone, which in the past would have been the ideal venue for the films Platinum Dunes is producing?

You will never kill the movie-going experience. I firmly believe that. There is something that is a shared experience. This movie is so much cooler in a big room where everyone screams. That is not what I am worried about. What kills you are the ancillary markets where you sell DVDs. That is where a lot of profits come from for a movie today.

Are you shocked or surprised at how easy it is to obtain the latest hit movies—your movies—off the street before they even hit theaters?

I got a copy of *Bad Boys II* that my contractor bought for eight bucks. And this company has this logo and it says, "We do the best DVDs." They pride themselves on how well they copy movies.

Do you think there is an answer? Perhaps go back to the way it was in the '70s, where you could just release a movie in a few theaters, distribute it regionally and just watch the good ones grow and grow?

I don't know. It's crazy. We have created it. It's killing movies because if you don't open huge your first weekend, it's like you're a piece of shit.

What's your take on DVD, just as a filmmaker and not a businessman?

I think DVDs were great in the beginning—as a film student, [I thought] they were great.

Your *Pearl Harbor* DVD set was pretty huge—four discs full of material. Do you think you went too far?

You do take away some of the magic by showing everything. They are interesting, but now it seems like everybody's doing it. Before it was kind of cool that some movies did it. I remember as a film student watching stuff. I was a little less involved in the *Bad Boys II* [DVD]. We did some things, and they wanted me to do a commentary track, but I had nothing to say. You just do not need to do a big, elaborate thing for every movie you do.

Pearl Harbor was also interesting because it contained an extended cut with more violence. Your work has often been criticized for its level of violence, fantasy or not—*The Rock,* the *Bad Boys* movies—and even as a producer on *Texas Chainsaw.* Do you feel the need to start getting away from that, or is Platinum Dunes, in a way, an opportunity to go for it even more?

Maybe it's because I took offense to the FTC coming into the Director's Guild and saying basically, "We're going to clean your act up if you don't clean it up yourselves." I am young in my career and for the government to say in kind of a back-handed way that you're not going to have a right to shoot R-rated movies—"We're trying to clean up R-rated movies!"—that is what they are saying. That kind of pisses me off.

There might be a little of that. Just a little. [Senator Joseph] Lieberman came in and that just bugged me.

What's it like for someone used to directing $100 million movies to move to producing little $10 million things? Is there any appeal in the freedom a low-budget can offer, especially given the political climate as you say above?

It's fun. I did have to call in some favors . . . but it serves the movies by making it low-budget because it adds that grunge factor.

A film like *Pearl Harbor* was certainly a behemoth. Do you ever think about going back to directing movies in the $60 million range or sticking with the mammoth $100 million-plussers? What is next for Michael Bay?

I want to reinvent myself. It's time for me to change it up. O

This Is Spinal Tap

DISTRIBUTOR: MGM Home Entertainment
DVD RELEASE: September 12, 2000
THEATRICAL RELEASE: March 1984
RUNNING TIME: 82 Minutes
MPAA RATING: R

This Is Spinal Tap doesn't annihilate its target. It nibbles away at it, gnawing at its edges. And when its over, all you're left with is the center. The heart. Even as the three core members of England's loudest band turn their amps to 11 or get lost on their way to the stage, their genuine love of music makes their gentle idiocy all the more endearing. When documentary film director Marty

> "It's such a fine line between stupid and clever."
>
> —David St. Hubbins

DiBergi (Rob Reiner) asks lead guitarist David St. Hubbins (Michael McKean) what he'd do if he weren't in rock and roll, he replies, "I'd be a full-time dreamer." Such dialogue is not why the film is funny, it's why the film endures.

That director Reiner and his merry band of mockumentarians have created one of the funniest movies ever made is not in dispute. Nor is their ability to absorb the mannerisms, nuances and mentality of a heavy metal band. Reiner, who in 1984 was known primarily as Meathead on the CBS sitcom *All in the Family,* made his directing debut here. He shot and edited the film like a documentary, which seems simple but is actually complicated. Miles of footage needed to be shot and whittled down to whatever is necessary to tell the story. And the frame is filled with numerous details and in-jokes that heighten the reality and require numerous viewings to appreciate.

The story is about the reuniting of the band for its first stateside tour in six years. Spinal Tap is led by the confused Nigel Tufnel (Christopher Guest), whose inability to notate "eighteen feet" on a cocktail napkin leads to one of the great sight gags in modern film. Tufnel's childhood friend and musical partner is lead guitarist David St. Hubbins, who seems to have his head on the straightest, until he insinuates his girlfriend Jeanine (June Chadwick) into the group, and she threatens to become Spinal Tap's version of Yoko Ono. Finally, there is bassist Derek Smalls (Harry Shearer), with his pipe, outlandish mustache and crotch-enhancing cucumber.

There is a wealth of perfectly cast supporting turns in the film. Some are name-actors, some are not. Of the former, look for Billy Crystal, Fran Drescher, Ed Begley Jr., Dana Carvey, Bruno Kirby, Paul Shaffer and Fred Willard. Aside from a brilliant troupe of actors ad-libbing their way through the film, what humanizes *This Is Spinal Tap* and makes it more than just a hilarious improv exercise is the quality of the music and, crucially, the point in the band's fictional career that Reiner and company focus on.

The songs featured in the film are, frankly, more tuneful than most real heavy metal, while the lyrics are good enough to seem real, but bad enough to be funny. Also, *This Is Spinal Tap* follows the band during their failed comeback tour. Watching them on the wane is funnier, more tragic and more interesting than watching them on the rise. Seeing the group react to getting second billing to a puppet show is undoubtedly funny. But knowing that with their dreams go the dreams of millions of air guitarists and garage bands makes the film universal.

The Goodies *This Is Spinal Tap* was originally released on DVD by Criterion in 1998. That edition, which featured a mountain of hilarious extras, has since become one of the most sought-after out-of-print DVDs, with fans frequenting online auction sites for a copy. In 2000, MGM finally released its own edition, which compares very favorably to the Criterion effort. There are almost two hours of special features and every single minute is worth watching.

In a risky creative move, the scene-specific audio commentary is done in character by the members of Spinal Tap, with Guest, McKean and Shearer reprising their roles. Even though we learn nothing about the making of the film, this gives three brilliant improv performers a chance to revisit their most beloved creation. For that alone, it was a risk worth taking, resulting in a unique and funny commentary.

Next is a brand-new, five-minute interview with director Marty DiBergi, who has been conspicuously absent since the film's 1984 release. It's insightful and essential for DiBergi fans, who'll discover that his directing debut was not *This Is Spinal Tap,* but the spoof "drama" *Kramer vs. Kramer vs. Godzilla.*

The DVD also contains over an hour of never-been-seen footage from the film. Spinal Tap completists will pore over every second, which include scene extensions as well as all-new sequences involving the band's visit to a radio station, Derek's divorce settlement and David talking about his son. The footage is terrific fun as a supplement but would have made the finished film a bit flabby.

The world that Reiner, Guest, McKean and Shearer created is admirably expansive and immersive, as evidenced by the amount of tangential footage they shot. Vintage Tap Materials contains a press conference for the release of "(Listen to the) Flower People" while Spinal Tap's appearance on *The Joe Franklin Show* shows two generations of entertainers coming together. There are also music videos for "Gimme Some Money," "(Listen to the) Flower People," "Hell Hole" and "Big Bottom." Other promotional material includes two trailers, three TV spots and one fictional commercial for a Spinal Tap album collection called Heavy Metal Memories. Finally, there are three television commercials for a British Hot Pockets–style food called Rock and Rolls. It all comes wrapped in humorous animated menus that recall classic scenes from the film.

The Presentation MGM's digital effort here stays true to *Spinal Tap*'s documentary conceit, while providing a better transfer than did the Criterion disc. The film sports a 1.85:1 widescreen picture and, at the risk of sounding like an apologist, what flaws remain work in favor of the presentation. Until the preponderance of digital video cameras, documentaries were often grainy, color-muted, 16mm affairs and that's the look re-created here. What MGM has done is smooth out transfer flaws and even out the colors.

Considering *This Is Spinal Tap* is a low-budget, shot-on-16mm film, the remastered Dolby Digital 5.1 surround track is surprisingly good. And while the added aural effort means little in most of the dialogue scenes, it does improve the concert scenes. In non-concert sequences, the surround channels lay dormant, except in the cocktail party scene and in scenes that take place backstage. In the musical numbers, the rears fill out the sound provided by the other speakers, resulting in a more enveloping concert experience.

Toy Story: The Ultimate Toy Box

DISTRIBUTOR: Buena Vista Home Entertainment

DVD RELEASE: October 21, 2000

THEATRICAL RELEASE: October 1995/November 1999

RUNNING TIME: 186 Minutes

MPAA RATING: G

If computers are only as smart as the people who program them, the people who programmed the computers that created the *Toy Story* films are very smart indeed. The 1995 original and its even superior sequel aren't just hollow exercises in cold, computer wizardry. They're tight and absorbing stories, with clever dialogue, brilliant voice acting and animated in-jokes that make them kids' movies only the most unrepentant Scrooge could dislike.

> **"To infinity and beyond!"**
> —Buzz Lightyear

In the original *Toy Story,* Woody (Tom Hanks) is a pull-string cowboy doll and the alpha toy in young Andy's bedroom. Other toys include a dinosaur (Wallace Shawn), a Mr. Potato Head (Don Rickles) and a Bo Peep (Annie Potts). Into this plastic fantastic world comes Andy's birthday present, a space ranger toy called Buzz Lightyear (Tim Allen). Woody is afraid Andy will consign him to the toy box of history in favor of this newfangled space hero. But Woody and Buzz learn to work together as they overcome life's obstacles, such as a sadistic next-door neighbor—a young boy who likes mutilating toys.

As magnificent as *Toy Story* was, the 1999 sequel was better. Advances in technology meant more sophisticated lighting effects and enhanced detail. Here, Woody is accidentally sold to a toy collector who discovers that the cloth cowboy is actually very valuable and intends to sell him to a Japanese toy museum. Buzz and his friends mount a daring rescue, which includes the almost impossible mission of crossing the street. The key characters introduced in the sequel are two toys from the same line as Woody's, a prospector named Stinky Pete (Kelsey Grammer) and cowgirl Jessie (Joan Cusack).

Both Toy Story movies are imaginative and delightful, but the sequel scores higher on an emotional level, making us acutely aware that toys "never forget kids, but [kids] they forget [toys]." It makes you want to go back and rediscover all the toys you loved and then later cruelly threw away. When Jessie sings Randy Newman's emotional "When She Loved Me," it's enough to make the most hard-hearted adult cry.

In May 2003, Sue Clayton, a film lecturer at the University of London, suggested that the perfect movie would consist of thirty percent action, seventeen percent comedy, thirteen percent good versus evil, twelve percent love/sex/romance, ten percent special effects, ten percent plot and eight percent music. Based on those criteria, *Toy Story 2,* she concluded, is as close as possible to the perfect movie. And while you may quibble with the science, you can't quibble with the conclusion.

The Goodies If you're buying *Toy Story: The Ultimate Toy Box* for your child, be warned, by the time they're finished watching every supplement, they'll be well into adulthood. There are dozens of deleted scenes, design sketches, music demos, storyboards and audio commentaries. In fact, the third disc, called "Supplemental Features," is so packed that it includes a two-page Navigational Overview insert to help you find everything.

The DVD containing the original *Toy Story* also includes the Oscar-winning short film *Tin Toy,* produced by Pixar, the revolutionary computer animation company responsible for the *Toy Story* films. There is also an audio commentary from a number of the film's creators, including director and cowriter John Lasseter. "The Story Behind *Toy Story*" is a great twenty-seven-minute look at every step in the film's production process. It's replete with test animations, interviews and behind-the-scenes footage of storyboard meetings. There are also fifty-two short blackout gags, which aired as ABC Saturday morning interstitials. Some are as short as ten seconds. Every last one is worth watching. Rounding out the first disc are "on-set interviews" with Buzz and Woody, the full-length Buzz Lightyear toy commercial seen in the film and a multilanguage reel showing clips from the film dubbed into foreign languages.

The DVD containing *Toy Story 2* includes 1986's *Luxo Jr.,* the first film produced by Pixar. Also on the disc are the "outtakes" seen over the end credits and a "Sneak Peek" at Pixar's 2001 film *Monsters, Inc.*

The third disc contains a dizzying array of supplemental features, broken up into sections for *Toy Story* and *Toy Story 2.* Notable extras include character design sketches, deleted animation, humorous rendering errors from *Toy Story,* John Lasseter's original treatment proposal to Disney, storyboard-to-film comparisons, trailers, TV commercials, posters, music videos and (too much) more. It'll take a fortnight to watch it all, but there are worse ways to spend a fortnight.

The Presentation As the DVDs here were created as direct digital transfers from computer to disc, both films sport near perfect 1.77:1 widescreen pictures. The image leaps off the screen. There are no print flaws, no pixelation, no compression errors, no edge enhancement and no smearing. Colors, which are bright and rich with a pastel tilt, are rendered as accurately as when the images were created. Everything is sharply in focus, and detail allows the viewer to read every toy box, poster and book cover. Simply awesome.

The same can be said for the audio. *Toy Story* comes in a very fulfilling Dolby Digital 5.1 surround, and *Toy Story 2* is presented with an EX mix. Either way, viewers are in for a treat. The THX-certified audio is dynamic, creative and a blast to experience. All speakers get quite the workout, with voices and effects flying in from all sides. Your ears perk up at the numerous directional effects. Both films include the ability to listen to the effects track only, without dialogue or music. Try it. The amount of detail and creativity is astounding. It's one of the most enveloping and engaging tracks the DVD format has to offer.

Additional Versions Both of the *Toy Story* films can also be purchased separately on DVD, in either widescreen or full-screen versions, with only a few of the extras included here. The third disc of supplemental material is only available in *The Ultimate Toy Box.*

Traffic

DISTRIBUTOR: The Criterion Collection
DVD RELEASE: May 28, 2002
THEATRICAL RELEASE: December 2000
RUNNING TIME: 147 Minutes
MPAA RATING: R

Sometimes the good guys don't win. Sometimes the bad guys get away with it. Sometimes you don't live to fight another day. Sometimes the smallest victory is all you have to hang your hopes on.

After hitting a nadir with 1996's *Schizopolis,* a stream-of-consciousness comedy so odd it was like he'd found someone to bankroll his career suicide, director Steven Soderbergh resuscitated himself with a furious creative streak that quickly reestablished him as an industry darling. His intelligence and originality gave a fresh, artistic voice to mainstream entertainments like *Out of Sight* (1998) and *Erin Brockovich* (2000). He was even able to pull a large audience to lower-budget side projects like his excellent 1999 drama *The Limey*.

But his crowning achievement and the film that made him an A-list director was *Traffic,* for which he won the 2000 Oscar for Best Director. In *Traffic,* Soderbergh mixes colors, so each storyline has its own hue, and he juggles interlocking stories and over a hundred speaking parts. But *Traffic* isn't about what Soderbergh does, it's about what Soderbergh does not do. He and writer Stephen Gaghan don't

> "If there is a war on drugs, then many of our family members are the enemy. And I don't know how you wage war on your own family."
>
> —Drug Czar Bob Wakefield

lecture the audience on the evils of drugs or how to solve the drug problem. While their ultimate conclusion is that the America's war on drugs is an expensive, ongoing failure that benefits those it should be punishing, it's simply where the story finally takes them.

Traffic is a movie filled with despair, yet it still leaves room for a glimmer of hope. As the film opens, Tijuana-based policemen Javier and Manolo (Oscar winner Benicio Del Toro and Jacob Vargas) intercept a truckload of heroin, but their haul is confiscated by General Salazar (an excellent Tomas Milian), whose interest in the heroin goes a little further than keeping it off the streets. On the American side of the border, Bob Wakefield (Michael Douglas) has just been appointed the president's drug czar, and he quickly emerges as a man eager to do good but naively unaware of his own naiveté: under his own roof, daughter Caroline (Erika Christensen) is freebasing cocaine. In San Diego, Drug Enforcement Agency agents Castro (the always wonderful Luiz Guzman) and Gordon (the equally wonderful Don Cheadle) nail a mid-level trafficker (Miguel Ferrer) who agrees to testify against drug kingpin Carlos Ayala (Steven Bauer), whose wife Helena (Catherine Zeta-Jones) is about to find out what her husband's real profession is. And the decision she makes with the knowledge will result in one of the film's best scenes.

As the film unfolds, the viewer begins to understand the complexity of the issue. For instance, Wakefield, the new drug czar, asks who his Mexican equivalent is. He's told there is none. And although he's the country's top antidrug mouthpiece, he is forced to acknowledge his wife's college-era experimentation, as well as his own borderline alcoholism.

Soderbergh takes all the story threads and intercuts them, layers them, and crisscrosses them, until we see that the drug problem is everybody's problem, from the rich, white high school kid who trolls downtown looking for a fix to an American government either too ignorant to realize the war on drugs isn't working, or too scared to admit it's not working. But ultimately, what this accomplished film proves is that drug lords like Carlos Ayala don't traffic in drugs. They traffic in human nature.

The Goodies Any Criterion release is a cause for celebration and here the company has taken a modern masterpiece and given it the deluxe treatment. The supplements help explain not only how *Traffic* was made, but also how all movies are made.

Three audio commentaries may seem like overkill (OK, it is overkill), but each track reveals important insights into the making of an important movie. The first is from Soderbergh and writer Gaghan. Those familiar with DVD supplements know that Soderbergh provides some of the best audio commentaries around, and he's great here: conversational and detail-oriented with just enough gossip. The second audio commentary is from producers Ed Zwick, Marshall Herskovitz and Laura Bickford and consultants Tim Golden and Craig Chretien. Finally, composer Cliff Martinez's commentary includes his edited-together thoughts as well as music cues not in the finished film.

The rest of the extras are on the second disc. The deleted scenes section is comprised of twenty-four cut scenes and one gag (between Zeta-Jones and a customs officer). A good chunk of the deleted material focuses on Helena and would have addressed the only valid criticism of the film: Helena's transition from ignorant country-club wife to scheming spouse is too abrupt. All the scenes contain optional audio commentary from Soderbergh and writer Gaghan.

"Demonstrations" is an interesting and instructive look at how Soderbergh and his team created the film's unique look and sound. It's broken down into "Film Processing" (how the color variances were achieved), "Editing" (how jump cuts helped sell the story) and "Dialogue Editing" (how light use of Automatic Dialogue Replacement cleaned up production sound difficulties).

"Additional Footage" contains extended takes of partly improvised scenes, including the cocktail party, where Bob Wakefield absorbs the varied opinions of actual U.S. senators. Finally, there is the usual bundle of trailers as well as a collection of trading cards created by U.S. Customs to honor its group of drug-detecting dogs.

The Presentation The techies who worked on the video transfer for *Traffic* must have been eyeing some illicit drugs themselves considering the varying looks and treated colors that Soderbergh utilizes. But their efforts were worth the trouble, because Criterion's new digital transfer is absolutely outstanding. Soderbergh famously employs different color schemes for different storylines, including steel blue hues for the Wakefield story thread and overexposed, dusty yellow/browns for the Tijuana scenes. It's all reproduced faithfully, with no grain (except where intended) and no edge enhancements. The print itself is extremely polished, with only a very rare speck, and only on stark, white backgrounds. Blacks are dead solid with impressive shadow detail. Presented in its original aspect ratio of 1.85:1, the *Traffic* video transfer is top-shelf.

Audio is available in a Dolby Digital 5.1 mix and a restricted dynamic range two-track. According to Criterion, the soundtrack was mastered from the original 24-bit print masters, so this rather uneventful, dialogue-driven mix sounds very nice. Cliff Martinez's effective score benefits most from what speaker separation is employed. Dialogue is easy to understand, while detail-oriented sounds like bedsprings and footsteps on staircases create a welcome dimension. It's a solid mix that wisely does not show off and is perfect for the material.

Additional Versions The first, movie-only DVD release of *Traffic* was produced in 2000 by USA Films and distributed through its home video arm, USA Home Entertainment. After the studio went under, Universal Studios Home Video reissued the film as a largely movie-only edition, with only a short featurette, still gallery and trailers. This version remains on the market, but despite its cheaper price, the Criterion edition is far superior.

The Treasure of the Sierra Madre

DISTRIBUTOR: Warner Home Video
DVD RELEASE: September 30, 2003
THEATRICAL RELEASE: January 1948
RUNNING TIME: 126 Minutes
MPAA RATING: Not Rated

John Huston's *The Treasure of the Sierra Madre* is an anomaly, the antiadventure adventure movie. It does not seek to entertain the conventional requirements of the genre, where we thrill to the hero's

> "You know, the worst ain't so bad when it finally happens. Not half as bad as you figure it'll be before it's happened."
>
> —Bob Curtin

dashing derring-do and revel in the last-minute rescue. Rather, it is of the tradition where its challenges and obstacles exist only to test the endurance and moral fiber of its protagonists. There is a little bit of humor, a little bit of fun, a little bit of smirking irony and a whole lot of bitterness. *The Treasure of the Sierra Madre* should not have been a very enjoyable movie. Instead, it has become, in its own strange, fascinating, utterly compelling way, one of the most iconic action-adventures of all time. Indiana Jones, where would you be without Fred C. Dobbs?

Dobbs (Humphrey Bogart) is a mercenary. A rather likable one, but dangle a golden carrot in front of his eyes, and he will do anything to get it. He is the classic drifter, stumbling into a search for gold in the mountains of the Sierra Madre, where he teams up with another aimless American, Bob Curtin (Tim Holt), after they steal a tip from the grizzled Howard (Walter Huston, father of John). If *Treasure* had climaxed with the pair discovering their booty, it may have just been another enjoyable if insignificant actioner. Instead, the acquisition of the treasure is just the beginning, because—of course—these two pals will become enemies once the power of money corrupts. "I know what gold can do to men's souls," Howard intones. Especially the soulless.

Lauren Bacall, wife of Bogart, revealed in her memoirs that Bogey, due to extreme hair loss, wore a wig throughout *The Treasure of the Sierra Madre*. But his courageous performance here is no ego-driven star turn. His Dobbs is strangely haunted, a grizzled shell of a man who has long since been deserted by idealism and hope. That neither he nor Curtin realizes that, by failing to trust each other, they have swindled themselves out of a treasure they have already obtained, adds an element of comedy. And when a third man, Jim Cody (Bruce Bennett), shows up, only to result in a game of truth and conscience tragic in its implications, we have lost *almost* all of our sympathy for these hopeless losers. But Bogart finds the palpable yearning and bleakness in Dobbs's heart that makes even his most foolish choices heartbreaking and poignant. And Huston's gorgeous canvas, lit by hot desert suns and stretching for eternity into nothingness, is the perfect setting for the adventure of a man about to implode.

The famous closing scenes of *The Treasure of the Sierra Madre* are strangely moving. Dobbs, with absolutely nothing left to lose or to give, must make the decision he was fated to—whether to leap into the abyss or save his soul. We realize he has become the tragic hero, one destroyed by his own frailties, insecurities and wrongdoing. But Dobbs will find only his conscience staring back at him . . . and laughing. The decision he ultimately makes earns *The Treasure of the Sierra Madre* its place as one of the true greats. And, perhaps, the most intelligent, important and landmark adventure in cinema history.

The Goodies After an appropriately laudatory introduction by Leonard Maltin, the extras on this extensive two-disc set show that it is possible to craft a top-flight special edition for a film half a century old. Bogart biographer Eric Lax provides a new audio commentary, which at first focuses almost entirely on the man and not the movie. But Lax is so knowledgeable and well researched that he creates the equivalent of an aural documentary; stories about the production of *Sierra Madre* are woven throughout, and there is hardly any redundancy with the included documentaries.

Originally produced for television, 1999's "John Huston: The Man, the Movies, the Maverick" and a second, all-new documentary. "Discovering Treasure: The Story of *The Treasure of the Sierra Madre*," are both excellent. The former is hosted by Robert Mitchum and chronicles Huston's long and varied career, from such early triumphs as *Madre* and *The Maltese Falcon* to his commercial reemergence with *Prizzi's Honor*. The second documentary is narrated by John Milius and is more traditional but just as grand; although it may be reality twice removed, as all of the stories were overheard or secondhand (including remembrances from such luminaries as Martin Scorsese, Robert Osbourne and Maltin), it is as close as you can get to actually being there.

An extensive array of additional supplements fill out this two-disc set: theatrical trailers for many of Bogart's best movies, a short film called "So You Want to Be a Detective," a Looney Tunes cartoon titled "Hot Cross Bunny," a fascinating Lux Radio Show adaptation (audio only) with Bogart and Huston recreating their famous roles, and a fairly comprehensive still gallery with assorted storyboards, production and publicity shots, and advertising materials.

The Presentation This is a very strong restoration, remastered here from a pristine source print. Defects are apparent in only a few scenes, namely a couple of nighttime sequences that are marred by long scratches. Otherwise, Ted McCord's sharp black-and-white photography is flush with detail and supported by excellent contrast and blacks. And unlike many remasters of vintage pictures, there appears to be little artificial processing applied to give the picture an overly sharp, "modern" look—*Sierra Madre* looks wonderfully film-like. The film's original mono track has not been remixed but has been nicely cleaned up with no audible anomalies and a full and pleasing sound.

TRON

DISTRIBUTOR: Buena Vista Home Entertainment
DVD RELEASE: January, 2002
THEATRICAL RELEASE: June 1982
RUNNING TIME: 98 Minutes
MPAA RATING: PG

In the title of his 1964 novel, author Philip K. Dick asked, *Do Androids Dream of Electric Sheep?* In 1982, the makers of *TRON* asked, "Do audiences dream of Ms. Pac-Man?" It was the year video games infiltrated the popular culture, when the kids of America stopped grooving to their parents' 8-tracks and instead played Pong and saw a future made up of digital bits and bytes. And it was the year that Walt Disney Studios was floundering. A decade worth of high-profile misfires left the once-mighty studio hopelessly unhip and uncool; kids would rather play "Space Invaders" at their local arcade than be caught dead at movie theater showing such disasters as *The Black Hole* (1979) or *The Watcher in the Woods* (1980). So when a young animator named Steve Lisberger pitched the story of a rebel programmer caught inside the world of the computer, told through a cutting-edge blend of animation and live action, the studio bit. It would be like nothing anyone had ever seen. And it would spark a revolution.

Walt Disney took a huge gamble on *TRON* . . . and lost. While not a bomb, it caused only a few faint ripples at the box office and was then quickly forgotten. But as with the rogue program of its title, a new generation of filmmakers raised on video games began to speak in breathless terms of its influence, hailing it as a seminal, unsung masterpiece. The impact of *TRON* could be traced through films as diverse as *The Matrix* (1999), the morphing T-1000 of *Terminator 2: Judgment Day* (1992) and the all-CGI wonders of Pixar (*Toy Story, Finding Nemo*). For nearly two decades *TRON* was an errant block of pixels lost in the Hollywood data stream. Now, on DVD, it has been rebooted.

> "Won't that be grand? Computers and the programs will start thinking and the people will stop."
>
> —Dr. Walter Gibbs

Most critics dismissed *TRON* as a fad movie, but beneath its computer screens and digitalized visuals beats the heart of a rebel. It is a subversive masterwork and the perfect movie for the techno-paranoid 1980s. In imagining a world where human molecules can be converted into computer bits and bytes, all at the mercy of an autocratic MCP (Master Control Program), *TRON* continues a science-fiction tradition that presupposes an inevitable war of man against machine—just as in *The Terminator,* which came out two years later and was all about computers that learn to think for themselves and try to kill us. It might not be very plausible, but it always works as a great science-fiction potboiler plot, and it fed directly into the early 1980s obsession with man overrun by computer.

One of the many ironies of *TRON*'s box office failure and later rediscovery is that because of the speed in which the computer revolution moves, *TRON* was dated the minute it was released. Many kids today find its antiquated effects and ancient technology cheesy. But *TRON* possesses a singular beauty; it created a one-of-a-kind universe that was both organic and artificial, a tapestry of light and sound. It is a true work of art. And for one brief, shining moment, it predicted the future . . . and was right.

The Goodies Disney has produced a lavish two-disc set for *TRON,* one of its best. The ironies begin with the menus, which were created with the kind of computer firepower kids today take for granted but that the animators of *TRON* would have needed five years of rendering time and ten office buildings full of computers to accomplish. The DVD dissects the film's unusual mode of moviemaking with a variety of supplements that are both linear and interactive, a perfect melding of the film's theme with the format's capabilities. A few of the materials are carried over from the acclaimed 1999 laserdisc box set release, but the majority are new.

The screen-specific audio commentary with Lisberger, Donald Kushner, Harrison Ellenshaw and Richard Taylor is excellent. A film as much about ideology as technology, *TRON* was produced while a massive shift in regime was taking place at the Walt Disney Studios, and the ramifications on the production are not lost on the participants. In the late 1970s, filmmaker Lisberger had an idea: use modern animation techniques to realize a full-length motion picture of the world inside a computer. After attracting the attention of Disney, Lisberger created the storyline by grafting ideas onto already-developed visual concepts and action sequences. Like the characters he created, Lisberger and his team soon became their own rogue programs within the vast Disney machine, left to their own devices to create a work few of the executives understood but all expected to become a blockbuster. A fascinating journey that makes for a fascinating commentary.

The ninety-minute documentary "The Making of *TRON*" is also excellent. The filmmakers and all of the primary cast return to recall the making of this most unusual experiment, including Jeff Bridges,

Cindy Morgan, Bruce Boxleitner and Barnard Hughes. Hilarious are recollections of making this "video game movie for Disney" and the utter silliness of wearing spandex, mouthing bizarre dialogue and throwing Frisbees across massive black-and-white sets. The realization of *TRON*'s visual world is dissected step by step, which occasionally gets very technical but is presented in a very accessible and comprehensive manner. Both the commentary and documentary are essential viewing.

A staggering amount of additional supplementary material is included that further breaks down the wonders of *TRON*. Ten vignettes examine the origins of the film's visual style, animation techniques and pioneering use of digital imaging. Hundreds of stills and storyboards further illustrate the extensive conceptualization process, from the characters and crafts, to the sets, costumes and gadgets. An intriguing extended prologue and multiple deleted scenes reveal many discarded concepts, while composer Wendy Carlos contributes a new interview discussing the various alternate scores that went unused in the film, and scoring key sequences including the famed Lightcycle game grid. A "Publicity" section wraps it up with over 150 additional promotional stills and a clutch of trailers and TV spots. An eight-page color booklet is the capper to a top-notch special edition.

The Presentation *TRON* is a singular visual experience. The techniques utilized to create its one-of-a-kind visuals are now ancient: composites, matte paintings and rotoscoping, all driven with the horsepower of an old Atari. This melding of animation, live action, and traditional and computer-based animation gives *TRON* a look that is both clean and dirty. The "inside the computer" sequences are the most bizarre: footage of the actors, clad in black-and-white and marching around black-and-white sets, went through a production process so complicated it takes a good chunk of the DVD to explain it. The result was weird but wonderful-looking. Blacks can be inconsistent, contrast fluctuates rapidly and grain is omnipresent throughout. But it is a tribute to this THX-certified, 2.2:1 anamorphic widescreen transfer that it looks as good as it does. Colors are very vibrant and oversaturated, as is intended, but there is no video noise or bleeding.

The film's aggressive Dolby Digital 5.1 soundtrack is both antiquated and exciting. Much of the film's rather cheesy sound effects sound dated, with a shrill, flat sound that lacks wide frequency response. But the aggressive surrounds turn *TRON* into a great, big cinematic video game. The Lightcycle sequence is the highlight, with exciting 360-degree pans and a powerful low end. Anything outside of the computer world is bland and boring. But once you put that quarter in, *TRON* really takes off.

Additional Versions Buena Vista Home Entertainment originally released *TRON* as a movie-only, non-anamorphic DVD edition in April 1998. It is now discontinued.

The Usual Suspects

DISTRIBUTOR: MGM Home Entertainment
DVD RELEASE: April 2, 2002
THEATRICAL RELEASE: August 1995
RUNNING TIME: 106 Minutes
MPAA RATING: R

Bryan Singer's *The Usual Suspects* is an elaborate, cinematic grift where the victim is surprised to find not only that he's been grifted, but also that he admires the grifter. Singer's first film, *Public Access,* won the Grand Jury Prize at the 1993 Sundance Film Festival, but it was a puzzling, inaccessible little number that did little to suggest he could pull off such an audacious, noir-inflected, crime thriller. However, in 1995, Hollywood's summer-season dance card was filled with oversold, overblown

> "Keaton always said, 'I don't believe in God, but I'm afraid of him.' Well, I believe in God. And the only thing that scares me is Keyser Soze."
>
> —Verbal Kint

films like *Waterworld, Batman Forever* and *Judge Dredd*. And while *Il Postino* kept the National Public Radio crowd chattering, there was really nothing staking out the middle ground, a movie smart enough for adults and cool enough for older kids.

So when *The Usual Suspects* was released in August 1995, it became a great success with its hard-boiled dialogue, macho posturing and Singer's ability to make a dense, dizzying storyline (almost) completely comprehensible. And while it's possible to enjoy the film by letting it simply wash over you, the real fun comes in accepting Singer's and screenwriter Christopher McQuarrie's challenge, which requires the viewer to unravel a complicated, tightly folded origami of a plot.

The film is told partially in flashback by Verbal Kint (Oscar winner Kevin Spacey), the only witness to a San Pedro boat explosion the previous evening. As he explains to Customs Agent Dave Kojan (Chazz Palminteri), Kint met four other "usual suspects" in a police lineup six weeks earlier. In addition to Verbal, the group consists of ex-cop Keaton (Gabriel Byrne), McManus (Stephen Baldwin), Hockney (Kevin Pollack) and Fenster (Benicio Del Toro). While in lockup, they decide to pull a job together, which eventually takes them to Los Angeles, where they're forced into the employ of Hungarian crime lord Keyser Soze, who is so mythic a figure that no one is sure he really exists. Of course, in Singer's tightly coiled world, nothing happens by coincidence and Soze really does exist. Or does he?

Summarizing *The Usual Suspects* is like writing Cliffs Notes for *The Big Sleep* on the back of a cocktail napkin. But that's what's impressive about Singer—he has complete mastery over what he's trying to accomplish. You may not understand it, but you have total confidence that he does. And allowing Del Toro to perform in a ridiculous, practically unintelligible accent shows an amazing amount of courage for a director attempting a mainstream breakout.

Of course, all lanes of this maze lead to the celebrated ending, which comes like a kick in the gut. Unlike the ending to *The Sixth Sense,* after which everything that came before it fell into place, the ending here makes the viewer want to see the movie again to further understand the endlessly complicated story. In fact, watching the film multiple times points out performance nuances and bits of information that begin to fill in the overall picture.

The Usual Suspects won Academy Awards for Best Original Screenplay and Best Supporting Actor. Singer went on to direct the surprisingly bad *Apt Pupil,* then the surprisingly good *X-MEN* films. But his best movie remains *The Usual Suspects,* a mystery where lies, not clues, lead to the truth.

The Goodies The story behind *The Usual Suspects* is told in comprehensive form, via two audio commentaries and a handful of informative documentaries and deleted scenes. The first commentary is by Singer and McQuarrie. The pair have been friends since high school and they provide a conversational track, filled with production information and, admirably, acknowledgments of mistakes made during filming. The second track is from editor and composer John Ottman. Ottman's duel role provided him a comprehensive understanding of why the film worked and how crucial its construction was to the final effect.

Five featurettes take the viewer through the entire filmmaking process, starting with "Pursuing the Suspects," in which the five leads explain how they were cast. "Doin' Time with the Suspects" chronicles principle photography and includes copious amounts of on-set footage, including some that shows the then twenty-seven-year-old Singer looking so young and baby-faced it is a miracle someone gave him $6 million to make a movie. "Keyser Soze—Lie or Legend" explores the development of the Soze character, and "Heisting Cannes with *The Usual Suspects,*" follows Singer and his lead actors at the 1995 Cannes Film Festival, where the movie became an unexpected sensation. Also included is the original electronic press kit, which is the standard behind-the-scenes featurette put out by the studio and is entirely skippable.

There are five deleted scenes introduced by Ottman and a gag reel introduced by Singer full of inside jokes but plenty of laughs. An easter egg in the "Special Features" menu reveals some funny out-

X MARKS THE SPOT: A CONVERSATION WITH BRYAN SINGER

Bryan Singer is the ultimate success story of young Hollywood. He began his career making 8mm short films and, after earning his degree from the esteemed University of Southern California School of Cinema-Television, went on to direct his first feature, the quirky *Public Access* (1993), at the tender age of twenty-seven. Then came *The Usual Suspects* (1995). An instant cult classic, this Christopher McQuarrie-penned masterpiece won two Oscars, including Best Original Screenplay and a Best Supporting Actor statuette for Kevin Spacey. The accomplished Stephen King adaptation *Apt Pupil* (1998) further proved Singer's impeccable craftsmanship and diversity, but it was the blockbuster *X-MEN* (2000) and its even more successful sequel *X2* (2003) that propelled Singer into the big leagues. Regardless of whether he makes a third trip to the land of the mutants, this self-proclaimed "nervous schoolboy" has firmly established himself as one of the preeminent filmmakers of his generation.

You have been one of the most active and inventive filmmakers when it comes to your work on DVD, as well as laserdisc. At what stage do you actively become involved with the DVD?

I have a great DVD producer, Rob Meyer Burnett. I've known him since we were students and I trust he'll find interesting things to put on the DVD. Beyond that, my focus is the film. In the back of your mind, you see it as a place to put something in case an outtake or a scene doesn't make it to the movie and you're proud of it in some way, or as a cautionary tale as to why it wasn't included in the movie.

You've shown a lot of courage in allowing the documentary team to invade your movie sets, especially on *X-MEN*. Did that take a big leap of faith on your part?

To be honest, on the first *X-MEN*, I had a really sweet guy who had a video camera who chronicled everything. And I found that to be a bit intrusive, so on *X2*, I regulated it more. Again, it's the fact that I trust the DVD producer, and I trust the people I'm working with and who are shooting the B-roll, that they're not going to exploit what they've shot or cut it in some humiliating way.

Ultimately, it is about control. You have good days and you have bad days, and sometimes the presence of a camera can be what I call the "Real World" effect. A friend of mine was editor of that show and he explained how people changed, their personalities changed and their behavioral patterns changed when they knew a camera was being pointed at them.

The danger is that it can turn your crew into actors?
You think it would temper one's temper, but it often works in a different way. "You're looking at me? Am I supposed to behave in a certain way?" And you feel like you're under scrutiny. I've worked about forty different jobs since I've been sixteen years old—I used to drive a bus for disabled kids. And my favorite part about the job was that, besides the aide who took care of the kids on the back of the bus, I didn't have a boss hovering over my head.

And when I make a movie, I don't have anybody looking over me—I'm the boss. But when there's a video camera, you feel like you're being scrutinized by an audience, which is your ultimate horror. You feel like they're watching you. Sometimes it's fun because when you're making a film, it's a kind of theater that only exists for that moment. Then the actors leave and the sets are taken down, and what remains is what's on film.

I want to be able to share that theater with other people, whether they're fans or students of film or friends. That's why I have a lot of friends visit the set—it's exciting. You see the scaffolding and the lighting—we had sixty miles of cable illuminating one of our set pieces. For that reason, you want to invite the cameras in there. But again, for moments of sensitivity when you're trying to be creative, it's hard to be under scrutiny. So I try to keep that balanced so as not to deprive the DVD of any value.

Do you think in a way your support of DVD is influenced by the fact that you are of a new generation of filmmakers who grew up in the age of video?
Yes, definitely. It reminds me of the times when I was a kid watching those Lou Mayfield "The Making Of" movies. Once I fell for the movie, just to see glimpses of the

people behind the scenes actually doing it was a real thrill. I don't recall it taking anything away from *Star Wars* or *Raiders of the Lost Ark*.

For me, there are really two kinds of DVDs and films: One is a biopic, so you can see actual footage of the events that are being dealt with in the movie, and the other is science-fiction/fantasy, because there is so much trickery going on in the making of these films that there's a lot to uncover, to show. When you get into standard drama, there is not much that is visually interesting, besides perhaps the audition process and the arguments in writing sessions and with producers.

DVD is a huge ancillary market now for the studios. Given the success you've had with *X-MEN*, does it inspire you or offer any leverage to attempt something a little riskier or more commercial for your next project?
I think that already existed with video. We as filmmakers think of DVD the same as video. It's that extra market that you know they're going to make bank on that you'll never see or know about. And you go in with that kind of confidence But you want to

do well in the theater. I'm ultimately a purist: I love the movie experience I love people going out to the theater and all that stuff. But I think it is almost thought of as the same as people catching it on video, so I'm just happy that the quality is better now.

Though I will say that with the film I'm negotiating to do next, a science-fiction film, it is a little more risky than an *X-MEN* film. It's maybe not as risky as the first *X-MEN*—that was very risky at the time—but certainly more risky than *X2*. But the genre is important. With science fiction, there's video game potential and other ancillary markets as well as DVD.

Both the *X-MEN* films and *The Usual Suspects* were huge successes. But in between you directed an adaptation of Stephen King's *Apt Pupil*, which wasn't a hit. Yet it seems to have been rediscovered on video, especially DVD. Is that a strange feeling for you as a filmmaker?
I've spoken to high school students and I'll ask how many have seen *The Usual Suspects* and you'll get a certain number of kids. Not that I do this that often, but anywhere from one-third to two-

thirds have gone back and seen this movie, and I'll ask the same thing about *Apt Pupil,* because my assumption is that because it didn't do well in theaters, there will be a much smaller percentage, but it's always the same amount. By slapping Brad Renfro in a graduation gown or Ian McKellan on the cover, suddenly it has got a life of its own.

Was video an important tool for you growing up as an aspiring filmmaker?

Sure. I discovered my favorite movies on video, really. My favorite movie is *JAWS.* I saw it in rerelease, because I wasn't allowed to see it when it first came out. And I thought, "Oh, this is cool!" But I ultimately didn't fall in love with it—or *A Clockwork Orange* or *The Shining* or all these movies—until I started watching them repeatedly on video. Which is a testament to story over spectacle. If the story is solid, then even on a small screen, you can fall in love with a movie, and then years later you can go back to it.

What are your feelings on the ever-shrinking DVD-to-video windows? Certainly, the success of the format has contributed to

films coming to video so fast if you don't catch it in the first few weeks, you have to see it on DVD. It's frustrating. Fifty percent of me thinks it should be a pure cinematic experience, [that] people should be encouraged to go theaters and see movies the way that they were meant to be seen. And fifty percent of me, as a student of films and as someone who understands the posterity of them, is all about the DVD and its special features. A movie should work on the small screen—maybe not as well, but it should work.

There are people I know who I run into that haven't seen *X2,* and they know me and they know the movie, but they're just very comfortable with the fact that they have a great DVD player and a great sound system, and they look forward to seeing it when it comes out.

So you wouldn't hold it against anyone who skipped your movie in the theater and went straight to the DVD?

I don't get hung up when people don't see my movies in the theater. Well, as long as they sit down, dim the lights and don't talk too much. ◉

takes from interviews conducted for the DVD, along with an eighteen-minute interview with Ottman.

Finally, the film's meager marketing comes by way of the original theatrical trailer (edited by Ottman), the international trailer and eight television spots.

The Presentation *The Usual Suspects* has been committed to DVD three times, of which only this special edition is worth the plastic it is printed on. Cinematographer Newton Thomas Sigel imbued the film with a vivid, noir-ish combination of light and shadow requiring the transfer to excel in color reproduction and detail. Thankfully, MGM's 2.35:1 anamorphic widescreen transfer honors the film's deep and varied color palette. Down converted from high definition, color saturation is excellent, with subtler background colors given their due along with the bolder, warmer hues. With the exception of some occasional grain, darker scenes are solid, with strong blacks and impressive shadow detail. Only a bit of noticeable edge enhancement distracts.

Also snappy is a strong Dolby Digital 5.1 remix. Benefiting the most is Ottman's excellent, atmospheric score, which sounds robust and enveloping. Dialogue comes mainly from the center speaker but is clear and understandable, while the rear speakers lack aggression but do nicely fill out the soundscape.

Additional Recommendations All of Singer's films are now available on DVD, including excellent two-disc special editions of *X-MEN* and its sequel, *X2: X-MEN United,* a movie-only *Apt Pupil* and, best avoided, a chintzy, bare-bones *Public Access,* which Singer claims he didn't even know had been released.

Valley Girl

DISTRIBUTOR: MGM Home Entertainment
DVD RELEASE: August 5, 2003
THEATRICAL RELEASE: April 1983
RUNNING TIME: 94 Minutes
MPAA RATING: R

Being a teenager has never been easy. And neither has being a teen film. Critical recognition remains elusive; kids will accept anything sold to them, so the line of reasoning goes, yet attempting to predict the next big teen trend is a fickle and foolish business. So the greatest teen epics remain underappreciated until decades later, when, at last, yesterday's adolescents are today's adults, the filmmakers and trendsetters

> JULIE: "Like, why don't you just punish me like Stacy's parents do?"
>
> JULIE'S MOM: "Bad karma, dear."

who define what's cool, hip and hot. Ahhh, sweet revenge.

The teen pics of the 1980s were no less original than those that came before and those that came after. But Martha Coolidge, the director of *Valley Girl,* was smart enough to realize that Andrew Lane and Wayne Crawford's script was a direct lift from classic Shakespeare, and all the better for it. Its greatest asset is its simplicity, pure "Romeo and Juliet" awash in day-glo colors and set to a new wave beat. Val chick Julie (Deborah Foreman) thinks Hollywood punk Randy (Nicolas Cage) is, like, totally hot. Her friends think he's grody to the max. They rebel and mash to "I Melt with You." So the Montagues and Capulets of Valley High plan to dethrone their once-mighty queen. Even the sage advice of Julie's ex-hippie parents (Fredric Forest and Colleen Camp, perfectly cast) can do little to prevent Julie from gagging herself with a spoon. What's a Val Girl in love supposed to do?

What makes *Valley Girl* so perceptive and winning is its innate understanding that teenagers, more than any other species, are entirely *of the now*. What may be trivial in retrospect is, to the acne-covered, gawky teenager experiencing it in the moment, of cataclysmic, melo-dramatic importance. *Valley Girl* was produced at the beginning of MTV's rising dominance of teen culture; the film is loosely struc-tured as a series of quick dialogue exchanges interspersed with music montages. But if the framework is slight, Coolidge allows her char-acters to seriously ponder their romantic dilemma, and in the process, be daring enough to confront such weighty issues as con-formity, intolerance and the courage to be different. What a wonder-ful message, and the fact that it comes wrapped up in a seemingly insignificant teen fad film only makes it more special. Why shouldn't the heartbreak of a seventeen-year-old be the stuff of high drama and classic pop art? Parents may never get it, but the little girls still un-derstand. *Valley Girl* is totally tripendicular.

The Goodies What is arguably the holy trinity of 1980s teen movies, *Valley Girl, The Breakfast Club* and *Fast Times at Ridge-mont High,* have all been released on DVD, but *Valley Girl* got the best disc. It attempts nothing less than to define the 1980s and just about succeeds. The sinister plot is revealed right from the menus: silly fonts, garish colors and groovy tunes instantly transport us back to 1983, a land of maxed-out credit cards and seriously stressed adverbs. But like the film, it is a DVD that doesn't mock its subject. Bitchin'.

Coolidge has recorded a new audio commentary and it is great fun, but it is also a tribute to the youthful filmmaker who seizes an opportunity and runs with it. Who would have a thought a film called *Valley Girl* could have any relevance at all? But lest anyone think shooting a sweet and winsome teen flick is an easy business, Coolidge had to quickly pass Filmmaking 101: "I knew if I wanted to shoot a feature film on only 60,000 feet of film, I had better have this thing planned. I knew it was going to be a one-take movie." Such feistiness and spirit continues with the VH-1–inspired "Pop Up Fact Track," loaded with factoids both profound and useless, and a cool video commentary. Turn it on and enjoy an extended branching ver-sion of the flick that breaks off on autopilot to newly recorded inter-view segments with Coolidge, Cage, and cast and crew. No one expected to ever be talking about this movie twenty years later, which is why these are such a gem.

Three additional featurettes smartly dissect the 1980s Val Girl phenomenon. All are surprisingly meaty. Coolidge and Cage sit down for the intimate "In Conversation," which is entirely free of condescension. Back in 1983, the newly christened Cage (previously Coppola) was out to prove himself as an actor, and he and Coolidge have a great time remembering the tough, short shoot that would launch both of their careers. "The Music of *Valley Girl*" pays tribute to the shamefully underrated pop gems of the time. Three of the acts that most enjoyed a career bump thanks to *Valley Girl* are profiled: Modern English, Josie Cotton and the Plimsouls. All were purveyors of great pop that have since been relegated to questions on *Rock 'N' Roll Jeopardy,* but they paved the way for the breakthrough of alternative music in the United States. And "Totally Tubular: 20 Years Later" fills in any of the missing gaps, a twenty-two-minute ode to Val greatness that's awesome, totally awesome.

Of the remaining supplements, the included storyboard-to-screen comparisons seem a bit superfluous but do aptly illustrate the magic you can make on a minuscule budget if you properly prepare. And what is a great 1980s teen flick without music videos? "I Melt with You" by Modern English and the Plimsouls' L.A. chestnut "A Million Miles Away" still hold up, and for some truly nostalgic fun, don't miss the cute theatrical trailer.

The Presentation *Valley Girl* was produced on a thrifty budget and shot in only three weeks. But you'd be hard-pressed to tell from this DVD. It looks, if not totally tubular, then at least splashy and colorful. The source material is in fine shape, with a clean if dated look and sharp detail throughout. The only drawback? MGM decided to cut corners when compressing the disc. The video commentary segments suffer from noticeable blockiness, but the main feature comes through more or less unscathed. Also quite sweet is the Dolby Digital 5.1 remix, which retains the spirit of the film's original flat mono mix with little surround use, but the clarity of the dialogue is greatly improved and the stellar tunes match the quality of the recently released soundtrack CDs. *Valley Girl* looks and sounds like the perfect pop that it is.

Additional Recommendations So many teen films, so little time. Must-see classics on DVD cross all decades and demographics: *Splendor in the Grass, Rebel Without a Cause, The Graduate, Breaking Away, Ordinary People, Dead Poet's Society, Porkys,* and the best of the John Hughes canon, *The Breakfast Club, Sixteen Candles, Weird Science* and *Pretty in Pink,* are all featureless; only Cameron Crowe's *Fast Times at Ridgemont High* receives any sort of extras, including a commentary and documentary; 8-tracks not included.

Vertigo

DISTRIBUTOR: Universal Studios Home Video
DVD RELEASE: March 31, 1998
THEATRICAL RELEASE: May 1958
RUNNING TIME: 128 Minutes
MPAA RATING: PG

Alfred Hitchcock's most personal film, *Vertigo* was for decades a lost masterpiece, the victim of critical indifference and audience apathy. Few knew what to make of Hitchcock's meditative thriller, a tale of a man haunted by obsession and wounded by betrayal. It was a box office flop upon release and languished for decades on the revival circuit, attracting a rabid, passionate cult following but little in the way of critical reevaluation. It was not until the 1980s and the rise of video, and, in 1996, a stunning restoration and theatrical rerelease, that *Vertigo* came to be considered one of Hitchcock's greatest achievements.

Hitchcock has long been criticized as the most controlling and misogynistic of filmmakers. His female characters are cold and remote. They manipulate weak men, are dressed up in elegant costumes and photographed beautifully, every detail attended to by Hitchcock with a gleeful fetishism. And they almost always meet the same fates: humiliated, run out of town or murdered. *Vertigo* feels largely confessional, the story of Scottie (James Stewart), another Hitchcock hero with handicaps emotional (fear of intimacy) and physical (fear of heights). He is inadvertently embroiled in a murder mystery when a childhood chum, Galvin (Tom Helmore), hires him to follow his wife Madeline (Kim Novak), who is strangely preoccupied with the past. Scottie falls in love with her—not the woman, but her image. And when he realizes he can't have her, he finds a replacement in Judy (also Novak), who he attempts to make over into a copy of Madeline. But the conspiracy that he has stumbled into is far more complex than Scottie could have ever expected, and will end in startling revelations, betrayal and murder.

> "Scottie, do you believe that someone out of the past—someone dead—can enter and take possession of a living being?"
>
> —Gavin Elster

The streets of San Francisco are as much of a character in *Vertigo* as are Scottie and Judy. As Scottie winds his way through the city's hills and valleys, obsessively tracking his haunted love, it is as if we are watching Hitchcock relive his past cinematic crimes, stalking the quintessential Hitchcockian woman he could never have, only fetishized and punished in his films. In *Vertigo,* he has created one of the most perverse and titillating love stories to come out of mid-century cinema. Is Scottie—and by extension, Hitchcock—a pervert, the perpetrator or the victim? The mystery at the heart of his story struggles with a single emotional paradox: if a man falls in love with a woman who does not exist, can he blame the real woman who is impersonating her for betraying him? Hitchcock was never more open, honest and naked as he was in *Vertigo*. It is a haunting, unforgettable masterpiece that asks tough questions and is often tough to watch. But it has the inexorable pull of a nightmare, and the title *Vertigo* is an apt metaphor: as the film climaxes, Scottie—and Hitchcock—stand high above the abyss. They hold on with one hand to their romantic ideal, and with the other for dear life. Neither choice seems a particularly good one.

The Goodies "Obsessed with *Vertigo*: New Life for Hitchcock's Masterpiece" is a marvelous documentary, narrated by Roddy Mc-Dowell and running fifty minutes. It is wonderfully comprehensive, from the conception of Hitchcock's most personal and assured masterpiece through its long location shoot in San Francisco, to the amazing, impeccable restoration, complete with before-and-after comparisons. Many modern filmmakers continue to be entranced by *Vertigo,* including Martin Scorsese, who appears here in a new interview along with many of the film's collaborators, including Novak, Barbara Bel Geddes, producer Herbert Coleman and Hitch's daughter, Pat. Also tucked into the documentary is a fascinating tale of the battle over the ending. Foreign censors asked for significant cuts to Hitchcock's downbeat finale; that butchered version is presented here, and it is both amusing and infuriating. A slew of rare still material, including production sketches and storyboards, is interspersed throughout.

There's also a very informative (if somewhat dry) audio commentary by Coleman and the restoration team of Robert A. Harris and James C. Katz. Harris and Katz often get highly technical, and some of the material discussed is difficult to conceptualize without the aid of before-and-after comparisons like those included in the documentary. Coleman offers many valuable insights into Hitchcock's creative process, and as a tribute to the amazing advances in restoration technology, this commentary is a must-listen for the curious. Rounding out the edition are some production notes, talent bios and the film's many theatrical trailers.

The Presentation *Vertigo* looks astounding. Despite a negative that suffered poorly throughout the years, Katz and Harris pulled out all the stops with a restoration that ranks with the best ever attempted. Colors are rapturous—the rich hues are simply stunning in depth and clarity. Lush purples, deep greens and sun-soaked oranges dazzle the eye. Detail is exquisite, with fine textures visible and only a slight shimmering to distract. There is still some minor grain and a little bit of print instability, but otherwise this is such a pristine presentation it is hard to image that *Vertigo* was made in 1958.

Also sensational is the new Dolby Digital 5.1 surround remix. Dialogue reproduction is still somewhat dated, but Bernard Hermann's highly influential score sounds absolutely amazing. Its dizzying cacophony of eerie sounds that fold back onto themselves is reproduced with a richness and clarity that is truly mesmerizing. Unfortunately, Universal Studios Home Video elected not to include a DTS option, despite the film being presented to great acclaim in the format during its theatrical rerelease.

West Side Story

DISTRIBUTOR: MGM Home Entertainment
DVD RELEASE: April 1, 2003
THEATRICAL RELEASE: October 1961
RUNNING TIME: 151 Minutes
MPAA RATING: G

When you're a kid, life is an opera. A grand adventure of oversized emotions. Your first love is the greatest love ever created—the one who makes your heart pound through your chest. Your friends would die for you, and you for them. Authority figures are puffy, clueless buffoons who don't understand you and your plans and your dreams. If only they'd leave you alone. If only they knew you planned to live forever.

When *West Side Story* debuted in movie theaters in 1961, it came at a particularly fertile time for stage-to-screen adaptations. The previous ten years had given audiences *Singin' in the Rain* (1952), *Oklahoma!* (1955), *The King and I* (1956) and *South Pacific* (1958). But *West Side Story* had more on its mind. It was an urban opera, where grit and grace mingled on sweaty basketball courts and in back alleys and outside brownstones. The teens who populate this pastel jungle are Puerto

> "You all killed him. And my brother and Riff. Not with bullets and knives. With hate. Well I can kill, too. Because now I have hate!"
>
> —Maria

Rican immigrants and American children of European immigrants, fumbling to stake their claim in a strange land. But the laws of the street don't allow for common ground. So on the streets of Leonard Bernstein and Jerome Robbins's New York, the Jets and the Sharks battle.

The Jets were founded by Riff (Russ Tamblyn) and Tony (Richard Beymer); the latter has slowly drifted away from gang life, having taken a job at Doc's Candy Store. At a dance scheduled at the local gym, Riff plans on issuing a challenge to Bernardo (George Chakiris), leader of the Sharks: an all-out rumble to decide who rules the neighborhood. Tony reluctantly comes to the dance and sees Maria (Natalie Wood), sister of Bernardo. The two instantly fall in love. Although the rules of the street command that their love can never be, they begin an affair. When Bernardo confronts Maria about her love for his rival, he asks, "Couldn't you see he's one of them?" Maria replies, "No. I saw only *him*."

West Side Story is a magnificent piece of entertainment and an essential experience for anyone who claims to love movies. The film, codirected by Robert Wise and Jerome Robbins, brims with dynamic choreography and some of the greatest songs ever heard on stage or screen, including *"America," "Maria"* and *"Tonight."* Bernstein's score combines the modern, clanking rhythms of the city with flowing love songs of such emotion, they seem written on the wind.

But *West Side Story* is more than just music, lyric and book—it's an inspired mix of urban setting and stylized dancing in a story that encompasses bigotry, rape, murder and gang warfare. At the top of Bernstein's personal copy of Shakespeare's *Romeo and Juliet,* there is the following annotation: "an out-and-out plea for racial tolerance." His own plea became a modern cinematic masterpiece.

The Goodies *West Side Story* won ten Academy Awards plus a Special Award for Robbins's extraordinary choreography. And MGM deserves its own award for creating such an outstanding DVD box set.

The second disc contains all the extras, starting with *"West Side* Memories," an excellent sixty-minute documentary. Almost all the surviving participants, including Wise, Sondheim and Moreno, reminisce with great reverence and honesty about the production. They describe Robbins as a brilliant but almost brutal taskmaster, and don't shy away from more controversial subjects, including the dismissal of the choreographer, who was deemed responsible for the film's budget overages. "*West Side* Memories" is also packed with archival video and audio, including original vocals from Natalie Wood, which were eventually replaced by vocals provided by Marni Nixon. Incredible 8mm footage of the filmmakers on set give the documentary a comprehensive feel.

Also on the supplements disc is a five-minute musical montage set to the visuals of Maurice Zuberano's storyboards, four trailers (the best being a dramatic animated trailer) and an admirably comprehensive "Photo Gallery," broken down into Production Design, Storyboard and Behind the Scenes.

Best of all is the collectable booklet, which almost qualifies as a real book. It contains Ernest Lehman's original screenplay (complete with colored pages), a reproduction of the original lobby brochure, as well vintage memos and reviews. The whole thing comes encased in an attractive, bright red slip-cover box.

The Presentation *West Side Story* deserved the grandest, most vibrant transfer possible and MGM certainly rose to the challenge, especially after the underwhelming 1998 edition (now discontinued). The Panavision 70mm print features fully saturated colors, including reds that are sharp with only a trace amount of smearing. The rest of the impressively broad palette, led by yellows and blues, is reproduced wonderfully. Blacks are dead-on and shadow detail is surprisingly excellent. The print is in well above-average shape for a forty-year-old movie, although the occasional print flaw is evident. The theatrical aspect ratio is preserved accurately at 2.20:1, which ensures a screen filled with dancing and detail.

A new Dolby Digital 5.1 surround track was produced exclusively for this DVD, but while the results are perfectly fine and honorable to the material, it's not a particularly enveloping experience. The three front speakers do most of the work, with dialogue coming largely from the center speaker and varying in quality—many of the actors spoke the words but did not sing the songs. As such, any number featuring a dubbed voice sounds less natural. The lefts and rights are put to marginal use, mostly to fill out the score, which sounds bright and loud if not completely fulfilling. There is also a bit of hiss, but overall, this is a very fine remix.

Willy Wonka and the Chocolate Factory

DISTRIBUTOR: Warner Home Video

DVD RELEASE: November 13, 2001

THEATRICAL RELEASE: December 1971

RUNNING TIME: 109 Minutes

MPAA RATING: PG

Willy Wonka and the Chocolate Factory is the scariest children's movie ever made. One can only imagine the horrified faces of parents in 1971 who took their children to see what they thought would be just another G-rated tale of wonder and instead got the first slasher flick for the preteen set. Watch as five unsuspecting contest winners get picked off one by one, all set to the beat of toe-tapping tunes like "Pure Imagination." That *Wonka*'s candy-colored wonderland ultimately resembles not so much a magical world of whimsy but a makeshift purgatory only adds to the demented fun. Never has a family entertainment been this subversive and sublime.

> **"The suspense is killing me! I hope it lasts."**
>
> **—Willy Wonka**

Based on the much-beloved 1964 novel *Charlie and the Chocolate Factory* by Roald Dahl, the retitled *Willy Wonka* was a box office bust upon first release but quickly became a perennial favorite via endless television airings. Dahl's dark satire has been cited as a major influence on everyone from Tim Burton (who threatens a remake) to shock rocker Marilyn Manson, and Gene Wilder's living embodiment of Wonka has become iconic. A sort of dark doppelganger to Santa Claus, he relishes in his grim task of deciding who's been naughty and who's been nice. But with the help of his demented band of Oompa Loompas, Wonka's hidden agenda will be made clear by journey's end. Each of the handpicked five has a lesson to learn, but not all the children, when put to the test, will rise to the challenge.

Embodying the purest essence of a Grimm's fairy tale ever seen on screen, *Willy Wonka and the Chocolate Factory* is a visual and aural delight. Harper Goff's imaginative designs for Wonka's factory are colorful, surreal masterpieces of ingenuity and invention (remember the candy flavored-wallpaper, or Wonka's office, where everything is cut in half?), and we breathlessly await the wonders to come around every corner. The memorable songs by Leslie Bricusse and Anthony Newley are infused with a truly glorious childlike wonder, from the signature "Candy Man" and "Pure Imagination" to the creepy, nursery rhymelike dirges of the Oompa Loompas. But what galvanizes the film is Wilder, who delivers one of his finest performances as the mischievous and seemingly sadistic Wonka. Bittersweet, not saccharine, he smartly avoids playing Wonka as a typical Disneyesque father figure but instead as an all-knowing, ultimately benevolent guardian angel. He understands, like Dahl, that although we may want life to always be as sweet as an Everlasting Gobstopper, eventually the pure innocence of youth must give way to the darker realities of adulthood. And that the gift of a golden ticket can be dangerous in the hands of the greedy, the lazy, the selfish and the impatient.

The Goodies *Willy Wonka and the Chocolate Factory* has always appealed to adults as much as, if not more than, children, and for this 30th Anniversary Edition, Warner Home Video has wisely created a batch of supplements free of most of the inane fluff that usually mars family titles on DVD. Reunited are all five of the film's golden ticket winners: Peter Ostrum (Charlie Bucket), Julie Dawn Cole (Veruca Salt), Denise Nickerson (Violet Beauregard), Paris Themmen (Mike TeeVee) and Michael Bollner (Augustus Gloop). Their group commentary is a real treat, as much a chance to marvel at the passage of time as to revel in the amusing anecdotes shared by all. Joining in for the thirty-minute documentary "Pure Imagination" are director Mel Stuart, producer Donald P. Wolper and Wilder, who, via new interviews, recount the story of a film largely dismissed upon first release but that has since become a part of the cultural vernacular. A smattering of never-before-seen footage includes a few surprises, including composer Newley unveiling the song "Pure Imagination" to Wolper, and a rare peek at the construction of the Goff's now-classic factory sets.

Other extras include a kid-friendly sing-along, complete with stylized on-screen lyrics, a fairly detailed still gallery with many photos from Wolper's private collection, and both the original and rerelease theatrical trailers.

The Presentation Warner Home Video's initial release of the 30th Anniversary Edition of *Willy Wonka* on DVD was full-frame-only and quickly drew ire from DVD enthusiasts on the Internet. The backlash was so fierce at the lack of a widescreen *Wonka* that a virtual petition amassed thousands of signatures in a mere few days. Warner soon relented, and Mr. Wonka himself would have been proud. Gloriously restored for its thirtieth anniversary, this transfer sports an image good enough to lick. Colors are sweet as cotton candy, and the print is nicely detailed and free from all the grain and dirt that marred previous video releases. The Dolby Digital 5.1 remix is also a wonderful confection, with classic tunes like "The Candyman" more luscious than ever. A pure delight.

Additional Versions Warner Home Video initially released *Willy Wonka and the Chocolate Factory* on DVD in 1997 in a movie-only edition, which has since been discontinued. Both the widescreen and full-screen 30th Anniversary Editions remain in print.

The Wizard of Oz

DISTRIBUTOR: Warner Home Video
DVD RELEASE: September 28, 2000
THEATRICAL RELEASE: August 1939
RUNNING TIME: 101 Minutes
MPAA RATING: G

The Wizard of Oz was a box office bomb upon first release in 1939 but became a perennial favorite and just may be the most-played film ever on television. It turned Judy Garland into a star. It gave the world "Over the Rainbow." It taught us that there is no place like home. And it was a film that traumatized me like no other. Often cited as the greatest family entertainment ever made, *The Wizard of Oz* is pretty grim stuff. Not like *The Texas Chainsaw Massacre,* but in a sneaky, sly way, it is a singularly frightening experience. And since it is a film that been analyzed to death, there is little new to say about Dorothy, Toto and their trip to *Oz.* So let's just look at the facts to determine why this is one of the most terrifying, mean-spirited and plain traumatic motion pictures of all time.

The film starts out in icky sepia tone, and Dorothy's neighbors sure are mean. What kind of person would steal a cute little dog like Toto? Then Dorothy's house is picked up by a *tornado.*

> **"Pay no attention to that man behind the curtain!"**
> —The Wizard

Unless you grew up in the Midwest, you are probably not familiar with the sight of a giant cyclone, traveling one hundred miles an hour, en route to demolish your house. And even the sudden switch to color offers no hope because when Dorothy's house lands, it kills someone. It seems like good ol' Dorothy is able to shrug off manslaughter pretty quickly ("Oh, look at the funny little Munchkins!"). For, without a care in the world, it is "off to see the Wizard, the wonderful Wizard of Oz!"

On her way she meets the Scarecrow, a gangly, creepy creature with no brain; the Tin Man, a pre-*Terminator* box of bolts with no heart, and a lion. The four skip and sing their way down the yellow brick road, with the Wicked Witch of the West hot on their trail. She is green, cackles with glee and flies through the air with an army of winged monkeys. Absolutely terrifying.

A facetious reading of *The Wizard of Oz,* maybe, but its beauty and brilliance stem from what the Brothers Grimm, Roald Dahl and Walt Disney all understood—that without dark there is no light, and that the passage from childhood to adulthood is fraught with danger, mystery and peril. And maybe *The Wizard of Oz* is so unnerving because of its nightmarish production. It took four tries to get it right: Victor Fleming is credited as sole director, but Richard Thorpe reportedly did some work on it, as did George Cukor and legendary silent film auteur King Vidor, who helmed the black-and-white sequences. It can feel schizophrenic and claustrophobic, surreal and trippy—the film became a favorite at midnight screenings, where drug-assisted moviegoers would lie on the floor in the front row, stare up at the screen and say "Far out." And its classic songs, including "Over the Rainbow," the most forlorn and emotionally naked of ballads, have an undercurrent of sadness and melancholia that is vaguely disturbing, especially as sung by Garland, who would eventually slide into drug and alcohol addiction. Poor Dorothy.

The Wizard of Oz is by all means a one-of-a-kind film experience and an all-time classic. But me? I still have not gotten over the trauma and I refuse to watch it alone. I, for one, can never go home again.

The Goodies The packaging of *The Wizard of Oz* is deceptive—its simple snapper case does not hint at the wonders inside. It is in fact loaded with excellent supplements. Angela Lansbury hosts the delightful fifty-minute documentary "The Wonderful *Wizard of Oz,*" which is a well-crafted blend of interview footage, never-before-seen stills and priceless, if brief, making-of footage. This documentary's sense of fun and curiosity is contagious. It may be designed for novices—many hardcore *Wizard* fans will already know this stuff— but it's a blast nonetheless.

This 60th Anniversary Edition includes a cornucopia of additional extras. A collection of deleted scenes includes the infamous "Jitterbug" scene that was excised due to length; it is a rather fantastic sequence, long but joyous, and a must for *Oz* fans. A "Behind-the-Scenes" section features an extensive selection of storyboards and sketches, as well as costume and makeup tests. The remaining still galleries are comprehensive, almost overwhelming: a portrait gallery, special effects stills, and a ton of production and publicity photographs. Some real finds include sections of Fleming's original cut that were excised from the final version, deleted early effects sequences and postproduction snapshots.

"*Oz* History" is a showcases of excerpts from the 1914 and 1925 silent film versions of the story, as well as a 1933 animated *Oz*. Next is "*Oz* Afterlife," an assortment of video- and text-based publicity materials, including 1979 interviews with Ray Bolger, Jack Haley and Margaret Hamilton, more publicity and poster art, and a vintage sequence from the 1939 Academy Awards ceremony. Also included here is an assortment of Chuck Jones's "Off to See the Wizard" animated bumpers from 1967.

But there is more: a colossal collection of audio supplements, including hilarious regular- and fast-speed versions of Munchkin dialogue, the entire score for the film, rough and alternate takes of songs from the film, and even an hour-long radio program produced for the original release of the movie. The navigation of these extras is a little tricky: you can't listen to small sections; you have to jump in for the long haul. But just click your remote three times—maybe it will take you back home.

The Presentation What a wonderful restoration of *The Wizard of Oz*! Lovely Technicolor hues and a clean new print make the trip from Kansas to the Emerald City well worth taking. Not surprising for a film over sixty years old, there is some wavering and inconsistencies to the print, and due to shrinkage, the three Technicolor "plates" don't always line up, which results in some softness and color "halos." But this is a very impressive transfer nonetheless; Warner utilized the latest in digital technology to greatly reduce such anomalies, and the image is smooth, sharp and filmlike.

Dorothy and her pals have been remixed in Dolby Digital 5.1 surround. It is a fairly artificially sounding mix and may be the only disappointment of this set. The surrounds have been processed to extract frequencies from the original mono source elements, which can sound false and echo-ey. Dialogue is generally crisp and clear, with the atmospheric effects benefiting the most from a more natural and full sound. Alas, the film's original mono soundtrack has not been included, the only oversight of an otherwise terrific special edition.

Additional Versions A deluxe, limited edition DVD package of *The Wizard of Oz* is also available, which includes the complete Sixtieth Anniversary Edition set, a screenplay reproduction, rare stills and color reproductions of the film's many posters. MGM Home Entertainment also released a movie-only edition of *The Wizard of Oz* on DVD in 1997; the rights have since reverted to Warner Home Video, and the previous MGM version is now out of print.

Appendix A:
The Shape of Things—
What Is an Aspect Ratio?

One of the most exciting advantages of the DVD format is its ability to present material in variable aspect ratios. Film buffs have long wanted to re-create the theatrical experience in their home, but for years, the vast majority of motion pictures shot in a widescreen picture format had to be heavily cropped and edited ("panned and scanned") when shown on broadcast television or presented on videotape. Now, with the advent of digital television and the growing availability of widescreen display devices, a revolution is taking place. And the DVD boom is largely responsible.

Yet as exciting as the possibilities are, the concepts of widescreen and aspect ratios are by far the most intimidating to the neophyte DVD consumer. What are those black bars? Why does the picture look squeezed? How do I set up my DVD player? You would not be alone in throwing down the remote in frustration, but have no fear: screens may come in all manner of shapes and sizes, but once you have the basics down, you'll be getting the most out of your home theater in no time. Below are eight steps to understanding aspect ratios, presented in a simple and accessible manner.

1. MAKING SENSE OF ASPECT RATIOS

> **aspect ratio** *noun:* a ratio of one dimension to another: **a:** the ratio of the width of a television or motion-picture image to its height

Simple, eh? So how about an example? Say you were to go see the latest blockbuster at your local gigaplex. You'd sit down with your popcorn and licorice, and marvel at the big, huge screen. (Oooh, ahhh!) And let's say the screen measured twenty feet wide and ten feet high. That would give it an aspect ratio of 20:10, expressed as 2:1. Same goes for your TV screen. A very nice home theater screen measuring four feet wide and three feet tall would give us an aspect ratio of 4:3.

See, there is nothing to be afraid of:

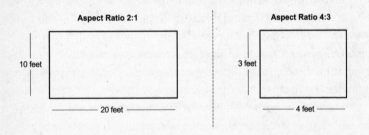

Important: The expression of an aspect ratio differs depending on the medium. Material produced for theatrical exhibition is almost always expressed as an integer, with the height a whole number. For example: 1.66:1, 1.85:1, 2.35:1, etc. Material produced for television broadcast is almost always expressed as two whole numbers, for example: 4:3, 16:9, etc. Why? The reasons are so long and convoluted that even industry professionals have forgotten. But it remains the industry standard, so we must accept it.

Also important: The expression of an aspect ratio refers to *units* only, not inches, feet or any other measurement. For example, say you buy a new DVD of your favorite movie and it is presented in an aspect ratio of 1.85:1. That means the image area you will see will measure out 1.85 times as wide as it is tall, regardless of the size of the screen you watch it on. For example, if your TV screen were one foot tall, that 1.85:1 aspect ratio means the image would measure out to be 1.85 feet wide. And if your screen were ten feet tall, it would be a very nice 18.5 feet wide. (Can I come over to your house?) Just remember that the aspect ratio always stays the same, even if the size of your TV doesn't.

2. RECTANGLES, BIG RECTANGLES AND VERY BIG RECTANGLES

It all started out so easy. For decades, the shape of both a motion picture and television screen was the same. In 1955, the National Television Society (NTSC) established a workable broadcast system—the same one we have today, in fact. Deciding on the shape of the TV screen was easy: 4:3, which is the equivalent of 1.33:1, or the shape of 35mm film, which was the dominant aspect ratio of film production at the time (also called Academy Standard or "flat"). Thus, converting film to video was pretty straightforward and there was no appreciable loss in image area; no cropping or other forms of manipulation were needed to squeeze a big-screen movie onto a television screen. They were already the same size!

But then the millions that bought shiny new television sets were also the millions that stopped going to the movies. Ticket sales plummeted so fast that by the end of the 1950s, many began to predict utter collapse for the film industry. The studios fought back, competing the only way they knew how: with chutzpah and showmanship. Gimmicks designed to get audiences back in theaters became commonplace and plentiful, from 3-D to "Odorama" to buzzers stuck under the seats. A few worked, most failed.

Widescreen was one of the few successes. The growing pains were lengthy (and costly), but by the start of the 1960s widescreen presentation was becoming the norm. Screens suddenly got bigger and wider. Aspect ratios as extravagantly wide as 2.55:1 proved overwhelming and intoxicating to audiences. But once the dust settled, only a few proved durable, and today, three basic sizes compromise the vast majority of motion pictures produced in North America: 1.85:1 (the most common), 2.35:1, and good old 1.33:1.

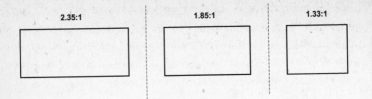

3. THE ADVENT OF PAN AND SCAN

As a result of the widescreen explosion, TV and eventually cable and home video, suffered. Something had to give—how do you squeeze a rectangle into a square? The solution was the most simple and obvious one: cropping. It was a seemingly benign process given a seemingly benign little name of "pan and scan." For decades, it would be the dominant method of transferring film to video.

So just how does pan and scan work? First let's take a look at how you would "fit" a film shot in an aspect ratio of 2.35:1 or 1.85:1 in a 4:3 television frame. Be warned, it gets ugly . . .

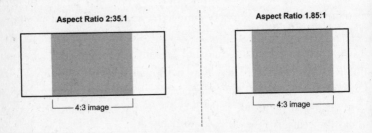

Yes, it is true. In the early days of film-to-video transfer (or *telecine*), films big and small were simply lopped off at the sides, often losing up to fifty percent of the total image area with little regard to composition or framing. Filmmakers fumed, but market considerations ruled. All of the blood, sweat and tears that went into composing big pictures for big screens was erased with just a few clicks of a button.

But then the pan and scan process gained favor as a more accept-able solution. Here, a more lengthy (and costly) process occurs: the pan and scan artist sits down with a film's director (and/or the direc-tor of photography) to go through the entire film—frame by frame—and recompose it for a 4:3 screen.

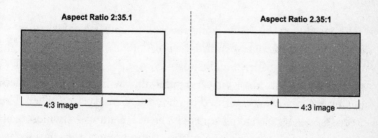

The pan-and-scan process created a whole new film grammar of its own. A shot of a couple talking suddenly became a single close-up. What was once a continuous long shot across a panoramic vista now became a jerky and distractingly rapid movement, as the 4:3 frame had to pan over the widescreen image area. Not only was com-position altered, but pacing was too. Home viewers may have sensed something was missing, but pan and scan became the standard. Until there came an alternative . . .

4. THE RISE OF LETTERBOXING

Enter the laserdisc. Originally conceived as an archival system and not a mainstream consumer video format, laserdisc became the first format to actively support "letterboxing," the process of preserving a film's original aspect ratio. Instead of cropping or panning and scan-ning an image, the full image area was placed unaltered inside the TV frame and the leftover image area filled in by a solid color, usu-ally black (although some early letterboxed presentations used vari-ous shades of gray). Hence, the oft repeated phrase, "those dreaded black bars!"

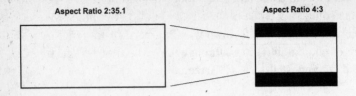

Aspect Ratio 2:35.1   Aspect Ratio 4:3

While widescreen found great favor with cineastes and critics—the kind of dedicated movie lovers who could afford laserdisc's high prices—it failed to attract mainstream consumers, and broadcast TV rarely supported it. Most viewers, unfamiliar with the film-to-video transfer process, were confused by the loss of image area. Their TV screens suddenly shrank, and aside from a handful of widescreen VHS releases and television broadcasts, letterboxing was confined to the niche laserdisc market.

5. DVD AND HD: A NEW ERA

Then came DVD and high-definition (HD) TV. With the adoption at last of a digital television (DTV) standard in the United States, the advent of widescreen monitors became widespread. Wider than the 4:3 NTSC standard, an aspect ratio of 16:9 (or 1.78:1) was chosen for DTV, one very near 1.85:1.

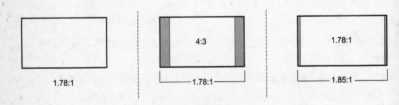

1.78:1   4:3 / 1.78:1   1.78:1 / 1.85:1

At last, motion pictures no longer needed to be cropped or panned and scanned. While material wider than 1.78:1 still continues to be letterboxed to retain its original aspect ratio, the blacked-out amount is slim to marginal on a film with an aspect ratio of 1.85:1, and the intrusiveness of the black bars greatly reduced even on a wide aspect ratio like 2.35:1.

Presenting 4:3 material in a 16:9 frame proves to be trickier; the most common solution has been "pillarboxing," applying black bars to the sides of an image. Some advanced widescreen television monitors offer alternatives, including the ability to "stretch" 4:3 images to 16:9 by applying digital distortion and/or cropping significant parts of an image.

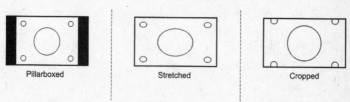

While the advent of DVD and DTV has greatly lessened the need for panning and scanning, there are many broadcast, digital cable and satellite content providers who still prefer to deliver widescreen images wider than 1.78:1 in compromised form, usually by cropping them down to 16:9 dimensions. (HBO's high-definition channel is a prime offender. As of this writing, it continues to broadcast 2.35:1 material panned and scanned at 1.78:1)

Even 4:3 material is not safe, undergoing what some call "reverse pan and scan," or "vertical pan and scan." Consumers bringing home that new widescreen are often surprised to discover that all of their local newscasters' heads are lopped off. There are even a few DVD presentations that have cropped 4:3 material to 16:9. While the practice of "vertical pan and scan" is not uncommon, as the understanding of the benefits of widescreen continues to grow, it will likely be severely tapered or abolished.

6. WHAT IS ANAMORPHIC?

DVD has at last made the world safe for widescreen. While the format is not capable of displaying true high-resolution, high-definition (HD) images, it does refine our current NTSC video system to the *nth* degree. DVD is not truly a widescreen medium—the actual aspect ratio of material that is stored on a DVD is still in the standard 4:3 aspect ratio—but, by making use of the *anamorphic* process, the format can maximize resolution and deliver the best picture possible.

First, let's talk about NTSC video. While well over fifty years old, this workhorse system still has a lot going for it, as the razor-sharp images of DVD can attest. NTSC video is capable of a maximum horizontal resolution of 525 horizontal lines, and DVD takes advantage of every last one of them. (However, only about 480 of them comprise what you will actually see on your screen; the rest fall in the unusable picture area or are victims of overscan—the part of the image that is not intended to be seen but that is needed to compensate for inconsistencies in the visible area of display devices.) By comparison, the VHS format delivered around 240 lines, the laserdisc, 425.

Now, these available "lines of resolution" are all well and good. And they fill up the 4:3 frame nicely. But what about those 16:9 televisions? DVDs look great on them. So how does it all work?

Before DVD, black bars of varying thickness were placed inside the 4:3 frame, say on a laserdisc or a VHS tape or an over-the-air broadcast, which meant that all that black area—empty picture space—ate up essential lines of resolution. Ultra-widescreen presentations, such as material composed for 2.35:1, suffered the most, with only a few lines left for the actual picture.

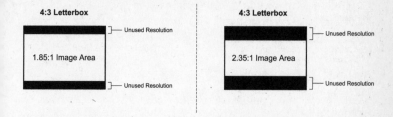

Thanks to the ingenuity of the DVD Forum (a consortium of manufacturers, replicators and studios who teamed up to define the DVD spec), the format has a neat workaround to maximize all those precious lines of resolution. How? By presenting widescreen material anamorphically, detail can be maximized.

But what does *anamorphic* actually mean? In layman's terms, it is taking an image, "squeezing" it horizontally and then unsqueezing it to utilize the most image area possible.

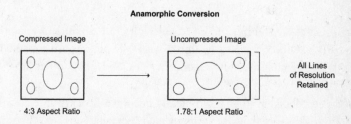

How is it done? To present material anamorphically, video is encoded on a DVD and horizontally compressed. This eliminates or greatly reduces the black bars of a widescreen presentation, which is valuable image area that would otherwise be lost. The DVD then outputs the image in its native squeezed state for unsqueezing by a widescreen display device. Presto! All those extra lines of resolution are retained and the image is as groovy as it can be.

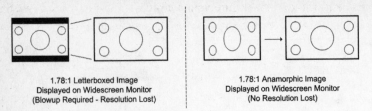

Anamorphic Versus Non-Anamorphic Conversion

1.78:1 Letterboxed Image
Displayed on Widescreen Monitor
(Blowup Required - Resolution Lost)

1.78:1 Anamorphic Image
Displayed on Widescreen Monitor
(No Resolution Lost)

But what if you don't have a widescreen TV? DVD solves that problem too. The player itself unsqueezes the material instead of outputting it in its native state, then takes the 1.78:1 image area, reduces it and extrapolates extra lines of resolution to expand the image vertically to 4:3.

Anamorphic Image Displayed on 4:3 Monitor

Compressed Image

Uncompressed Image

Letterboxed Image

4:3 Aspect Ratio

1.78:1 Aspect Ratio

4:3 Aspect Ratio

So, what do you have to do to enjoy the full benefits of anamorphically encoded movies? Nothing! All DVD players are capable of displaying anamorphically encoded titles and can output images properly regardless of what screen shape your display device is. While the decision to anamorphically encode a DVD disc rests with the producer, the majority of major and independent DVD distributors have adopted the practice as standard.

7. HOW DO I SET UP MY PLAYER?

Setting up your DVD player properly requires some time, patience and a willingness to consult your player's manual. It is easy—anyone can properly set up both the DVD player and TV with a minimum of fuss and hassle. Here's a few helpful hints.

Go to the screen-size setup screen (consult your manual for proper instructions) and make sure your player is set for either 4:3 or 16:9 depending on your display device. Then sit back, watch and enjoy. Easy, huh?

But what happens if your player is set for 16:9 and you have a 4:3 display device? The player, doing strictly what it is told, will output the material directly to your set still squeezed. Hence, people become really skinny and tall. Again, consult your manual and properly set up your player for your screen shape. If you have a standard television set, your display device is 4:3.

8. WIDESCREEN IS YOUR FRIEND

Despite the significant benefits, there continues to be a backlash among many consumers and retailers against widescreen presentation. The drawbacks cited are many and certainly valid: the reduced image area as a result of letterboxing (especially on very wide aspect ratios, such as 2.35:1), the loss in resolution and the expense of having to purchase a widescreen television to enjoy the full experience. And the home video industry has done little to educate the public on the benefits of widescreen and the differences between pan and scan, letterboxing and anamorphic. Even relatively few filmmakers have taken a public stance on the issue; aside from vocal widescreen proponents like Martin Scorsese, Hollywood has been surprisingly mum on the issue.

It is the position of this author that widescreen is the preferable format for watching theatrical motion pictures at home. Except for those with the smallest of display devices (say, under twenty-seven inches), the drawbacks are far outweighed by the benefits—primarily the opportunity to see the entire image. You may be surprised at how quickly you will become accustomed to those black bars, and investing in a widescreen TV enhances the experience exponentially. Letterboxing is virtually eliminated or greatly reduced, even on material as wide as 2.35:1. And gone is all that distracting panning and scanning. Those black bars are a small price to pay for—at last—seeing classic films in the manner in which they were originally intended.

Or just think of it in the reverse: imagine going to the movies and having the theater owner open the curtains only halfway. Wouldn't you ask for your money back?

Appendix B:

Glossary of Terms

.1 LFE Refers to the low-frequency (subwoofer) channel in a multichannel soundtrack. Capable of delivering only low-bass frequencies, to be decoded by a surround processor and directed to the subwoofer.

2-3 pulldown The process of converting 24-frames-per-second film to video. (See Appendix A for details.)

AC-3 Acronym for the Dolby Digital 5.1 surround audio coding system. Primarily associated with the laserdisc format, the term is no longer used outside of technical and standards documentation.

access time The length of time it takes for a player or drive to access data on a disc and begin transferring it. The quicker a player or drive's access time, the faster the user can navigate menus, skip chapters and access supplements. Generally measured in seconds.

analog A signal created by making small changes to physical media, such as a needle riding a groove on a vinyl album, particles arranged on a strip of magnetic tape, or sound waves generated by a speaker cone. Analog signals suffer from real-world degradation, interference and decay. (See also "digital.")

anamorphic widescreen The process of compressing an image during storage then uncompressing it upon display to increase resolution. (See Appendix A. See also "aspect ratio," "letterbox" and "widescreen.")

angle In DVD parlance, an angle is a different camera view or video segment that can be accessed during viewing. Most commonly used for "multi-angle" supplemental presentations and music programs.

artifact Generalized term for an effect or distortion not present in the original video or audio. Caused by an external agent, process or anomaly, an artifact can result from any part of the DVD production chain: telecine, transmission errors, interference or digital compression. Some artifacts can result from intentional tweaking or processes applied during the production. Common MPEG artifacts can include video noise, compression pixel break-up (blocking) and mosquitoes. (See also "edge enhancement.")

aspect ratio The ratio of an image, expressed as width-to-height. Broadcast aspect ratios are generally expressed as whole numbers, such as 4:3 (4x3 is also generally accepted), pronounced "four by three"; film aspect ratios as decimals (such as 1.85:1, 2.35:1, etc., pronounced "one eight five-to-one" and "two three five-to-one," respectively). Aspect ratios with a height of one are often abbreviated by omitting the *:1*. (See Appendix A for details. See also "anamorphic widescreen," "widescreen" and "letterbox.")

authoring The process of creating and encoding DVD material. Today's all-in-one, one-stop DVD authoring houses have come to include creating, collecting, designing and quality controlling materials, such as menus and even supplemental content. For DVD-ROM, authoring can also include the creation of extensive multimedia and other applications.

bit Short for *binary digit,* the smallest measurement of digital data; the building block of DVD.

bit rate Volume of data as measured over time. Usually expressed as kilobits per second (kbps), megabits per second (mbps) or gigabytes per second (gbps). Same as "data rate."

blocking Term for a common MPEG-related artifact that results in a blocky "break up" of pixels, usually caused because the compression is so high that the averaging of pixels becomes visible. A true blocking artifact will always occur in the same place and at the same time. Dirty or damaged discs can also cause blocking, which is usually correctable by cleaning the disc or repairing it.

Blu-Ray A disc-based optical format, still in development, capable of delivering true full-resolution, high-definition prerecorded content.

caption Representation in text form of the audio portion of a program. Can be a permanent part of the visible picture, but more often encoded as a subpicture element. Although technically incorrect, captions are often used interchangeably with subtitles; captions, however, are generally intended for the hearing impaired and include additional text to identify the person speaking, offscreen sounds, music, etc. (See also "subtitles," "closed captions" and "subpicture element.")

CGI Acronym for computer generated imagery.

channel One part of an audio track. Generally one channel corresponds to one speaker in a home theater audio setup. A DVD audio track can contain up to six separate channels. (See also "downmixing.")

closed captions Video overlays encoded as part of a video signal but not actually part of the visible picture. Stored in an unused line of the video signal, to then be decoded by a built-in or outboard decoder. Generally, closed captions display white or light yellow text over a black background. This is the method of captioning preferred by the hearing impaired, as it allows for easier reading of text as well as additional text to identify the speaker, offscreen sounds, etc. In the United States, the official NTSC closed caption standard requires that all televisions larger than thirteen inches include decoders to display caption information stored in the video signal. (See also "subtitles," "captions," and "subpicture element.")

compression A reduction of the amount of digital data to be stored or transmitted by removing like or redundant information. There are two types of compression: "lossless" compression removes only enough information to ensure an exact recreation of original data; "lossy" compression sacrifices additional data but is able to achieve higher rates of compression. (See also "perceptual coding.")

data rate See "bit rate."

decibel A unit used to measure human aural or visual perception; abbreviated as dB. Expressed as a ratio (negative or positive); reference level is 0 dB.

decode To take encoded material (such as compressed data) and reverse the transformation process, then output it for storage, access and display. A decoder is the actual circuit or device that does the decoding. (See also "encode.")

digital A signal created by numerical representations of analog values. Digital technology is binary based and not susceptible to most of the inherent defects of analog technology, including decay, wear and tear, and interference. (See also "analog.")

digitize To convert analog information (audio or video) into digital information.

discrete surround sound Refers to each channel in an audio stream being stored separately from other channels. Allows for specific direction of a channel to a loudspeaker, greater control of the soundfield, and the precise simulation of moving sounds from speaker to speaker. A discrete surround soundtrack also generally allows for the full frequency response in all channels, aside form the .1 LFE (low-frequency) channel. (See also ".1 LFE" and "Dolby Surround.")

DIVX Digital Video Express. A pay-per-view variant of the DVD format that required specially encoded discs and players. Launched in late 1997 to much fanfare, it failed to reach mass commercial acceptance and was quietly discontinued in 1999.

Dolby Digital Developed by Dolby Labs, a perceptual coding system that allows for up to 5.1 channels of discrete audio. The mandatory audio compression system used for NTSC DVD-Video. (See also "PCM" and "DTS.")

Dolby Pro Logic Developed by Dolby Labs, a circuit-based technology that allows for limited-fidelity audio channels to be extracted from a 2.0 channel soundtrack. Often used interchangeably (and erroneously) with Dolby Surround encoding technology. (See "Dolby Surround.")

Dolby Surround Developed by Dolby Labs, a circuit-based technology used to matrix-encode additional channels into a 2.0 channel mix, often called "matrixed surround" A matrixed soundtrack can then be decoded by a circuit, such as Dolby Pro Logic. Dolby Digital is compatible with Dolby Surround. (See "Dolby Pro Logic" and "Dolby Surround EX.")

Dolby Surround EX Developed by Dolby Labs, a version of Dolby Digital decoding that allows for an additional rear center channel of audio. Similar to Dolby Pro Logic, the rear center channel is matrix-encoded into the two rear channels of a Dolby Digital soundtrack. Requires a Dolby Surround EX decoder. (See "Dolby Digital," "Dolby Pro Logic" and "DTS ES.")

downmix The ability of DVD circuitry to combine multiple channels of audio into two or less. Most common application is to convert a 5.1 audio track into two-channel stereo. Downmixing can cause a reduction in quality and fidelity, thus some DVD releases are encoded with both 5.1 and 2.0 audio tracks to eliminate need for downmixing.

DTS Digital Theater Sound. A perceptual coding system that allows for up to 5.1 channels of discrete audio. A competitor of Dolby Digital, it is an optional sound format for both DVD-Video and DVD-Audio. Requires a DTS-compatible DVD player and DTS decoder. (See also "DTS ES.")

DTS ES Digital Theater Sound Expanded. A version of DTS decoding technology that allows for an additional rear center channel of audio. There are two varieties of DTS ES: matrixed and discrete. Requires a DTS-ES decoder. (See also "DTS.")

D-VHS Digital Video Home System. A tape-based format developed by JVC that is capable of delivering full-resolution, high-definition content. Currently the only way to watch prerecorded high-definition content (such as full-length motion pictures) at home.

edge enhancement Umbrella term used to describe any digital encoding, compression or quality control process used to artificially increase the apparent sharpness of an image. Often used as a derogative to imply negative side effects, such as ringing around sharply contrasted objects, noise or an overly digital appearance to an image to which edge enhancement has been applied.

encode To transform data based on an encoding method (such as compression) for transmission or storage. Most encoding methods are applied to maximize storage efficiency by reducing like or redundant material. An encoder is the actual circuit or device that does the encoding. (See also "decode.")

enhanced viewing mode The capability of DVD to add interactive elements to a program in progress, such as the ability to branch off to related video segments and then return to the same point on the disc, to overlay icons or other graphics, or to access alternate angles or material.

FCC Federal Communications Commission.

field In the NTSC video system, a field is one set of alternating scan lines in an interlaced video picture. Two fields make up one video frame. (See also "frame.")

fps Frames per second.

frame In the NTSC video system, a frame is one complete set of scan lines that makes up a video image. In an interlaced video picture, a frame is made up of two fields of alternating scan lines. (See also "field.")

GB Gigabyte.

Gbps Gigabytes per second.

HDCD High-definition compact disc. A proprietary enhancement for audio CDs that offers improved quality.

HDTV High-definition television. Used loosely (and sometimes erroneously) to describe the U.S. DTV standard, which can also encompass digital television that does not contain high-resolution material. True HDTV is generally considered to be a digital picture presented in a 16:9 aspect ratio and with resolution at least one-and-a-half to twice the resolution of a conventional NTSC television.

HTML Hypertext markup language. A globally accepted language for formatting text for transmission and display on the Internet. Most DVD-ROM applications are based in HTML to ensure universal compatibility between operating systems and web browsers.

horizontal resolution The measurement of the number of lines of horizontal detail in a video picture. The resolution of VHS is generally accepted as 240 lines, laserdisc at 425, and DVD at around 525. Note that a portion of horizontal resolution is often reserved for nonvisible information, giving DVD an apparent (or visible) resolution of 480 lines. (See also "vertical resolution" and "scan line.")

hue The color of light or a pixel (such as red, green, blue, etc.).

IDTV Improved-definition television. Televisions that can, regardless of aspect ratio or signal source (analog or digital) improve the apparent quality of a picture via digital processing techniques. Not the same as true high-definition television.

interlace A scanning system that creates a complete video picture (a frame) by transmitting in rapid succession two separate fields, each with alternating scan lines. In an interlaced video signal, two fields make up one frame. In terms of quality, an interlaced picture is regarded as inferior to progressive scan. (See also "progressive scan.")

jewel box Plastic casing used to hold CDs. Gained some support in the early days of the format as a storage device for DVDs; quickly abandoned in favor of other packaging options, such as the keepcase and "snapper" case.

karaoke A cultural sensation that originated in Japan consisting of amateur sing-alongs to popular hit tunes and standards, usually in a public setting. In DVD terms, a generic term for a music-only track without lyrics, coupled with a subtitle stream. "Karoake-enabled" players usually include a microphone input.

KB Kilobyte.

Kbps Kilobytes per second.

laserdisc A 12-inch optical disc-based format that delivered analog video and analog or digital audio. Gained popularity with cinephiles in the mid- to late-1990s but failed to achieve mainstream acceptance. Rendered obsolete by the arrival of DVD.

letterbox The process of applying black horizontal mattes to an image to alter the aspect ratio, usually to achieve a widescreen image. A letterboxed (or widescreen) image is generally employed to eliminate the need for panning and scanning. An image with vertical mattes applied (to create, for example, a traditional 4:3 TV aspect ratio in a widescreen frame) is called pillarboxing; to matte all four sides of an image is called windowboxing. (See Appendix A for details. See also "matte," "aspect ratio," "widescreen" and "anamorphic widescreen.")

lossless compression A process of reduction that still allows all original data to be recreated without any loss. (See also "lossy compression.")

lossy compression A process of reduction that can achieve very high rates of compression that retain most significant information but still permanently remove data. (See also "lossless compression.")

mastering Specific to DVD, refers to the actual chemical process of replicating an optical disc. However, this term has also begun to be used in a more generalized (if arguably inaccurate) manner to include the entire physical manufacturing process, such as authoring, encoding and even quality control.

matrix encoding The combining of additional channels of audio information into a traditional two-channel mix. (See also "Dolby Surround.")

matte An area of an image covered or replaced (usually with black). Most matting is done directly in the source (such as letterboxing), but the DVD spec allows for mattes to be generated by the player. For motion pictures, when the process is done optically or during exhibition it is referred to as "soft matting," whereas when the original source is being permanently altered, it is called "hard matting." (See also "letterbox.")

menu Navigation screens from which titles, chapters, audio and video options, and supplements can be selected. The initial or "top" menu is usually referred to as the main menu; additional screens that can be accessed from the main menu are generally referred to as submenus.

MPEG Moving Picture Experts Group. This international organization developed the MPEG compression standard. (See also "compression.")

multi-angle See "angle."

multiregion player A player or drive able to circumvent region coding and playback discs encoded in more than one region (aside from Region 0). (See "What Is Region Coding," page 15 for details.)

multiformat player See "universal DVD player."

multiplexing The process of combining multiple data streams into a single stream.

noise All-purpose term used to describe any unwanted, erroneous information added to or inherent in a signal.

NTSC National Television Systems Committee. A committee founded in 1941 by the Electronic Industries Association to develop a unified commercial television broadcast standard in the United States.

overscan Refers to the area at the edges of a television image that is obscured or covered, either during transmission or by the monitor itself (such as a display device's plastic frame or the rounded edges of a TV set). Overscan is generally about four to five percent of total picture area, and broadcast material is often composed with overscan in mind. (See "TV safe.")

parental control Also called "parental management." Refers to the ability of DVD to allow a DVD player to prohibit the playback of discs encoded with a specific parental level, and/or allow access to alternate versions of a program more suitable to a specific audience. Parental control requires a DVD title to be encoded with parental level instructions and alternate program material to access different versions.

PCM Pulse code modulation. An uncompressed, 2.0 channel stereo digitally encoded soundtrack. Preferred by purists and audiophiles, considered to be the highest-quality audio the DVD can deliver, especially on music-based material. (See also "Dolby Digital" and "DTS.")

perceptual coding A compression technique that identifies and removes "redundant" information that is least likely to be missed by the average viewer. (See also "compression.")

pillarbox See "letterbox."

PIP Picture in picture. A feature on some display devices and DVD players that allows for more than one video source to be displayed on the screen, often in various sizes and configurations. (See also "picture outside picture.")

pixel A single dot of picture information, an array of which makes up a video image. A pixel is the smallest picture element of an image. (See also "resolution.")

POP Picture outside picture. A feature on some 16x9 display devices that allows for the unused area outside of a 4:3 image to display picture information from more than one video source. Often confused with PIP. (See also "picture in picture.")

progressive scan A scanning system that creates a complete video picture (a frame) by transmitting all scan lines in one pass. In terms of quality, a progressive scan image is considered superior to an interlaced picture. (See also "interlace.")

QC Quality control. The systematic process of assuring quality via extensive checking, testing and verifying of a DVD's video, audio, menu navigation and authoring.

RAM Random access memory. In terms of DVD-RAM, refers to a recordable format that is able to read and write at any point on the disc. (See "What Kinds of DVDs Are There" page 8 for details.)

redundancy See "compression."

reference quality Generalized term referring to the best possible quality, a benchmark standard against which all others are measured.

region code A code identifying one of the eight regions used to restrict DVD playback and compatibility. Used interchangeably with "regional code." (See "What Is Region Coding," page 15 for details.)

replication In terms DVD manufacturing, the process of manufacturing and reproducing a DVD disc from its master.

resolution The measurement of the total numbers of pixels, or pixel elements, of a video image. (See also "pixel.")

ROM Read-only memory.

RSDL Reverse-spiral dual-layer. (See "What Kinds of DVDs Are There," page 8 for details.)

sampling The process of converting analog information into a digital representation. Multiple samples are taken at regular intervals across time, then encoded as numerical values.

saturation The vividness or intensity of a color.

scan line A single line traced out by the scanning system of NTSC video. (See also "horizontal resolution" and "vertical resolution.")

seamless branching The capability of the DVD format to access another portion of a disc and jump back to the same point with no interruption in playback, such as an alternate cut or version of a film. Used interchangeably with "seamless playback."

stream A continuous flow of digitally encoded data on a DVD. Used interchangeably with "bit stream."

submenu See "menu."

subpicture element Graphic overlays that can create subtitles, captions, highlight effects (for menus) and icons. Subpicture elements are favored over "burned in" or hard-matted subtitles due to their flexibility, and encoded data can usually be turned on or off by the user (such as toggling on/off a subtitle track).

substrate A substance which forms a physical DVD disc. The substrate is made up of a clear polycarbonate upon which data layers are imprinted.

subtitles Representation in text form of the audio portion of a program. Can be a part of the picture itself (often called "burned in" subtitles), but the preferred method is to encode as a subpicture element. Not to be confused with captions or true closed captions, which are intended for the hearing impaired and usually include additional text information. (See also "captions," "closed captions" and "subpicture element.")

surround sound Refers to a multichannel audio setup that allows for simultaneous playback of multiple channels of sound, usually placed both in front of and behind the listener, and often other angles.

telecine Refers to both the process and the equipment used to transfer film-based material to video.

title In general terms, refers to a specific DVD movie, music video, etc. In strict technical terms, a title is the largest unit contained on a DVD disc and sits at the top of the navigation hierarchy. A DVD-Video disc can hold up to ninety-nine titles per side, and a title can include multiple chapter stops, subtitle streams or alternate angles. Titles cannot contain other titles.

top menu See "menu."

track An element of audiovisual information encoded on a DVD disc, specifically the actual picture and individual soundtracks. DVD-Video can contain one track of video (with multiple angles), up to eight tracks of audio (including alternate languages and audio commentaries) and thirty-two subpicture tracks (such as subtitles).

TV safe The technique of composing broadcast or prerecorded video material within a more confined aspect ratio to compensate for overscan. (See "overscan.")

universal DVD player A player or drive that can playback DVDs of different formats, such as both DVD-Video and DVD-Audio discs. Also often called a multiformat player. (Not to be confused with a multiregion player; see also "multiregion player.")

vertical resolution The measurement of the number of lines of vertical detail in a video picture. (See also "horizontal resolution" and "scan line.")

VHS Video Home System. Until DVD, the most popular prerecorded consumer home video format in history.

Video CD An optical disc-based format that delivered VHS-level quality using MPEG-1 compression. It never gained mainstream acceptance in the United States but was extremely popular in other parts of the world, especially Asia.

watermark A digital marker hidden in a video or audio signal. Usually used to track or identify a disc to aid copy protection or version control.

widescreen An image wider than the standard 4:3 NTSC aspect ratio. Also often used to describe a DVD presented with a letterboxed or anamorphically encoded transfer. (See also "aspect ratio," "letterbox" and "anamorphic widescreen.")

windowbox See "letterbox."